. . . for lo, the eternal and sovereign luminous space,
where rule the unnumbered stars,
is the air we breathe in
and the air we breathe out.
And in the moment betwixt the breathing in
and the breathing out
is hidden all the mysteries
of the Infinite Garden.

—Essene Gospel of Peace

How to

A Primer on the Life-Giving Sustainable
GROW BIOINTENSIVE®
Method of Organic Horticulture

*than you ever thought possible

Grow More Vegetables*

(and fruits, nuts, berries, grains, and other crops)

by John Jeavons

Ecology Action of the Midpeninsula

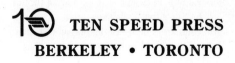 **TEN SPEED PRESS**
BERKELEY • TORONTO

on less land than you can imagine

Ten Speed Press
P.O. Box 7123
Berkeley, California 94707
www.tenspeed.com

Distributed in Australia by Simon & Schuster
Australia, in Canada by Ten Speed Press Canada,
in New Zealand by Southern Publishers Group, in
South Africa by Real Books, in Southeast Asia by
Berkeley Books, and in the United Kingdom and
Europe by Airlift Book Company.

Library of Congress
Cataloging-in-Publication Data

Jeavons, John.
    How to grow more vegetables : and fruits,
nuts, berries, grains, and other crops than you
ever thought possible on less land
than you can imagine / by John Jeavons.
       p. cm.
Includes bibliographical references and index.
    ISBN 1-58008-233-5
    1. Vegetable gardening. 2. Organic gardening.
I. Title.
    SB324.3 .J424 2002
    635—dc21

                              2001006451

Cover design by Larissa Pickens
Interior design by Linda Davis, Star Type,
        based on a design by Brenton Beck,
        Fifth Street Design Associates
Major illustrations by Pedro J. Gonzalez
Illustrations on pages 10 through 12 by Ann Miya,
        based on illustrations by Pedro J. Gonzalez
Illustrations on pages vi, vii, 2, 6, 22, 34, 49,
        62, 65, 66, 74, 121, 142, and 156 by Susan
        Stanley
Illustrations on pages 66 (top) and 78 (bottom)
        by Sue Ellen Parkinson
Other illustrations by Betsy Jeavons Bruneau
Copyediting by Shirley Coe

Printed in the United States

2 3 4 5 6 7 8 9 10 — 06 05 04 03

Drawing of the original Common Ground Garden in Palo Alto, California, provided by Landal Institute, Sausalito, California.

Contents

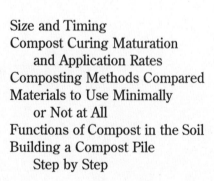

A Perspective
for the Future

"Population will increase rapidly, more rapidly than
in former times, and 'ere long the most valuable of
all arts will be the art of deriving a comfortable
subsistence from the smallest area of soil."
— Abraham Lincoln

"They're making more
people every day, but
they ain't makin' any
more dirt."
—Will Rogers

There is an exciting challenge ahead of us. How can we
revitalize our extraordinary planet, ensuring life and
health for the environment, the life-forms of a myriad
of ecosystems, humankind, and future generations? The answer
is as close to each of us as the food we consume each day.

We can begin to create a better world from right where we
are—in home gardens and mini-farms, in virtually all climates
and soils. Millions of people are already doing this in over
one hundred countries around the world, using sustainable
GROW BIOINTENSIVE® mini-farming techniques.

We "farm" as we eat. For example, if we consume food that
has been grown using methods that inadvertently deplete the
soil in the growing process, then *we are responsible for depleting
the soil*. If, instead, we raise or request food grown in ways that
heal the Earth, then *we are healing the Earth and its soils*. Our
daily food choices will make the difference. We can *choose* to
sustain ourselves while increasing the planet's vitality. In the
bargain we preserve resources, breathe cleaner air, enjoy good
exercise, and eat pure food.

It has been estimated that about 1/3 of the health care costs
in the United States could be eliminated through an increase in
exercise and by eating a nutritious diet. Gardening and mini-
farming provide both of these, resulting in a win-win proposi-
tion. By doing something that is wondrous and fun—growing
food—each individual becomes important again in the face of
an otherwise overwhelming global environmental challenge.
The Earth, the soils, and each individual will be better as a
result of these efforts.

What are the dimensions of this challenge? Current agricultural practices reportedly destroy approximately 6 pounds of soil for each pound of food produced.[1] United States croplands are losing topsoil about 18 times faster than the soil formation rate. This is not sustainable. In fact, worldwide only about 42 to 84 years' worth of topsoil remains.[2]

Why is this happening? Conventional agricultural practices often deplete the soil 18 to 80 times more rapidly than nature builds soil. This happens when the humus (cured organic matter) in the soil is used up and not replaced, when cropping patterns are used that tend to deplete the soil's structure, and when minerals are removed from the soil more rapidly than they are replaced. Even organic farming probably depletes the soil 17 to 70 times faster than nature builds it by importing organic matter and minerals from other soils, which thereby become increasingly depleted. The planetary result is a *net reduction* in overall soil quality.

Ecology Action is in its 31st year of rediscovering the original principles behind the highly effective, resource-conserving, and sustainable 4,000-year-old Chinese Biointensive way of farming. One to two millennia ago, cultures in Latin America, Europe, and other parts of Asia developed similar approaches. Ecology Action developed the GROW BIOINTENSIVE growing method, which is patterned after nature's own intensive biological plantings. Based on over 10,000 years of field trials, the features of GROW BIOINTENSIVE include:

- *Deep soil preparation*, which develops good soil structure. Once this structure is established, it may be maintained for several years with 2-inch-deep surface cultivation (until compaction once again necessitates deep soil preparation).
- *The use of compost* (humus) for soil fertility and nutrients.
- *Close plant spacing*, as in nature. (How surprised we would be to find natural meadows, forests, and fields growing in rows, with the area between the rows resembling long strips of desert.)
- *Synergistic planting of crop combinations* so plants that are grown together enhance each other.
- *Carbon-efficient crops*—planting approximately 60% of the growing area in dual-purpose seed and grain crops for the production of large amounts of carbonaceous material for compost and significant amounts of dietary calories.
- *Calorie-efficient crops*—planting approximately 30% of the growing area in special root crops, such as potatoes, burdock, garlic, and parsnips, which produce a large amount of calories for the diet per unit of area.

1. Developed from U.S. Department of Agriculture statistics.

2. Developed from P. Buringh, "Availability of Agricultural Land for Crop and Livestock Production," in D. Pimentel and C. W. Hall (eds.), *Food and Natural Resources* (San Diego: Academic Press, 1989), pp. 69–83, as noted in "Natural Resources and an Optimum Human Population," David Pimentel, et al., *Population and Environment: A Journal of Interdisciplinary Studies,* Vol. 15, No. 5, May 1994; and with statistics from the United Nations.

- *Open-pollinated seed use* to preserve genetic diversity.
- *A whole, interrelated farming system.* The GROW BIOINTENSIVE food-raising method is a whole system, and its components must all be used together for the optimum effect. If you do not use all of its elements together, the method's high yields can rapidly deplete the soil. In this book you will see the terms GROW BIOINTENSIVE and Biointensive. The latter refers to individuals, projects, and programs before Ecology Action's 1999 trademark registration of GROW BIOINTENSIVE and/or not using all of the GROW BIOINTENSIVE features.

It is interesting to note that during the last 50 years, since mechanized and chemical agricultural approaches have been used in China (as opposed to traditional Biointensive practices), China has lost as much as 33% of her farmland.[3] In contrast, when properly used, GROW BIOINTENSIVE sustainable mini-farming's *miniaturization of agriculture* can build the soil up to 60 times faster than in nature,[4] while making possible

- a 67% to 88% *reduction* in water consumption per unit of production;
- a 50+% *reduction* in the amount of purchased fertilizer required per unit of production;
- a 99% *reduction* in the amount of energy used per unit of production;
- a 100+% *increase* in soil fertility, while productivity increases and resource use decreases;
- a 200% to 400% *increase* in caloric production per unit of area;
- a 100+% *increase* in income per unit of area.

Up to 6 billion microbial life-forms can live in one 5-gram amount of cured compost, about the size of a quarter. Life makes more life, and we have the opportunity to work together with this powerful force to expand our own vitality and that of this planet.

Gandhi observed that "To forget how to dig the earth and tend the soil is to forget ourselves." In *Candide*, Voltaire points the way: "The whole world is a garden and what a wonderful place this would be, if only each of us took care of our part of the Garden!" Each of us is needed. Building a *truly* sustainable agriculture is an essential part of building sustainable communities. As we build soils, we also build a culture made up of healthy living and effective farming, as well as enduring communities. In order to accomplish this, we need to shift our agricultural perspective. We need to *stop growing crops* and *start growing soils!* Granted, in order to grow soil, we need to grow crops. But rather than growing crops for the sole purpose of

---

3. *New York Times*, March 27, 1994.
4. "Worldwide Loss of Soil and a Possible Solution," Ecology Action, 1996.

consumption, the goal changes to one of giving and creating life—producing, in the process, an abundance of food.

We must begin by educating ourselves, then sharing what we have learned by teaching *people to understand the importance of growing soil*. This new challenge will be to discover how to live *better* on fewer resources. It is possible! The way humankind is currently living and increasing in population, *we will not be able to provide for our own food needs soon if we do not grow soils*. The information on page xiii illustrates how, in as little as 12 years, there may be an average of just 9,000 square feet (or less) of farmable land per person to feed most people on Earth. But regardless of the amount of arable land available, as early as 1992, many countries had only enough water to irrigate 4,000 square feet per person. However, GROW BIOINTENSIVE sustainable mini-farming can make it possible to grow all the food for one's own nutrition, as well as food for the soil, on as little as 4,000 square feet. This may be accomplished at intermediate yield levels, which can be obtained without a great amount of difficulty.

It is important to note from the examples given that at some point during the years 2014 to 2021, there probably will not be enough land to produce all the nutrition needed for most of the world's population using current standard agricultural practices. These practices currently require about 7,000 to 63,000 square feet of farmable land, and most people will have access to only 9,000 square feet of arable soil as early as 2014. Further, most of the current practices are growing only *food* in the areas indicated, yielding insignificant net amounts of organic matter to produce the soil-nurturing humus needed to ensure the development of a healthy soil. With many of these practices, an additional equal area will be needed to produce the amount of organic matter necessary to sustain soil fertility for both the food-growing farm area and the organic matter-growing farm area.

However, GROW BIOINTENSIVE sustainable mini-farming alone (or any other sustainable farming practice) is not the answer. If not used properly, GROW BIOINTENSIVE practices can deplete the soil more rapidly than other farming practices because of the high yields. In contrast, when used properly—so all wastes are recycled and enough organic matter is grown to ensure that each farm can produce enough compost to create and maintain sustainable soil fertility—*GROW BIOINTENSIVE sustainable mini-farming can create soil rapidly and maintain sustainable soil fertility*. It is *how* each one of us uses GROW BIOINTENSIVE, or other food-raising practices, that makes a living difference!

On the other hand, to use only one agricultural approach to grow food could be unhealthy. This would be another form of "monocropping" in a living world ecosystem that needs diversity. Agriculture in the future will probably be a synthesis, a *sustainable* collage, of:

- GROW BIOINTENSIVE mini-farming
- agroforestry
- no-till Fukuoka food raising
- traditional Asian blue-green algal wet rice farming
- natural rainfall "arid" farming
- indigenous farming

Also, to preserve the plant and animal genetic diversity upon which we all depend, we need to keep ⅓ of the world's farmable land in wild.

As we begin to use sustainable, land- and resource-conserving food-raising approaches, more wilderness areas can remain untouched so more of the endangered plant and animal diversity on this Earth can be preserved. This wealth of genetic diversity is necessary if the planet on which we live is to support abundance.

Alan Chadwick, the horticultural genius who taught us the basis for GROW BIOINTENSIVE sustainable mini-farming practices, guided us: "Just grow one small area, and do it well. Then, once you have got it right, grow more!" Each of us can begin in this way to revitalize ourselves, the soil, and the Earth—one small growing area at a time. Before we know it, we will all live on a thriving, vibrant Earth consisting of many personal and community *mini-preserves*, reestablished with health as a vital, dynamic whole!

Each one of us has tremendous potential to heal the Earth. Let us begin.

APPROXIMATE AREA REQUIRED TO GROW ONE PERSON'S DIET USING CONVENTIONAL MECHANIZED *CHEMICAL* OR *ORGANIC* TECHNIQUES

High Meat Diet (fossil fuels available) currently	31,000–63,000 sq ft
Average U.S. Diets[5] (fossil fuels available) currently	15,000–30,000 sq ft
Average U.S. Vegan (fossil fuels available) currently	7,000 sq ft
Average U.S. Vegan Diet (no animal products) (post-fossil fuel era)	21,000–28,000 sq ft
Average of actual areas needed for diets eaten in developing nations, using actual agricultural practices (fossil fuels available)	1977: 30,000 sq ft
	1988: 22,000 sq ft
	2000: 16,000 sq ft

5. Assuming average amounts of vegetables, fruits, grains, beans, eggs, milk, cheese, and meat are eaten.

ESTIMATED ARABLE LAND AVAILABLE TO GROW ONE PERSON'S DIET WITH DIFFERENT LEVELS OF WATER AVAILABILITY IN THE FUTURE

Year 2000, Developing Nations (where 80% of the world's population will be living) with water available	16,000 sq ft
Year 2014–2021, Developing Nations (where 90% of the world's population will be living) with water available	9,000 sq ft
Year 2000, in water-scarce areas around the world	4,000 sq ft

AREA REQUIRED TO GROW ONE PERSON'S DIET WITH THE GROW BIOINTENSIVE METHOD, INCLUDING CROPS THAT PRODUCE A HIGH LEVEL OF CALORIES PER UNIT OF AREA (SEE PAGES 31–32)

GROW BIOINTENSIVE intermediate yields with soil fertility sustained	4,000 sq ft

By the year 2014–2021 with an average of 9,000 square feet available (see above), sufficient land and resources may be available in many developing-nation areas with GROW BIOINTENSIVE, leaving up to 5,000 square feet surplus farmland for the preservation of plant and animal genetic diversity in adequate water situations.

WILL THERE BE ENOUGH LAND TO GROW A COMPLETE DIET FOR ONE PERSON USING CONVENTIONAL MECHANIZED CHEMICAL OR ORGANIC TECHNIQUES OR USING THE GROW BIOINTENSIVE METHOD?

Land Available with Different Levels of Water	*Diet* / *Agricultural Technique*	High Meat / Conventional or Organic	Avg. U.S. / Conventional or Organic	Vegan / Conventional or Organic	Vegan / Conventional or Organic (post fossil fuel)	Vegan with special root crops / GROW BIOINTENSIVE (Intermediate yields/sustainable)
16,000 sq ft (year 2000, water available)		Insufficient	Insufficient	Sufficient land and 9,000 sq ft surplus[6]	Insufficient	Sufficient land and 12,000 sq ft[6] surplus
9,000 sq ft (year 2014–2021, water available)		Insufficient	Insufficient	Sufficient land and 2,000 sq ft surplus[6]	Insufficient	Sufficient land and 5,000 sq ft[6] surplus
4,000 sq ft (year 2000, water scarce)		Insufficient	Insufficient	Insufficient	Insufficient	Sufficient land and no surplus

6. Number of square feet represents the area that is in surplus, not needed for food production, that could be left in a natural state to preserve plant and animal genetic diversity and ecosystems.

How to Grow Made Simple

The table of contents has special notations to make this book especially easy to use for the beginning gardener. One of the advantages of *How to Grow More Vegetables* is that *it describes a complete general approach to gardening.* As you learn the basics of soil preparation, the simple joys of gardening will gain depth. Bed preparation, fertilization, composting, seed propagation, transplanting, watering, and weeding are performed essentially the same way for *all* crops. Only the seedling flat and growing bed spacings are different from one crop to another (these are given in columns H, L1, and M2 of each section of the Master Charts beginning on page 87). *So, once you know how to grow lettuce, you know most of the basics for growing onions, tomatoes, wheat, apple trees, and even cotton!*

Remember to enjoy gardening while you are working— experience the warmth of the sun, the touch of a breeze, the scent of a flower, the smell of freshly turned soil, a bird's song, and the beauty of it all. Above all, have fun!

One way to harvest your fullest enjoyment is to garden with your family or friends. Light conversation makes the time pass quickly during even the most difficult tasks. Consider having a barbecue or picnic after double-digging, holding a neighborhood compost building party, or inviting your children to join in the harvesting! And preserving the year's harvest through drying, freezing, or canning vegetables and fruits is always a social occasion. Gardening together is half the fun of this practical experience of learning and sharing.

If you are a *beginning gardener or mini-farmer* reading *How to Grow More Vegetables,* you may want to skip most of the tables except for column H in the Master Charts for planning on pages 87–115, which lists plant spacings. You will probably start by growing vegetables and a few flowers and herbs, and many of these crops can be bought as seedlings from a local

nursery. Starting your own seedlings is a higher skill level that you may not want to try until your second or third year.

If you are an *intermediate gardener,* you will begin to use more of the tables and charts and to grow some compost crops, grains, and fruit trees. The bibliography (beginning on page 165) is a source of additional information on topics of interest that you may like to pursue as your skill as a mini-farmer grows.

Ten years in the garden will produce a *fully experienced food grower.* You can now draw on all of the information provided in this book as you work on growing most or all of your family's food at home, plant a mini-orchard in the front yard, begin an economic mini-farm, or teach others the skills you have already mastered.

As you begin to grow GROW BIOINTENSIVEly, be sure to grow *sustainable soil fertility crops*—which we are calling carbon-and-calorie crops (see pages 27–29)—as part of your garden. We need to grow crops that *feed the soil* as well as ourselves. There are many such soil fertility crops. Examples are corn, millet, wheat, oats, barley, cereal rye, and amaranth. These crops grow a lot of carbonaceous material for the compost pile, which in turn feeds the soil with humus, as well as provides a great deal of *nutritious food to eat.* Be sure to try a few soil fertility crops in your garden or mini-farm this year. Information about these *dual-purpose crops,* which provide both dietary calories *and* compost materials, is included in the Master Charts section beginning on page 87 of this book and in the compost crop sections of Ecology Action's Self-Teaching Mini-Series Booklets 10, 14, 15, 25, and 26.

It is important to grow calorie crops in your garden or mini-farm. About 90% of your diet-growing area should eventually be planted in these nutritious crops. There are two kinds—crops that are *area-efficient* in the production of calories, and crops that are *weight-efficient* for calories.

Area-efficient crops produce *a large number of calories in a given area* because of their high yields per unit of area. Examples of these farming-efficient crops are potatoes, sweet potatoes, garlic, parsnips, burdock, and salsify.

Weight-efficient crops contain *a large number of calories per pound of food*, but have lower yields per unit of area. Examples of these kitchen-efficient crops are wheat, millet, oats, cereal rye, barley, and corn. Each garden or mini-farm should optimally contain some of both kinds of these calorie crops.

For more information about these concepts, also see *One Circle*, published by Ecology Action, and *The Sustainable Vegetable Garden*, published by Ten Speed Press. Important information about calorie crops is included in the Master Charts as well as in Ecology Action's Self-Teaching Mini-Series Booklets 14, 15, 25, 26, and 28.

How to Grow More Vegetables provides you with everything you need to create a garden symphony—from the basic techniques to advanced planning skills for a beautifully planted backyard homestead. But the real excitement is that each of us will never know everything! Alan Chadwick, after he had been gardening for 50 years, said, "I am still learning!" And so are we all. We have a lifetime of growing before us, and the opportunity to continually improve our understanding of the living canvas we are painting.

A General Preface

Ecology Action Goal: Act as a catalyst,
teach teachers, and train students

The Common Ground Garden was started in California in 1972 to determine what agricultural techniques would make food-raising by small farmers and gardeners more efficient. We call the results "mini-farming." Mini-farms can flourish in nonagricultural areas such as mountainous regions, arid areas, and in and around urban centers. Food can be produced where people live. With knowledge and skill, the yield per hour can be high without using the expensive machinery that is the preoccupation of our current agriculture. Mini-farming is available to everyone.

We began by concentrating on the exciting possibilities presented by the Biointensive method—does this method really produce four times the yield, as Alan Chadwick claimed? If so, does it take more water? Does it consume vast amounts of fertilizer and organic matter? Does it exhaust the soil? Or the people working? The only way to answer these questions was to plunge in and try it. Initially, we worked mainly on the quantitative aspects, developing the tools and data to maximize yields within the framework of Biointensive's life-giving approach. This involved experimentation with and evaluation of plant spacings, fertilizer inputs, various watering methods, and other variables.

The work has always been worthwhile despite the continuing challenge of attracting strong, ongoing support. The biggest single asset to this undertaking is John Jeavons' unfailing stamina and dedication. Over and over, when we all ask, "Can it work?" he answers, "How are we going to make it work?" It is becoming increasingly clear that sustainable GROW BIOINTENSIVE mini-farming will be an important part of the solution to starvation and malnutrition, dwindling energy supplies, unemployment, and exhaustion and loss of arable land, if the social and political challenges can be met.

After 30 years of testing, GROW BIOINTENSIVE farming has produced amazing benefits, but a lot of work is still to be done.

Yields can average 2 to 6 times those of U.S. agriculture and a few range up to 31 times as high. The full potential for all areas has probably not yet been reached. We are still working to develop an optimally healthy soil system. *Calorie* and *compost crops* present the most challenges because they are crucial in meeting the nutritional needs of people and the soil. Experiments include soybeans, alfalfa, fava beans, wheat, oats, cardoon, and comfrey. So far our yields are from 1 to 5 times the U.S. average for these crops. *Water* use is well below that of commercial agriculture per pound of food produced, and is about 33% to 12% that of conventional techniques per unit of land area.

Energy expenditure, expressed in kilocalories of input, is 1% of that used by commercial agriculture. The human body is still more efficient than any machine we have been able to invent. Several factors contradict the popular conception that this is a labor-intensive method. Using hand tools may seem to be more work, but the yields more than compensate. Even at 25¢ a pound *wholesale*, zucchini can bring as much as $9 to $16 per hour depending on the harvest timing because it is easy to grow, maintain, and harvest. Time spent in soil preparation is more than offset later in less need for weeding, thinning, cultivation, and other chores per unit of area and per unit of yield. Hand watering and harvesting appear to take the most time. *Initial* soil preparation, including fertilization and planting, may take 5 to 9½ hours per 100-square-foot raised bed. Thereafter, the time spent decreases dramatically. A new digging tool, the U-bar, has reduced subsequent bed preparation time to as little as 20 minutes when that is desirable. A new hand watering tool that waters more quickly *and* more gently is also being developed.

Nature has answered our original queries with an abundance even greater than expected, and we have narrowed our research to the most important question that can be asked of any agricultural system: Is it sustainable? The GROW BIOINTENSIVE method currently uses ½ or less the purchased *fertilizer* that commercial farmers use. Can we maintain all nutrient levels on site, once they have been built up and balanced? Or is some outside additive always necessary? We need to look more closely at all nutrients: nitrogen, phosphorus, potash, calcium, and trace minerals. Anyone can grow good crops on good soil, cashing in on nature's accumulated riches. The GROW BIOINTENSIVE method appears to allow anyone to take "the worst possible soil" (Alan Chadwick's appraisal of our original Palo Alto research site) and turn it into a bountiful garden or mini-farm. Preliminary monitoring of our soil-building process by a University of California soil scientist was probably the most important information garnered about our initial site. Continued monitoring will unlock new secrets and provide hope for people with marginal, worn-out, or desertified soils. However, a complete answer to the long-term question of sustainable soil fertility will require at least 50 years of observation as the living soil system changes and grows! We continue to work on that issue.

Nine years of growing and testing in Ecology Action's urban garden mini-farm came to an end in 1980 due to the termination of our lease and new construction on that land. Like so much other agricultural land in the United States, our lovingly tended beds succumbed to the press of urbanization. The city growing area prepared us for a rural site. The facilities of grocery store and electric lines were exchanged for open skies and room to grow more herbs, flowers, vegetables, beans, grains, and compost crops than we ever imagined. At the Common Ground mini-farm in Willits, California, we are enjoying a permanent site where we can grow trees of all kinds—for food, fuel, and beauty. Other projects include a self-fertilizing lawn composed of fragrant herbs and clovers, and a working mini-farm. In 1973, we initially estimated that a one-person small holding ($\frac{1}{8}$ to $\frac{1}{2}$ acre) could grow crops bringing in a net income of $5,000 to $20,000 a year (about $100 to $400 a week) after 4 to 5 years. However, one woman in Vancouver, British Columbia, was later earning about $400 a week growing gourmet vegetables for restaurants on $\frac{1}{16}$ of an acre 20 years after we began. At first she thought it could not be done, but when she tried growing crops for income it worked. She then passed her skills on to 12 other women. Crops grown may include collards, chard, beets, mangels, spinach, green onions, garlic, radishes, romaine and Bibb lettuce, zucchini, patty pan squash, cucumbers, and lavender. Rather than solely looking to Ecology Action for answers, we hope you will dig in and try GROW BIOINTENSIVE for yourself! The techniques are simple to use, as this book shows. No large capital expenses are necessary to get started. The techniques work in varied climates and soils. American farmers are feeding the world, but mini-farming can give people the knowledge to feed themselves.

Posted on the wall of our local environmental center, there once was a tongue-in-cheek guide called "50 Really Difficult Things You Can Do to Save the Earth." The second item was to "grow all your own vegetables." We had to laugh. We moved up to our new mini-farm in Willits with a plan for short-term food self-sufficiency. That was about 20 years ago. We still take a neighborly ribbing for racing down to the farmers' markets to buy sweet corn, carrots, and other vegetables and fruits to feed an extended family of staff, apprentices, interns, and friends at our research site. Research priorities often interfere with growing all our vegetables and fruits, but we are attempting to grow significant amounts of calories and compost crops. It is difficult to research, write, publish, teach, do outreach around the world, and farm—all at the same time!

Robin Leler Jeavons said, "My first garden was a total failure. I planned, dug, and planted, but I had not really learned how to garden yet. Now my favorite class to teach is compost. I bring a glass jar of waste—a slimy brew of potato peels, coffee grounds, and last week's rotting roses. The other jar has compost—sweet smelling, earthy, and alive and, by the way, nothing like the sifted and homogenized product sold at garden centers. These two jars remind me of the magical transformation of a garden: health from garbage, riches out of waste. I can 'see' that magic immediately, though it may take me years to fully comprehend it!"

Betsy Jeavons Bruneau, a senior staff person at Ecology Action, has an affinity for tiny life-forms. She taught us to appreciate the infinitely variable lichens that cling to bare rock and fallen trees, creating soil for larger life-forms to follow. People used to bring insects into our store for identification. Betsy's first response was usually a hushed "How beautiful!" She still marvels at the intensely colorful tomato hornworms, the intricate markings on the shells of wise old snails, and the fact that earwigs are wonderful mothers.

We live in an age of consumption, when we are constantly exhorted to measure ourselves by our possessions. Yet no matter how rich we manage to become, something human in us says our true worth is reflected by what we ourselves create. Why not make it full of life and beauty rather than pollution? Our neighbor Ellen spent all day putting up jars of string beans and picalilli, then worked until midnight to finish up a batch of raspberries. One of her notes reads, "There is no rest for the gardener . . . but there is always dessert!"

Gardening is not always easy, but the rewards are personal and fun. For most of us, the environment is what is around us, separate from human activity. Gardening offers the chance to become partners with nature. The reward is not just a salad from the backyard or a gleaming jar of peaches. Gardening is the process of digging the soil, starting small seeds, watching an apple tree grow. Gardening is *an education in observation, harmony, honesty, and humility—in knowing and understanding our place in the world.*

But the impact is also global. Alan Chadwick felt that gardening was the only way to prevent another world war—to bring *a living, active peace* on Earth by working with healthy, creative, positive life forces. In doing this, we become one with those life forces. The homegrown tomato requires no fuel for transportation, no packaging to be sent to the landfill, no political decisions about who will be allowed to work the fields or what level of pollutants is acceptable in our groundwater. Nature is not always a Garden of Eden. Some partnership is required to bring out the best in both nature and people. "Give to Nature, and she will repay you in glorious abundance," was one of Chadwick's favorite sayings. Gardening and mini-farming

give us the opportunity to participate in the subtle transformation of desert to "dessert." All we need to do is to start with one
growing bed and tend it well, and we have begun the exciting,
expansive, giving process of enlivening and healing the earth
and ourselves.

Ecology Action Staff
January 2, 2002

An Historical Introduction

In September 1971, Larry White, Director of the Nature and Science Department for the City of Palo Alto, invited Stephen Kafka, Senior Apprentice at the University of California Santa Cruz Student Garden, to give a 4-hour class on the biodynamic/French intensive method of gardening. Two years before, the city had made land available to the public for gardening, and residents appeared eager to hear more about this method. Alan Chadwick had brought the method to Santa Cruz 5 years earlier, and with love, vision, and apparent magic, the master horticulturist had converted a barren slope into a Garden of Eden. Vegetables, flowers, and herbs flourished everywhere. The method's techniques were primarily available through training in a 2-year apprentice program at Santa Cruz and through periodic classes given by Alan Chadwick or Stephen Kafka. However, neither detailed public classes nor vegetable yield research were being conducted regularly at Santa Cruz or in Palo Alto.

In January 1972, Ecology Action's board of directors approved a Biointensive research and education project. The purposes of the Ecology Action project were to:

- teach regular classes;
- collect data on the reportedly fourfold yields produced by the environmentally sound horticultural method;
- make land available for gardening to additional midpeninsula residents;
- publish information on the method's techniques.

In May, after a 5-month search for land, the Syntex Corporation offered 3¾ acres of their grounds in the Stanford Industrial Park with all the water needed for the project at no cost. Frank Koch, Syntex Public Affairs Director, told Dr. Alejandro Zaffaroni of the Alza Corporation about the project, and Dr. Zaffaroni subsequently contributed the first money to the project, $5,000, without which we never could have begun. Commitment by Frank Koch, Don Keppy, Chuck and Dian Missar, Ruth Edwards, Ibby Bagley, numerous other individuals, several corporations, and the Point Foundation enabled the project to continue.

Alan Chadwick soon visited the garden site and gave us basic advice on how to proceed. We then attended a series of lectures given by Mr. Chadwick in Saratoga, California. Using the classes taught by Alan Chadwick and Stephen Kafka as a base, we began teaching our own classes in the spring of 1972.

Further study and experience in the garden made it possible to increase the original class to a 5-week series. The classes led to the development of information sheets on topics such as vegetable spacings and composting techniques. Many people asked for a book containing all the information we gathered. Those who were unable to attend our Saturday classes or who had friends living outside the area were especially insistent. This book was the result. Robin Leler Jeavons, Betsy Jeavons Bruneau, Tom Walker, Craig Cook, Rip King, Bill Spencer, Claudette Paige, Keven Raftery, Marion Cartwright, Paka, Phyllis Anderson, Wayne Miller, Paul Hwoschinsky, Dave Smith, Steve and Judi Rioch, Louisa Lenz, Bill Bruneau, Dean Nims, Tommy Derrick, Carol Cox, John Beeby, Cynthia Raiser Jeavons, Dan Whittaker, Shirley Coe, members of Ecology Action, and friends have all made important contributions to the book's content and spirit.

I assume responsibility for any inaccuracies that may have been included; they are mine and not Alan Chadwick's or Stephen Kafka's. This book is not intended to be an exhaustive work on the subject, but rather one of simple completeness. Most of us at Ecology Action are only beginning to intermediate GROW BIOINTENSIVE gardeners. The purpose of this book is to turn on as many people as possible to a beautiful, dynamically alive method of horticulture and life. I had hoped that the great interest this book stimulated would encourage Alan to write an extensive work on the many sophisticated techniques that only he knew well. Because of his untimely death in 1980, this is no longer possible.

Our initial research indicates that GROW BIOINTENSIVE can produce an average of 2 to 6 times more vegetables per acre than the amount grown by farmers using mechanized and chemical agricultural techniques. The method also appears to use 33% to 12% the water, 50% to no purchased nitrogen fertilizer, and 1% the energy consumed by commercial agriculture per pound of vegetable grown.[7] The vegetables usually taste

7. Figures for yield and water and fertilizer consumption are based on data collected through 1979. The 1% energy consumption figure is from a November 2, 1973, letter from Richard Merrill, Director of the New Alchemy Institute—West, Pescadero, California. Energy data were collected and evaluated by Mr. Merrill and Michael J. Perelman, Assistant Professor of Economics, California State University at Chico. The data are for a growing area with a

excellent, and there are indications that their nutritive value can be higher than that of commercially grown vegetables. This method is exciting to me because each of us becomes important as we find our place *in relation* to nature.

One person annually consumes in food the energy equivalent (in calories or British Thermal Units) of 32.6 gallons of gasoline.[8] In contrast, the most efficient economy car will use that much gas in a month or two of ordinary driving. Imagine the fuel consumed by a tractor or industrial machine in a year! People are not only beautiful, they are very capable and efficient. We believe GROW BIOINTENSIVE can produce more net income per acre than commercial agriculture. With GROW BIOINTENSIVE we help provide for the needs of the plants instead of trying to dominate them. When we provide for these real needs, the plants bounteously provide more food. In striving for quality gardening, a person will be able to provide a diet and income more than sufficient for his or her needs. The effort will produce a human renaissance and a cornucopia of food for all.

Our work grows out of a personal concern about worldwide starvation and malnutrition. If we could determine the smallest amount of land and resources needed for one person to supply all of his or her own needs in a *sustainable* way, we might have a *personal solution*. What if a person could, in a tiny area, easily raise all the crops that would supply all food, clothes, building materials, compost materials, seeds, and income for an entire year? We asked whether others knew the smallest area required to do this, and no one did—so we began our 30-year quest to help settle an ongoing problem and make possible a better quality of life.

Generally, the challenges of world hunger, soil depletion, and diminishing resources seem so overwhelming that we tend to look for big solutions, such as massive grain shipments, breeding high-yield miracle crops, or establishing infrastructures—bank loans, machinery and fertilizer purchases, markets, and roads. These solutions create long-term dependency. What is so exciting about a personal approach is that it seeks to answer the question: "How do we enable ourselves to take care of our own needs?" Personal solutions will have as many varied applications as there are people, soils, climates, and cultures. Our work is one way for people to begin to develop those solutions.

---

proper humus content after a 5-year development period. The data are a qualitative projection and have been assembled during a 3-year period of tests performed on root and leaf crops (except brassicas) grown by hand cultivation in the Santa Barbara area with its 9-month growing season. (The 1/100 figure does not include the energy required to get the soil system to the point noted above and does not include unproductive plants that constituted 10% of the area under cultivation.)

8. Michael Perelman, "Efficiency in Agriculture: The Economics of Energy," in Richard Merrill (ed.), *Radical Agriculture* (New York: Harper & Row, 1976), p. 86.

Universal scientific principles operate within GROW BIOINTENSIVE sustainable mini-farming's biological systems. Yet our gardening results change each time we modify our system. For example, the microbial life levels and yields differ depending on whether we prepare the soil 7 inches, 12 inches, or 24 inches deep. Why? We do not know all the reasons yet. As we explore, we will come to understand the underlying principles, and a whole new world will unfold. We will be able to make changes to improve the health, fertility, effectiveness, and sustainability of the way we farm for an even better life on this planet.

Much new material is included in this latest revision: some improved techniques, understandings, and approaches; updated yield and seed information; corrected and updated planning data; and a greatly expanded bibliography. That is, more information to add to your fun as you grow past the beginning stage of GROW BIOINTENSIVE mini-farming in depth and breadth! This edition represents 30 years of working with plants, soils, and people—in virtually all climates and soils around the world. The result is for your benefit. I hope it will make your path easier.

John Jeavons
January 2, 2002
Willits, California

"Nothing happens in living nature that is not in relation to the whole."

—Goethe

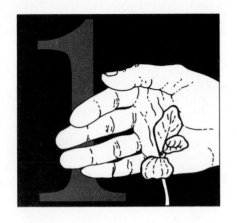

History and Philosophy

Goal: Learn from the experiences of farmers through time

Winter lettuce growing in an 1890s cloche (bell-glass). The standard diameter is 16¾ inches.

The GROW BIOINTENSIVE method of horticulture is a quiet, vitally alive art of organic gardening that relinks people with the whole universe—a universe in which each of us is an interwoven part of the whole. People find their place by relating and cooperating in harmony with the sun, air, rain, soil, moon, insects, plants, and animals rather than by attempting to dominate them. All of these elements will teach us their lessons and do the gardening for us if we will only watch and listen. We become gentle shepherds providing the conditions for plant growth.

The GROW BIOINTENSIVE method is a combination of two forms of horticulture practiced in Europe during the 1800s and early 1900s. *French intensive techniques* were developed in the 1700s and 1800s outside Paris. Crops were grown on 18 inches of horse manure, a fertilizer that was readily available. The crops were grown so close to each other that when the plants were mature, their leaves would barely touch. The close spacing provided a mini-climate and a living mulch that reduced weed growth and helped hold moisture in the soil. During the winter, glass jars were placed over seedlings to give them an early start. The gardeners grew up to nine crops each year and could even grow melon plants during the winter.

Biodynamic techniques were developed in the early 1920s by Rudolf Steiner, an Austrian genius, philosopher, and educator. Noting a decline in the nutritive value and yields of crops in Europe, Steiner traced the cause to the use of the newly introduced synthetic chemical fertilizers and pesticides. An increase was also noticed in the number of crops affected by disease and insect problems. These fertilizers were not complete and vital meals for the plants, but single, physical nutrients in a soluble salt form. Initially, only nitrogen fertilizers were used to stimulate growth. Later phosphorus and potassium were added to strengthen the plants and to minimize disease and insect problems. Eventually, trace minerals were added to the chemical larder to round out the plants' diet. After breaking down nutrients into their component parts for plant food, people found it necessary to recombine them in mixtures approximating a balanced diet. This attempt might have been more successful if the fertilizers had not caused chemical changes in the soil that damaged its structure, killed beneficial microbiotic life, and greatly reduced its ability to make nutrients already in the air and soil available to the plants.

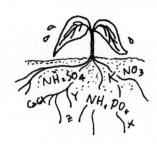

Artificial fertilization.

Rudolf Steiner returned to the more gentle, diverse, and balanced diets of organic fertilizers as a cure for the ills brought on by synthetic chemical fertilization. He stressed the holistic growing environment for plants: their rate of growth, the synergistic balance of their environments and nutrients, their proximity to other plants, and their various companion relationships. He initiated a movement to scientifically explore the relationship that plants have with each other. From centuries of farmer experience and from tests, it has been determined that certain flowers, herbs, weeds, and other plants can minimize insect attacks on plants. Many plants also benefit one another. Strawberries and green beans produce better when grown together. In contrast, onions stunt the growth of green beans. Tomatoes are narcissists; they prefer to be grown alone in compost made from tomato plants.

Natural fertilization.

The biodynamic method also brought back raised planting beds. Two thousand years ago, the Greeks noticed that plant life thrives in landslides. The loose soil allows air, moisture, warmth, nutrients,[1] and roots to properly penetrate the soil.

French gardeners at lettuce beds in the early 1900s.

1. Alan Chadwick used to call these *nutriments,* the things that "nourish or promote growth and repair the natural wastage of organic life." He used the term to distinguish them from *nutrients,* which are merely "nourishing substances or ingredients." He did this in particular to note the importance of multinutrient organic fertilizers, which break down over a period of time and nourish microbial life growth. In contrast, chemical fertilizers generally break down rapidly and cause inefficient decomposition of organic matter. This organic matter is the microbial life's food source. In this book, *nutrient* has both meanings.

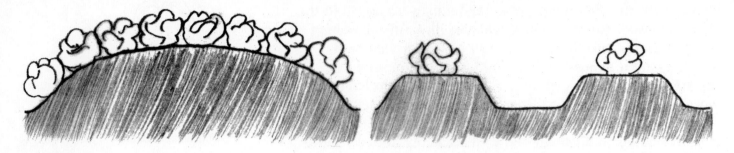

(*Left*) GROW BIOINTENSIVE raised bed; (*right*) traditional rows.

The curved surface area between the 2 edges of the landslide bed provides more surface area for the penetration and interaction of the natural elements than a flat surface. The simulated landslides or raised beds used by biodynamic gardeners are usually 3 to 6 feet wide and of varying lengths. In contrast, the planting rows usually made by gardeners and farmers today are only a few inches wide with wide spaces in between. The plants have difficulty growing in these rows due to the extreme penetration of air and the greater fluctuations in temperature and moisture content. During irrigation, water floods the rows, immerses the roots in water, and washes soil away from the rows and upper roots. Consequently, much of the beneficial microbiotic life around the roots and soil, which is so essential to disease prevention and to the transformation of nutrients into forms the plants can use, is destroyed and may even be replaced by harmful organisms. (About 3/4 of the beneficial microbiotic life inhabits the upper 6 inches of the soil.) After the water penetrates the soil, the upper layers dry out and microbial activity is severely curtailed. The rows are then more subject to wide temperature fluctuations. Finally, to cultivate and harvest, people and machine trundle down the trough between the rows, compacting the soil and the roots, which eat, drink, and breathe—a difficult task with someone or something standing on the equivalent of your mouth and nose!

Row plants are more susceptible to soil compaction.

These difficulties are also often experienced at the edges of raised beds prepared in clay soils during the first few seasons. Until the soil texture becomes friable, it is necessary to level the top of the raised bed to minimize erosion (see chapter on Bed Preparation), and the soil on the sides of the beds is sometimes too tight for easy planting. Increased exposure to the elements occurs on the sides, and the tighter soil of the paths is nearby. The plants along the sides usually do not grow as vigorously as those further inside the bed. When raised beds are prepared in friable soil, the opposite is true. The top of the bed can now be curved and erosion will not be a problem. The soil is loose enough for plants to thrive along the sides. The edges of the beds are included in the mini-climate effect created by closely spaced plants, and the water that runs from the middle of the bed provides the extra moisture the edges need.

Between the 1920s and 1930s, Alan Chadwick, an Englishman, combined the biodynamic and French intensive techniques into the biodynamic/French intensive method. The United States was first exposed to the combination when Mr. Chadwick brought the method to the 4-acre organic Student Garden at the University of California's Santa Cruz campus in the 1960s. Chadwick, a horticultural genius, had been gardening for half a century and was also an avid dramatist and artist. He studied under Rudolf Steiner, the French gardeners, and George Bernard Shaw, and worked as a gardener for the Union of South Africa. The site he developed at Santa Cruz was on the side of a hill with poor, clayey soil. Not even "weeds" grew well there—except poison oak, which was removed with pickaxes. By hand, Chadwick and his apprentices created a good soil in 2 to 3 years. From this soil and vision, a beautiful, wondrous and real Garden of Eden was brought into existence. Barren soil was made fertile through extensive use of compost, with its life-giving humus. The humus produced a healthy soil that grew healthy plants less susceptible to disease and insect attacks. The many nuances of the biodynamic/French intensive method —such as transplanting seedlings into a better soil each time a plant is moved and sowing by the phases of the moon—were also used. The results were beautiful flowers with exquisite fragrances and tasty vegetables of high quality. As an added bonus for all the tender loving care they received, the vegetable plants produced yields four times greater than those produced by commercial agriculture.

As the biodynamic/French intensive gardening method has continued to evolve and be simplified by Ecology Action, so has its name. It is now known simply as GROW BIOINTENSIVE gardening.

Lush growing beds at Common Ground make optimal use of garden space.

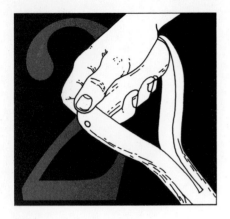

Bed Preparation

Goal: Develop soil structure so the plants will have a "living sponge cake" in which to thrive

Proper soil structure and nutrients allow uninterrupted and healthy plant growth.

Preparing the raised bed is the most important step in GROW BIOINTENSIVE gardening. Proper soil *structure* and nutrients allow uninterrupted and healthy plant growth. Loose soil with good nutrients enables roots to penetrate the soil easily, and a steady stream of nutrients can flow into the stem and leaves. How different from the usual situation when a plant is transferred from a flat with loose soil and proper nutrients into a hastily prepared backyard plot or a chemically stimulated field. Not only does that plant suffer from the shock of being uprooted, it is also placed in an environment where it is more difficult to grow. The growth is interrupted, the roots have difficulty getting through the soil and obtaining food, and the plant develops more carbohydrates and less protein than usual. Insects like the carbohydrates. The plant becomes more susceptible to insect attack and ultimately to disease. A debilitating cycle has begun that often ends in the use of pesticides that kill soil life and make the plants less healthy. More fertilizers are then used in an attempt to boost the health of the plants. Instead, the fertilizers kill more soil life, damage the structure of the soil further, and lead to even sicker plants that attract more insects and need more toxic "medicines" in the form of additional pesticides and fertilizers. Well-documented reports tell us that a wide variety of commercial pesticides kill beneficial invertebrate predators while controlling pest populations. These pesticides exterminate earthworms and other invertebrates that are needed to maintain soil fertility. The pesticides also destroy microorganisms that provide symbiotic relationships between the soil and plant root systems. Why not strive for good health in the first place!

Unless you are lucky enough to have loose soil, *preparing and planting a raised bed initially* can take a lot of time—as much as 6½ to 11 hours for a 100-square-foot bed the first time.

As you become skilled, the double-dig often takes 2 hours or less. After the first crop, however, only 4 to 6½ hours should be required on an *ongoing* basis for the whole preparing and planting process, because the soil will have better structure. Once the beds are planted, only about 30 minutes a day are required to maintain a 200-square-foot area—an area large enough to provide one person with vegetables 12 months a year in an area with a 4- to 6-month growing season.[1] Even less time per day and only a 100-square-foot area may be required in an area with an 8- to 12-month growing season. Beginning gardeners may require a larger area for the same yield, but we recommend a new gardener use only 100 square feet and allow the soil to gradually produce more food as his or her skills improve.

The square footage required to provide the vegetable supply for one person is approximate since the exact amount varies depending on whether the individual likes corn (which takes up a lot of space per pound of edible vegetable grown) or a lot of carrots, beets, potatoes, and tomatoes (which require much less area per pound of food produced). Using the tables in "Making the Garden Plan" (based on yields produced by the GROW BIOINTENSIVE method for all vegetable crops), you can determine the actual area needed for each crop. Be patient in this soil-building process. It takes 5 to 10 years to build up a good soil (and one's skills). Actually, this is very rapid. Nature often requires a period of 2,000 years or more to build a soil!

Instructions for the initial preparation of a 100-square-foot bed in a heavy clay, very sandy, or good soil are given below. Instructions for the repreparation of a bed are also given. After the soil has been initially prepared, you will find that the GROW BIOINTENSIVE method requires less work than the gardening technique you presently use. The Irish call this the "lazy bed" method of raising food. It has the added benefit of producing tasty vegetables and an average of 4 times more vegetables than your current yield! Or, if you wish to raise only the same amount of food as last year, only ¼ the area will have to be dug, weeded, and watered.

INITIAL PREPARATION PER 100 SQUARE FEET

First, perform a soil test (see the soil test section in "Fertilization"), then do the following:

1. If needed, soak the area to be dug for *2 hours* with a sprinkler (for hard, dry clays).

2. Let the soil dry out partially for *2 days*.

3. Loosen 12 inches of soil with a spading fork, and remove weeds. *1 to 2 hours*.

4. Water gently by hand for *5 minutes,* and let the soil rest for *1 day.* If your soil has particularly large clods, wait several extra days,

1. Two hundred square feet can yield over 300 pounds of vegetables and soft fruits in a 4- to 6-month growing season at intermediate GROW BIOINTENSIVE yields. The average person in the United States consumes about 322 pounds of vegetables and soft fruits annually.

- 1 cubic foot = 1.5 5-gallon buckets
- 1 5-gallon bucket = 0.67 cubic feet
- The *most* cured compost that can be added per 100-square-foot area per 4- to 6-month growing season on a *sustainable* basis is probably 8 cubic feet (including 50% soil by volume). This amount has been added with good results historically in Europe. However, in various situations, 1.6 to 2.8 to 5.6 cubic feet of cured compost (that is 50% soil by volume) may be a sufficient and sustainable amount to be added the same growing season. More research is needed to determine which amounts produce the best results in different climates and soils.

and let nature help do the work. The warm sun, cool nights, wind, and water will help break down the clods. Water the bed lightly every day to aid the process.

5. At this time, sand may be added to a bed with clayey soil, or clay to a bed with sandy soil, to improve texture. Normally you should not add more than a 1-inch layer (8 cubic feet) of sand or clay. (More sand may allow the water-soluble fertilizers to percolate down too rapidly.) Mix the sand or clay thoroughly into the loosened 12 inches of soil with a spading fork. *1 hour.*

6. Up to a 1-inch layer (8 cubic feet or 12 5-gallon buckets) of cured compost—whatever is available—is spread onto and incorporated into the surface of a bed that has good soil. (You may add up to a 2-inch layer [16 cubic feet per 100 square feet] of compost [preferably] or aged manure[2] to soil with poor [very sandy or very clayey] texture *on a one-time basis only*.) *1/2 hour.*

7. Water gently by hand for *5 minutes,* and let the soil rest for *1 day,* if needed.

8. Remove 7 5-gallon buckets of soil from the upper level of the first trench (assuming a 5-foot-wide growing bed—see drawing on page 21). Use 6 buckets of soil to make compost (these will eventually be returned to the growing beds in the form of added compost) and 1 bucket of soil to make flat soil to grow seedlings in. Even though you have removed one upper trench of soil, there will be enough soil at the end of the double-dig process to fill in the last trench, due to the expansion of the soil's volume as air is incorporated into the soil during the dig.

9. Double-dig the soil with a flat spade and a spading fork (see pages 10–14 for double-digging instructions). Be sure to use a digging board to avoid unnecessary soil compaction. *2 to 4 hours.* Be sure to dig trenches across the *width* of the bed. It helps to level the soil with a rake after every 3 to 4 trenches during the digging process.

10. Level and shape the bed, filling last trench with soil. *1/2 hour.*

11. Sprinkle organic nitrogen, phosphorus, potash, calcium, and trace mineral fertilizers (such as alfalfa and kelp meals, wood ash, and eggshells) as indicated by your soil test evenly over the surface of the bed after leveling and shaping it. Include any desirable levels of pH modifiers (such as special leaf or pine needle compost to make the soil less alkaline, or lime to make the soil less acid) as indicated by your soil test. Sift in fertilizers and pH modifiers only 2 to 4 inches deep with a spading fork (2 inches if surface cultivation is being used—see page 59). After sifting in fertilizers, do no further raking to avoid disturbing the even distribution of fertilizers and compost. (If there seems to be an excess of air in your soil, tamp the soil down by placing your digging board on various sections of the bed and then standing on it. This removes excess air from the upper few inches of the bed.) *1/2 to 1 hour.*

12. Plant or transplant. *1 to 2 hours.*

Total: 6½ to 11 hours for *initial* soil preparation, fertilization, and transplanting.

2. Two-year-old steer or cow manure, or 2-year-old horse manure that originally contained a lot of sawdust, or 2-month-old horse or chicken manure not containing much sawdust.

The proper tools will make the work easier and more productive.

FOR SOIL PREPARATION

FOR SEED PROPAGATION

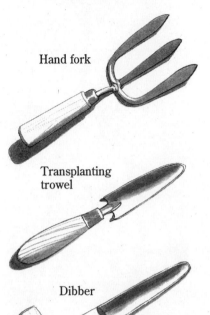

Hand fork

Transplanting trowel

Dibber

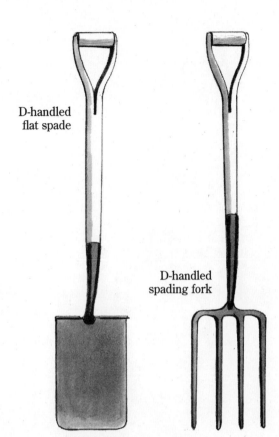

D-handled flat spade

D-handled spading fork

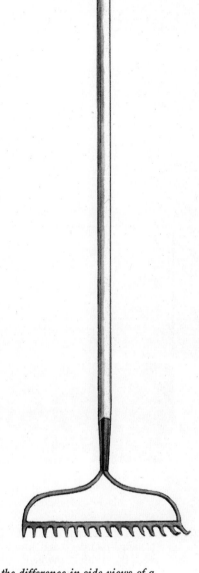

Bow rake

ONGOING PREPARATION FOR REPLANTING PER 100 SQUARE FEET—BEFORE EACH NEW CROP

1. Remove remaining vegetation, if necessary. Remove 7 5-gallon buckets of soil from the upper level of the first trench. Use 6 buckets of soil to make compost (they will eventually be returned to the growing bed in the form of added compost) and 1 bucket of soil to make flat soil.[3] Double-dig the soil. *2 to 3 hours.*

2. Level and shape the bed. *1/2 hour.*

3. Add any fertilizers and pH modifiers indicated by a soil test to the surface of the bed, and then add up to a 1-inch layer (8 cubic feet or 12 5-gallon buckets) of compost per 4-month growing season to the surface of the bed.[4] Sift in materials 2 to 4 inches deep with a spading fork. *1/2 to 1 hour.* (Adding the compost *after* the double-dig for *ongoing* soil preparation minimizes problems caused by water-soluble nitrogen leaching in increasingly loose soil.)

4. Plant or transplant. *1 to 2 hours.*

Total: 4 to 6½ hours for *ongoing* soil preparation, fertilization, and transplanting.

Note the difference in side views of a shovel and a spade.

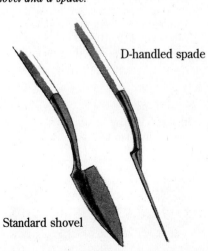

D-handled spade

Standard shovel

3. If you are digging only 25 rather than 100 square feet, only hold out 1¾ 5-gallon buckets of soil for making compost and flat soil, and return 5¼ 5-gallon buckets of soil into the bed.

4. Do this at least once a year—normally at the beginning of the main growing season. Generally our practice for autumn crops is to only single-dig and to add no compost or fertilizers.

The *Initial* Double-Dig Process

Step by Step

1.

2.

1. Spread a layer of compost over the entire area to be dug.
2. Using a spade, remove the soil from a trench 1 foot deep and 1 foot wide across the width of the bed, and put the soil into buckets or a wheelbarrow for use in making compost and flat soil. If the bed is 5 feet wide, the soil will fill 7 5-gallon buckets. (The trench is being dug across the *width* of the bed.)

Sides of bed may be dug outward into path.

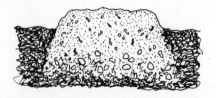

The goal of double-digging is to loosen the soil to a depth of 24 inches below the surface. The first year, you may only be able to reach 15 to 18 inches with reasonable effort. Be satisfied with this result. Do not strain yourself or your tools. More important than perfection the first year or two is going in the right direction. Nature, the loose soil, worms, and the plant roots will further loosen the soil with each crop so digging will be easier each year and the depth will increase 3 to 6 inches annually.

For all-around ease, D-handled flat spades and D-handled spading forks of good temper are usually used for bed preparation. (Poor tools will wear out rapidly while you are preparing your garden area.) D-handles allow you to stand straight with the tool directly in front of you. You must frequently hold a long-handled tool to your side. This position does not allow for simple, direct posture and leverage. When digging for long periods of time, many people find the use of a D-handled tool less tiring (though it will probably take the digging of 3 beds to

get used to!). However, people with back problems may need long-handled tools. In fact, people with back problems and those not in good health should check with their physician before proceeding with the physically active process of double-digging.

The flat spade has a particular advantage in that it digs equally deep all along its edge rather than in a pointed V pattern. This is especially important in the double-dig since all points in the bed should be dug to an equal depth. The blade on the flat spade also goes into the soil at less of an angle and without the usual shovel's curve. This means the sides of the bed can be dug perpendicular or even diagonally outward into the path, a plus for root penetration and water flow.

You should only dig when the soil is evenly moist. It is easier and also better for the soil. Digging a hard, dry soil breaks down the structure, and it is difficult to penetrate. Wet soil is heavy and easily compacted. Compaction destroys friable structure and minimizes aeration. These conditions kill microbiotic life. The main reason for drying-out periods after watering the

3a. Loosen the soil an additional 12 inches with a spading fork by digging the tool in to its full depth and then pushing the tool handle downward so the fork tines will lever through the soil, loosening and aerating it. (See illustrations on page 12 for loosening compacted soil.)

4. Dig out the upper part of a second trench 1 foot deep and 1 foot wide. Move each spadeful of soil forward (into the first trench), mixing the soil layers as little as possible.

3b(i).   3b(ii).

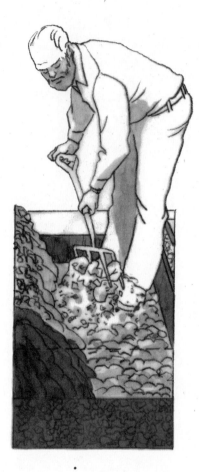

3b(i). *For compacted soil:* While standing in the trench, loosen the soil an additional 12 inches with a spading fork by digging in the tool to its full depth and lifting out a tight soil section on the fork pan.

3b(ii). Then, by moving your arms upward in a small jerk, the soil will break apart as it falls downward, hits the fork tines, and falls into the hole below.

soil is to attain the proper moisture level and to make digging enjoyable and beneficial. Soil is too dry for digging when it is loose and will not hold its shape after being squeezed in the palm of your hand (in the cases of sands or loams) or when it is hard and dry and cannot be penetrated by a spade (in the case of clays). Soil is too wet when it sticks to the spade as you dig.

Double-digging is the term used for the process of preparing your soil 2 spades deep (about 24 inches). To begin, mark out a bed 3 to 5 feet wide and at least 3 feet long. Most people prefer a bed 5, 10, or 20 feet long, but the maximum is up to you. To double-dig, remove the soil from a trench 1 foot deep and 1 foot wide across the width of one end of the bed. Use a ⅝-inch-thick plywood board, 2 to 3 feet long by 3 to 5 feet wide, to stand on. Place it on top of the 1-inch compost layer you spread over your bed, and advance it along the bed 1 foot at a time as you prepare to dig each new trench. Move 7 5-gallon buckets of soil from the beginning of the bed to a soil storage area for use in making compost and flat soil.

You can move the soil with the spade, in buckets, or by wheelbarrow. Make as few motions and use as little muscle as possible in this process. This will conserve your energy and involve less work. In fact, as you dig the soil, you will discover you can use an Aikido-like economy of motion and energy in which you are virtually just *shifting your balance and weight* rather than digging. (For a visual representation of this, see the *Dig It!* video carried by Ecology Action's Bountiful Gardens international mail-order service.)

Now, standing in the trench, dig down another 12 inches (if possible) with a spading fork, a few inches at a time if the soil is tight. Leave the fork as deep as it has penetrated, and loosen the subsoil by pushing the fork handle down and levering the tines through the soil. If the soil is not loose enough for this process, lift the chunk of soil out of the trench on the fork tines. Then throw the chunk slightly upward, and allow it to fall back on the tines so it will break apart. If this does not work, use the points of the fork tines to break the soil apart. Work from one end of the trench to the other in this manner.

Next, dig another trench behind the first one, moving each spadeful of the top 12 inches of soil forward into the first trench. Sometimes you will have to work over a trench a second or third time to remove all the soil and obtain the proper trench size. Repeat the subsoil loosening process in the second trench. Dig a third trench, and so on, until the entire bed has been double-dug. (When you are through double-digging, the aerated soil in the bed will be enough to fill in the last trench at the end of the bed, and you will have added some soil to the bed in the form of cured compost.) It helps to level the soil with a rake after every 3 to 4 trenches during the digging process.

When you are sliding the soil forward from one trench into another, notice two things. First, some of the compost layer you have added to the surface of the bed before beginning to dig slides 3 to 6 inches down into the trench creating a small mound of soil or landslide. This approximates the way nature adds leaves, flower bodies, and other decaying vegetation to the top of the soil, where they break down and their essences percolate into the soil. Second, the *upper* layer of soil—the top 12 inches—should not be turned over during the double-dig and succeeding double-digs. Most of the microbiotic life lives in the upper 6 inches of the soil. Also, the natural layering of the soil that is caused by rainfall and leaching, leaf litter, temperature, gravity, and other natural forces is less disturbed when the soil is not generally mixed, even though the soil is loosened up and disturbed somewhat. Aim for a balance between nature's natural stratification and the loosened landsliding soil. (As a goal, strive not to mix the soil layers. The goal is important even though it will never be reached and significant mixing sometimes occurs. Without this goal, however, excessive disruption of the soil layers will occur.)

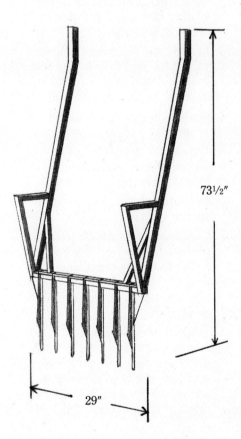

73½"

29"

The U-bar (see pages 15 and 17).

TYPES OF DEEP SOIL PREPARATION

Simplified Side Views

Ecology Action uses four basic types of deep soil preparation processes: the initial double-dig, the ongoing double-dig, the complete texturizing double-dig, and the U-bar dig. Following are simplified side views of each of these processes. The first two are described in the text.

The complete texturizing double-dig was developed to improve soil quality more rapidly and is used one time only. It is used usually in place of the initial double-dig, but it can be used

Initial Double-Dig

1. When the soil is lightly moist, loosen the top 12 inches of the entire area to be dug with a spading fork, and remove any weeds.

2. Spread a 1-inch layer of compost over the entire area to be dug (after mixing in a 1-inch layer of sand or clay 12 inches deep; optional, see page 8).

3. Remove the soil from the upper part of the first trench, and place it in a soil storage area for use in making compost and flat soil.

4. Loosen the soil an additional 12 inches.

5. Dig out the upper part of the second trench, and move it forward into the first trench.

6. Loosen the lower part of the second trench.

7. Continue the double-digging process (repeating steps 3, 4, 5, and 6) for the remaining trenches. Rake after each 3–4 trenches to ensure even bed height.

8. Shape the bed by raking it. Then evenly spread any needed fertilizers over the entire area, and sift them in 2 to 4 inches deep with a spading fork. The double-dug bed is now completed.

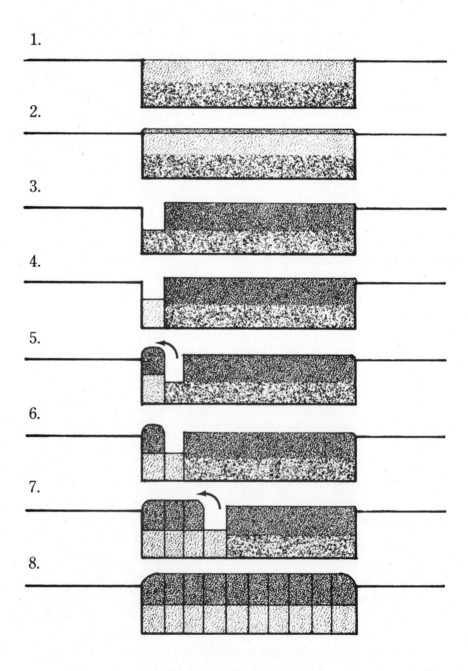

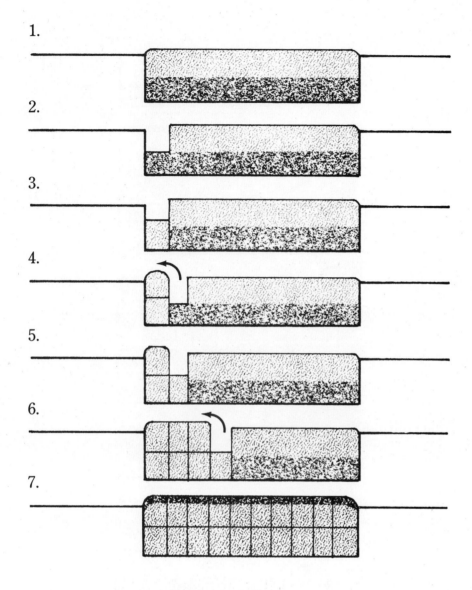

1.

2.

3.

4.

5.

6.

7.

A primary difference between the ongoing and the initial double-dig is that the compost is put on *after* the digging process in the ongoing double-dig.

1. The bed is shown after harvest with a slightly raised mound of partially recompacted soil and residual compost. When the soil is lightly moist, loosen the entire top 12 inches of the area to be dug with a spading fork, and remove any weeds.

2. Remove the soil from the upper part of the first trench, and place it in a soil storage area for use in making compost and flat soil.

3. Loosen the soil an additional 12 inches. (See Note below.)

4. Dig out the upper part of the second trench, and move it forward into the first upper trench.

5. Loosen the lower part of the second trench.

6. Continue the double-digging process (repeating steps 4 and 5) for the remaining trenches. Rake after each 3–4 trenches to ensure even bed height.

7. Shape the bed by raking it. Evenly spread a 1-inch layer of compost and any needed fertilizers over the entire area. Sift in compost and any fertilizers 2 to 4 inches deep with a spading fork.

Note

After the lower trench has been loosened, potatoes may be placed on its surface on 9-inch centers using offset spacing (see "Seed Propagation," pages 63–65). The soil from the next trench's upper level may then be moved forward onto them. This is the easiest way we have found to plant potatoes. (Mark the location of the potatoes with stones or sticks in the outside paths before covering them with soil. This will indicate where potatoes should be placed on the surface of each succeeding lower trench.)

at a later point in time. We have found this soil preparation process greatly improves plant health and yields immediately in poor, compacted and heavy soil. It is often worth the extra digging time involved. However, it does use an *insustainable* amount of organic matter.

The U-bar dig can be used as a substitute for the ongoing double-dig in soil that is in reasonably good shape. This usually means after one normal double-dig or more. The 18-inch-long U-bar tines (see page 13) do not prepare the soil as deeply as a spade and a spading fork used to double-dig 24 inches deep, but the lower 12 inches of the growing bed compact more slowly over time than the upper 12 inches. Also, the U-bar appears to have the advantage of mixing up the soil strata much less than double-digging with a spade and a spading fork. It aerates the soil less, however. This is an advantage in looser, sandier soil and can be a problem in tighter clays. If you use a U-bar regularly, do a normal double-dig as often as increased compaction

Complete Texturizing
Double-Dig

One time only for compacted heavy soils.

1. When the soil is lightly moist, loosen the top 12 inches of the entire area to be dug with a spading fork, and remove any weeds.

2. Spread a 1-inch layer of compost over the entire area to be dug (after mixing in a 1-inch layer of sand or clay 12 inches deep; optional, see page 8).

3. Thoroughly mix in compost 12 inches deep.

4. Remove the soil from the upper part of the first trench and place it in a soil storage area for use in making compost and flat soil.

5. Loosen the soil an additional 12 inches.

6. Spread a 1-inch layer of compost on the loosened soil in the first trench.

7. Thoroughly mix the compost placed on top of the lower first trench into the soil 12 inches deep.

8. Dig out the upper part of the second trench, and move it forward into the first trench.

9. Loosen the lower part of the second trench.

10. Spread a 1-inch layer of compost on the loosened soil in the second trench.

11. Thoroughly mix in the compost on the lower second trench 12 inches deep.

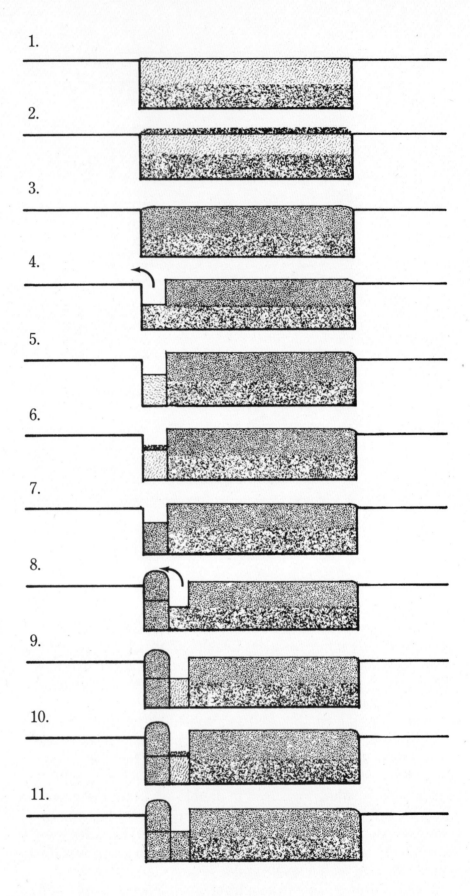

1.

2.

3.

4.

5.

6.

7.

8.

9.

10.

11.

12.

13.

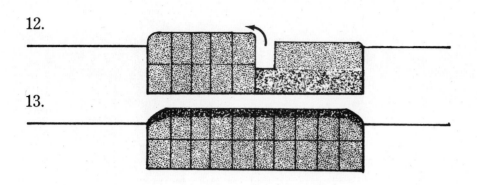

12. Continue the complete texturizing double-digging process (repeat steps 8 through 11) for the remaining trenches. Rake after each 3–4 trenches to ensure even bed height.

13. Shape the bed by raking it. Then evenly spread any needed fertilizers over the entire area, and sift them in 2 to 4 inches deep with a spading fork. The complete texturizing double-dug bed is completed.

1.

2.

3.

4.

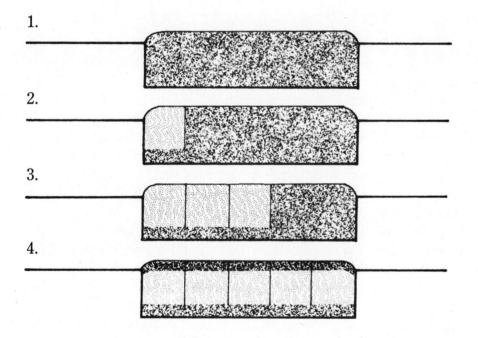

U-Bar Dig

1. After harvest, if necessary, weed the entire slightly raised bed.

2. When the soil is lightly moist, begin U-barring the soil along the length of the bed. No digging board is used. The soil will be loosened ¾ as deep as in the double-dig.

3. Continue U-barring until the bed is done. Two or three U-bar passes along the length of the bed may be necessary epending on the bed's width. The U-bar is about 2 feet wide and loosens the soil 2 to 2½ feet wide. See the drawing on page 13.

4. Break up any remaining large clumps with a spading fork. Shape the bed by raking it. Then evenly spread compost and any needed fertilizers over the entire area, and sift them in 2 to 4 inches deep with a spading fork.

Note

See *Backyard Homestead, Mini-Farm and Garden Log Book* on the proper techniques for using a U-bar.

indicates. U-barring is quicker and easier than using a spade and a spading fork, though some knowledge of how your soil is improving, or not improving, is lost with the decreased personal contact with the soil. (For detailed plans on how to build a U-bar, see Ecology Action's *Backyard Homestead, Mini-Farm and Garden Log Book*.) At Ecology Action, we prefer to double-dig, as we learn more from it and stay more in touch with the soil.

SELECTED VEGETABLE ROOT SYSTEMS SHOWN IN SCALE

Feet   sweet corn   lettuce   tomato

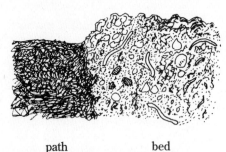

path   bed

Soil in the path is subject to compaction; soil in the bed remains loose.

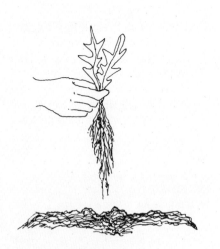

The loosened soil of the planting bed makes weeding easier.

Once the bed is prepared, you will truly appreciate its width. The distance between the tips of your fingers and your nose is about 3 feet when your arm is extended out to the side. Thus a 3- to 5-foot-wide bed can be fertilized, planted, weeded, and harvested from each side with relative ease, and insects can be controlled without walking on the bed. A 3- to 5-foot width also allows a good miniclimate to develop under closely spaced plants. You may wish to use a narrower bed, 1½ to 2½ feet wide, for plants supported by stakes, such as tomatoes, pole beans, and pole peas, for easier harvesting.

Try not to step on the growing beds once they have been prepared. To do so compacts the soil and makes it more difficult for the plants to grow. If the bed must be walked on, use the double-digging board. This will displace your weight over a large area and minimize the damage. Plants obtain much of their water and nutrients through the contact of their root hairs with the soil. If they do not develop an abundant supply of root hairs, less water and nutrients are taken in. The root hairs are more numerous and vigorous in looser soil, so keep your soil loose.

When weeding, note that the entire weed root usually comes up out of loosened raised-bed soil. This is a welcome change to weeding, and, if you get all the root, you will not have to weed as often. Also, you do not need to cultivate the soil of raised beds as much as other gardens. The *living mulch* shade cover provided by mature plants helps to keep the soil surface loose. If the soil compacts between young plants before the mini-climate takes effect, you should cultivate.

carrot   cauliflower   beet

Once this beautifully alive bed is prepared, it should be kept evenly moist until and after planting so the microbiotic life and plants will stay alive. The bed should be planted as soon as possible so the plants can take advantage of the new surge of life made possible by bringing together the soil, compost, air, water, sun, and fertilizers.

A good growing bed will often be 2 to 10 inches higher than the soil's original surface. A good soil contains 50% air space. (In fact, adequate air is one of the missing ingredients in most soil preparation processes.) Increased air space allows for increased diffusion of oxygen (which the roots and microbes depend on) into the soil, and of carbon dioxide (which the leaves depend on) out of the soil. The increased "breathing" ability of a double-dug bed is a key to improved plant health. Thus, the prepared depth will be as much as 34 inches in clayey soil. A sandy soil will probably not raise as high as clayey soil at first.

If the bed raises higher than 10 inches as you are double-digging, be sure to level it out with a rake as you go along. Otherwise you will end up with a very wide and deep trench at the end of the bed. Then you will have to move a large amount of soil from one end of the bed to the other to even it out when you are tired. This would also cause a disproportionate mis-placing of topsoil into the subsoil area. Whenever you re-dig a bed (after each crop or season), the 24-inch depth of the bed should be measured from the top of the bed, rather than from the path surface. We currently reprepare the soil after each

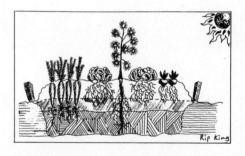

The GROW BIOINTENSIVE raised bed. A balance between nature's natural stratification and our loosened land-sliding soil.

For different types of ongoing soil cultivation practices to use after digging, refer to the "Cultivation" information sheet in the *Gardening Techniques* information packet (see page 228).

crop, except for autumn compost crops. Some people prefer to do this only once each year. As your soil improves and the large clods disappear, your bed may not raise as high as initially. Do not worry about this. It is just a sign that you and your soil are successful. The goal of double-digging is not the height of the bed, but the looseness and *good structure* of the soil.

Once a *good structure* has been established by double-digging, it may be better to use *surface cultivation* (the loosening of the upper 2 inches of the soil with a cultivating tool) for several years. In this way, the developed structure and soil organic matter are better preserved. One simple way to determine whether your soil has good structure follows. Squeeze a sample of reasonably moist soil firmly in your hand. Then open your hand. If the soil falls apart easily, it does not have good soil structure. If it holds the shape of your hand even when you press it gently with the fingers from your other hand, it does not have good soil structure. If the soil breaks apart into small clumps when you press it with your fingers, it probably has good soil structure.

When surface cultivation is used, *compost made without soil* will be used, because soil will not be removed from the bed during the soil preparation process. Whenever the lower soil becomes compacted, the bed may be double-dug again to encourage reestablishment of a well-aerated structure.

The soil's *texture* is determined by its basic ingredients: silt, clay, and sand particles. Its *structure* is the way its ingredients hold together. With your assistance, "threads" exuded by microbial life and "glue" exuded by plant roots help to loosen a clay soil and improve a sandy soil. The goal is to create a sumptuous *"living sponge cake."* Bon appétit![5]

5. For more information on growing soil quality and soil structure, also see "Table 20.1—Qualitative Soil Health Indicators," in U.S. Department of Agriculture/Agriculture Research Service, *Soil Quality Test Kit* (Washington, DC: U.S. Department of Agriculture/Agriculture Research Service, 1999); and Fred Magdoff and Harold van Es, *Building Soils for Better Crops*, 2nd edition (Burlington, VT: Sustainable Agriculture Network, 2000).

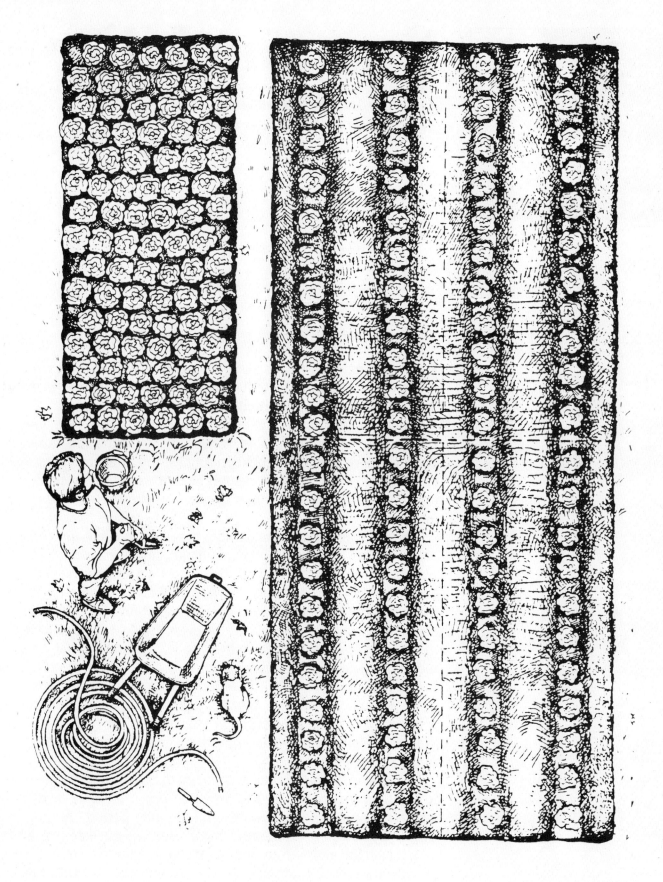

Good soil preparation makes GROW
BIOINTENSIVE fertility possible—up to 4
times the productivity per unit of area!

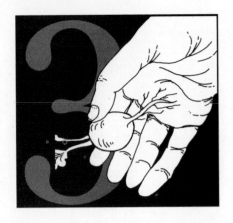

Sustainability

*Goal: Grow and maintain
sustainable soil fertility*

"The grandfather keeps sheep,
the son keeps goats,
the grandson keeps nothing."
— Richard St. Barbe Baker, *My Life, My Trees*

Sustainability means living in such a way that there are enough resources to live well in an alive, diverse, thriving environment—indefinitely.

Sustainability *is* possible—individual people, families, and communities accomplish this frequently all around the world. Yet most people find this challenging. Many of us are living on 6 times—or more—the resources that would be available to each person in the world, if the resources were divided up equally!

We often think of sustainability in terms of using *nonrenewable resources* carefully. More important, however, is using *renewable resources* well. If all the earth's agriculture became organic tomorrow, it would be wonderful and challenging. A more healthy resource-conserving, food-raising, and planetary ecosystem would be possible. However, the cost of purchasing the cured compost needed to grow food organically would be too high because the demand would exceed current supply. For that reason, we need to properly preserve, manage, and develop our renewable resources. Soil, for example, needs a given level of humus, or cured compost, in order to thrive. We each need to make sure we grow enough organic matter for our own needs.

For a garden or mini-farm to be sustainable, it must be able to produce sufficient crops to provide the gardener or farmer with what she or he needs over an indefinite period of time. This is possible *only* if the mini-farm's soil is kept fertile in a way that relies neither on nonrenewable resources, such as petroleum, nor on the nutrients or health of another soil. Most chemical fertilizers and pesticides are created in part from petroleum, which also fuels tractors, processing machinery, and transport vehicles. While organic fertilizers may seem to be a good alternative, their production relies on another farm's soil being able to produce the raw materials, such as alfalfa, cottonseed, and feed for animals that provide bone and blood meals. With these materials constantly taken away from the soil that produces them, these soils lose nutrients and eventually become depleted and infertile.

When our focus is on harvesting as much as we can from the soil, we forget to give the soil what it needs to remain fertile. We must grow *soil* in a way that is sustainable. Only then can it continue to provide us with abundant food. If we farm in a way that *does not* sustain soil fertility, the soil that is currently used to grow crops will soon be able to grow only fodder for sheep, later only scraggly weeds for goats, and then nothing at all.

The Loss of Soil Nutrients and Humus

When soil grows crops, it loses the nutrients the crops extract as well as the humus that the soil microorganisms consume. To maintain the soil's fertility, the nutrients and humus must be replenished. Both of these requirements can be met simultaneously when the crop and all other residues from those who consumed the edible portion of the crop are composted and returned to the soil. The cured compost will have almost all of the nutrients that the crop contained and, depending on the crops that are grown, enough humus to replenish the soil's supply. (Also, see *Future Fertility*.)

The carbon that left the soil in the form of carbon dioxide will be returned if plants that store a lot of carbon in their bodies (such as corn, amaranth, wheat, and rice) are grown and added to the soil as cured compost. These kinds of compost crops should optimally be grown on about 60% of the farm area over the course of a year in order to generate enough cured compost to maintain the soil's fertility.

Initially Adding Nutrients and Humus to the Soil

Not all soils naturally have all of the nutrients they need for their optimum health and crop productivity. Deep-rooted crops such as alfalfa and comfrey can be grown to bring up nutrients from below the range of most roots, then composted and added to the topsoil. However, if the needed nutrients are not in the deeper regions of the soil, they will not be present in the cured compost. On the other hand, when cured compost *is* added to the soil, nutrients that were previously unavailable in the soil may be made available by the biogeologic cycle.

In the biogeologic cycle, *humic acid*—which is produced from the decomposition process and is contained in the cured compost—along with the *carbonic acid* developed around the plant's roots, can increase soil microbial activity, decompose larger minerals, and possibly alter soil pH so that previously unavailable nutrients are made available. However, if the nutrients are not in the soil in the first place, even in an unavailable form, *the cured compost made from plants grown on the nutrient-deficient soil will not contain the deficient nutrient, and the soil will still be unbalanced after the cured compost is added.* Therefore, in some cases, you may need to bring nutrients in the form of organic fertilizers into the mini-farm from the outside, but probably only on a one-time basis, before the mini-farm can be maintained sustainably.

You may also need to bring carbonaceous materials into the garden or mini-farm in the beginning so sufficient humus can be added to the soil. Humus is the food of soil microorganisms that are responsible for creating good soil structure and soil fertility. It also helps hold the nutrients in the soil. If there is not enough humus (about 4% to 6% organic matter in temperate regions; about 3% organic matter in tropical ones), nutrients that are returned to the soil in the form of cured compost may leach out.

Losses = Gains?

Some nutrients will escape from the garden or mini-farm, whether from leaching, from rainfall runoff, or from the wind picking them up and carrying them away (although water and wind erosion are usually not a problem when the soil's humus supply is maintained and all of the GROW BIOINTENSIVE techniques are used). At the same time, however, nutrients are added naturally to the mini-farm through rainfall, wind, the breakdown of the soil's parental rock material, and the upsoaking of groundwater. With GROW BIOINTENSIVE sustainable gardening and mini-farming, the gain in nutrients may eventually be approximately *equal* to the loss of nutrients, and *the soil's nutrient balance may be maintained if all nutrients are recycled.*

100% Sustainability *Impossible*

According to the Second Law of Thermodynamics, all systems proceed toward a state of entropy or disorder. Therefore, no system, including agriculture, can be sustained indefinitely. At the extreme, all mini-farms will cease, as will all life as we know it, when the sun burns out millions of years from now. However, until this happens, we can maintain our soils at a level close to complete sustainability (instead of close to complete *insustainability,* as is now the situation with most agricultural systems). Within a garden or mini-farm, some soil nutrients may not be replenished by natural forces, or the same natural forces may add soil nutrients in excess. In both situations, if proper soil nutrient maintenance is not pursued, the soil may cease to be able to grow significant amounts of crops in a very short period of time.

The Need for up to "99%" Sustainability

At Ecology Action, we are looking for the quickest, most effective, most resource-conserving, and most ecologically sound ways to replenish and balance soil nutrients. Once the soil's nutrient base has been properly built and balanced, we need to learn how best to maintain those nutrients in our gardens and mini-farms. One promising approach is to grow all of our own compost materials in sufficient quantities so that the cured compost we add to the soil contains as many of the nutrients the crops removed from the soil as possible, as well as enough humus to feed the soil microbes and prevent nutrient leaching. In this way, our food-raising area becomes *a source*—rather than *a sink*—of carbon, nutrients, and fertility. (The *net* loss of carbon dioxide, or "leakage," from the system is a key concern. Worldwide, the loss of carbon from our soils—and plants in the form of harvested trees and their use for fuel—is a situation causing increasing problems.)

Keeping the nutrients within the mini-farm, as well as learning how to minimize the amount of nutrients we need to bring in from the outside, are important tasks if we are to grow all of our food, clothing, and building materials on the 9,000 square feet (or about 1/5 of an acre) that may soon be all that is available to each man, woman, and child living in developing nations (see "A Perspective for the Future"). Soon we simply will not have the luxury of taking nutrients from one soil to feed another.

With about 42 to 84 years' worth of topsoil remaining in the world, learning how to enrich, improve, and maintain soil— in a way that is sustainable—is of vital importance if we, as a species, are to survive. If they can only provide food for about a century before they deplete the soil, the agricultural systems that have brought us to where we are now are clearly not sustainable. Ancient civilizations sustained their soils to feed large populations for lengthy periods of time. China's soils, for example, remained productive for 4,000 years or more until the adoption of mechanized chemical agricultural techniques that have been responsible, in part, for the destruction of 15% to 33% of China's agricultural soil since the late 1950s. Many of the world's great civilizations have disappeared when their soil's fertility was not maintained. Northern Africa, for example, used to be the granary for Rome until overfarming converted it into a desert, and much of the Sahara Desert was forested until it was overcut.

Ecology Action's Pursuit of Sustainability

When Ecology Action began the Common Ground Mini-Farm in Willits, California, the soil was so infertile that many carbonaceous compost crops did not grow well. In an effort to improve the soil so it could grow all of the carbonaceous compost material needed to provide the mini-farm with sufficient cured compost, carbonaceous compost material (straw) and nutrient-containing horse manure were imported to the mini-farm. This approach eventually did not feel appropriate because we were *importing* a significant amount of carbon. Consequently, we limited our compost building to include materials produced by the mini-farm whenever possible. However, because many crops we were testing did not contain much carbon, the mini-farm produced significantly less carbonaceous compost material than was needed to increase and maintain the soil's fertility. Without sufficient cured compost, the soil began losing the humus it had, and its ability to grow sufficient organic matter declined.

While we still chose to grow some experimental crops that did not produce a significant amount of carbonaceous compost material, we grew *more* of our own compost material than before and supplemented our supply of carbonaceous compost material with purchased straw, goat litter (primarily from outside fodder inputs), and/or straw from noncrop areas.

We have been getting closer to achieving closed-system soil humus sustainability *within the limits of the mini-farm* and are now working toward closed-system soil humus sustainability by using compost materials grown primarily *within the limits of the growing beds* that receive cured compost. In the future, we will be emphasizing the growing of an even larger percentage of the carbonaceous compost material we need each year, and will continue to do so until we are growing *all* of this material ourselves in our own growing beds. In addition, we are exploring different *levels* of maintaining sustainable soil fertility. These methods involve using different amounts of cured compost (depending on its availability), with different corresponding crop yield levels resulting.

Current Goals of Understanding and Achieving "99%" Sustainability

Our goals are to understand how a garden or mini-farm can
- produce all of its own compost material initially *without having to import any straw, manure, or other carbonaceous material* for the soil's humus sustainability,
- maintain *nutrient* sustainability.

Because we are not currently returning the nutrients in our human urine and manure to the mini-farm's soil, we need to import some organic fertilizers to maintain the nutrient levels and balance in the soil. However, for the future, we *are* exploring ways to safely, effectively, and legally return the nutrients in our waste to the soil from which they came.

How to Better Sustain Your Soil's Fertility

In order to more easily sustain the fertility of your soil, you should divide your growing area as follows:

- approximately *60%* in *carbon-and-calorie crops* that produce large amounts of carbon for compost and that also produce food in the form of significant amounts of calories (To grow the nitrogen needed to make a good compost, legumes will need to be interplanted with these crops; for example, fava beans among wheat in winter and bush beans with corn in summer. See *The Complete 21-Bed Biointensive Mini-Farm* and *One Basic Mexican Diet* for more details.)
- approximately *30%* in special root *diet crops* that produce large amounts of calories
- a maximum of *10%* in *vegetable crops* for additional vitamins and minerals (Up to ¾ of this area may be planted in *income crops* if the missing needed vitamins and minerals are provided by ¼ of the area.)

See the information on pages 28 and 29 for details. We hope these guidelines will make your path to sustainability easier.

In order to mini-farm sustainably, the following goals should be taken into account as you grow compost crops and apply compost:

COMPOST AND SUSTAINABLE SOIL FERTILITY GOALS

Per 100 Square Feet Per 4- to 6-Month Growing Season

| | Cured Compost* | | | Pounds Dry Matter to |
	Cubic Feet	5-Gallon Buckets	Inches	Grow per 100 Sq Ft
Recommended by Ed Glenn, Environmental Research Lab, University of Arizona. Southern Arizona sandy soil inside greenhouse. Thought sustainable for that specific site, application and cropping pattern.	1.6	2.4	0.2	
GROW BIOINTENSIVE amount for a *beginning* level of sustainable soil fertility.	2.0	3.0	0.25	15
"Good" amount of compost for soil fertility and productivity, according to one expert.	2.8	4.2	0.35	
GROW BIOINTENSIVE amount for an *intermediate* level of sustainable soil fertility.	4.0	6.0	0.5	15+ to 30
GROW BIOINTENSIVE amount for a *high* level of sustainable soil fertility.	8.0	12.0	1.0	30+ to 60

*including approximately 50% soil

The GROW BIOINTENSIVE Sustainable Mini-Farm

Approximate Crop Area Percentages for Sustainability: 60/30/10

Approximately 40 beds (4,000 sq ft) for one person
(~5,000 sq ft including paths)

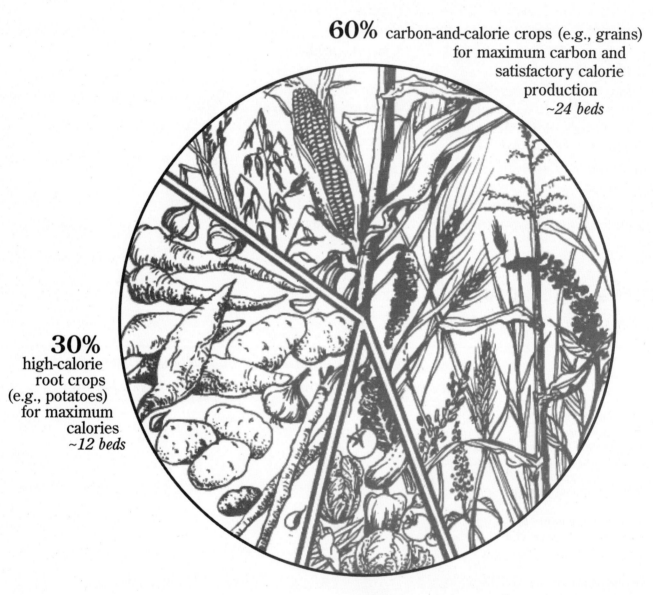

60% carbon-and-calorie crops (e.g., grains) for maximum carbon and satisfactory calorie production
~24 beds

30% high-calorie root crops (e.g., potatoes) for maximum calories *~12 beds*

10% vegetable crops (e.g., salad crops) for vitamins and minerals *~4 beds*

If desired, 50% to 75% of the vegetable crops area may be used for income crops.

CLARIFICATIONS AND EXAMPLES FOR THE 60/30/10 CROP AREA MODEL

General Aids for Planning Your Diet

60% to 65% of the area: Carbon-and-calorie crops for maximum carbon and satisfactory calorie production with weight-efficient* crops

> Grains: wheat, cereal rye, oats, barley, triticale, corn, sorghum, amaranth, quinoa, etc.
> Fava beans (grown to maturity for dry bean and dry biomass production)
> Sunflowers (sunflower seeds are very high in fat; maximum to avoid copper toxicity = 0.62 pound per day)
> Jerusalem artichoke (if stored for a long time—almost weight-efficient and minimally carbon-efficient)
> Filberts
> Raisins

30% of the area: High-calorie root crops for maximum calories with area- and weight-efficient crops*

> (Area in 100-square-foot beds / Weight in pounds)
> *For example, it takes 15.7 beds of potatoes to produce the 2,400 calories per day needed by an average person, who would have to eat 8.6 pounds of potatoes per day.*

BOTH AREA- AND WEIGHT-EFFICIENT	WEIGHT-EFFICIENT (trade-off of increase in area)	AREA-EFFICIENT (trade-off of increase in weight)
Potatoes (15.7 / 8.6) (Maximum to avoid potassium toxicity = 2.5 pounds per day)	Peanuts (34.2 / 0.9) (Very high in fat)	Onions, regular (14.0 / 15.3) (assuming 2 crops are possible OR yield is two times intermediate)
Burdock (14.6 / 5.6) (assuming carrot yield)	Beans (56.5 / 4.5) Soybeans (59.9 / 3.9)	Leeks (14.8 / 19.5)
Sweet potatoes (14.2 / 6.4)	Cassava (22.9 / 3.5) (May produce modest amounts of carbon)	Turnips + tops (9.0 / 9.8) (assuming 2 crops are possible OR yield is two times intermediate)
Garlic (13.3 / 4.4)		Rutabaga (12.4 / 13.6)
Parsnips (12.6 / 8.2)		
Salsify (6.8 / 7.4) (if stored for some time)		

> For diet diversity, you may choose crops that are *less* weight-efficient, in which case you need to have a significant amount of food from crops that are *more* weight-efficient and/or increase your design area.

> Root crops that are not good choices *for this category:*
> carrots (37.4 / 15.4); beets/mangels (roots only) (58.1 / 17.5); radishes (63.5 / 34.8)

5% to 10% of the area: Vegetable crops for vitamins and minerals

---

*As defined for this approach, a crop is considered to be "area efficient" if the annual area needed for total calories is 16 beds (1,600 square feet) or less, assuming *intermediate* yields; it is considered to be "weight efficient" if the daily weight of food to be eaten for total calories is 9 pounds or less. As stated in the book *One Circle,* by David Duhon, an area-efficient crop can provide total calories with 700 square feet or less (550 square feet for a woman, 850 square feet for a man), and a weight-efficient crop can provide total calories in 6 pounds or less for a man or 5.5 pounds or less for a woman.

Sustainability Worldwide

Nature grows plants close together rather than in rows. That's why so many weeds grow between the rows in commercial agriculture. The GROW BIOINTENSIVE method of growing food takes advantage of Nature's propensity to fill any void with living plants through maximizing yields by growing bountiful crops on a minimal amount of area.

The Chinese miniaturized agriculture in a similar way over 4,000 years ago! They grew food by closely spacing plants and maintaining soil fertility (using nutrient- and carbon-containing compost) for thousands of years without depleting their resources. As recently as 1890 this process enabled the Chinese to grow all the food for one person on about 5,800 to 7,200 square feet, including animal products used at the time. Other people in different areas of the world—Greece, Bolivia, Peru, Nepal, Guatemala, Mexico, and Japan—independently developed miniaturized forms of agriculture 2,000 years ago. How does this apply to our modern world? Recently, this kind of miniaturized crop-raising has appeared in Russia, Ireland, and other parts of Europe.

Ecology Action has built on the work of the Chinese, Mayans, and others by using traditional agricultural techniques that are thousands of years old, discovering the universal scientific principles that underlie them. We have spent years making mistakes, learning and relearning, as we attempted to streamline these techniques and make them available to other people (including developing written how-to materials that are easy to understand). The worldwide results of our research and information outreach have been amazing and rewarding.

The people in Biosphere II, a closed-system living project in Arizona during the 1990s, used techniques based on those rediscovered by Ecology Action: They raised 80% of their food for two years within a closed system. Their experience demonstrates that a complete year's diet for one person could be raised on the equivalent of just 3,403 square feet! In contrast, it currently takes commercial agriculture 15,000 to 30,000 square feet to do the same. Moreover, commercial agriculture has to bring in large inputs from other areas and soils just to make this possible, depleting other soils in the process. To raise all the food for one person in a developing nation takes about 16,000 square feet, given the diets eaten and the food-raising practices used.

The Environmental Research Laboratory at the University of Arizona performed the first tests for Biosphere II, documenting the status of the soil and crop yields over time. In the Human Diet Experiment, all crop tests involved sustainable Biointensive crop rotations including grains, legumes, and green manures, and all crop residues were returned to the soil after harvest and composting. Dr. Ed Glenn, who conducted the tests, stated:

"Although funding was not available to continue these experiments for the number of years necessary to draw final conclusions, the results supported the hypothesis that sustainable food production with few or no outside inputs will not only continue to produce high yields but will improve rather than deplete the organic constituents in the soil."

In **India,** just one copy of *How to Grow More Vegetables* became the textbook for a gardening program at an alternative technologies training center, Shri A.M.M. Muragapa Chettier Center in Madras State. That program evolved over a 15-year period into preparations for a national Biointensive program. We recently received word that village women who have been gardening the Biointensive way on their own small plots were able not only to raise food to feed their families but also to raise an annual income by growing crops in a small area.

In all 32 states of **Mexico**, millions of people are currently using Biointensive methods to grow food for *nutrition intervention* for themselves and their families. Each year, new people are taught these processes by extension agents, universities, governmental entities, communities, and organizations, or by those already using the techniques. It is estimated that 1.6 million people are currently using these practices. In addition, many Spanish publications and videos are spreading Biointensive techniques throughout Latin America.

In **Kenya,** the Manor House Agricultural Centre has been directly and indirectly responsible for training well over 40,000 mini-farmers in just a 16-year period. The Centre gives 2-year apprentice training to individuals who are sent by their villages to learn Biointensive techniques so they can go back and teach these methods to their whole village. There are also shorter training periods, and a local outreach program sends teachers out to surrounding areas on a frequent basis to educate members of the communities. The Centre has now opened its training program to international students.

In the **Philippines,** Biointensive publications, conferences, and workshops given by the International Institute for Rural Reconstruction resulted in the initiation of a mandated national Biointensive educational program for all grade school and high school students.

There is also the beginning of a GROW BIOINTENSIVE network in the **United States.** Ecology Action's 3-day introductory workshops have drawn many people who are committed to sharing their own enthusiasm for GROW BIOINTENSIVE techniques with other people. This has been true of the 3-day workshop held in Seattle in September 1992, the one at Stanford University in March 1993, the one given in San Diego in November 1993, as well as more recent ones in Willits and around the United States. To date, 1,163 people from 45 states, the District of Columbia, and 20 countries have been trained in these workshops. People from different parts of the country who have taken Ecology Action workshops have gone on to teach GROW BIOINTENSIVE techniques to other people. One woman's correspondence with Habitat for Humanity has developed into that organization's support of an associated project, Gardens for Humanity, which includes GROW BIOINTENSIVE practices.

A group in Seattle has developed a rural Community Supported Agriculture project to sustainably grow all the food for people in urban areas with the Biointensive method.

We hear from people all over the country that they are starting to seriously use GROW BIOINTENSIVE techniques, some to produce income as well as food for their families.

Even though we are pleased that so many people and programs have adopted GROW BIOINTENSIVE practices, there is still a *challenge to be met.* Many people are successfully using GROW BIOINTENSIVE farming techniques to grow food for nutrition intervention, but few are trying to grow all their calorie food needs on a basis that *also* feeds the soil adequately. When people say they are growing all of their own food, they generally mean that they are growing 5% to 10% of their diet (the vegetables that they can produce during the growing season). *Calorie and sustainable soil fertility mini-farming and gardening* is the next step, which needs to be catalyzed by each of us! The Ecology Action publications *One Circle, The Sustainable Vegetable Garden,* and the Self-Teaching Mini-Series Booklets 14, 15, 25, and 26 deal with growing a complete diet. Once this additional 90% of calorie-growing area has been established in the garden, it only takes an average of about 15 minutes or less each day *per bed* to maintain the garden!

There has been a great shift in human consciousness since Ecology Action first set up its research garden mini-farm 30 years ago. This shift has come about because many individuals have begun to realize that although they might not be able to change the world, they can change the way they do things in their own lives. Raising food in a gentle and conscious manner is one change that has made a difference.

Being disconnected from our food base has separated us from the soil and the life of the Earth. Producing food from a small area is a strengthening, slowing-down process—a way of tuning in to the Earth's needs as we meet our own. We put life into the soil, and the soil enriches our lives.

We as humans are part of the Earth's nutrient cycle, just as the plants and animals are. The Earth welcomes us by creating what we need. The trees are a wonderful example of this: they absorb our carbon dioxide and give us back oxygen to breathe. As we become more aware of and attuned to our place in the circle of life, then *it will seem natural to plant at least 60% of our growing area in carbon-producing crops, which also produce calories. In this way our crops will give life back to the Earth that has fed us.* As we become more responsible for our place in this exciting nutrient flow, we will want to grow *all* of our diet.

Despite its worldwide impact, Ecology Action has remained a small organization, believing that small is effective and human. We consider ourselves to be a catalyst: Our function is to empower people with the skills and knowledge necessary to enable them to improve their lives and thus transform the world into a garden of health and abundance. The message is to live richly in a simple manner—in a way we can all enjoy.

You can assist Ecology Action in this work by finding 5 friends and getting them involved in GROW BIOINTENSIVE sustainable mini-farming and/or other sustainable food-raising practices. Together we can make a significant difference in the world, one small area at a time. This is our opportunity. It is fun to be part of the *whole* picture and part of the long-term world environmental solution! A healthy soil grows healthy crops, which grow healthy people, who can grow a healthy planet and ecosystem.

Compost

Goal: Maximize quality and quantity of cured *compost produced per unit of compost built and maximize* microbiodiversity

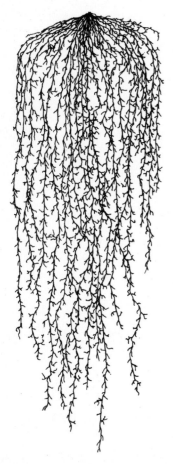

Cereal rye roots grow to six feet deep.

A "Natural" System

In nature, living things die, and their death allows life to be reborn. Both animals and plants die on forest floors and in meadows to be composted by time, water, microorganisms, sun, and air to produce a soil improved in structure and nutrients. Organic plant growing follows nature's example. Leaves, grass, weeds, prunings, spiders, birds, trees, and plants should be returned to the soil and reused—not thrown away. Composting is an important way to recycle such elements as carbon, nitrogen, magnesium, sulfur, calcium, phosphorus, potash, and trace minerals. These elements are all necessary to maintain the biological cycles of life that exist naturally. All too often we participate instead in agricultural stripmining.

Composting in nature occurs in at least 3 ways: (1) in the form of manures, which are plant and animal foods composted inside an animal's body (including earthworms) and then further aged outside the animal by the heat of fermentation. Earthworms are especially good composters. Their castings are 5 times richer in nitrogen, 2 times richer in exchangeable calcium, 7 times richer in available phosphorus, and 11 times richer in available potassium than the soil they inhabit;[1] (2) in the form of animal and plant bodies that decay on top of and within the soil in nature and in compost piles; and (3) in the form of roots, root hairs, and microbial life-forms that remain and decay beneath the surface of the soil after harvesting. It is estimated that one rye plant in good soil grows 3 miles of roots a day, 387 miles of roots in a season, and 6,603 miles of root hairs each season![2]

1. Care must be taken to avoid overdependence on worm castings as a fertilizer; the nutrients in them are very available and can therefore be more easily lost from the soil system.

2. Helen Philbrick and Richard B. Gregg, *Companion Plants and How to Use Them* (Old Greenwich, CT: Devin-Adair Company, 1966), pp. 75–76.

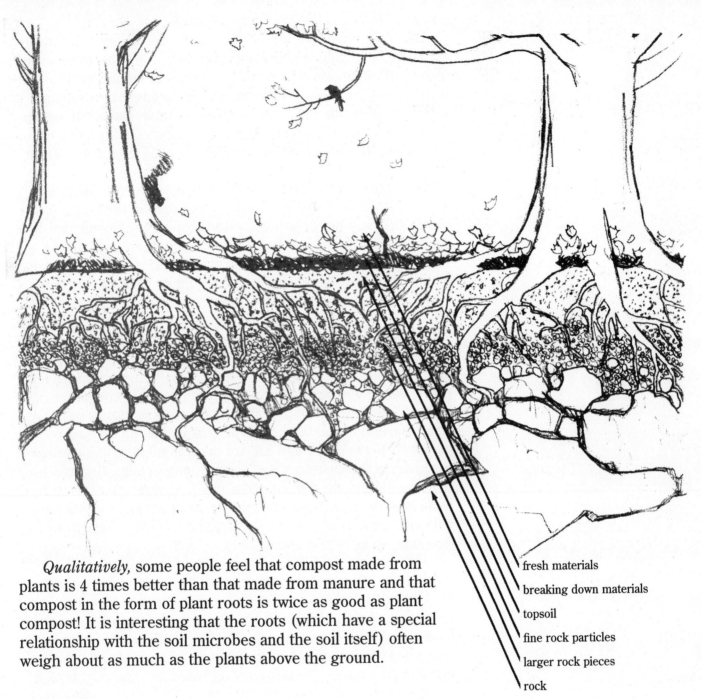

fresh materials

breaking down materials

topsoil

fine rock particles

larger rock pieces

rock

Qualitatively, some people feel that compost made from plants is 4 times better than that made from manure and that compost in the form of plant roots is twice as good as plant compost! It is interesting that the roots (which have a special relationship with the soil microbes and the soil itself) often weigh about as much as the plants above the ground.

Functions

Compost has a dual function. It improves the *structure* of the soil. This means the soil will be easier to work, will have good aeration and water-retention characteristics, and will be resistant to erosion. Compost also provides *nutrients* for plant growth, and its organic acids make nutrients in the soil more available to plants. Fewer nutrients leach out in a soil with adequate organic matter.

Improved structure and nourishment produce a healthy soil. A *healthy soil* produces healthy plants better able to resist insect and disease attacks. Most insects look for sick plants to eat. The best way to control insects and diseases in plants is with a living, healthy soil rather than with poisons that kill beneficial soil life.

Compost keeps soil at maximum health with a minimum expense. Generally, it is unnecessary to buy fertilizers to be able to grow healthy plants. At first, organic fertilizers may have to be purchased so the soil can be brought to a satisfactory level of fertility in a short period of time. Once this has been done, the soil's health can be maintained with compost, good crop rotation, and the recycling of plant residues into the compost pile.

It is important to note the difference between *fertilization* and *fertility*. There can be plenty of fertilizer in the soil, and plants still may not grow well. Add compost to the soil, and the organic acids it contains will release the hidden nutrients in a form available to the plants. This was the source of the amazing fertility of Alan Chadwick's garden at Santa Cruz.

The Process

Compost is created from the decomposition and recombination of various forms of plant and animal life, such as leaves, grass, wood, garbage, natural-fiber clothes, hair, and bones. These materials are *organic matter*. Organic matter is only a small fraction of the total material that makes up the soil—generally between 1% and 8%. Yet organic matter is absolutely essential to the sustenance of soil life and fertility. Organic matter refers to dead plant and animal residues of *all* kinds and in *all* stages of breakdown or decay. Inseparable from these decaying dead residues are the living microorganisms that decompose, or digest, them.

Microscopic life-forms (bacteria and fungi) in the soil produce the recombining process, which creates the warmth in the compost pile. Most of the decomposition involves the formation of carbon dioxide and water as the organic material is broken down. You can monitor the temperature of your compost pile with a compost thermometer. You can also do this by inserting a 1-inch by 1-inch piece of wood into the pile, removing it periodically and feeling the warmth with your hand. You can judge whether the latest measurement is hotter or cooler than before.

As the available energy is consumed, microbial activity slows down, their numbers diminish—and the pile cools. Most of the remaining organic matter is in the form of *humus compounds*. Humus is the living and dead bodies of microbial life. As humus is formed, nitrogen becomes part of its structure. This stabilizes nitrogen in the soil because the humus compounds are resistant to decomposition. They are worked on slowly by soil organisms, but the nitrogen and other essential nutrients are protected from too rapid solubility and dissipation. Organic matter includes humus and some undecomposed organic matter.

Humus also acts as a site of nutrient adsorption and

exchange for plants in the soil. The surfaces of humus particles carry a negative electric charge. Many of the plant nutrients—such as calcium, sodium, magnesium, potassium, and most trace minerals—carry a positive electrical charge in the soil solution and are thereby attracted to and adhere to the surface of humus. Some of the plant nutrients—such as phosphorus, sulfur, and the form of nitrogen that is available to plants—are not positively charged. Fortunately, a good supply of these nutrients becomes available to the plants through biological transformation in the compost pile and soil.

As plant roots grow through the soil in search of nutrients, they feed on the humus. Each plant root is surrounded by a halo of hydrogen ions that are a by-product of the roots' respiration. These hydrogen ions also carry a positive electric charge. The root actually "bargains" with the humus, exchanging some of its positively charged hydrogen ions for positively charged nutrient ions stuck onto the surface of the humus. An active exchange is set up between humus and roots, the plants "choosing" which nutrients they need to balance their own inner chemistry.

Therefore, humus is the most reliable plant food, and plants pull off whatever combinations of nutrients they choose from its surface. GROW BIOINTENSIVE practices rely on this natural, continual, slow-releasing biological process for nutrient release to the plants, rather than making available all the season's nutrients chemically at one time.

The beauty of humus is that it feeds plants with nutrients that the plants pick up on its surface and it also safely stores nutrients in forms that are not readily leached. The humus contains much of the remainder of the original nitrogen that was put in the compost pile in the form of grass, kitchen wastes, and so on. The humus was formed by the resynthesizing activity of numerous species of microorganisms feeding off that original "garbage."

The microorganisms in the soil then continue to feed on the humus after the finished compost is spread on the soil. As the microorganisms feed, the core nutrients in the humus are released in forms available to plant roots. Thus, the microorganisms are an integral part of the humus, and one cannot be found without the other. The only other component of the soil that holds onto and exchanges nutrients with plant roots is clay, but humus can hold onto and exchange a far greater amount of these nutrients.

"Give back to the soil as much as you have taken—and a little bit more—and Nature will provide for you abundantly!"
—Alan Chadwick

Soil and Other Materials in the Compost Pile

It is important to add soil to your compost pile. The soil contains a good starter supply of microorganisms. The organisms help in several ways. Some break down complex compounds into simpler ones the plants can utilize. There are many species of free-living bacteria that fix nitrogen from the air in a form available to plants. Many microorganisms tie up nitrogen surpluses. The surpluses are released gradually as the plants need nitrogen. An excessive concentration of available nitrogen in the soil (which makes plants susceptible to disease) is therefore avoided. There are predaceous fungi that attack and devour nematodes, but these fungi are only found in large amounts in a soil with adequate humus.

The microbial life provides a living pulsation in the soil that preserves its vitality for the plants. The microbes tie up essential nutrients in their own body tissues as they grow, and then release them slowly as they die and decompose. In this way, they help stabilize food release to the plants. These organisms are also continuously excreting a whole range of organic compounds into the soil. Sometimes described as "soil glue," these excretions contribute to the building of the soil structure. The organic compounds also contain disease-curing antibiotics and health-producing vitamins and enzymes that are integral parts of biochemical reactions in a healthy soil.

Note that at least *3 different materials of 3 different textures* are used in the GROW BIOINTENSIVE method compost recipe and in many other recipes. The varied textures will allow good drainage and aeration in the pile. The compost will also have a more diverse nutrient content and greater microbial diversity. A pile made primarily of leaves or grass cuttings makes the passage of water and air through the pile difficult without frequent turning because both tend to mat. Good air and water penetration are required for proper decomposition. The layering of the materials further promotes a mixture of textures and nutrients and helps ensure even decomposition.

Microbe diversity is very important in the growing soil. Many microbes produce antibiotics that help plants resist diseases, and healthy plants have fewer insect challenges. Each microbe tends to have a food preference—some prefer beet refuse, others wheat straw, and so on. Therefore, a way to maximize microbe diversity in the compost pile is to build your compost pile with a large variety of materials.

Building the Pile

One recipe for GROW BIOINTENSIVE compost is, **by weight:** *¹/₃ dry vegetation* (which becomes rehydrated to full weight as you water the compost pile), *¹/₃ green vegetation* (including *kitchen wastes*), and *¹/₃ soil*[3]—though we have found with our heavy clay soil that less soil produces better results. These material amounts by volume are approximately equal parts of green and dry materials to ¹/₄ part of soil. It is *not* necessary to

3. See Ehrenfried E. Pfeiffer, *The Compost Manufacturer's Manual* (Philadelphia: The Pfeiffer Foundation, 1956), especially pp. 23–48.

Tip

Always be sure to add at least 3 different kinds of crops to your compost piles. Different microbes flourish in specific kinds of crops. The result of this crop diversity is *microbe diversity* in the soil, which ensures better soil and plant health.

Tip

You will probably want to build some *compost without soil* for your perennial growing areas. This is because you cannot easily take soil from these areas to build compost piles. Also, the perennial roots will necessitate *surface cultivation* to an approximately 2-inch depth in most cases.

rehydrate the dry material until it is added to the compost pile. Each layer should be watered well as it is created. This $\frac{1}{3}$ to $\frac{1}{3}$ to $\frac{1}{3}$ recipe will give you a carbon-nitrogen ratio in your built compost pile of about 30 to 1, and will produce compost with a significant amount of higher quality, short-term humified carbon. The result will be a hotter (thermophilic: 113° to 149°F) pile with faster-releasing cured compost that generally releases nutrients over a 3-month to 2-year period. A lot of the carbon in this type of compost pile is lost, however, and the resulting cured compost only contains about $\frac{1}{3}$ to $\frac{1}{2}$ the cured compost that a *cooler* (mesophilic: 50° to 113°F) 60-to-1 compost pile will produce. A 60-to-1 pile is built with approximately 2 parts dry vegetation to $\frac{1}{2}$ part green vegetation (including kitchen wastes) and $\frac{1}{4}$ part soil. The result of this pile will be a slower-releasing cured compost that generally releases nutrients over a 3-month to 5,000-year period— especially if the sources of dry matter contain a large amount of lignin, such as corn and sorghum stalks. This can be a way to build up your soil fertility on a long-term basis, but the more readily available nutrients in the cured compost from a 30-to-1 pile will be important for the good growth of most vegetables. We make separate compost piles of small tree branches, since they can take 2 years to decompose.

The ground underneath the pile should be loosened to a depth of 12 inches to provide good drainage. Next, lay down roughage (brush, corn stalks, or other materials) 3 inches thick, if available, for air circulation. The materials should optimally be added to the pile in 1- to 2-inch layers with the dry vegetation on the bottom, the green vegetation and kitchen wastes second, and the soil third (in a $\frac{1}{4}$- to $\frac{1}{2}$-inch layer). You can, however, build a pile spontaneously, adding materials daily or so, as they become available. This kind of pile will usually take a little longer to cure, but can be built more easily. Always be sure to cover kitchen waste and fresh manures with soil to avoid flies and odors!

Green vegetation is 95% more effective than dry vegetation as a "starter" because its higher nitrogen content helps start and maintain the fermentation process. Dry vegetation is high in carbon content. It is difficult for the microbes in the compost pile to digest carbon without sufficient amounts of nitrogen. Unless you have a large household, it may be necessary to save your kitchen scraps in a tight-lidded unbreakable container for several days to get enough material for the kitchen waste layer. You may want to hold your breath when you dump them because the stronger-smelling *anaerobic* form of the decomposition process has been taking place in the closed container. The smell will disappear within a few hours after reintroducing air. All kitchen scraps may be added except meats and sizable amounts of oily salad scraps. Be sure to include bones, tea leaves, coffee grounds, eggshells, and citrus rinds.

Note
We are finding that cold compost piles, which are built with more carbon and can take up to one year to fully cure, *may* produce much more cured carbon (humus) and compost per unit of carbon added to the pile after the built point. This could be essential to maintaining sustainable soil fertility, since sufficient humus is the essential factor in making this fertility possible. You may wish to experiment with this!

KEY ORGANIC MATTER FUNCTIONS

1. Organic matter feeds plants through nutrient exchange and through nutrient release upon its decomposition.

2. It is a continual slow-release source of nutrients for plants.

3. Organic acids in humus help dissolve minerals in the soil, making the mineral nutrients available to plants. Organic acids also increase the permeability of plant root membranes and therefore promote the plant roots' uptake of water and nutrients.

4. Organic matter is the energy source for the soil's microbial life-forms, which are an integral part of soil health. In 1 gram of humus-rich soil there are several *billion* bacteria, 1 million fungi, 10 to 20 million actinomycetes, and 800,000 algae.

5. The microbes that feed on organic matter in the soil temporarily bind the soil particles together. The fungi, with their *thread-like* mycelia, are especially important. They literally sew the soil together. The microbes secrete compounds into the soil as they live, metabolize, and ultimately decompose. Their secretions are a bacterial *glue* (polysaccharides) that holds soil particles, thus improving the soil's structure. Structure is vital to soil productivity because it ensures good aeration, good drainage, good water retention, and erosion resistance.

6. Organic matter is the key to soil structure, keeping it safe from severe erosion and keeping it in an open, porous condition for good water and air penetration.

There are more than 6 billion microbial life-forms in only 1 level teaspoon of cured compost—more than the number of people on Earth!

Soil is added to a compost pile after green vegetation and a kitchen waste layer.

Add the soil layer immediately after the kitchen waste. It contains microorganisms that speed decomposition, keeps the smell down to a minor level, and prevents flies from laying eggs in the garbage. The smell will be difficult to eliminate entirely when waste from members of the cabbage family is added. In a few days, however, even this soil-minimized odor will disappear. Also, the soil in the compost pile becomes "like compost." It holds compost juices, microbes, and minerals that would otherwise leach out of the pile. It is one way to get "more" compost.

Watering the Pile

As each layer is added, water it thoroughly so the pile is *evenly* moist—like a wrung-out damp sponge that does not give out excess water when squeezed. Sufficient water is necessary for the materials to heat and decompose properly. Too little water results in decreased biological activity, and too much simply drowns the aerobic microbial life. Water the pile, when

CROSS SECTION OF A GROW BIOINTENSIVE COMPOST PILE

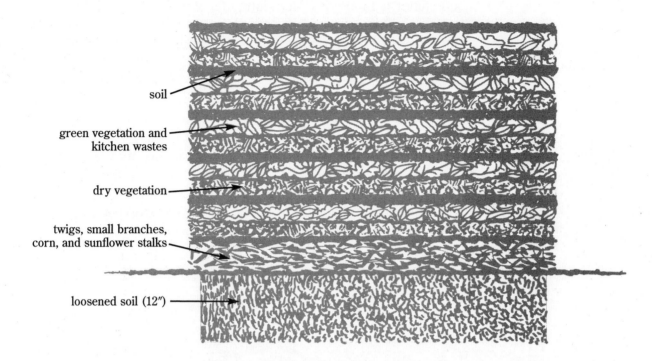

soil

green vegetation and kitchen wastes

dry vegetation

twigs, small branches, corn, and sunflower stalks

loosened soil (12″)

necessary, as you water your garden. The particles in the pile should glisten. During the rainy season, some shelter or covering may be needed to prevent waterlogging and the less optimal anaerobic decomposition that occurs in a waterlogged pile. (The conditions needed for proper functioning of a compost pile and those required for good plant growth in raised beds are similar. In both cases, the proper mixture of air, soil nutrients, structure, microorganisms, and water is essential.)

Locating the Pile

Compost piles can be built in a pit in the ground or in a pile above the ground. The latter is preferable, since during rainy periods a pit can fill up with water. A pile can be made with or without a container. We build our compost piles without using containers. They are unnecessary and use wood and metal resources.

The pile should optimally be built under a deciduous oak tree. This tree's nature provides the conditions for the development of excellent soil underneath it. And compost is a kind of soil. The second-best place for a compost pile is under any other kind of deciduous tree (with the exceptions of walnut and eucalyptus). As a last resort, you can build your pile under evergreen trees or any shady place in your backyard. The shade and windbreak provided by the trees help keep the pile at an even moisture level. (The pile should be placed 6 feet away from the tree's trunk so it will not provide a haven for potentially harmful insects.)

The least expensive type of compost container is homemade.

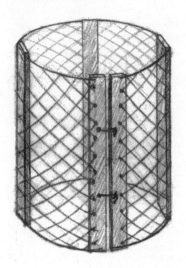

For those who wish to use them, containers can help shape a pile and keep the materials looking neat. The least-expensive container is made of 12-foot-long, 3-feet-wide pieces of 1-inch mesh chicken wire with 5 3-foot-long, 1-inch-by-2-inch boards and 2 sets of small hooks and eyes. The boards are nailed along the 2 3-foot ends of the wire and at 3-foot intervals along the length of the wire (see illustration). The hooks and eyes are attached to the 2 end boards as shown. The unit is then placed as a circle on the ground, the hooks attached to the eyes, and the compost materials placed inside. The materials hold up the circle. After the pile is built, the wire enclosure may be removed and the materials will stay in place. You may now use the enclosure to build another pile, or you may use it later to turn the first pile into if you want to speed up the decomposition process. We rarely try to accelerate this natural process.

Some other kinds of compost piles.

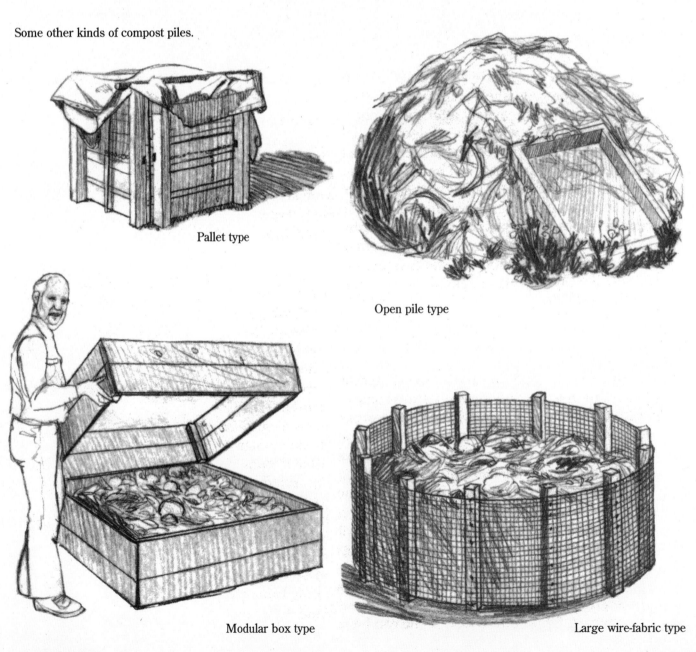

Pallet type

Open pile type

Modular box type

Large wire-fabric type

Size and Timing

A minimum compost pile size of 3 feet by 3 feet by 3 feet (1 cubic yard of lightly moist, built compost, weighing about 1,000 pounds) is recommended. (In colder climates a minimum compost pile size of 4 feet by 4 feet by 4 feet will be needed to properly insulate the heat of the composting process.) Smaller piles fail to provide the insulation necessary for appropriate heating (up to 140°F) and allow too much air to penetrate. It is all right to build up piles slowly to this size as materials become available, though it is best to build an entire pile at one time. A large compost pile might be 4 feet high, 5 feet wide, and 10 feet long. A pile will cure to ⅓ to ¼ of its original size, depending on the materials used.

The best time to prepare compost is in the *spring or autumn,* when biological activity is highest. (Too much heat or cold slows down and even kills the microbial life in the pile.) The two high-activity periods conveniently coincide with the maximum availability of materials in the spring, as grass and other plants begin to grow rapidly, and in the autumn, as leaves fall and other plant life begins to die.

Compost Curing Maturation and Application Rates

Usually, a compost pile needs one turning to adjust the moisture level and make the mixture more homogeneous for complete breakdown. This should be done at about the 3-week point, after the *temperature* of the compost pile has *peaked and fallen.* A *decrease in moisture* usually occurs at the same time, the color begins to change to *brownish* from the original green and yellow, and the compost's odor begins to change from musty to an *earthy, freshly plowed soil aroma.* The compost will normally be ready about 2 months later.

Compost is ready to use when it is dark and rich looking and it crumbles in your hands. The texture should be even, and you should not be able to discern the original source of materials. Mature compost even smells good—like water in a forest spring! A GROW BIOINTENSIVE pile should be ready in 3 to 6 months.[4]

An abundant garden starts with good compost made of "waste products" such as vegetable peelings, weeds, and straw. With some knowledge and planning, the garden can produce all its needed fertilizer and organic matter.

Notes
- When you turn a compost pile, make the base of the new pile smaller than the original base to give the turned pile more mass.
- If you are not ready to use your compost when it is fully cured, stop watering it and spread it out to dry. (See Ecology Action's booklet, *Biointensive Composting.*)

---

4. If for some reason you need compost cured quickly, there are 3 ways to speed up the decomposition rate in a compost pile—though they will probably leave you with much less *cured* compost per unit of material added to your pile originally, rather than the greatest quantity of life-enhancing compost you must seek. One way is to *increase the amount of nitrogen.* The ratio of carbon to nitrogen is critical for the breakdown rate. Materials with a high carbon-nitrogen ratio—such as dry leaves, grain, straw, corn stalks, and small tree branches—take a long time to decompose alone since they lack sufficient nitrogen, which the bacteria depend upon for food. To boost the rate of decay in carbonaceous materials, add nitrogen-rich materials such as newly cut grass, fresh manure, vegetable wastes, green vegetation, or a fertilizer such as alfalfa meal. Twelve to 20 pounds of alfalfa meal per cubic yard of compost will fortify a compost pile with a high carbon content. Lightly sprinkle these fertilizers on each layer as you build your compost pile.

A second method is to *increase the amount of air* (aeration). Beneficial aerobic bacteria thrive in a well-aerated pile. Proper layering and periodic turning of the pile will accomplish this.

Third, you may *increase the surface area of the materials.* The smaller the size of the materials, the greater the amount of their exposed surface area. Broken-up twigs will decompose

In the garden a *maximum* maintenance dressing of 1 inch of compost should be added to the soil before each crop per 4-month growing season. Guidelines for *general* maintenance dressings are a ¼- to 1-inch layer of compost (2 to 8 cubic feet) per 100 square feet,[5] if available.

Composting Methods Compared

The GROW BIOINTENSIVE method of making compost differs in particular from the *biodynamic method* in that the GROW BIOINTENSIVE method is simpler, normally uses no manure, and usually uses no herbal solutions to stimulate microorganism growth.[6] Manure, used continually and in large amounts in biodynamic compost piles, is an imbalanced fertilizer, although it is a good texturizing agent because of its usual decomposed sawdust content. Rather than using herbal solutions, GROW BIOINTENSIVE practices sometimes use weeds, such as stinging nettle, and other plants, such as fava beans, as part of the ingredients in compost piles. Special compost recipes may be created in GROW BIOINTENSIVE to meet particular pH, structure, and nutrient requirements.

The GROW BIOINTENSIVE method of making compost differs from the *Rodale method;* we use little or no manure and usually no rock powder fertilizers or nitrogen supplements.[7] Fertilizers do not need to be added to the pile since successful compost can be made from a mixture of ingredients. The nitrogen supplements do, however, speed up the decomposition process. Both the biodynamic and Rodale methods are good ones, proven by use over a long period of time. Chadwick's Biointensive recipe seems simpler to use and equally effective.

Some people use *sheet composting,* a process of spreading uncomposted organic materials over the soil and then digging them into the soil where they decompose. The disadvantage of this method is that the soil should not be planted for 3 months or so until decomposition has occurred. Soil bacteria tie up the nitrogen during the decomposition process, thereby making it unavailable to the plants. Sheet composting may be beneficial if it is used during the winter in cold areas because the tie-up prevents the nitrogen from leaching out during winter rains.

---

more rapidly than twigs that are left whole. We discourage the use of power shredders because nature will do the job in a relatively short time, and everyone has sufficient access to materials that will compost rapidly without resorting to a shredder. The noise from these machines is quite disturbing and spoils the peace and quiet of a garden. They also consume increasingly scarce fuel.

5. Current research indicates that this amount may eventually be significantly reduced with the use of a high-quality compost containing higher concentrations of carbon and nutrients than are obtained in many composting processes. (See Ecology Action's Self-Teaching Mini-Series Booklet 23, *Biointensive Composting,* for more details.)

6. For the biodynamic method of compost preparation, see Alice Heckel (ed.), *The Pfeiffer Garden Book* (Stroudsburg, PA: Biodynamic Farming and Gardening Association, 1967), pp. 37–51.

7. For the Rodale method of compost preparation, see Robert Rodale (ed.), *The Basic Book of Organic Gardening* (New York: Ballantine, New York, 1971), pp. 59–86.

Other people use *green manures*—cover crops such as vetch, clover, alfalfa, beans, peas, or other legumes, grown until the plants are at 10% to 50% flower. The nitrogen-rich plants are then dug into the soil. By using these legumes in this manner, a maximum of nitrogen is fixed in their root nodules. (The nitrogen is taken from the nodules in the seed-formation process. You can tell whether the nodules have fixed nitrogen by cutting one in half with a fingernail. If the inside is pink, they have fixed nitrogen.) This is one way to bring unworked soil into a better condition. These plants provide nitrogen without your having to purchase fertilizer and they also help you dig. Their roots loosen the soil and eventually turn into humus beneath the earth. Fava beans are exceptionally good for green manuring if you plan to plant tomatoes; their decomposed bodies help eradicate tomato wilt organisms from the soil.

However, we find that green-manure crops are much more effective when used as compost materials, and their roots still have their good effect in the soil. There are several reasons for this. Due to their high nitrogen content, green manures decompose rapidly and even deplete some of the soil's humus. Another disadvantage of the green manuring process is that the land is not producing food crops during the period of cover crop growth and the 1-month period of decomposition. Additionally, green manures generally produce only about ¼ the carbon in a given area that carbonaceous compost crops do, and carbon in the form of *humus* is the most limiting and essential element in maintaining sustainable soil fertility (by serving as the food for microbial life and holding minerals in the soil so they cannot easily leach out of it).

The advantage of the small-scale GROW BIOINTENSIVE method is that backyard composting is easily feasible. When you use compost crops without digging in the crop residues, the growing process will put nitrogen into the soil and make it possible to grow plants, such as corn and tomatoes, that are heavy nitrogen feeders. (See "Companion Planting.") And the plant residues are valuable in the compost pile.

Materials to Use Minimally or Not at All

If you need to use manures and/or less desirable materials in your compost pile, they should make up only ⅙ of your pile by volume so their less optimum effects will be minimized. Some materials should not be used in the preparation of compost, including

- Plants infected with a disease or a severe insect attack where eggs could be preserved or where the insects themselves could survive in spite of the compost pile's heat
- Poisonous plants, such as oleander, hemlock, and castor beans, which harm soil life
- Plants that take too long to break down, such as magnolia leaves
- Plants that have acids toxic to other plants and microbial life, such as eucalyptus, California bay laurel, walnut, juniper, acacia, and cypress
- Plants that may be too acidic or contain substances that interfere with the decomposition process—such as pine needles, which are extremely acidic and contain a form of kerosene (However, special compost piles are often made of acidic materials, such as pine needles and leaves. This compost will lower the soil's pH and stimulate acid-loving plants like strawberries.)
- Ivy and succulents, which may not be killed in the heat of the decomposition process and can regrow when the compost is placed in a planting bed
- Pernicious weeds, such as wild morning glory and Bermuda grass, which will probably not be killed in the decomposition process and will choke out other plants when they resprout after the compost is placed in a planting
- Cat and dog manures, which can contain pathogens harmful to infants. These pathogens are not always killed in the heat of the compost pile

Plants infected with disease or insects and pernicious weeds should be burned to be destroyed properly. Their ashes then become good fertilizer. The ashes will also help control harmful soil insects, such as carrot worms, which shy away from the alkalinity of ashes. (Use ashes in moderate amounts.)

Parts of a regular compost pile that have not broken down completely by the end of the composting period should be placed at the bottom of a new pile. This is especially true for twigs and small branches that can use the extra protection of the pile's height to speed up their decomposition in a situation of increased warmth and moisture.

FUNCTIONS OF COMPOST IN THE SOIL

Improved Structure—compost breaks up clay and clods, and binds together sandy soil. Helps make proper aeration in clayey and sandy soil possible.

Moisture Retention—compost holds 6 times its own weight in water. A soil with good organic matter content soaks up rain like a sponge and regulates the supply to plants. A soil stripped of organic matter resists water penetration, thus leading to crusting, erosion, and flooding.

Aeration—plants can obtain 96% of the nutrients they need from the *air, sun, and water.* A loose, healthy soil assists in diffusing air and moisture into the soil and in exchanging nutrients. Carbon dioxide released by organic matter decomposition diffuses out of the soil and is absorbed by the canopy of leaves above in a raised bed mini-climate created by closely spaced plants.

Fertilization—compost contains some nitrogen, phosphorus, potassium, magnesium, and sulfur but is especially important for trace elements. The important principle is to return to the earth, by the use of plant residues and manures, all that has been taken out of it.

Nitrogen Storage—the compost pile is a storehouse for nitrogen. Because it is tied up in the compost-breakdown process, water-soluble nitrogen does not leach out or oxidize into the air for a period of 3 to 6 months or more—depending on how the pile is built and maintained.

pH Buffer—a good percentage of compost in the soil allows plants to grow better in less-than-optimal pH situations.

Soil Toxin Neutralizer—important recent studies show that plants grown in organically composted soils take up less lead, heavy metals, and other urban pollutants.

Nutrient Release—organic acids dissolve soil minerals and make them available to plants. As organic matter decomposes, it releases nutrients for plant uptake and for the soil microbial population.

Food for Microbial Life—good compost creates healthy conditions for organisms that live in the soil. Compost harbors earthworms and beneficial fungi that fight nematodes and other soil pests.

The Ultimate in Recycling—the earth provides us with food, clothing, and shelter, and we close the cycle in offering fertility, health, and life through the shepherding of materials.

Note
In order to maintain good soil fertility, approximately 4% to 6% (by weight) organic matter is needed in temperate soils. About 3% is desirable in tropical soils. It is noteworthy that the soil organic matter level used to be measured 11 inches deep many years ago. Later, the measurement level was reduced to $6^2/_3$ inches. Today, it has been further reduced to less than 6 inches deep.

BUILDING A COMPOST PILE STEP BY STEP

1. Under the pile area (3 or 4 square feet), loosen the soil to 12 inches deep with a spading fork.

2. Lay down *roughage* (brush, corn stalks, or other material), 3 inches thick, if it is available, for air circulation.

3. Put down a 2-inch layer of *dry vegetation*—dry weeds, leaves, straw, dry grass clippings, hay, and old garden wastes. Water it thoroughly.

4. Put down a 2-inch layer of *green vegetation and kitchen wastes*—fresh weeds, grass clippings, hedge trimmings, green cover crops, and kitchen wastes you have saved. Water well.

5. Cover lightly with a ¼- to ½-inch layer of *soil* to prevent flies and odors. Moisten the soil.

6. Add new layers of dry vegetation, green vegetation, kitchen waste, and soil as materials become available until the pile is 3 to 4 feet high.

7. Cover the top of the pile with a ½- to 1-inch layer of soil.

8. Water the completed pile regularly until it is ready for use.

9. Let the completed pile cure 3 to 6 months while you are building a new pile. Turn the pile once for faster decomposition. For planning purposes, remember that a 4-foot-high compost pile will be 1 to 1⅓ feet high when it is ready to use.

Note

We sometimes build a compost pile on an unused growing bed so the next crop grown in that bed will pick up and utilize any nutrients leached out from the pile into the soil. The next season we build compost on another unused growing bed.

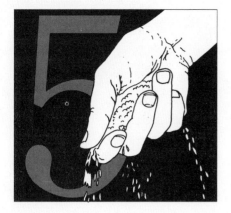

Fertilization

Goal: Build and maintain proper levels of and balances among soil nutrients

T he *first* goal of adding fertilizers to your soil is to build nutrients up to their proper levels and balances for your particular type of soil type, rainfall, climate, sun exposure, altitude, and cation-exchange capacity (that is, a measurement of the availability of nutrients in a given soil). The *second* goal is to keep those nutrients in your food-raising area by composting properly and recycling all wastes. A *third* goal is to use *enough* nutrients, water, and compost in your growing area.

During a drought years ago, several women in India grew food using Biointensive methods. Their production was double that of others who used single-dug row cropping practices. One woman got even higher yields than other Biointensive gardeners by using her one unit of water, fertilizers, and seed on *one* growing area. Hoping for higher yields, the others had spread their single units of resources over 7 to 15 units of growing area. The woman with the best results got more total production in $\frac{1}{7}$ to $\frac{1}{15}$ the area. She had benefited by Alan Chadwick's observation, "Begin with one bed and tend it well! Then expand your growing area."

Over the years we have seen gardeners in many countries obtain excellent, good, and fair yields using GROW BIOINTENSIVE techniques, depending on the care taken with the resources and on what results individuals believed they would obtain. A good level and balance of nutrients in your soil will help your garden flourish and make it optimally healthy and productive.

Taking a soil sample.

Soil Testing

A professional soil test performed by a laboratory will provide you with the most complete evaluation. Unfortunately, because of variation in soil types, climates, cultivation practices,

The La Motte soil test kit is a home kit.

SOIL TEST

Date performed: _____

Performed by: _____

Test	Results	Recommendations per 100 Square Feet
Nitrogen		
Phosphorus		
Potassium		
pH (6.5 or slightly acid is optimum)		
Remarks (including texture)		

NITROGEN (N), PHOSPHORUS (P), AND POTASSIUM (K)

Pounds of fertilizer to add per 100 square feet. Pounds of *pure* nutrients added are given in parentheses.
Note: The goal is to reduce the nutrient deficiencies in the soil slowly over time. (If you add large amounts of readily available nutrients all at once, nutrients not in short supply in the soil may become unavailable.)

Test Rating	Nitrogen (N)	Phosphorus (P)	Potassium (K)
Very High[1]	(.1) 4.2 lbs alfalfa meal	(.2) 4.5 lbs phosphate rock or 4.5 lbs soft phosphate	(.15) 1.5 lbs wood ashes[2] and 1.5 lbs crushed granite[3]
High[1]	(.2) 8.4 lbs alfalfa meal	(.3) 6.8 lbs phosphate rock or 13.6 lbs soft phosphate	(.2) 1.5 lbs wood ashes[2] and 2.5 lbs crushed granite[3]
Medium High	(.25) 10.5 lbs alfalfa meal	(.35) 8 lbs phosphate rock or 16 lbs soft phosphate	(.25) 1.5 lbs wood ashes[2] and 3.5 lbs crushed granite[3]
Medium	(.3) 12.6 lbs alfalfa meal	(.4) 9 lbs phosphate rock or 18 lbs soft phosphate	(.3) 1.5 lbs wood ashes[2] and 4.5 lbs crushed granite[3]
Medium Low	(.35) 14.7 lbs alfalfa meal	(.45) 10.2 lbs phosphate rock or 20.4 lbs soft phosphate	(.35) 1.5 lbs wood ashes[2] and 5.5 lbs crushed granite[3]
Low	(.4) 16.8 lbs alfalfa meal	(.5) 11.4 lbs phosphate rock or 22.8 lbs soft phosphate	(.4) 1.5 lbs wood ashes[2] and 6.5 lbs crushed granite[3]
Very Low	(.5) 18.9 lbs alfalfa meal	(.6) 13.6 lbs phosphate rock or 27.2 lbs soft phosphate	(.5) 1.5 lbs wood ashes[3] and 8.5 lbs crushed granite[3]

1. Addition of nutrients at these levels is optional.
2. Wood ash application should be used with care for soils with a pH above 6.5.
3. Finely ground.

rainfall, altitude, sun exposure, drainage conditions, the types of crops grown, and cation-exchange capacity, no standard added nutrient formula will work in all situations.

If you can, test your soil for major nutrients and trace minerals, including pH (the acidity or alkalinity level of your soil), before choosing fertilizers. The major minerals, those that plants utilize in relatively large amounts, include nitrogen, phosphorus, potassium, sulfur, magnesium, and calcium. Trace minerals—such as zinc, boron, copper, and iron—are important elements that are required in very small quantities. For professional soil testing, we use the *Timberleaf* soil testing service.[4] It specializes in testing for organic farmers and gardeners, with an emphasis on Biointensive fertility. The service analyzes all soil and plant minerals and the soil's physical characteristics and can provide follow-up review and advice on your year's experience in the garden. If you are unable to arrange a professional soil test, purchase a home test kit. The best such kit is the *La Motte kit*.[5] With the home kit you will be limited to testing nitrogen, phosphorus and potassium content, and pH.

To take a soil sample from your yard, use a nonferrous trowel or a stainless steel spoon to dig a vertical soil slice from 8 inches below the surface. Take samples from 6 to 8 representative areas and mix them together well in a clean plastic bucket. Make sure you do not include residues, such as roots and surface organic litter, in the composite sample. Also, do not sample for 30 days after adding any fertilizers, manure, or compost to the area. The samples normally should be taken at the end of a growing season or just before one. You will need a total soil volume of 1 pound for professional testing or 4 heaping tablespoons for the home test kit. Remember that soil tests can save you a lot of money, since they all guard against overapplication of fertilizers, allow you to account for nutrients already available in your soil for good plant growth, and increase yields.

To use the *Timberleaf* service, ship your composite sample as instructed in its soil test packet without drying the soil. For a home test kit, let samples dry in a small paper bag in indirect sunlight—*not* in the sun or an oven. When you are ready to begin testing, follow the included with the kit. Record home test results on a photocopy of the chart on page 50. Once you have completed the test, use the information page 45 to determine a general fertilization plan for your garden.

As you become more skilled, you may want to use John Beeby's book *Test Your Soil with Plants* to test your soil. This is how people used to learn about their soil's nutrient needs for thousands of years before chemical soil tests became available. Eventually each of us should have a *living soil test* of plants

---

4. *Timberleaf,* 39648 Old Spring Road, Murieta, CA 92563-5566.
5. La Motte Chemical Products, Box 329, Chestertown, MD 21620: Model STH.

grown in a small area that is "read" to determine existing nutrient levels in the soil of that area! Until about 100 years ago, this is how farmers determined soil nutrient needs. It will take many years to fully rediscover and develop all these skills.

ANALYSIS OF RECOMMENDED ORGANIC SOIL AMENDMENTS[6]

N, P, and K refer to three of the major nutrients that plants need. According to law, any product sold as a fertilizer must provide an analysis upon request for these three minerals. *Nitrogen* contains proteins, is a food source in compost piles, and causes green growth. *Phosphorus* gives plants energy and is necessary for the growth of flowers and seeds. *Potassium* aids in protein synthesis and the translocation of carbohydrates to build strong stems. Plants also need a good supply of *organic matter* to give them additional nitrogen, phosphorus, sulfur, copper, zinc, boron, and molybdenum, and they need 8 other nutrients. Only under *ideal conditions* do native soil minerals provide these nutrients naturally. Plants need a full meal of nutrients, and as good stewards of the soil we are responsible for providing them. Be aware that laboratory analysis to determine fertilizer amendments does not always show *all* of the actual needs of the soil plant system. Also, the composition may vary for products from various sources. Be sure to check the analyses on the bags.

NITROGEN

Alfalfa Meal
2% to 3% N, .7% P, 2.25% K. Lasts 3 to 4 months. Use up to 19 lbs (16¾ qt)/100 sq ft. A quick-acting source of nitrogen and some potassium. (If not organic, it can contain methoxichlor pesticide residues.)

Fish Meal
9% to 10.5% N, 6% P, 0% K. Lasts 6 to 8 months. Use up to 5 lbs (3⅔ qt)/100 sq ft. Good combined nitrogen and phosphorus source. (Caution: Some can contain significant amounts of toxic heavy metals.)

PHOSPHORUS

Phosphate Rock
~11.5% to 17.5% total P. Lasts 3 to 5 years. Use up to 9 lbs (2⅔ qt)/100 sq ft. Very slow releasing.

Note
Remember that too much nitrogen in your soil can cause the soil's all-important organic matter to break down too quickly.

---

6. Note: GROW BIOINTENSIVE no longer uses many organic fertilizers because of disease, pesticide residue, or heavy metal toxicity challenges.

Soft Phosphate (Colloidal)
~8% total P; ~2% available P. Lasts 2 to 3 years. Use up to 18 lbs (2⅔ qt)/100 sq ft. Clay base makes it more available to plants than the phosphorus in phosphate rock, though the two are used interchangeably.

POTASSIUM

Wood Ash
1% to 10% K. Lasts 6 months. Use up to 1.5 lbs (1¾ qt)/100 sq ft. Ash from wood is high in potassium and helps repel maggots. Ash also has an alkaline effect on the soil, so use it with care if your soil pH is above 6.5. *Black* wood ash is best. Wood ash provides strength and plant essence, aids in insect control, and is a flavor enhancer for vegetables, especially lettuce and tomatoes. You can produce it with a controlled, soil-covered, slow-burning fire built during a soft drizzle or rain. This ash is higher in potassium and other minerals because they do not readily escape into the atmosphere as the wood is consumed by fire. Wood ash should be stored in a tight container until it is used; exposure to air will destroy much of its nutrient value. *Grey* wood ash from a fireplace may be used if it is from wood and not from colored or slick paper.

Crushed Granite (Finely Ground)
3% to 5% K. Lasts up to 10 years. Use up to 8.5 lbs (3½ qt)/100 sq ft. It is a slow-releasing source of potassium and trace minerals.

SOIL MODIFIERS

Dolomitic Lime
~25% Ca. ~6% to 14% Mg. A good source of calcium and magnesium to be used when both are needed. Do not use dolomitic lime in a soil with an adequate or high level of magnesium. Do not use lime to "sweeten" the compost pile as doing so will result in a serious loss of nitrogen. A layer of soil will discourage flies and reduce odors. 1 qt = about 3 lbs 8 oz.

High Calcium Lime (Calcite)
A good source of calcium when magnesium levels are too high for applying dolomitic lime. Oyster shell flour lime (~34% to 36% Ca) is a good substitute. 1 qt = about 30 oz.

Gypsum (Calcium Sulfate)
~23% Ca. ~19% S. Used to correct excess levels of exchangeable sodium. Apply only when recommended by a professional soil test. 1 qt = about 1 lb 4 oz.

Crushed Eggshells
High in calcium. Especially good for cabbage family crops.

Eggshells help break up clay and release nutrients tied up in alkaline soils. Use up to 2 lbs (1¼ qt)/100 sq ft. Dry them first.

Manure (All Types)
A good source of organic matter in the garden. The nutrient levels in each manure will depend on proper management of the curing process and on the amount of straw or sawdust in the manure. Optimally, do not use more than 4 cubic feet (6 5-gallon buckets) of aged manure per year (about 136 lbs dry weight, or a ½-inch layer). It is best to use manure that contains little undecomposed sawdust. Approximately 2 cubic feet (3 5-gallon buckets) of manure (50 lbs dry weight) applied per 100 square feet can lower the pH *one* point. Manure is a microbial life stimulant and an animal and plant essence that has been "composted" both inside the animal and outside in a curing pile. Avoid using too much manure because manures that do not contain much sawdust or straw can contain excess salt and imbalanced ratios of nitrogen, phosphorus, and potassium. The GROW BIOINTENSIVE method uses as much (or more) phosphorus and potassium as nitrogen. This results in stronger, healthier plants. It is one difference between the GROW BIOINTENSIVE method and the French intensive approach that depended heavily on the use of horse manure, which is about 3 parts nitrogen to 1 part phosphorus to 3 parts potassium. This ratio is unbalanced in favor of nitrogen, which in time results in weak and rank plant growth more susceptible to disease and insect attack. A ratio of 1 part nitrogen to 1 part phosphorus to 1 part potassium is better. Using a large amount of composted or aged manure is recommended as an alternative to compost only when compost is not available.

Caution
In order to obtain a 1-inch layer of aged steer manure for use as compost on a 100-square-foot area, fodder for the animal to eat must be grown on a 500-square-foot area. This means an area four times as large as your growing area is being depleted of trace minerals and life-sustaining humus! Such a practice is not sustainable if used over a long period of time. When the proper *compost crops* are used instead, the compost materials for your 100-square-foot garden can be grown in just your 100-square-foot garden itself!

MANURES—SOLIDS
(approximate)

Chicken—Fresh	1.50% N	1.00% P	.50% K
Chicken—Dry	4.50% N	3.50% P	2.00% K
Dairy Cow	.56% N	.23% P	.60% K
Horse	.69% N	.24% P	.72% K
Pig—Fresh	.50% N	.32% P	.46% K
Sheep	1.40% N	.48% P	1.20% K
Steer	.70% N	.55% P	.72% K

Compost
Good compost is the most important part of the garden. It aerates soil, breaks up clay, binds together sand, improves drainage, prevents erosion, neutralizes toxins, holds precious moisture, releases essential nutrients, and feeds the microbiotic life of the soil, creating healthy conditions for natural antibiotics, worms, and beneficial fungi. Each 4-month growing season, use

up to an inch of cured compost (8 cubic feet/100 square feet), which is about ⅓ of a cubic yard. (One cubic yard equals 27 cubic feet. Two cubic feet of cured compost will cover 100 square feet ¼ inch deep.) Generally, use only a maximum 8 cubic feet cured compost made with equal amounts by weight of dry material, green material, and soil (or 4 cubic feet cured compost made without soil) per 100 square feet per 4- to 6-month crop to avoid using more than a sustainable amount of compost.

You should note the heavy emphasis that the GROW BIOINTENSIVE method places on compost. The demand for organic fertilizers is increasing while the supply available to each person in the world is decreasing. Soon, few fertilizers will be available at reasonable prices. Also, the materials used to produce chemical fertilizers are becoming less available. Materials for GROW BIOINTENSIVE compost, on the other hand, are plants and soil, which can be produced in a sustained way by a healthy garden. These compostable materials can be produced indefinitely if we take care of our soils and do not exhaust them. In fact, 96% of the total amount of nutrients needed for plant growth processes are obtained as plants use the sun's energy to work on elements already in the air and water.[7] Soil and compost provide the rest.

GROW BIOINTENSIVE compost (see "Compost") is high in most major and trace minerals. It also contains nitrogen and, when made properly, can be high in nitrogen. A thin layer of manure added to the soil during the fertilization stage can also provide nitrogen. Periodically growing legumes—such as peas, beans, clover, alfalfa, and vetch—in the planting beds will provide nitrogen, too. The nitrogen that the legumes fix from the air is released when their roots, stems, and leaves decompose. Compost, manure, wood ash, nitrogen from legumes, and nutrients from the growth of certain kinds of herbs and weeds in the beds (see "Companion Planting") supply the 4% of a plant's diet not provided by the air and water.

What a Home Soil Test Will Not Tell You

A *professional soil test* is an excellent tool for analyzing deficiencies, excesses, and the relative balance of all plant nutrients in your garden's soil. A *home test kit*, however, is very limited and only points out pH level and deficiencies of nitrogen, phosphorus, and potassium. If you have difficulty growing healthy plants in your garden, a home test kit may not provide the solution. Plants grown in soil lacking any of the major or trace minerals show their deficiency in yellowed leaves, stunted growth, purple veins, or any number of other ways.

7. Joseph A. Cocannouer, *Farming with Nature* (Norman, OK: University of Oklahoma Press, 1954), p. 50.

SOIL pH SCALE

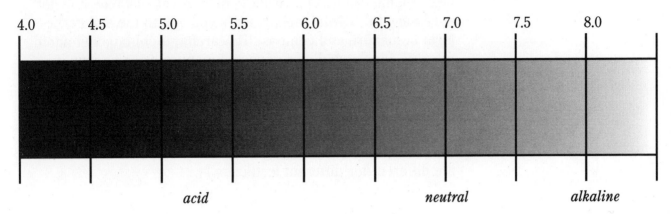

4.0   4.5   5.0   5.5   6.0   6.5   7.0   7.5   8.0

acid   *neutral*   *alkaline*

pH

A pH reading tells you the relative acidity or alkalinity of the soil water, generally called the soil solution. Nutrient availability for vegetable plants, soil microbial activity, and soil structure are all affected by pH. Most vegetables grow best in a slightly acidic soil with a pH of 6.8. A range of 6.0 to 7.0 is fine for most crops.

More important than the actual pH reading is the quality of the pH. This is determined by testing for the amount of plant-available potassium, magnesium, calcium, and sodium in your soil. Only a professional soil test can determine the soil's mineral balance. You should have this information before you apply pH modifiers to your soil. For instance, limestone is a common pH modifier; however, all limestones do not have the same mineral composition. An application of a dolomitic instead of a calcitic lime to a soil with a high magnesium content could disrupt your soil balance and adversely affect plant growth.

Soil-applied organic matter and manure can alter the pH over time. When adequate organic matter is used, we find crops will tolerate a wider pH range. Leaf mold, pine needles, and sawdust produce an acidic compost that can lower the pH. Manures may be alkaline and raise the pH, although they may lower the pH *one* point in some cases. Compost can be either acidic or alkaline. Using the proper limestone with the correct mineral balance is the least expensive and most practical way to increase pH. Mined sulfur, a soil nutrient deficient in many soils, is an excellent amendment to lower the pH. Although you can use organic matter to alter pH, you will need to know your soil mineral structure, the existing soil pH, and the pH of the applied material in order to apply it accurately and in an effective amount.

The Analysis of Recommended Organic Soil Amendments, beginning on page 53, gives the mineral nutrient content of many commonly used organic fertilizers. This information will help you determine the amounts of each fertilizer to add if you are using a home test kit and are unable to have a professional soil test performed. In your calculations, it is not necessary to *subtract* the nutrients you add to the soil in the form of manure and compost. Be careful, though, about adding manure. Much aged or composted manure actually contains little nitrogen and may have a substantial amount of nitrogen-demanding sawdust. If you use a lot of manure containing large amounts of sawdust as a soil texturizer, you may want to add some additional nitrogen fertilizer, such as 4 extra pounds of alfalfa meal per 100 square feet. (Notice that the release times are different for different fertilizers.)

Shaping the Bed

The bed should be shaped before adding fertilizers. If your soil is in good condition, use a rake to shape the bed into a mound. The soil will not easily wash off or erode from beds shaped in this manner, once the structure of the soil is improved. While you are still improving the structure of heavy clay soils, you may want to form a *flat-topped bed* with a small lip on the outer edges of the bed. This will minimize erosion caused by watering. The sides of the bed should have about a 30-degree slope; a sharper angle will encourage erosion. When you have shaped the bed, tamp the soil down before planting, if necessary, by placing the digging board on all parts of the

Broadcasting fertilizers.

(*Left*) Raking soil outward from the inside for a lip; (*right*) raking the soil up from the side for a lip.

bed and walking across the board. If you add a lip to the bed, do it after tamping down the soil.

Adding Fertilizers and Compost

Add fertilizers and other amendments one at a time. Avoid windy days, and hold the fertilizer close to the bed surface when spreading. Use the different colors to help you. The soil is dark, so sprinkle on a light-colored fertilizer (such as oyster shell flour) first, then a darker fertilizer (such as alfalfa meal), and so on. It is better to underapply the fertilizers because you can go back over the bed afterward to spread on any leftover, but it is difficult to pick up fertilizer if too much falls in one place. Aim for even distribution. Next, add compost and/or aged manure. After all are applied, sift in the fertilizers and other amendments by inserting a spading fork 2 to 4 inches deep at a slant, then lifting it upward with a slight jiggling motion.

Several things should be noted about the nutrients added to the upper 3 to 4 inches of soil. (1) The nutrients are added to the upper soil layer as they occur in nature. (2) The nutrients are relocated through the soil when larger soil organisms and when water flows downward. (3) Organic fertilizers break down more slowly than most chemical fertilizers. By utilizing natural nutrient cycles, plant-available minerals are released over an extended period of time.

(*Left*) Casting fertilizer onto a bed's surface; (*right*) sifting in fertilizers with a spading fork. (A "twist dig" is now being used to sift in fertilizers also. It is easier on the back and does not require bending over as far. This method requires three motions at once: [1] a slight up-and-down motion with the left hand, [2] a twist back and forth holding onto the D-handled spade with the right hand, and [3] a slight pushing in and out of the handle through the left hand with the right hand. Develop this skill by practicing.) Do not rake the bed to smooth it out after sifting in fertilizers, as this usually creates irregular concentrations of fertilizers that were previously spread evenly.

More-Sustainabile Fertilization

Each gardener should strive to use less and less fertilizer brought in from outside his or her own garden area. This will be especially true when such amendments become scarce due to the increased number of people using them. There are at least 4 ways to create a more "closed system" garden, to which few resources are imported:

1. Use most of the food you grow *at home*, so all the residues are returned to your soil. "Export" as little as possible of your valuable soil resource.

2. Grow some trees. Their deep root systems will bring up nutrients from far down in the subsoil into the topsoil and even into the tree leaves. These nutrients would not otherwise become available for use as plant food.

3. "Grow" your own fertilizers by raising plants that produce good amounts of compost material, which concentrates the nutrients required in a form that plants can use. For beginning information on plants to use, see Ecology Action's Self-Teaching Mini-Series Booklet 12, *Growing and Gathering Your Own Fertilizers* (see Ecology Action Publications, page 225), Bargyla and Gylver Rateaver's *Organic Method Primer*, and Ehrenfried Pfeiffer's *Weeds and What They Tell* (see pages 184 and 199 in the bibliography, respectively). If everyone were to use organic fertilizers, there would be a worldwide shortage; eventually the key will be growing our own and recycling *all* wastes. Deep-rooting alfalfa (as deep as 125 feet) and comfrey (up to 8 feet) also help bring up leached-out and newly released nutrients from the soil strata and rocks below.

4. Maintain at least a 4% to 6% organic matter level in at least the upper 6 inches of soil in temperate zones and 3% organic matter level in tropical ones. This will encourage microbial life growth, which can keep nutrients from leaching out of the soil.

The GROW BIOINTENSIVE method has roots 4,000 years into the past in Chinese intensive agriculture, 2,000 years into the past in the Greek use of raised beds and, more recently, in European farming. Similar practices are still used today in the native agriculture of many countries, such as Guatemala. GROW BIOINTENSIVE will extend its roots into a future where environmentally balanced resource usage is of the utmost importance.

The balanced ecosystem:
"Nothing happens in living
nature that is not in relation to
the whole."

—Goethe

Seed Propagation

Goal: Enhanced and uninterrupted plant growth

Now that we know a little about the body and soul of our Earth, we are ready to witness the birth of seedlings. Just for a moment, close your eyes, and pretend you are the seed of your favorite plant, tree, vegetable, fruit, flower, or herb. You are all alone. You can do nothing in this state. Slowly you begin to hear sounds around you. The wind, perhaps. You feel warmth from the sun, feel the ground underneath you. What do you need for good growth? Think like a seed, and ask yourself what a seed needs. It needs an entire microcosm of the world—air, warmth, moisture, soil, nutrients, and microorganisms. Plants need all these things, as do birds, insects, and animals.

Generally, the elements needed for growth fall into two categories: terrestrial (soil and nutrients) and celestial (air, warmth, moisture). The celestial elements cannot be completely categorized, however, since air, warmth, and moisture come from the heavens to circulate through the soil, and plants can take in air through their roots as well as through their leaves. Nutrients can also be borne upon air currents. In fact, citrus trees take in the important trace mineral zinc more readily by their leaves than by their roots. See "Companion Planting" for further information on the parts that other elements in the plant and animal worlds play—the parts of other plants and insects, for example.

Seed Planting

Seeds should be planted as deep as the thin vertical dimension of each side. Lima and fava beans may be planted on their sides. Their root systems, which emerge from an eye, can grow straight down. The seeds should be covered with humus-containing flat soil, which is similar to the soil with decomposed plant matter found over germinating seeds in nature. The compost stimulates the germination process.

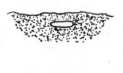

A seed is planted at a depth equal to its vertical dimension.

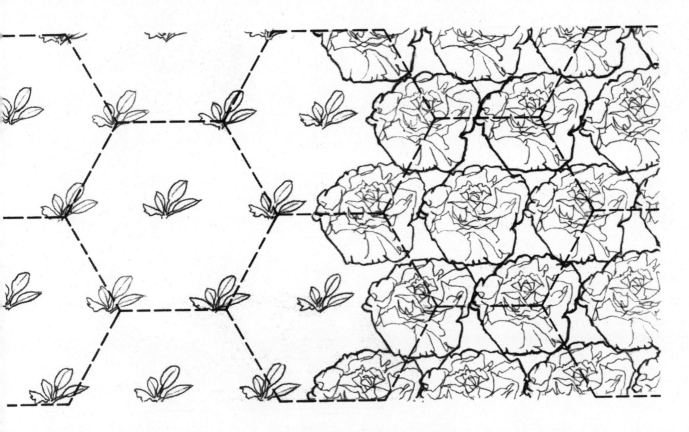

Hexagonal spacing:
Leaf lettuce is spaced on 8-inch centers.

Seeds, whether they are planted in beds or in flats, should be planted in a diagonally offset or hexagonal spacing pattern with an equal distance between each seed. The Master Charts later in this chapter tell how far apart to space different types of plants. When plants are mature in flats or planting beds, their leaves should barely touch. Appropriately spaced plants form a *living mulch*, which retards weed growth, aids in the retention of soil moisture by shading the soil, and creates the living mulch miniclimate under their leaves so essential to balanced, uninterrupted growth. When spacing seeds in flats, place the seeds far enough apart that the seedlings' leaves will barely touch when the seedlings are transplanting size. Try 1-inch to 2-inch spacings depending on the size of the seedling at its transplanting stage (see the Master Charts at the end of this chapter). In general, the plant spacings listed in the Master Charts for vegetables, flowers, and herbs are equal to the "within the row" spacings listed on the back of seed packets, or sometimes ¾ of this distance. *Disregard* any "between row" spacings. You will have to establish spacing for plants grown on hills by experimentation. The Master Charts list our best spacing determinations to date for these plants.

To make the placement of seeds in planting beds or flats easier, use frames with 1-inch or 2-inch mesh chicken wire stretched across them. The mesh is built on a hexagonal pattern, so the seeds can be dropped in the center of a hexagon and be on the proper center. Or, if a center greater than 1 inch is involved and you only have 1-inch mesh, just count past the proper number of hexagons before dropping the next seed.

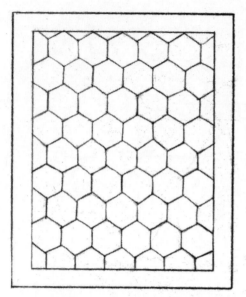

A spacing frame aids in placing seeds in flats. Place one seed in the center of each space.

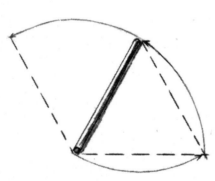

Use a spacing stick for placing seeds in beds. 3-inch to 36-inch sizes are used according to the crop planted. Triangulation is the way we plant most seeds and transplant seedlings.

Use a triangular spacing template for placing seeds in beds.

When transplanting or planting seeds on spacings of 3 inches or more, try using measuring sticks cut to the required length to determine where each plant should be located. Transplant or sow a seed at each point of the triangulation process. You will eventually be able to transplant with reasonable accuracy without measuring!

Once you get the feel for plant spacing, you may want to practice broadcasting seeds by hand in flats for some crops, such as lettuce and flowers. Broadcasting was the method that Alan Chadwick and his apprentices used with flats. Be sure the seeds end up ¼ to ½ inch apart in the first flat so the seeds can take advantage of their complete miniclimate for early growth stimulation and health. This method does, however, require more time to do several prick outs. When these seedlings' leaves are barely touching, prick them out (transplant them) into other flats on 1- to 2-inch centers. One flat of these broadcasted seeds will fill approximately 4 flats after pricking out.

Cover the seeds in their flats with a layer of the flat soil mixture described later in this chapter. When broadcasting seeds onto a growing bed, gently "chop" them in afterward with a bow rake to a depth equal to their diameter (when they are lying flat on a surface). Be sure to chop the rake only up and down; do not pull it toward you. If you pull, seeds, fertilizers, and compost may concentrate irregularly over the bed rather than remain evenly spread. Or you may poke large seeds into the soil to their proper depth with your index finger. Fill the hole by pushing soil into it with your thumb and index finger.

Use your digging board as a planting board to minimize compaction. As you move it along the bed, reloosen the soil underneath with a hand fork.

Now that you have prepared your GROW BIOINTENSIVE bed and have spread the compost, you have a choice as to whether to sow seeds directly into the bed or to use seedlings.

Transplanting seedlings involves more advance planning and more time, but in a small garden, this has several advantages:

- Transplanted seedlings make better use of bed space. Seeds can take from 5 days to 12 weeks or more to reach transplanting size. If that growing is done in a flat, something else can be growing in the bed in the meantime.

- You can be reasonably sure that each transplanted seedling will grow into a healthy mature plant. Not all seeds germinate, so no matter how carefully you sow seeds directly in the bed, you can end up with gaps between plants and, therefore, bare soil that allows evaporation.

- Plants grow better if they are evenly spaced. Some seeds are sown by broadcasting, scattering them over the soil. Broadcast seeds—no matter how evenly you try to scatter them—will inevitably fall in a random pattern, with some closer and some farther apart than the optimal spacing for best plant growth. Plants that are too close together compete with each other for light, water, and nutrients. When plants are too far apart, the soil around them may become compacted, more water may evaporate, and space is wasted.

The roots of evenly spaced transplanted seedlings can find nutrients and grow more easily, and their leaves will cover and protect the soil, creating a good miniclimate with

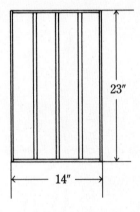

A bottom view of full-sized seedling flat construction. Leave ⅛ inch between board pieces for drainage.

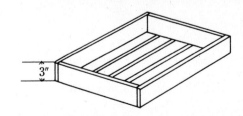

Seedling flat ends are 1 inch by 3 inches redwood. A 3-inch-deep, full-sized flat with evenly moist flat soil and plants weighs about 45 pounds.

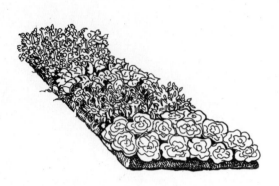

A GROW BIOINTENSIVE bed.

The leaves are roots in the air . . .

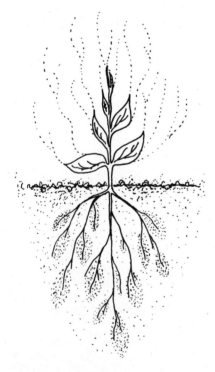

Roots are leaves in the ground . . .

better protection for the soil. Carbon dioxide is captured under the leaf canopy of closely spaced plants, where the plants need it for optimal growth.

- Transplanting stimulates growth. When you transplant a seedling into a double-dug, composted bed that is fluffy, aerated, and full of nutrients, you give it a second "meal" of nutrients, air, and moisture after its first meal in the flat. If the seeds are sown directly in the bed, the soil will begin to recompact after its initial digging while the seeds are germinating and growing into seedlings. Therefore, the soil will not be as loose for the plants to grow in once the seedling stage is reached.

- Seedlings in a flat require much less water ($\frac{1}{2}$ gallon per day) than seedlings in a bed (10 to 20 or more gallons per 100 square feet per day).

Flats

If you build your own flats, the standard flat size is 3 inches deep by 14 inches wide by 23 inches long (interal dimensions). For smaller home gardens, and people with less sturdy backs, half-sized flats may be more convenient. The depth is critical since an overly shallow flat allows the seedling roots to touch the bottom too soon. When this occurs, the plants believe they have reached their growth limit, and they enter a state of "premature senility." In this state the plants begin to flower and fruit even though they are only transplanting size. We have experienced this with broccoli and dwarf marigolds; the broccoli heads were the size of the nail on a little finger. The flat's length and width are not as critical. They should not become too large, however, or the flat will be hard to carry. If plants must remain in a container more than 4 to 6 weeks, use a half-sized flat that is 6 inches deep.

When planting seeds or seedlings, remember that the most important areas for the plant are the 2 inches above and the 2 inches below the surface of the flat or planting bed. The miniclimate created under the plants' leaves and the protection of the upper roots in the flat or the bed by the soil is critical. Without proper protection, the plants will develop tough necks at the point where the stem emerges from the soil. A toughened neck slows the flow of plant juices and interrupts and weakens plant growth. These few inches are also important because in a very real sense the roots are *leaves in the soil* and the leaves are *roots in the air*. The roots "breathe in" (absorb) gases in significant amounts as if they were leaves, and the leaves absorb moisture and nutrients from the air. Also, plant life activity varies above and below the ground according to monthly cycles. Root growth is stimulated more during the third quarter of each 28-day period, and leaf growth is stimulated more during the second quarter, in accordance with the phases of the moon. (See pages 71–74.)

The critical distance above and below the surface of the planting bed is not exactly 2 inches. Obviously it will be different for radishes than for corn, since their leaves begin at different heights from the soil surface and because their root systems have different depths. Generally speaking, though, the 2-inch/ 2-inch guideline helps us develop a sensitivity to the plants' needs above and below ground. (The need for proper conditions above and below ground was also noted in the comparison between the normal use of rows in gardening and farming and the use of raised beds for growing plants, discussed on pages 3 and 4.) In particular, this miniclimate protects feeder roots and microbial life, which are both concentrated in the upper soil.

Once you have planted a flat, there are several locations—depending on the weather—where you can place it while the seeds germinate and grow:

- In a greenhouse or miniature greenhouse if the weather is cold
- In a cold frame for two days when the seedlings are almost transplanting size as part of their hardening off (acclimatization to the cooler outside) for transplanting in cold weather
- In the open for two more days to complete the hardening off process before transplanting
- In the open during warm and hot weather
- In the shade to slow down their growth in hot weather

You may want to build flat covers to protect seedlings from birds and mice. An easy way to do this is to build a flat similar to the ones the seedlings will be in, but *without* the wooden bottom. We use ½-inch galvanized wire fabric on the "bottom." Then we turn the unit upside down and place it on top of the flat to protect the seeds and seedlings.

Flat Soil

You are now ready to prepare the soil in which to grow seedlings. *A good simple flat soil mix is one part sifted compost and one part bed soil* (saved from the first trench when you double-dug) by volume. "Old" flat soil, which has been used to raise seedlings, can be stored in a bin. Although some of the nutrients will have been depleted, it will still be rich in nutrients and organic matter, so it can be used to make a new flat mix. In this case, the recipe would be one part old flat soil, one part sifted compost, and one part bed soil. Compost for the flat soil mix should be passed through a sieve of ½-inch or ¼-inch wire fabric. As your bed soil and your compost improve, your flat soil and seedlings also will improve.

Remember to completely fill your flat with soil, or even mound it slightly above the edge of the flat, so the seedlings will have as much depth as possible to grow in. If available, line the bottom of the flat with a ⅛-inch layer of oak leaf mold (partially

A seedling flat.

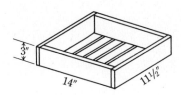

Half-sized flats are easier to carry. This shallow flat, with evenly moist flat soil and plants, weighs about 22½ pounds.

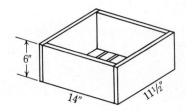

A half-sized deep flat (6 inches deep) ensures a manageable weight. This flat, with evenly moist flat soil and plants, weighs about 45 pounds.

Pricking Out

Lift the first seedling out of the first flat.

Open the planting space in the new flat while . . .

. . . placing the seedling in the hole.

Gently sweep the soil into the hole.

Evenly spaced pricked-out seedlings.

decayed oak leaves) for drainage and additional nutrients. You may place crushed eggshells above the oak leaf mold for calcium-loving plants such as carnations and members of the cabbage family. Lightly sprinkle the eggshells to cover 1/4 of the total surface area.

Alan Chadwick's *classic* planting mixture for starting seeds in flats is one part each *by weight*: evenly moist compost (sifted, if possible), sharp (gritty) sand, and turf loam. These three ingredients provide a fertile, loose-textured mixture. Turf loam is made by composting sections of turf grass grown in good soil. The sections of grass are composted alternating grass sides together and soil sides together within the pile (see the illustration, opposite). Good garden soil, from the first trench of a double-dug bed, for example, can be substituted for turf loam. Thoroughly mix the compost, sand, and garden soil or turf loam and place them in the flat on top of the oak leaf mold.

Some Causes of Poor Germination

When seeds fail to germinate or plants hardly grow at all after germination, some common causes are:

- Using redwood compost. This compost is widely available as a mulch or soil conditioner but contains growth inhibitors that can keep seeds from germinating or plants from growing well. (This is how redwood trees reduce competition.)

- Planting too early or too late in the season. Seeds and seedlings wait for the right temperature and length of day to start and continue growth.

- Using weed killers or soil sterilizers. Many weed killers are short-lived, but they can limit growth in a garden long after they are supposed to degrade. Some people use them to minimize or eliminate yard care, but they can continue to have an effect for 2 years. There is never any reason to use these poisons in your yard. Also, dumping used motor oil can destroy valuable growing areas. Take it to a service station for recycling.

- Using old seeds. Check your source.

- Planting in soil that is too wet. Wet soil restricts oxygen, which is required for root growth. Plants can die in fertile soils when soil oxygen is too low to sustain growth.

Pricking Out

The GROW BIOINTENSIVE method continually seeks to foster uninterrupted plant growth. Part of this technique is embodied in the "Breakfast-Lunch-Dinner!" concept that Alan Chadwick stressed. If seedlings are raised in very good soil—with good nutrients and a good structure—only to be transplanted into an area that has few nutrients and a poor structure, the plants

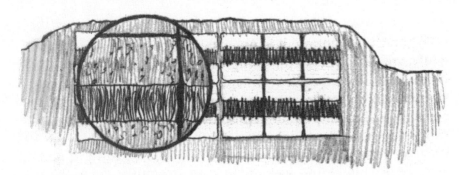

Loose soil with good nutrients enables roots to penetrate the soil easily, and a steady stream of nutrient flows into the stem and leaves.

will suffer root shock. Results are better when seedlings are pricked out from a flat with a good planting mixture "breakfast" into a second flat with a "lunch" consisting of fresh flat soil. The plant will forget the trauma of being pricked out when it tastes the delectable new lunch treats in the second flat. This process minimizes shock and even fosters growth. Finally, a splendid GROW BIOINTENSIVE "dinner" greets the plant in the growing bed! With this kind care and stimulated healthy plant growth, there is less likelihood of insect and disease damage. In the GROW BIOINTENSIVE method, pricking out and transplanting can stimulate growth rather than slowing it down.

Seedlings from broadcast seed are ready to be pricked out after their cotyledons (the first "seed leaves" that appear, although they are not true leaves) have appeared and before their roots are too long to handle easily. You should do the second pricking out (if it is called for) when the seedlings' leaves have just begun to touch each other.

To prick out seedlings, fill a 3-inch- or 6-inch-deep flat with flat soil, and mound the soil slightly (remember to fill in the corners). Use a widger or kitchen knife to loosen the soil under the seedlings so you can lift out one seedling at a time, holding it by its cotyledons and keeping as much soil on the roots as possible.

Place the widger or kitchen knife into the soil of a second flat at a slight backward angle, just behind where the seedling should be, and pull the widger toward you to open a hole.

Drop the seedling into the hole by its roots, placing it a little deeper than it was in the first flat.

Lift out the widger, and let the soil fall around the seedling. It is often not necessary to spend time carefully pushing the soil up around the seedling; when you water the flat, the soil will settle in around the stem and roots. If soil does need to be added to the hole into which the seedling is placed, just gently sweep the soil into the hole with a widger with one motion. Arrange the seedlings on offset, or hexagonal, centers to maximize the space in the flat and to optimize the miniclimate that will develop around the seedlings as they grow.

Hold a seedling by its leaves.

The hand fork.

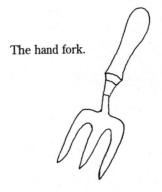

Transplanting

A Biodynamic gardener once had a row of broccoli plants. Only two plants had aphids, but both were quite infested. The

Unpot a seedling correctly.

Note

Seedlings are transplanted when they are 2 to 3 inches high except for those marked "LG" in column L4 and M4 of the Master Charts on pages 87–115. The LG seedlings are transplanted when they are 6 to 9 inches high.

Spread root-bound plant roots out before transplanting them into a bed.

For best bulb formation, do not plant onions too deeply; instead, plant as shown here.

two plants were dug up, and the gardener discovered that the plants had experienced root damage during transplanting. The healthy broccoli, which had experienced uninterrupted growth, were untouched by the insects, while nature eliminated the unhealthy plants.[1]

When transplanting, it is important to handle the seedlings gently and to touch them as little as possible. Plants do not like their bodies to be handled, though they do like to have human companionship and to have dead leaves removed from their stems. You should hold them only by the tips of their leaves (if the plant must be touched) or by the soil around their roots. If you have grown the seedlings in a flat, use a hand fork to gently separate a 4-inch-square section of soil and plants from the rest. Using the fork, gently lift that section from the flat and place it on the ground. Then carefully pull away one plant at a time from the section for transplanting. If it is particularly dry, hot, or windy, place the section on a wet towel. Always keep as much soil around the roots as possible when transplanting. If the seedling has been grown in a pot, turn the pot upside down, letting the plant stem pass between your second and third fingers, and tap firmly on the bottom of the pot with your other hand. Or tap the lip of the pot on something solid.

In all cases, if the plants are root bound (the roots being so tightly grown together from having been kept in a starting flat or pot so long that with the soil they constitute a tight mass), gently spread the roots out in all directions. This process is important because the plant should not spend critical growth energy sending out a new, wide-ranging root system for eating and drinking when a good root system has already been produced. Instead, the plant's energy will go into the natural flow of continuous growth.

Be sure to place the seedling into a large enough hole so that the plant can be buried up to its first set of true leaves. Water the seedlings after transplanting to help settle the soil around the roots, to eliminate excess air spaces, and to provide an adequate amount of water for growth. As the soil is packed down under the pressure of watering, the final soil level will remain high enough to cover the upper roots. The plant's roots need firm contact with the soil to properly absorb water and nutrients. Press the soil firmly around the seedling, if necessary, but not too tightly. Tight packing will damage the roots and will not allow the proper penetration of water, nutrients, and air. Soil that is too loose will allow air and moisture to concentrate around the roots. This will cause root burn and decay.

Transplanting seedlings up to their first true leaves prevents them from becoming top-heavy and bending over during their early growth period. (This is especially true for members of

1. John and Helen Philbrick, *Gardening for Health and Nutrition* (New York: Rudolph Steiner Publications, 1971), p. 93.

the cabbage family.) If a plant bends over, it will upright itself, but will develop a very "tough neck" that will reduce the quality and size of the plant and crop. Onions and garlic, however, do better if the bulb does not have much soil weight to push up against.

Optimally, transplanting should be done in the early evening so the seedlings get settled into their new home during more moderate weather conditions. If transplanting is performed during the day some temporary shading may be needed. In our hot, summer weather, we shade newly transplanted seedlings with 30% shade netting or Reemay, a "row cover" cloth, for several days to minimize transplanting shock and wilt.

Transplanting is preferable to directly sowing seeds. More importantly, transplanting improves plant health. Beds become compacted as they are watered and the soil will not be as loose for a seed that is planted directly in the bed. Some compaction will have occurred by the time it is a "child" a month later and, in some cases, so much so after 2 months, when it is likely to be an "adolescent," that its "adulthood" may be seriously affected. If, instead, you transplant the 1-month-old "child" into the growing bed, a strong adult root system can develop during the next 2 months, and a good adult life is likely. In fact, a study at the University of California at Berkeley in the 1950s indicated that a 2% to 4% increase in root health can increase yields 2 to 4 times.[2]

Spotting

Some newly transplanted seedlings may die for various reasons or be eaten by animals or insects. Therefore, we usually save the surplus seedlings left in the flats after transplanting. We use these seedlings during the next 10 days to fill in the holes or "spots" in the miniclimate. This process has been named "spotting."

Planting by the Phases of the Moon

One of the most controversial aspects of the GROW BIOIN-TENSIVE method is Alan Chadwick's method of planting seeds and transplanting seedlings according to the phases of the moon. *Short- and extra-long–germinating seeds (which take approximately 1 month to germinate)* are planted *2 days before the new moon*, when significant magnetic forces occur, and up to 7 days after the new moon. *Long-germinating seeds* are planted *at the full moon* and up to 7 days afterward. *Seedlings are transplanted at the same time.* Both planting periods take advantage of the full sum of the forces of nature—which are greatest at the new moon—including gravity, light, and

2. Charles Morrow Wilson, *Roots: Miracles Below—The Web of Life Beneath Our Feet* (Garden City, NY: Doubleday, 1968), p. 105.

Most vegetables should be transplanted up to their first two true leaves.

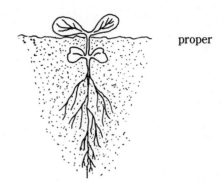
proper

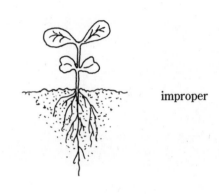
improper

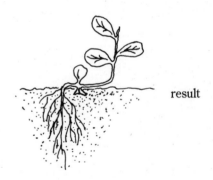
result

Tip
When the stems of cucumbers, melons, squash, pumpkin, and gourds grow into the path, turn the stems back into the bed's growing area to keep walkways clear. The stems prefer the more humid miniclimate in the growing area and will stay there.

magnetism. The lunar gravitational pull that produces high tides in the oceans and water tides in the soil is very high at the new moon. And the moon, which is dark, gets progressively lighter. (See the drawings.) The exact day on which you plant or transplant is not as important as generally taking advantage of the impetus provided by nature.

If you place short-germinating seeds in the ground 2 days before the lunar tide forces are greatest, the seed has time to absorb water. The force exerted on the water in the seed helps create a "tide" that helps burst the seed coat in conjunction with the forces produced by the seed's swelling. No doubt you have wondered why one time beet seeds come up almost immediately and another time the germination process takes 2 weeks in the same bed under similar conditions. Temperature and moisture differences, pH changes, and humus levels may influence the seeds in each case, but the next time you note a marked difference in germination time, check your calendar to determine the phase the moon was in when you sowed the seeds. You may find the moon had an influence.

Looking at the drawing of the moon's phases, you can see that there are both increasing and decreasing lunar gravitational and light force influences that recur periodically during the lunar month. Sometimes the forces work against each other, and sometimes they reinforce one another. When the lunar gravitational pull decreases and the amount of moonlight increases during *the first 7 days of the lunar cycle*, plants undergo a period of balanced growth. The decreasing lunar gravity (and the corresponding relative increase in Earth's gravity) *stimulates root growth*. At the same time, the increasing amount of moonlight stimulates leaf growth.

During *the second 7 days of the lunar cycle*, the lunar gravitational force reverses its relative direction, and it increases. This pull *slows down the root growth* as Earth's relative gravitational pull is lessened. The moonlight, on the other hand, continues to a peak, and *leaf growth is especially stimulated*. If root growth

PLANTING BY THE PHASES OF THE MOON

2 days before new moon

First 7 days

Second 7 days

Plant short- and extra-long–germinating seeds (most vegetables and herbs) in flats and/or beds

Balanced increase in rate of root and leaf growth

Moonlight +
Lunar Gravity –

Increased leaf growth rate

Moonlight +
Lunar Gravity +

has been sufficient during previous periods, then the proper amounts of nutrients and water will be conveyed to the above-ground part of the plant, and balanced, uninterrupted growth will occur. This time of increasing gravitational, moonlight, and magnetic forces gives seeds that have not yet germinated a special boost. Seeds that did not germinate at the time of the new moon should do so by the full moon. Alan Chadwick said it is during this period that seeds cannot resist coming up, and mushrooms suddenly appear overnight.

During *the third 7 days of the lunar cycle*, the amount of moonlight decreases along with the lunar gravitational pull. As the moonlight decreases, above-ground *leaf growth slows down*. The *root growth is stimulated again*, however, as the lunar gravitational pull decreases. This is a good time to transplant, since root growth is active. This activity enables the plant to better overcome transplant shock and promotes the development of a good root system while leaf growth is slowed down. Then, 21 days later, when leaf growth is at a maximum, the plant will have a developed root system that can provide it with sufficient nutrients and water. This is also the time to plant long-germinating seeds that take approximately 2 weeks to germinate; they will then be ready to take advantage of the boost from the high gravitational pull of the new moon.

During *the last 7 days of the lunar cycle*, the lunar gravitational force increases, and *root growth slows down*. The amount of moonlight decreases and also *slows down leaf growth*. This period is one of a balanced decrease in growth, just as the first 7 days in the lunar month is a period of balanced increase in growth. The last 7 days, then, is a rest period that comes before the bursting forth of a period of new life. Short-, long-, and extra-long-germinating seed crops are listed in the Master Charts later in this chapter.

A planted seed bursts its seed coat around the 28th day of the lunar month and proceeds into a period of slow, balanced, and increasing growth above and below ground, passes into

KEY:

● New Moon

◐ First Quarter

○ Full Moon

◑ Fourth Quarter

+ = Increasing

− = Decreasing

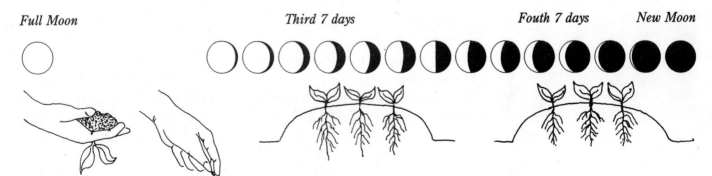

Full Moon   *Third 7 days*   *Fouth 7 days*   *New Moon*

Transplant short- and extra-long–germinating seedlings from flats into beds and plant extra-long–germinating seeds (most flowers) in flats and/or beds

Increased root growth rate
Moonlight –
Lunar Gravity –

Balanced decrease in rate of root and leaf growth (resting period)
Moonlight –
Lunar Gravity +

English Haws watering can.

Special upward-pointing Haws watering rose.

Ross watering fan attached to a valve unit.

Ross watering fan attached to a variable water pressure gun.

a period of stimulated leaf growth, then goes into a period of stimulated root growth (getting ready for the next period of stimulated leaf growth), followed by a time of rest. This plant growth cycle repeats itself monthly. Plants are transplanted at the full moon so they may begin their life in the growing bed during a time of stimulated root growth to compensate for the root shock that occurs during transplanting. (It is also vital that the plant's root system be well developed so it can later provide the leaves, flowers, vegetables, fruits, and seeds with water and nutrients.) The transplanted plant then enters a time of rest before beginning another monthly cycle. The workings of nature are beautiful.

Planting by the phases of the moon is a gardening nuance that improves the health and quality of plants. If you do not follow the moon cycles, your plants will still grow satisfactorily. However, as your soil improves and as you gain experience, each gardening detail will become more important and will have a greater effect. Try this one and see.

Watering

When beds and flats are watered, the GROW BIOINTENSIVE method approximates rainfall as much as possible. The fine rain of water absorbs beneficial airborne nutrients as well as air, helping the growth process. For seeds and seedlings in flats, you can use a special English Haws sprinkling can, which has fine holes in the sprinkler's "rose."[3] The rose points up so that when you water, the pressure built up in the rose first goes up into the air, where much of the pressure is dissipated as it flows through the air. The water then softly falls on the plants from above like rain, with only the force of gravity pulling the water down. When watering planting beds, you may employ the same method of spraying water into the air and letting it fall back down, using a water gun or a valve unit with a fan spray nozzle attached.[4] (If you use a water gun or a valve unit, you may need a heavy duty hose to contain the water pressure.) This gentle method of watering packs down the soil in the bed less, and the plants are not hit and damaged by a hard water spray. If you choose to point the fan downward, stand as far away from the plants as possible and/or keep the water pressure adjusted to a low point to minimize soil compaction and water damage.

Some plants, such as those in the cabbage family, like wet leaves. It is all right, and in fact beneficial, to water these plants from overhead. Other plants, such as tomatoes, peas, and members of the squash and melon families, can suffer from wilt and mildew, and their fruit may rot when their leaves are wet, espe-

3. Available by mail order from Walter F. Nicke, Box 667G, Hudson, NY 12534.
4. A Ross No. 20 is best.

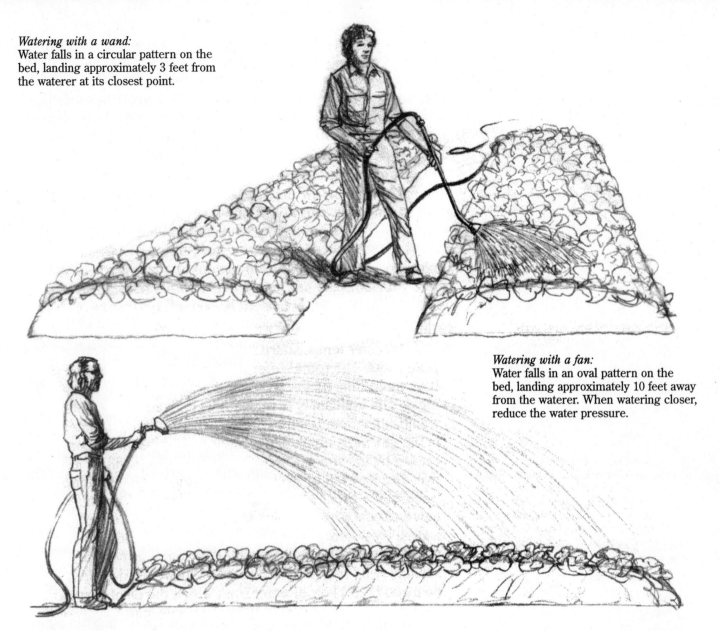

Watering with a wand:
Water falls in a circular pattern on the
bed, landing approximately 3 feet from
the waterer at its closest point.

Watering with a fan:
Water falls in an oval pattern on the
bed, landing approximately 10 feet away
from the waterer. When watering closer,
reduce the water pressure.

cially in foggy or humid climates. Take care when watering
these plants to water only the soil around them whenever
possible. (In drier climates it probably will not matter.) To avoid
spraying a plant's leaves, hold the fan just above the soil and
point it sideways. A better method is to use a watering wand,
which will allow you to more easily direct the water under the
plant's leaves.

Water the beds sufficiently each day to keep them evenly
moist. Daily watering washes the dust, grime, and insects from
plant leaves and creates a deliciously moist atmosphere
conducive to good plant growth and thriving microbial life.
(Watering may be more or less frequent when the weather is
warmer or cooler than normal.)

Water mature plants in beds when the heat of the day first
subsides. This is about 2 hours before sunset during the summer and earlier during the winter. However, weather conditions,
especially cloud cover, may necessitate earlier watering. The
soil, warmed during the day, warms the cool water from the

Watering tomato plants using a wand.

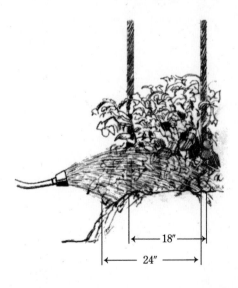

hose so it is more temperate by the time it reaches the plant roots. The roots suffer less shock, and the soil and plants have more time to absorb water during the cooler, less windy night. Also, plants do a significant amount of their growing at night, and this ensures they will have plenty of water to do so. If you water early in the morning, much of the water will be lost in evaporation caused by the sun and wind, and the watering will be less effective. The loss will be even greater if you water at midday. If you water in the evening, the plants will be more susceptible to mildew and rust problems due to unevaporated water left on their leaves. By watering in the late afternoon, the water can percolate into the soil for 12 hours or more before the sun and wind reappear in strength. When they do, the bed will have a good reservoir of water from which the plants can draw before their next watering.

Seeds and seedlings in flats and immature plants in the growing beds may have to be watered in the morning and at noon as well as late in the afternoon. Until the living mulch effect occurs, the flats and beds dry out more rapidly. When the leaves grow closer together, less watering will be required.

To determine how much water to give a bed each day, strive for a ½- to 15-second "shiny."[5] When you first begin to water, a *shiny layer* of excess water will appear on top of the soil. If you stop watering immediately, the shiny layer will disappear quickly. You should water until the shiny layer remains for ½ to 15 seconds after you have stopped watering. The actual time involved will differ depending on your soil's texture. The more clayey the texture, the longer the time will be. A newly prepared bed with good texture and structure will probably have enough water when a ½- to 3-second shiny is reached. A newly prepared clayey bed may indicate that it has enough water with a 3- to 5-second shiny, since a clayey soil both retains more moisture and lets the water in less rapidly. A month-old bed (which has compacted somewhat due to the watering process) may require a 5- to 8-second shiny, and beds 2 to 3 months old may require more than that. A 2- to 4-month-old bed may require a longer shiny.

Eventually the watering process will become automatic, and you will not have to think about when the bed has received enough water; you will know intuitively when the point has been reached. Remember to allow for the different natures of plants. Squash plants, for instance, will want a lot of water in comparison to tomato plants. One way to determine whether you have watered enough is to go out the next morning and poke your finger into the bed. If the soil is evenly moist for the

---

5. Another simple way to estimate the amount of water a bed is receiving is to first measure the gallons delivered per minute. Turn the hose on, and point the spray into a 1-gallon jar or a 4-quart watering can. If, for example, it takes 15 seconds to fill the jar, then you know you are delivering 4 gallons per minute to the bed. Currently, in our moderately heavy clay, we find each 5-feet by 20-feet bed will take anywhere from 5 to 20 gallons daily (10 gallons on the average), depending on the weather, the type of plant, the size of the plants, and the tightness of the soil.

first 2 inches and continues to be moist below this level, you are watering properly. If the soil is dry for part or all of the first 2 inches, you need more shiny. If the soil is soggy in part or all of the upper 2 inches, you need less shiny.

Remember also to adjust your watering according to the weather. A bed may lose more moisture on a cloudy, windy, *dry* day than on a hot, clear, *humid*, and still one. And there are times when the flats and beds need no water or need watering twice a day. It is important to note these differences and to become sensitive to the plants' needs. You should water for good fruit, flower, and seed production, not just so the plant will stay alive. Be sure to water the sides and ends of the planting beds more than the middle. These areas, which many people miss or underemphasize, are critical because they are subject to more evaporation than the middle of the bed. Newly dug but still unplanted beds should be watered daily so they will not lose their moisture content. A transplant in a bed that has a low moisture level (except in the recently watered upper 2 inches or so) will have difficulty growing well because of the dry pan below. If you wait until plants are wilting and drooping before you water them, they will revive but they will have suffered some permanent damage—an open invitation for pests and diseases. Slight drooping, however, is not usually a sign that you should water. Plants are just minimizing water loss (due to transpiration) when they droop on a hot day, and watering them at this time will increase water loss rather than lessen it. It will also weaken the plant through too much pampering.

Shade Netting

After you have watered your newly planted bed, in hot weather you may want to consider covering this area with 30-percent shade netting from approximately 10 A.M. to 5 P.M. Use shade netting that is 3 feet wider and 3 feet longer than your growing bed, so the netting can drape down around the edges to provide shade on the sides as well as the top. We generally insert 3-foot-long pieces of 1-inch by 1-inch wood on a 45-degree angle into the soil at the four corners of the bed and every 5 feet along and perpendicular to the sides. Headless nails are hammered part way into the top end of the sticks so the shade netting can be held in place. At 5 P.M. we unhook the netting from the long eastern side of the bed and hook its edges over the nails on the other side several times to secure the netting and keep it out of the paths and the bed. We reverse this process at 10 A.M. the next day. Make sure the nails do not jut into the path where they can be a hazard to you.

We also use shade netting to protect newly transplanted grains in the fall and winter from birds. In this case, we leave the shade netting on for 10 days and use long pieces of ⅝-inch

Note
It is important to realize that we are *watering the soil*, so that it may thrive as a *living sponge cake*. We are not watering the plants. The soil in turn then "waters" the plants. Keeping the soil alive will help retain water and minimize the water consumed.

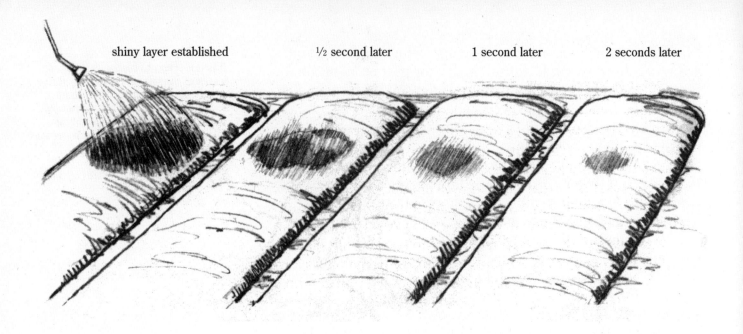

shiny layer established　　　½ second later　　　1 second later　　　2 seconds later

A newly prepared bed is properly watered when the *shiny layer* of excess water disappears within ½ to 3 seconds after the watering stops.

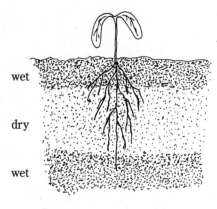

wet

dry

wet

Dry pan.

rebar to hold down the edges of the netting so birds cannot enter the growing area. We adjust the 1-inch by 1-inch sticks so the netting edges lie on the ground with the rebar along the edges. After 10 days, the shade netting is removed because at this point the plants are less tasty and, therefore, are not attractive to the birds.

Mini-Greenhouses

A mini-greenhouse made from plastic sheeting and wood[6] can increase the temperature of the soil and the air surrounding plants and allow you to get an early start on the growing season in the spring and to lengthen the growing season in the autumn. Our design has double-walled construction, which can keep the inside temperature above the freezing point when the outside temperature falls as low as 20°F. This makes the unit a good season-extender for crops.

A mini-greenhouse.

6. For plans and instructions, see *Backyard Homestead, Mini-Farm and Garden Log Book* (Willits, CA: Ecology Action, 1993).

KEY WATER FACTORS

The GROW BIOINTENSIVE method is especially important for areas with scarce water. Though much more experimentation is needed in this area, the information below should assist you.

- Seventy-five percent of the Earth's land surface where food is generally grown receives 10 inches of rainfall or more annually. About *one-half* of this rainfall can be retained in soil properly prepared for plant use. To grow a good yield, 20 inches of rain are needed annually. In an area receiving only 10 inches of rainfall, the rain a growing area receives can be increased to 20 inches in the "bent bed" examples at the bottom of this page and in the margin on page 80.

- The GROW BIOINTENSIVE method uses an average of 10 gallons (a 5- to 20-gallon range) per day per 100 square feet while commercial food raising consumes an average of 20 gallons per day for the same area. GROW BIOINTENSIVE produces
4 times the food in the same area as commercial agricultural practices.

- Research by academic institutions has shown that soil that has living compost as 2% of its volume in the upper 11 inches of soil can *reduce* the rainfall or *irrigation* required for poor soils *by as much as 75%*. (Poor soils have about ½ of 1% living compost in the upper soil area.) GROW BIOINTENSIVE encourages maintaining more than 2% compost.

- Even under arid conditions, soil that is shaded can *reduce evaporation up to 63%*, depending on soil type. The *miniclimate* created by closely spaced plants provides good shading.

- *Plants transpire* water, which can be *reduced by as much as 75%* in soils that have sufficient and well balanced nutrients in the soil water. The GROW BIOINTENSIVE method prepares the soil so it provides for a high level of fertility.

Tip

To conserve water, raise your seedlings in flats until transplanting size (usually for the first 2 to 4 weeks). For many crops, one flat, which needs only about ½ gallon of water each day, will plant one 100-square-foot growing area. When planted, this growing area will need about 10 to 20 gallons of water daily during the main growing season. The water savings in one month (compared with direct sowing of seeds in the growing area) is about 285 to 585 gallons of water!

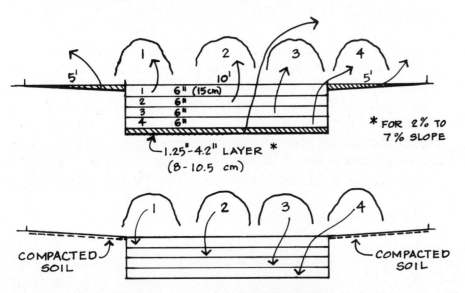

One way to prepare a 5-by-20-foot "bent bed" for the concentration of rainwater in your growing area.

Sloped beds on flat ground (side view) can be used for water harvesting.

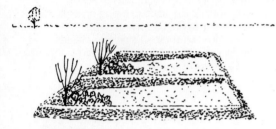

Native American type of "bent bed" is used to capture rainfall effectively. This is a key *water-harvesting* technique.

Note

Twenty inches of rainfall over a 4-month growing season is an average of .167 inch per day.

- If you combine the last three factors listed above, water consumption can sometimes be reduced to $1/32$ the level ($1/4 \times 1/2 \times 1/4$) plants normally require. We have found that GROW BIOINTENSIVE can reduce water consumption on average to $1/8$ that of normal methods per pound of vegetable produced and to about $1/3$ that of normal methods per pound of grain produced once the soil is in reasonable shape.

- Native people in some parts of Africa have been using a deeply prepared bed approach successfully with grains. They triple-dig(!) the soil, incorporating a lot of organic matter into it just before the seasonal rains. Immediately after the rains stop, they plant their seeds. No more rain falls, yet crops are harvested at the end of the season. Others in the area reportedly are unable to grow crops well during this season.

- GROW BIOINTENSIVE techniques should produce at least 4 times the yield under natural rainfall conditions (when not irrigating) that would be obtained under the same conditions with commercial techniques. Let us know what works for you.

- Native Americans in the southwestern United States have used a number of approaches to grow food in limited rainfall areas. One method is to create large diamond-shaped growing areas on a slight slope, with one point each being at the top and the bottom of the slope. Crops are planted in the bottom $1/4$ to $1/2$ of each diamond—depending on the amount of rainfall. (More water per unit of soil area is concentrated in the bottom part of the diamond.)

  With this method, use the following information to determine how much of the diamond to plant: Well-prepared soil needs to retain approximately 10 inches of water per unit of area (623 gallons per 100 square feet) to grow one complete crop during a 4-month growing season. To retain this much water, the soil needs about 20 inches of rainfall (1,246 gallons per 100 square feet) per season. If only 10 inches fall, you would have only $1/2$ the water needed, and you would plant only the bottom $1/2$ of each diamond. If you had only 5 inches of rain, you would only have $1/4$ the water needed for a crop, and you would only plant the bottom $1/4$ of the diamond (more or less). Experimentation will be required before you have optimum success. Be careful not to overplant. A completely dry soil does not rewet or absorb water easily, which will lead to erosion. To be on the safe side, start with a small area and plant $1/4$ less crop than the above recommendations to ensure that the soil retains some moisture. Once you achieve success, you can increase the area under cultivation. Please share your experiences with us and others so this approach can be better understood.

- See John A. Widtsoe's *Dry Farming* (see page 169 in the bibliography) for more information on dry farming.

Weeding

Intensively planted raised beds do not require weeding as often as other types of gardens due to the living mulch that the plants create. Usually, our beds only need to be weeded once, about a month after the bed is planted. A bed prepared in a new area may have to be weeded more often at first, however, since many dormant seeds will be raised to a place in the soil where they can germinate readily. Over time, as the soil becomes richer and more alive, you will probably have fewer weeds, since they tend to thrive more in poor and deficient soils than in healthy ones.

There really is no such thing as a "weed." A weed is just a plant that is growing in an area where you, the gardener, do not want it to grow. In fact, many so-called weeds, such as stinging nettle, are quite beneficial to the soil and to other plants. (This will be discussed in more detail in "Companion Planting.") Instead of weeding indiscriminately, you should learn the natures and uses of the different weeds so you can identify and leave some of the most beneficial ones in the growing beds. Until they are removed, weeds help establish a more quickly nourishing miniclimate for your current crop. Add the weeds you pull to the compost pile. They are rich in trace minerals and other nutrients and will help grow good crops next season.

Weeds are generally hardier than cultivated plants since they are genetically closer to their parental plant stock and nearer to the origin of the plant species. They tend to germinate before broadcasted cultivated plants. You should usually wait to remove these plants from the beds until the cultured plants catch up with the weeds in height or until the cultured plants become established (about transplanting size)—whichever comes first. Weeding before this time is likely to disturb the germinating cultured plant seeds or disturb the developing new root systems, causing interrupted plant growth and weakened plants. However, be sure to remove any grass plants that develop in the beds after the first weeding. These plants put out incredibly large root systems that interfere with other plants in the competition for nutrients and water.

Planting in Season

Vegetables, flowers, and herbs—all plants for that matter—should be planted in season. This is a good way to love your plants. If they are forced (grown out of season), much of their energy is used up straining to combat unseasonable weather in the form of cold, heat, rain, or drought. Less energy is left for balanced growth, and a plant with limited energy reserves—not unlike people—is more susceptible to disease and insect attacks. Also, for the best crop health and yields, be sure to keep your plants harvested! To determine the best time to plant various crops, see the information on page 82.

Appropriate posture can make weeding easier.

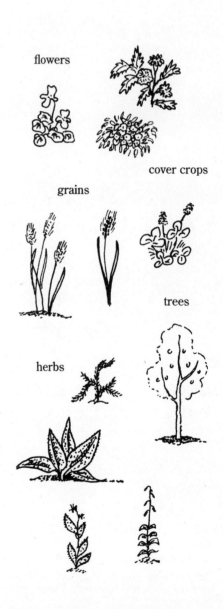

flowers

cover crops

grains

trees

herbs

SATISFACTORY (AND OPTIMAL) PLANT-GROWING TEMPERATURE RANGES[7]

Determine the Planting-Range Calendar for Your Area

Crop Season	Temperature Range	Optimal Temperature Range	Plant
Cool-Season Crops[8]	30°F		Asparagus • Rhubarb
	40°–75°F	(60°–65°F)	Beet • Broad bean • Broccoli • Brussels sprouts • Cabbage • Chard • Collard • Horseradish • Kale • Kohlrabi • Parsnip • Radish • Rutabaga • Sorrel • Spinach • Turnip
	45°–75°F	(60°–65°F)	Artichoke • Carrot • Cauliflower • Celeriac • Celery • Chicory • Chinese cabbage • Endive • Florence fennel • Lettuce • Mustard • Parsley • Pea • Potato
	45°–85°F	(55°–75°F)	Chicory • Chive • Garlic • Leek • Onion • Salsify • Shallot
Warm-Season Crops	50°–80°F	(60°–70°F)	Bean • Lima bean
	50°–95°F	(60°–75°F)	Corn • Cowpea • New Zealand spinach
	50°–90°F	(65°–75°F)	Pumpkin • Squash
	60°–90°F	(65°–75°F)	Cucumber • Muskmelon
Hot-Season Crops	65°–85°F	(70°–75°F)	Sweet pepper • Tomato
	65°–95°F	(70°–85°F)	Eggplant • Hot pepper • Okra • Sweet potato • Watermelon

7. From James Edward Knott, *Handbook for Vegetable Growers* (New York: John Wiley & Sons, 1957), pp. 6–7.

8. Try these crops in shady areas in the summer. Remember, crops need *at least* 4 hours of direct sunlight to grow. Seven hours are preferred, and 11 hours are even better.

SOIL TEMPERATURE CONDITIONS FOR VEGETABLE SEED GERMINATION[9]

Crop	Minimum	Optimum Range	Optimum	Maximum
Asparagus	50°F	60°–85°F	75°F	95°F
Bean	60°F	60°–85°F	80°F	95°F
Bean, Lima	60°F	65°–85°F	85°F	85°F
Beet	40°F	50°–85°F	85°F	95°F
Cabbage	40°F	45°–95°F	85°F	100°F
Carrot	40°F	45°–85°F	80°F	95°F
Cauliflower	40°F	45°–85°F	80°F	100°F
Celery	40°F	60°–70°F	70°F*	85°F*
Chard, Swiss	40°F	50°–85°F	85°F	95°F
Corn	50°F	60°–95°F	95°F	105°F
Cucumber	60°F	60°–95°F	95°F	105°F
Eggplant	60°F	75°–90°F	85°F	95°F
Lettuce	35°F	40°–80°F	75°F	85°F
Muskmelon	60°F	75°–95°F	90°F	100°F
Okra	60°F	70°–95°F	95°F	105°F
Onion	35°F	50°–95°F	75°F	95°F
Parsley	40°F	50°–85°F	75°F	90°F
Parsnip	35°F	50°–70°F	65°F	85°F
Pea	40°F	40°–75°F	75°F	85°F
Pepper	60°F	65°–95°F	85°F	95°F
Pumpkin	60°F	70°–90°F	95°F	100°F
Radish	40°F	45°–90°F	85°F	95°F
Spinach	35°F	45°–75°F	70°F	85°F
Squash	60°F	70°–95°F	95°F	100°F
Tomato	50°F	60°–85°F	85°F	95°F
Turnip	40°F	60°–105°F	85°F	105°F
Watermelon	60°F	70°–95°F	95°F	105°F

*Daily fluctuation to 60 degrees or lower at night is essential.

9. From James Edward Knott, *Handbook for Vegetable Growers* (New York: John Wiley & Sons, 1957), p. 8.

Master Charts

The Master Charts that follow should help your gardening efforts. The charts for grains, compost crops, trees, and other crops provide a picture of what you can accomplish in your own backyard or small farm-holding. (Also see Ecology Action's *Backyard Homestead, Mini-Farm and Garden Log Book.*) Additional information about special seed sources and harvesting, cleaning, grinding, storing, and preserving these crops will be included in the future. The charts are largely based on our many years of experience and are generally complete and accurate.

Ecology Action continues to study the spacings and other growing information for grains, fodder crops, fibers, bush and dwarf fruit trees, other tree crops, berries and grapes, and compost crops. As testing continues, the information is revised and the chance of error reduced. (A good explanation of the information in these charts is given in the planning section of *The Sustainable Vegetable Garden.*)

It should be noted that:

- You may not reach maximum yields in the first year. Also, one plant, grown alone, will probably not produce as large a yield as one plant grown among several plants under mini-climate conditions.

- Seeds grown out of season will take longer to germinate and/or may decompose before they do germinate unless grown under special mini-greenhouse or shade netting conditions.

- Closer spacing may be needed during the winter to make up for slower plant growth during this period and to create a balanced winter miniclimate. (Try ¾ or ½ the usual spacing with lettuce in the winter.) Closer spacing can also promote faster, balanced growth by more rapidly creating a miniclimate. Thin extra plants to make room for larger plants. (Baby carrots and beets are a delicacy.)

- You may need wider spacings in the humid tropics during the wetter months.

One of the exciting things about the GROW BIOINTENSIVE method is its emphasis on the soil. Once you know how to prepare soil well for vegetables, a whole world of crops becomes available to you. The bed preparation, fertilization, and watering approaches remain essentially the same—only the plant spacings are different!

These charts will help you expand from growing only vegetable crops to including plants from the following broad groups:

- grains, protein sources, and vegetable oil crops
- compost, organic matter, and fodder crops. Some compost crops, such as pearl millet, sorghum, and corn, can produce very high yields of biomass and should be fully recycled

through composting whenever possible to minimize the potential for soil depletion.

- tree and cane food crops
- energy, fiber, paper, and miscellaneous crops

Eventually, we hope to add tree crops for fuel and building materials. If you seek more information than is contained in these detailed charts, refer to the books listed in the bibliography.

There is a convenient soil improvement succession that is good to know. Vegetables from one year improve soil for grains the next year, and this leads to soil that supports more permanent tree crops the third year. If you want to study this process more closely, see Ecology Action's *Backyard Homestead, Mini-Farm and Garden Logbook* crop-testing chapter for vegetable, grain, fodder, and tree crops, and read our "Soybean Test" booklet.

The importance of the soil is especially apparent with a permanent crop-growing system. Even biological and tree cultivation systems can be environmentally unsound if improperly used. Dr. Hans Jenny, soil scientist emeritus at the University of California, Berkeley, pointed to this in *Science* magazine:

> At the turn of the century, farsighted agricultural experiment stations set up permanent cultivation plots and monitored for decades the nitrogen and carbon balances. Stirring soil and removing crops initiated profound declines in nitrogen, carbon, and humus substances and caused deterioration of soil structure. Under these circumstances water infiltration is reduced and runoff and sheet erosion are encouraged. Crop yields suffer. While applications of nitrogen fertilizers boost yields, they have not restored the soil body. In central Europe, farmers used to remove forest litter and put it on their fields for manuring. Tree production declined markedly, documented by Aaltonen.[10] . . .
>
> I am arguing against indiscriminate conversion of biomass and organic wastes to fuels. The humus capital, which is substantial, deserves being maintained because good soils are a national asset. The question will be raised, How much organic matter should be assigned to the soil? No general formula can be given. Soils vary widely in character and quality.

Growing crops must be approached, then, with a sensitivity to how *the way* they are being grown affects the sustainability of the soil's vitality and health. Understanding this proper relationship will take time and eventually will involve growing many different crops, including a large number of trees. Trees beneficially modify our climate, bring up and make available nutrients from deep down in the soil, protect the soil from erosion, help maintain healthy water tables, and provide us with food and building materials.

Food value columns have been added to the Master Charts for protein, calories, and calcium for each crop. These are important, but so are many other food values—including iron, vitamins, and amino acids. See the reference books listed in the

Note

Microbial life-forms thrive and greatly increase in activity when the nighttime air temperature reaches a minimum of 60°F. The next time you go out in the morning early in the season and notice that your garden has grown a foot overnight and is a darker, lush green, check the previous night's temperature. You may be surprised!

Other Key Air Temperatures

32°F:	Nitrogen release begins in the soil.
50°F:	Significant nitrogen release occurs in the soil.
86°–95°F:	The maximum nitrogen release point is reached in the soil.
90°F:	The pollination process begins to decrease.
95°–104°F:	A significant decrease in nitrogen release occurs in the soil.
131°F:	Nitrogen release stops in the soil

10. V. T. Aaltonen, *Boden und Wald* (Berlin: Parey, 1948).

Note

GROW BIOINTENSIVE techniques can be used to grow important protein crops. Experiments with wheat, soybeans, grains, beans, and other seeds have worked well. For information on how to grow your own open-pollinated seeds in the smallest area while preserving genetic diversity, see Ecology Action's Self-Teaching Mini-Series Booklet *Growing to Seed*.

bibliography if you want to pursue this further. Be sure to explore growing compost crops in between your trees to increase the soil's friability and its nitrogen and organic matter content. Try medium red clover. It has beautiful red flowers.

Increasingly, more people want to grow food. One hundred square feet of grain may yield 4, 8, 12, or more pounds of edible seed. If you are in a cooler climate and wish to grow beans for eating, try varieties such as the peanut, yellow-eye, and cranberry beans available from the Vermont Bean Seed Company. Dwarf fruit trees, if nurtured properly, can yield 50 to 100 pounds of fruit annually at maturity. Two trees on 8-foot centers in 100 square feet can have a combined yield of up to 200 pounds, and the average person in the United States eats only about 162 pounds of tree fruit per year. Fava beans may yield the greatest amount of organic matter. Alfalfa and clover are also fun to raise as nitrogen-fixing legumes to improve your soil's fertility.

Our goal with wheat is to eventually get 2 26-pound crops in an 8-month period. This would yield 1 1-pound loaf of bread for every week in the year from only 100 square feet! Then we could literally raise our own bread in our backyards. Sound impossible? Yields close to this are already occurring in some parts of the world. Wheat can be threshed easily with a mini-thresher[11] made available by a public organization in your area. Our highest wheat yield to date is at the rate of about 21 pounds per 100-square-foot bed, using about 10 inches of water for the whole season, with compost we grew ourselves for fertilizer and a small amount of purchased organic fertilizer. The Zulus in South Africa use a technique similar to the GROW BIOINTENSIVE method and grow grains with natural rainfall. See what you can do! Let us know if you get to 26 pounds— and tell us how you do it!

When planning your garden, remember to look closely at *all* the factors involved. For example, sesame seeds are very high in nutrition, but they usually have low yields (compared with other protein crops), are somewhat difficult to harvest, and exhaust the soil. So on a per-square-foot, sustainable nutrition yield basis, sesame seeds are not particularly superior to other protein sources, even though they are great nutritionally and good to eat. A large harvest of sesame seeds would also require a very large growing area. It is important to examine each crop's total *practicality*.

When you begin to produce intermediate yields, another factor to consider is the quantity of nutrients each crop takes from the soil. Many "heavy givers" of nitrogen can exhaust the soil of other nutrients over time. Soybeans are "heavy giving" legumes, but continuous cropping of them has been demonstrated to wear out the soil. It is important to develop and work within natural sustainable cycles.

11. One good foot-treadle–powered mini-thresher is available from CeCe Co., P.O. Box 8, Ibaraki City, Osaka, Japan.

Master Charts

LETTER CODES

A — Approximate germination rate as sold by seed companies. No known minimum legal germination rate. Can be higher or lower.

AA — Each "seed" contains about 3 seeds, of which half germinate.

AC — Harvest alfalfa and clover 2 to 4 inches above the growing crown (sheep shears work well for this), loosen the soil with a border fork, water the bed, and cover the growing area with shade netting cloth for 1 to 2 weeks.

B — In beds.

BB — Soak seeds overnight for best germination.

BC — Broadcast.

C — Centers.

c — Cups.

CA — Cantaloupe.

D — Do not know yet.

E — Spacing increases with warmth of climate.

EL — Extra-long–germinating seed (22 to 28 days).

F — In flats.

FA — Fall.

G — Best "seed" is a seed packet of 2 to 6 seeds, of which approximately 1.62 germinate.

H — Honeydew.

I — Transplant into 1- to 5-gallon container as appropriate. Raise sapling until 1 year old. Then transplant into soil.

J — Germination average in laboratory.

K — Straw weight is generally 1 to 3+ times harvested and cleaned seed weight for GROW BIOINTENSIVEly grown grains, 1 to 2 times for grains grown with commercial agriculture (Roger Revelle in *Scientific American,* September 1976).

L — Long-germinating seed (8 to 21 days).

LG — Transplant seedling when larger— about 6 inches tall.

M — Cook to minimize oxalic acid, calcium tie-up.

N — Narrow bed (2 feet wide) will produce better yields due to improved pollination.

P — Perennial.

Q — Celery is pricked out into a third flat, 6 inches deep, on 2-inch centers, where it grows for a further 4 to 6 weeks until it is ready to be transplanted. The seedlings may be 4 inches tall. Overall, it takes 3 to 4 months from sowing until transplanting.

qt — Quarts.

R — Replant at points where germination fails. We call this "spotting."

S — Short-germinating seed (1 to 7 days).

SN — During hot weather, cover with shade netting cloth between approximately 10 A.M. and 5 P.M. for better results.

SP — Spring.

SU — Summer.

T — Tablespoon.

t — Teaspoon.

TO — 18 inches for cherry tomatoes; 21 inches for regular tomatoes; 24 inches for large tomatoes. Sequential information in columns D, H, and I should be used according to spacing chosen.

U — A 1-pound loaf of bread requires ⅔ pound flour (2½ cups).

V — Approximate minimum.

W — 12 or 15 inches for midget varieties; 18 inches for 5- to 7-pound varieties; 21 inches for 10- to 15-pound varieties; 24 inches for largest varieties.

WI — Winter.

Y — Estimate.

Z — Based on Ecology Action experience, half of the garlic cloves are large enough to use, on the average.

* — Digestible protein for animals.

** — Depending on variety selected.

— — Not applicable.

\# — First set of figures: summer sowing in lathhouse for fall set-out or winter sowing in areas with a less cold winter and a greenhouse for spring set-out.

Second set of figures: winter sowing in a good greenhouse or a miniature greenhouse in areas with very cold winters for spring set-out.

Harden off for 2 days outside in flat before transplanting into bed.

\## — If direct sowing on centers, rather than broadcasting, plant 2 seeds per center to compensate for low germination rate.

\+ — Yield may be significantly higher.

++ — Given harvest time in column O.

VEGETABLES AND GARDEN CROPS

	SEED			YIELD		
PLANT A	B Approx. No. Seeds per Ounce [12] (range: larger–smaller seed)	C Minimum Legal Germination Rate [13]	D Ounces / Volume Seed per 100 Square Feet (adj. for germ. rate, offset spacing, and curv. surf.) [14, 15, 16]	E Possible GROW BIOINTENSIVE Yield in Pounds per 100-Square-Foot Planting [17]	F Possible GROW BIOINTENSIVE Yield in Pounds per Plant [18, 19]	G Average U.S. Yield in Pounds per 100 Square Feet [20, 21]
1 Artichoke, Jerusalem	Sprouted 2 oz tuber pieces	—	10.5 lbs / —	Tubers: 100 / 206 / 420+ Biomass, air-dry: ~7.5 / ~15 / ~30	Tubers: 1.20–5.00+	D
2 Artichoke, Regular	From divided roots or seeds	Seeds: .70[A]	3 roots / —	D	D	20.7
3 Asparagus	875–1,250	.70	.32 / 1 t or 159 roots	9.5 / 19 / 38	.06–.24	6.2
4 Basil	12,000	.60	.09 / 1 t	35 / 75 / 150	.06–.24	D
5 Beans, Lima, Bush	Baby: 75–94 Regular: 25–38	.70	Regular: 35.5–23.3 / 6⅗–3¾ c	Dry: 11.5 / 17.2 / 23	0.02–.04	4.6
6 Beans, Lima, Pole[N]	Baby: 35–90 Regular: 25–38	.70	Regular: 18.3–12 / 3³⁄₁₆–2 c	Dry: 11.5+ / 17.2+ / 23+	.04+–.07+	4.6+
7 Beans, Snap, Bush	100–125	.70	8.8–7.0 / 1½–1⅛ c	30 / 72 / 108	.05–.17	12.9
8 Beans, Snap, Pole[N]	100–125	.70	8.8–7.0 / 1½–1⅛ c	30+ / 72+ / 108+	.05+–.17+	12.9+
9 Beets, Cylindra	1,500–1,625	.65	1.4–1.3 / 6 T[AA]	Roots: 110 / 220 / 540 Greens: 55 / 110 / 270	.08–.40 .04–.20	"68.0" D
10 Beets, Regular	1,500–1,625	.65	1.4–1.3 / 6 T[AA]	Roots: 55 / 110 / 270 Greens: 55 / 110 / 270	.04–.20 .04–.20	"34.0" D
11 Broccoli	9,000	.75	.01 / ¹⁄₂₄ t	Heads: 26 / 39 / 53 Leaves: 52+ / 78+ / 106+	.31–.63 .62–1.26	29.6 D
12 Brussels Sprouts	9,000	.70	.01 / ¹⁄₂₄ t	71 / 106 / 142	1.34–2.68	36.7
13 Burdock	1,700	.60	1.3 / 4 T	75 / 150 / 300	.06–.22	D
14 Cabbage, Chinese	9,000	.75	.03 / ⅛ t	96 / 191 / 383	.48–1.91	72.1
15 Cabbage, Regular	9,000	.75	.023 / .012 / .007 / ¹⁄₂₄ t	96 / 191 / 383	.60–7.22	"72.1"
16 Carrots	18,750–25,000	.55	.2 / 1¼ t[BB]	Roots: 100 / 150 / 400+	.04–.16	76.2
17 Cauliflower	9,000	.75	.01 / ¹⁄₂₄ t	44 / 100 / 291	.52–3.46	35.8
18 Celery	72,000	.55	.016 / ¹⁄₂₄ t	240 / 480 / 959+	.39–1.54	152.0
19 Chard, Swiss	1,500	.65	33 / 1½ T[AA]	200 / 405 / 810	.62–2.5	D
20 Collards, Annual & Perennial	9,000	.80	.022 / ⅛ t	96 / 191 / 383	.60–2.41	D
21 Corn, Sweet	112–156	.75	1.0–.72 / 2–1 c	Shelled, wet: 17 / 34 / 68 Biomass, air-dry: 12 / 24 / 48	15″ C: .20–.81	25.5
22 Cucumbers	938–1,000	.80	.2 / 1¼ T	158 / 316 / 581	1.00–3.65	45.2
23 Eggplant	6,500	.60	.014 / ¹⁄₁₂ t	54 / 108 / 163	1.02–3.08	55.1
24 Garlic	Cloves: 12	.5[Z]	20 lbs / 10 qt bulbs	60 / 120 / 240+	.04–.18+	33.3
25 Horseradish	Live roots used	—	159 roots / —	D	D	D
26 Kale	9,000	.75	.01 / ¹⁄₂₄ t	76 / 114 / 153	.90–1.82	"16.0"
27 Kohlrabi	9,000	.75	.20 / ¹⁄₁₆ t	67 / 135 / 270	.05–.20	D
28 Leeks	12,500	.60	.1 / ⅜ t	240 / 480 / 960	.39–1.55	D
29 Lettuce, Head	25,000	.80	.008 / ⅛ t	75 / 150 / 300	.47–1.89	73.5
30 Lettuce, Leaf	25,000	.80	.016 / .012 / ¼ t	135 / 202 / 540	8″ C: .42–1.69 9″ C: .54–2.18	51.2

	BEDS/FLATS											MATURITY		FOOD NEEDED	SEED YIELD
H	**I**	**J**	**K**	**L¹**	**L²**	**L³**	**L⁴**	**M¹**	**M²**	**M³**	**M⁴**	**N**	**O**	**P**	**Q**
				FIRST FLAT—3 INCHES DEEP				SECOND FLAT							
In-Bed Spacing (inches)	Maximum No. Plants per 100 Square Feet [15]	Short/Long/Extra-Long Germination Time	Plant Initially in Flats/Beds (in order of preference)	Spacing in First Flat (inches) or Broadcast (BC)	Approx. No. Plants per Flat (adj. for germ. rate) [22]	Division Factor to Determine Flats to Broadcast [23]	Approx. No. Weeks in First Flat [24]	Depth of Second Flat (inches)	Spacing in Second Flat (inches)	Approx. No. Plants per Flat [22]	Approx. No. Weeks in Second Flat [24]	Approx. No. Weeks to Maturity in Ground [25]	Approx. No. Weeks in Harvesting Period	Pounds Consumed per Year by Average Person in U.S. [21,26]	Approx. Maximum Pounds Seed Yield per 100 Square Feet [27]
15 centers 6 depth	84	L	F / B	Use 6-inch-deep flat. Put tubers as close as possible.			3–4	—	—	—	—	17–26	—	D	Tubers: 420+
72	3	L	Seeds: F Roots: B	Seeds 1	Seeds 175	—	Seeds 3–4	6	2	60	12–16	D, P	8	D	D
12	159	L	Seeds: F Roots: B	1	175	—	D	6	2	60	D	Seeds: 4 yrs. Roots: 1 yr.	8	.8	8.7
6	621	L	F	BC	175	4	1–2	3	1.5	111	3	6–8	12	D	D
6	621	S	F	1	175	—	1–2	—	—	—	—	9–11	12	}"1.3"	23
8	320	S	F	1	175	—	1–2	—	—	—	—	11–13	12		23+
6	621	S	F	1	175	—	1–2	—	—	—	—	8	12	}1.7	17.0
6	621	S	F	1	175	—	1–2	—	—	—	—	8–9	12		29.7
4	1,343	S	F / B^R	1	162	—	3–4	—	—	—	—	8–9	—	}"1.9"	30.6
4	1,343	S	F / B^R	1	162	—	3–4	—	—	—	—	8–9	—		30.6
15	84	S	F	1	187	—	2–3# 3–4	6	2	60	3–4# 5–6 LG	8–9	4–6	5.6	5.5
18	53	S	F	1	175	—	2–3# 3–4	6	2	60	3–4# 5–6 LG	11–13	12	".3"	2.8
4	1,343	S	F	1	150	—	3–4+	—	—	—	—	Up to 42	8–12	D	D
10	201	S	F	1	187	—	2–3# 3–4	6	2	60	3–4# 5–6 LG	7–11**	—	D	6.1
12 / 15 / 18**	159 / 84 / 53	S	F	1	187	—	2–3# 3–44	6	2	60	3–4# 5–6 LG	9–16**	—	8.9	3.6
3	2,507	S	F / B##	BC	137	3	3–4	—	—	—	—	9–11	4+	13.6	17.8
15	84	S	F	1	187	—	2–3# 3–4	6	2	60	3–4# 5–6 LG	8–12**	—	1.6	1.0
6	621	L / EL	F	BC	137	4	4–6	3	1	250	4–6Q	12–16	—	6.2	9.9
8	320	S	F	1	162	—	3–4	—	—	—	—	7–8	44	D	29.0
12	159	S	F	1	200	—	2–3# 3–4	6	2	60	3–4# 5–6 LG	12	24	D	D
15	84	S	F	1	187	—	3–5 days	—	—	—	—	9–13**	—	Shelled, wet: 9.0	22.6
12	159	S	F	2	48	—	2–3# 3–4	—	—	—	—	7–10	7–14	Reg: 6.7 Pickles: 4.4	4.1
18	53	L / EL	F	1	150	—	5–6	6	2	60	4–6 LG	10–11	13	".5"	.6
4	1,343	L	B	—	—	—	—	—	—	—	—	17–44	—	2.5	Bulbs: 240
12	159	L	B	—	—	—	—	—	—	—	—	26	—	D	D
15	84	S	F	1	187	—	2–3# 3–4	6	2	60	3–4# 5–6 LG	8–9	17	D	3.8
4	1,343	S	F	1	187	—	2–3# 3–4	—	—	—	—	7–8	—	D	20.1
6	621	S	F	BC	150	2	8–12	—	—	—	—	19	—	D	9.8
12	159	S	F	BC	200	4	1–2	3	1.5	111	2–3	11–13	1–3	22.8	1.2
8 WI / 9 SP–FA	320 / 248	S	F	BC	200	4	1–2	3	1.5	111	2–3	6–12**34	1–3	7.4	4.0

VEGETABLES AND GARDEN CROPS (continued)

PLANT AA	FOOD NEEDED BB *Pounds You Select*	MATERIALS NEEDED			
		CC *Approx. No. Plants You Need* [28]	DD *Approx. Square Feet You Need* [29]	EE *Approx. No. Flats You Need* [30]	FF *Approx. Ounces Seed You Need* [31]
1 Artichoke, Jerusalem					
2 Artichoke, Regular					
3 Asparagus					
4 Basil					
6 Beans, Lima, Bush					
7 Beans, Lima, Pole[N]					
8 Beans, Snap, Bush					
9 Beans, Snap, Pole[N]					
10 Beets, Cylindra					
11 Beets, Regular					
12 Broccoli					
12 Brussels Sprouts					
13 Burdock					
14 Cabbage, Chinese					
15 Cabbage, Regular					
16 Carrots					
17 Cauliflower					
18 Celery					
19 Chard, Swiss					
20 Collards, Annual & Perennial					
21 Corn, Sweet					
22 Cucumbers					
23 Eggplant					
24 Garlic					
25 Horseradish					
26 Kale					
27 Kohlrabi					
28 Leeks					
29 Lettuce, Head					
30 Lettuce, Leaf					

YIELDS		MISCELLANEOUS			NUTRITION			NOTES
GG	**HH**	**II**	**JJ**	**KK**	**LL**	**MM**	**NN**	**OO**
Your Actual Yield per 100 Square Feet	_Your Yield Compared with U.S. Average_ [32]	_Especially Good Varieties, Possible Seed Sources, and Remarks_	_Heavy Giver (HG), Light Feeder (LF), Low Nitrogen User (LNU), Heavy Feeder (HF)_ (see p. 145)	_Time of Year to Plant (SP, SU, FA, WI)_	_Protein Content per Pound in Grams (g) (454g per pound)_ [33]	_Calorie Content per Pound_ [33]	_Calcium Content per Pound in Milligrams (mg)_ [33]	
		35	HF	SP	7.2	Fresh: 22 Stored: 235	44	:Raw. 31% refuse. Used in alcohol production for gasohol. Good source of organic matter. Harvest when top is dead.
		—	HF	FA	5.3	Fresh: 16 Stored: 85	93	:Raw.
		—	HF	SP	6.4	66	56	:Raw. 44% refuse.
			HF	SU	D	D	D	
		—	HG	SU	} 92.5	1,565	327	}:Dry seeds.
		—	HG	SU				} Pick when beans are bulging through pods so plants will set more beans.
			HG	SP, SU	} 7.6	128	124	}:Raw. 12% refuse.
			HG	SP, SU				
			LF	SP, SU, FA	} 5.1	137	51	}:Roots, raw. 30% refuse. Excellent tops often mean too much nitrogen fertilizer and poor root growth. Cylindra variety twice the weight of regular beets.
		—	LF	SP, SU, FA	5.6	61	302M	:Greens, raw.
		36	HF	SP, FA	12.7 / 13.6	113 / 158	364 / 1,189	:Head, raw. 22% refuse. :Leaves, raw. Contain more nutrition than heads.
		—	HF	SP, FA	20.4	188	150	:Raw. 8% refuse. When sprout node begins to bulge, remove leaf below it for best growth.
		—	LF	SP, FA	9.4	400	225	Sow Watanabe in spring for summer harvest and Takinogawa in spring or fall for late summer or following spring harvest, respectively.
		—	HF	SP, FA	5.3	62	189	:Raw. 3% refuse.
		—	HF	SP, FA	5.3 / 8.2	98 / 127	200 / 171	:Green, raw. 10% refuse. :Red, raw. 10% refuse.
		—	LF	SP, SU, FA	4.1	156	134	:Raw, without tops. 18% refuse. Excellent tops often mean too much nitrogen fertilizer and poor root growth.
		37	HF	SP, FA	12.2	122	113	:Raw. Cauliflower head often develops in just a few days.
		—	HF	SP, FA	5.3	62	189	:25% refuse.
		Burpee Fordhook	HF	SP, SU, FA	10.0	104	367M	:Raw. 8% refuse. Harvest sequentially as leaves mature. Good organic matter crop at high yields.
		38	HF	SP, FA	16.3	181	921	:Leaves and stems, raw. Harvest sequentially as leaves mature.
		—	HF	SU	8.7	240	7	:Raw. 45% refuse (cob). Harvest when fluid in kernel is halfway between clear and milky. Air-dry biomass can be as much as for flour corn if plants are left to grow 4 weeks after harvest of ears.
		—	HF	SU	3.9	65	108	:Raw, whole. 5% refuse. Harvest when swollen, but not yellowing for sweetest taste.
		—	HF	SU	4.4	92	44	:Raw. 19% refuse.
		—	LF	SP, FA	24.8	547	116	:12% refuse. Most bulb growth occurs in last 45 days. Contains antibiotics. Amount of seed depends on size of bulbs and cloves.
		—	LF	SP, FA	10.6	288	464	:Raw. 27% refuse.
		—	HF	SP, FA	14.1	128	601	:Raw leaves and stems. 26% refuse. Good vitamin and mineral content.
		—	LF	SP, FA	6.6	96	136	:Raw. 27% refuse.
		—	LF	SP, FA	5.2	123	123	:Raw. 48% refuse.
		SN	HF	SP, FA	3.9	56	86	:Raw. 5% refuse. Harvest in very early morning for best taste.
		SN	HF	SP, SU, FA, WI	3.8	52	197	:Raw. 36% refuse. Harvest in very early morning for best taste. Winter growing in double-walled mini-greenhouse.

Letter codes on page 88, footnotes on page 116.

VEGETABLES AND GARDEN CROPS (continued)

PLANT	SEED			YIELD		
A	**B** Approx. No. Seeds per Ounce[12] (range: larger–smaller seed)	**C** Minimum Legal Germination Rate[13]	**D** Ounces / Volume Seed per 100 Square Feet (adj. for germ. rate, offset spacing, and curv. surf.)[14, 15, 16]	**E** Possible GROW BIOINTENSIVE Yield in Pounds per 100-Square-Foot Planting[17]	**F** Possible GROW BIOINTENSIVE Yield in Pounds per Plant[18, 19]	**G** Average U.S. Yield in Pounds per 100 Square Feet[20, 21]
31 Mangels	1,600	.65	.41 / 3.4 T[AA]	Roots: 200 / 400 / 800+ Greens: 100 / 200 / 400+	Roots: .46–1.85 Greens: .23–1.11	Roots: "68.0" Greens: **D**
32 Melons	1,000–1,250	.75	.09–.1 / ½ t	50 / 72 / 145	.60–1.73	49.1[CA] 44.1[H]
33 Mustard	15,000	.75	.055 / ¼ t	180 / 225 / 270	.29–.43	**D**
34 Okra	500	.50	.64 / 3½ t	30 / 60 / 120	.19–.75	**D**
35 Onions, Bunching	11,250–12,500	.70	.29–.32 / 5⁄16 t	100 / 200 / 540	.04–.21	**D**
36 Onions, Regular	8,125	.70	.2 / 3⁄16 t	100 / 200 / 540	.07–.40	} 91.1
37 Onions, Torpedo	8,125	.70	.2 / 3⁄16 t	200 / 400 / 800+	.15–.60+	
38 Parsley	18,000	.60	.08 / ½ t	45 / 91 / 182 (4- to 6-mo. harvest)	.05–.22	**D**
39 Parsnips	12,000	.60	.19 / ⅔ c	119 / 238 / 479	.09–.36	**D**
40 Peas, Bush	94–156	.80	2–1.25 lbs / 2–1¼ c	Fresh: 25 / 53 / 106 Dry: 4 / 10 / 24	Fresh: .01–.04 Dry: .001–.01	} Fresh: 6.8 Dry: 4.4
41 Peas, Pole[N]	94–156	.80	1.1 lbs–10.7 oz / 1⅒–⅔ c	Fresh: 25+ / 53+ / 106+ Dry: 4 / 10 / 24	Fresh: .02–.08+ Dry: .003–.02	
42 Peppers, Cayenne	4,500	.55	.064 / ⅜ t	5 / 10 / 20 Dry	.03–.13	**D**
43 Peppers, Green	4,500	.55	.064 / ⅜ t	36 / 83 / 197	.23–1.24	59.0
44 Potatoes, Irish	—	—	23.25–31 lbs / 12–16 qt	100 / 200 / 780	.40–3.15	78.7
45 Potatoes, Sweet	—	—	12 lbs / —	82 / 164 / 492	.33–1.98	34.0
46 Pumpkin	94–250	.75	.75–.07 / ⅒ T	Whole: 48 / 96 / 191 Seeds without hulls: 1 / 2 / 4	Whole: 18″ C: .91–3.60 30″ C: 3.42–13.64 Seeds: 18″ C: .02–.08 30″ C: .07–.29	**D**
47 Radishes	2,500–3,125	.75	2.5–3.1 / 4⅔ T	Roots: 100 / 200 / 540	.02–.09	**D**
48 Rhubarb	1,700[Y]	.60[Y]	.025 / ⅔ t	Stalks: 70 / 140 / 280	2.69–10.77	**D**
49 Rutabagas	9,375–11,875	.75	.09 / ¼ t	200 / 400 / 800+	.32–1.29	"68.0+"
50 Salsify	1,900	.75	1.7 / ½ c	100 / 200 / 400+	.04–.16	**D**
51 Shallots	8[Y] (bulbs)	.75[Y]	14.0 / 7 qt (bulbs)	60 / 120 / 240+	.04–.18+	**D**
52 Spinach, New Zealand, Malabar	350	.40	1.14 / 6 T	180 / 225 / 270	1.13–1.70	**D**
53 Spinach, Regular	2,800	.60	.37 / 2 t	50 / 100 / 225	.08–.36	29.8
54 Squash, Crookneck	218–281	.75	.5–.4 / 2–1½ T	35 / 75 / 150	.42–1.79	**D**
55 Squash, Patty Pan	300	.75	.37 / 1⅓ T	75 / 150 / 307	.89–3.65	**D**
56 Squash, Winter	100–250+	.75	12″ C: 2.12–.84 / 9½–3¾ T 15″ C: 1.12–.45 / 5–2 T 18″ C: .71–.28 / 3⅕–1¼ T	50 / 100 / 350	12″ C: .31–2.20 15″ C: .60–4.17 18″ C: .94–6.60	**D**
57 Squash, Zucchini	300	.75	.24 / 2.4 t	160 / 319 / 478+	3.02–9.02	**D**
58 Tomatoes	10,000–12,000	.75	.006 / .004 / .003 / 1⁄25–1⁄40 t	100 / 194 / 418	18″ C: 1.89–7.89 21″ C: 2.89–11.94 24″ C: 3.85–16.08	Fresh: 61.5 Processing: 143.9
59 Turnips	9,375–12,500	.80	.18–.13 / ⅔ t	Roots: 100 / 200 / 360 Greens: 100 / 200 / 360	Roots: .07–.27 Greens: .07–.27	**D**
60 Watermelon	Small seed: 500–625 Large seed: 187–312	.70	Small seed: 12″ C: .45–.36 / 3–2⅝ t 18″ C: .15–.12 / 1⅛–¾ t 21″ C: .10–.08 / ⅝–½ t 24″ C: .07–.06 / 7⁄16–⅜ t Large seed: 12″ C: 1.2–.73 / 2¾ T 18″ C: .4–.24 / 2⅝–1⅝ t 21″ C: .27–.16 / 1¾–1 3⁄16 t 24″ C: .20–.12 / 1⅜–¾ t	50 / 100 / 320	.31–12.30	50.0

H (In-Bed Spacing (inches))	I (Maximum No. Plants per 100 Square Feet [15])	J (Short/Long/Extra-Long Germination Time)	K (Plant Initially in Flats/Beds (in order of preference))	L1 (Spacing in First Flat (inches) or Broadcast (BC))	L2 (Approx. No. Plants per Flat (adj. for germ. rate) [22])	L3 (Division Factor to Determine Flats to Broadcast [23])	L4 (Approx. No. Weeks in First Flat [24])	M1 (Depth of Second Flat (inches))	M2 (Spacing in Second Flat (inches))	M3 (Approx. No. Plants per Flat [22])	M4 (Approx. No. Weeks in Second Flat [24])	N (Approx. No. Weeks to Maturity in Ground [25])	O (Approx. No. Weeks in Harvesting Period)	P (Pounds Consumed per Year by Average Person in U.S. [21,26])	Q (Approx. Maximum Pounds Seed Yield per 100 Square Feet [27])
7	432	S	F	1	162	—	3–4+	—	—	—	—	8–12+	—	D	20.0+
15	84	S	F	2	45	—	3–4 LG	—	—	—	—	12–17**	13	11.3CA 12.4H	2.9
6	621	S	F	1	187	—	3–4	—	—	—	—	5–6	8	D	5.7
12	159	L	F	1	125	—	6–8	6	2	60	3–4	7–8	13	D	9.3
3	2,507	S	F	BC	175	2	6–8	—	—	—	—	8–17	—	D	39.6
4	1,343	S	F	BC	175	2	6–8# 8–10	—	—	—	—	14–17	—	} 18.6	10.3
4	1,343	S	F	BC	175	2	6–8# 8–10	—	—	—	—	14–17	—		10.3
5	833	L / EL	F	BC	150	2	2–3	3	2	60	6–8	10–13	17–26	D	24.8
4	1,343	L	F	1	150	—	3–4	—	—	—	—	15	—	D	24.8
3	2,507	S	F	1	200	—	1–2	—	—	—	—	8–10	12	} "4.1"	24
4	1,343	S	F	1	200	—	1–2	—	—	—	—	10–11	12		24
12	159	L / EL	F	1	137	—	2–3	6	2	60	3–4# 5–7 LG	9–11	17	D	.1
12	159	L / EL	F	1	137	—	2–3	6	2	60	3–4# 5–7 LG	9–12	17	6.4	.3
9 centers 9 depth	248	L	39	39	—	—	—	—	—	—	—	9–17	—	47.8	Tubers: 780
9 centers 9 depth	248	L	40	40	30–60	—	4–6	—	—	—	—	13–17 (3-mo. var.) 26–34 (6-mo. var.)	—	4.1	492
18 / 30	53 / 14	S	F	2	45	—	3–4 LG	—	—	—	—	14–16	—	".6"	5.1
2	5,894	S	B	—	—	—	—	—	—	—	—	3–9**	—	D	20.6
24	26	L	Seeds: F Roots: B	1	150	—	D	6	2	60	D	Seeds: 3 yrs. Roots: 1 yr.	D	.03	D
6	621	S	F	1	187	—	3–4	—	—	—	—	13	—	D	5.4
3	2,507	S	F	1	187	—	3–4	—	—	—	—	17	—	D	27.7
4	1,343	L	B	—	—	—	—	—	—	—	—	17–26	—	D	Bulbs: 240
12	159	L	F	2	24	—	3–4	—	—	—	—	10	42	D	17.2
6	621	S	F	1	150	—	3–4	—	—	—	—	6–7	—	1.0	10.8
15	84	S	F	2	45	—	3–4 LG	—	—	—	—	10	17+	D	6.1
15	84	S	F	2	45	—	3–4 LG	—	—	—	—	7	17+	D	6.1
12 / 15 / 18	159 / 84 / 53	S	F	2	45	—	3–4 LG	—	—	—	—	11–17**	4+	D	5.7
18	53	S	F	2	45	—	3–4 LG	—	—	—	—	7–9	26	D	6.1
18 / 21 / 24TO	53 / 35 / 26	S	F	1	187	—	4–6	6	2	60	3–4 LG	8–13	17+	Canned: 75.6 Fresh: 17.4	5.5
4	1,343	S	F	1	200	—	2–3	—	—	—	—	5–10**	—	D	14.7
12 / 18 / 21 / 24W	159 / 53 / 35 / 26	S	F	2	42	—	3–4 LG	—	—	—	—	10–13	13	14.5	2.6

Letter codes on page 88, footnotes on page 116.

VEGETABLES AND GARDEN CROPS (continued) PLANT AA	FOOD NEEDED BB _Pounds You Select_	MATERIALS NEEDED CC _Approx. No. Plants You Need_[28]	DD _Approx. Square Feet You Need_[29]	EE _Approx. No. Flats You Need_[30]	FF _Approx. Ounces Seed You Need_[31]
31 Mangels					
32 Melons					
33 Mustard					
34 Okra					
35 Onions, Bunching					
36 Onions, Regular					
37 Onions, Torpedo					
38 Parsley					
39 Parsnips					
40 Peas, Bush					
41 Peas, Pole[N]					
42 Peppers, Cayenne					
43 Peppers, Green					
44 Potatoes, Irish					
45 Potatoes, Sweet					
46 Pumpkin					
47 Radishes					
48 Rhubarb					
49 Rutabagas					
50 Salsify					
51 Shallots					
52 Spinach, New Zealand, Malabar					
53 Spinach, Regular					
54 Squash, Crookneck					
55 Squash, Patty Pan					
56 Squash, Winter					
57 Squash, Zucchini					
58 Tomatoes					
59 Turnips					
60 Watermelon					

YIELDS		MISCELLANEOUS			NUTRITION			NOTES
GG _Your Actual Yield per 100 Square Feet_	**HH** _Your Yield Compared with U.S. Average_ [32]	**II** _Especially Good Varieties, Possible Seed Sources, and Remarks_	**JJ** _Heavy Giver (HG), Light Feeder (LF), Low Nitrogen User (LNU), Heavy Feeder (HF)_ (see p. 145)	**KK** _Time of Year to Plant (SP, SU, FA, WI)_	**LL** _Protein Content per Pound in Grams (g) (454g per pound)_ [33]	**MM** _Calorie Content per Pound_ [33]	**NN** _Calcium Content per Pound in Milligrams (mg)_ [33]	**OO** Δ Approximately 12% of the calories, 8% of the protein, and 18% of the calcium eaten worldwide is in the form of potatoes grown on 2.4% of the cropland. Harvest when tops are dead.
		Yellow Intermediate [41]	LF	SP, SU, FA	**D**	**D**	**D**	
		42	HF	SU	1.6 2.3	68 94	32 32	:Cantaloupe. 50% refuse. :Honeydew. 37% refuse.
		—	HF	SP, FA	9.5	98	73	:Raw. 30% refuse.
		—	HF	SU	9.4	140	359	:Raw. 14% refuse.
		—	LF	SP, SU, FA	6.5 1.8	157 76	222 67	:Raw. Bulb and entire top. 4% refuse. :Raw. Bulb and white portion of top. 63% refuse.
		Ishikura [43]	LF	SP, FA	6.2	157	111	:Dry. Raw. 9% refuse.
		44	LF	SP, FA	6.2	157	111	:Dry. Raw. 9% refuse.
		—	HF	SP, FA	16.3	200	921	:Raw.
		—	LF	SP, FA	6.6	293	193	:Raw. 15% refuse.
		—	HG	SP, FA	10.9	145	45	:Green. 62% refuse (pods). Harvest when seeds are bulging in pods.
		—	HG	SP, FA	109.4	1,542	290	:Dry. Try sugar snap edible variety.
		—	HF	SU	45	1,371	681	:Dry (including seeds). 4% refuse.
		—	HF / LNU	SU	4.5 5.1	82 112	33 47	:Green. 18% refuse. :Red. 20% refuse.
		45, 39, SN	LF	SP, SU	7.7	279	26	:Raw. 19% refuse. Green parts poisonous. }See above Δ
		46	LF / LNU	SU	6.6 6.2	375 430	118 118	:Jewel (firm). :Puerto Rican (soft). 19% refuse.
		47	HF	SU	3.2 131.5	83 2,508	67 231	:Raw fruit. 30% refuse. :Seeds. Hulls 30% of unhulled weight.
		48	LF	SP, FA	4.1	69	122	:Raw, without tops. 10% refuse.
		—	HF	SP	2.3	62	374	:Raw, without leaves. 14% refuse. Green parts poisonous.
		—	LF	SP, FA	4.2	177	254	:Raw. 15% refuse. Very flavorful when GROW BIOINTENIVEly grown.
		—	LF	SP, FA	11.4	51	185	:Fresh. Caloric content rises to 324 after being stored for some time.
		—	LF	SP, FA	10.0	287	148	:Raw. 12% refuse.
		Drought-resistant	HF	SP, SU, FA	10.0	86	263	:Raw.
		—	HF	SP, FA	10.5	85	304 [M]	:Raw. 28% refuse.
		Bush	HF	SU	5.3	89	124	:Raw. 2% refuse.
		Bush	HF	SU	4.0	93	124	:Raw. 2% refuse. Harvest the white variety when bone white with only a tinge of green left.
		Bush and vine	HF	SU	5.2 4.4 4.2	152 171 117	107 102 57	:Acorn, raw. 24% refuse. :Butternut, raw. 30% refuse. } Harvest when neck stem is dry. :Hubbard, raw. 34% refuse.
		Bush and vine	HF	SU	5.2	73	121	:Raw. 5% refuse. Harvest when 10 inches long.
		—	HF	SU	5.0	100	59	:Raw.
		—	LF / LNU	SP, FA	3.9 13.6	117 127	152 1,116	:Roots, raw. :Greens, raw.
		49	HF	SU	1.0	54	15	:Raw. 54% refuse.

CALORIE, GRAIN, PROTEIN SOURCE, AND VEGETABLE OIL CROPS

For protein, also see: Beans, Lima; Buckwheat; Collards; Corn, Sweet; Garlic; Peas; Potatoes, Irish and Sweet

PLANT	SEED			YIELD		
A	**B** *Approx. No. Seeds per Ounce* [12] *(range: larger–smaller seed)*	**C** *Minimum Legal Germination Rate* [13]	**D** *Ounces / Volume Seed per 100 Square Feet (adj. for germ. rate, offset spacing, and curv. surf.)* [14, 15, 16]	**E** *Possible GROW BIOINTENSIVE Yield in Pounds per 100-Square-Foot Planting* [17]	**F** *Possible GROW BIOINTENSIVE Yield in Pounds per Plant* [18, 19]	**G** *Average U.S. Yield in Pounds per 100 Square Feet* [20, 21]
1 Amaranth, Grain and Leaf	25,000–53,400	.70[A]	.035–.017 / ⅓–⅙ t .009–.004 / 1⁄40–1⁄80 t	Edible greens-type: 68 / 136 / 272+; Seed: 4 / 8 / 16+ Biomass, air-dry (stalks): 12 / 24 / 48 Biomass, wet: 53 / 132 / 317	Greens: .08–.30 Seed: .11–.44+	Seed: "4" Biomass, air-dry: "6"
2 Barley	500 hulled	.70[A]	2.4 / 6⅓ T	Seed: 5 / 10 / 24[K, U] Biomass, air-dry: 12 / 30 / 72	Seed: .006–.03 Biomass, dry: .01–.09	Seed: 6.6 Biomass, dry: est. 9.9
3 Beans, Fava, Cold-Weather	15–70	.75	28.4–6.1 / 7.5–1.6 c	Seed: 5 / 9 / 18 Biomass, air-dry: 18 / 36 / 72 Biomass, wet: 90 / 180 / 360	Seed: .02–.06 Biomass, dry: .06–.23	**D**
4 Beans, Fava, Hot-Weather	15–70	.75	55.2–11.8 / 14.5–3 c	Seed: 2 / 3 / 6 Biomass, air-dry: 6 / 12 / 24 Biomass, wet: 30 / 60 / 120	Seed: .003–.01 Biomass, dry: .01–.04	**D**
5 Beans, Kidney	50	.70[A]	17.7 / 1 9⁄10 c	Seed: 4 / 10 / 24	.006–.04	"4.0"
6 Beans, Mung	500	.70[A]	3.8 / 7.6 T	Seed: 4 / 10 / 24	.003–.02	3.6
7 Beans, Pinto	70	.70[A]	12.7 / 1 4⁄10 c	Seed: 4 / 10 / 24	.006–.04	3.6
8 Beans, Red Mexican and Black	50–100	.70[A]	17.7–8.9 / 2 1⁄10–1 1⁄10 c	Seed: 4 / 10 / 24	.006–.04	3.6
9 Beans, White	90–180	.70[A]	9.9–4.9 / 1¾–⅚ c	Seed: 4 / 10 / 24	.006–.04	3.6
10 Cassava	—	—	**D**	Root: 30 / 60 / 120	1.67–6.67	**D**
11 Chickpea (Garbanzo)	50	.70[A]	38.4 / 6 c	Seed: 4 / 10 / 24	.003–.02	**D**
12 Corn, Flour or Fodder, Dry	100–200	.70[A]	1.2–.6 / 3–2 T	Seed: 11 / 17 / 23+ Biomass, air-dry: 24 / 48 / 96 Biomass, wet: 107 / 214 / 428	Seed: .13–.27+	Seed: 17.3
13 Cowpea	150	.75	1.5–.25–.17 / 3½ T–1¼ T	Seed: 2.4 / 4.5 / 9 Green hay: 91 / 183 / 366	Seed: .02–.50 Green hay: .57–20.33	**D**
14 Lentils	600	.70[A]	3.2 / 6½ T	Seed: 4 / 6 / 8+	.003–.006+	2.8
15 Millet, Japanese	10,000	.70[A]	.06 / ¾ t	Seed: 3 / 7 / 13+[K] Biomass, air-dry: 12 / 30 / 72	Seed: .002–.03+	Seed: "3.4"
16 Millet, Pearl	2,200 unhulled	.70[A]	.3 / **D**	Seed: 3 / 6 / 12 Biomass, air-dry: 15 / 40 / 75 Biomass, wet: 70 / 185 / 350	Seed: .01–.03 Biomass, dry: .03–.17	**D**
17 Millet, Proso	2,200 unhulled	.70[A]	.28 / ⅘ T	Seed: 3 / 6 / 12+ [K] Biomass, air-dry: 6 / 15 / 36	Seed: .002–.03+	Seed: 4.1
18 Oats	90 hulled	.70[A]	1.25 / 3 T	Seed: 3 / 7 / 13+[K, U] Biomass: air-dry: 12 / 30 / 72	Seed: .004–.02 Biomass, dry: .01–.09	Seed: 4.4 Biomass, dry: est. 6.6
19 Peanuts	20–70 unshelled 30–90 shelled	.70[A]	11.8–3.9 / 4.4–1.5 c shelled	Seed: 4 / 10 / 24	.02–.10	6.2
20 Pigeon Pea	**D**	.70[A]	**D**	Seed: 2 / 4 / 16+	.50–4.00	**D**
21 Quinoa	10,000	.70[A]	.023 / ⅙ t	Seed: 6 / 13 / 26 Biomass, air-dry: 18 / 39 / 78	Seed: .04–.16	**D**
22 Rapeseed	8,000	.70[A]	.04 / 2 t	Seed: 5 / 10 / 20	.02–.08	3.1
23 Rice	1,100 unhulled	.70[A]	1.7 / 3⅗ T	Seed: 8 / 16 / 32[K, U] Biomass, air-dry: 24 / 54 / 96	Seed: .006–.02 Biomass, dry: .02–.07	Seed: 13.0 Biomass, dry: est. 19.5
24 Rye, Cereal	500 hulled	.70[A]	2.4 / 5⅖ T	Seed: 4 / 10 / 24 [K, U] Biomass, air-dry: 12 / 30 / 72	Seed: .005–.03 Biomass, dry: .01–.09	Seed: 3.7 Biomass, dry: est. 5.6
25 Safflower	640 unhulled	.70[A]	1.8 / 2.6 c	Seed: 4 / 9 / 17+ Biomass, air-dry: 5 / 10 / 20	Seed: .005–.02+	Seed: 3.3
26 Sesame	11,000	.70[A]	.08 / ⅕ T	Seed: 1.5 / 3 / 6+	Seed: .002–.01+	**D**
27 Sorghum	1,000	.65[A]	Reg. type: .66 / 1⅔ T Broom type: 1.9 / 6⅘ T	Reg. type: Seed: 6 / 12 / 24 Biomass, air-dry: 25 / 50 / 100+ Biomass, wet: 88 / 175 / 350+	Reg. type: Seed: .01–.06 Biomass, dry: .06–.23	Reg. type: Seed: 8.6 Biomass, wet: 52.3
28 Soybeans	100–250	.75	8.2–3.3 / 1⅛–½ c	Dry seed: 4 / 8 / 14+	.006–.02+	5.3
29 Sunflowers	650 in shell[Y]	.50+[Y]	.08 / .76 / ⅓–3 T	Seed, hulled: 24″ C: 2.5 / 5 / 10 Stalks, air-dry: 9″ C: 20 / 40 / 80	Seed: 24″ C: .10–.38 Stalks: 9″ C: .08–.32	Seed, hulled: 3.5
30 Wheat, Durum	500 hulled	.70[A]	2.4 / **D**	Seed: 4 / 10 / 26 [K, U] Biomass, air-dry: 12 / 30 / 72	Seed: .005–.03 Biomass, dry: .01–.09	Seed: 5.1 Biomass, dry: est. 7.7
31 Wheat, Early Stone Age	800 unhulled	.70[A]	1.5 / **D**	Seed: 4 / 10 / 17[K, U] Biomass, air-dry: 12 / 30 / 51	Seed: .005–.02+ Biomass, dry: .01–.06	**D**
32 Wheat, Hard Red Spring	500 hulled	.70[A]	2.4 / 6⅓ T	Seed: 4 / 10 / 26[K, U] Biomass, air-dry: 12 / 30 / 72	Seed: .005–.03 Biomass, dry: .01–.09	Seed: 4.8 Biomass, dry: est. 7.2
33 Wheat, Red Winter	500 hulled	.70[A]	2.4 / 6⅓ T	Seed: 4 / 10 / 26[K, U] Biomass, air-dry: 12 / 30 / 72	Seed: .006–.03 Biomass, dry: .01–.09	Seed: 6.5 Biomass, dry: est. 9.8
34 Wheat, White	500 hulled	.70[A]	2.4 / 6⅓ T	Seed: 5 / 10 / 24[K, U] Biomass, air-dry: 12 / 30 / 72	Seed: .005–.03 Biomass, dry: .01–.09	Seed: "3.7" Biomass, dry: est. 5.6

H	I	J	K	L¹	L²	L³	L⁴	M¹	M²	M³	M⁴	N	O	P	Q
BEDS/FLATS												**MATURITY**		**FOOD NEEDED**	**SEED YIELD**
				FIRST FLAT—3 INCHES DEEP				SECOND FLAT							
In-Bed Spacing (inches)	Maximum No. Plants per 100 Square Feet [15]	Short/Long/Extra-Long Germination Time	Plant Initially in Flats/Beds (in order of preference)	Spacing in First Flat (inches) or Broadcast (BC)	Approx. No. Plants per Flat (adj. for germ. rate) [22]	Division Factor to Determine Flats to Broadcast [23]	Approx. No. Weeks in First Flat [24]	Depth of Second Flat (inches)	Spacing in Second Flat (inches)	Approx. No. Plants per Flat [22]	Approx. No. Weeks in Second Flat [24]	Approx. No. Weeks to Maturity in Ground [25]	Approx. No. Weeks in Harvesting Period	Pounds Consumed per Year by Average Person in U.S. [21,26]	Approx. Maximum Pounds Seed Yield per 100 Square Feet [27]
Greens: 6 Seed: 12	621 159	S	F	BC	175	4	1	3	1.5	111	3	Greens: 6 Seed: 12	Greens: 4+ Seed: —	D	16+
5	833	S	F	1 or BC	175	2	1–2	—	—	—	—	9–10	—	.7	24
8	320	S	F / B^R	1	187	—	2	—	—	—	—	17–43	—	D	18
6	621	S	F / B^R	1	187	—	2	—	—	—	—	13–17	—	D	6
6	621	S	F	1	175	—	1–2	—	—	—	—	12	8		24
4	1,343	S	F	1	175	—	1–2	—	—	—	—	12	8		24
6	621	S	F	1	175	—	1–2	—	—	—	—	12	8	All dry edible beans: "13.5"	24
6	621	S	F	1	175	—	1–2	—	—	—	—	12	8		24
6	621	S	F	1	175	—	1–2	—	—	—	—	12	8		24
36	18	—	B	—	—	—	—	—	—	—	—	26–52	D	D	D
4	1,343	S	F	1	175	—	1–2	—	—	—	—	9	8	D	24
15	84	S	F	1	175	—	3–5 days	—	—	—	—	11–16	—	152.3	23+
12 / 24 / 36^E	159 / 26 / 18	S	F	1	187	—	2	—	—	—	—	9–12	8	D	9
4	1,343	S	F	1	175	—	1–2	—	—	—	—	12	8	—	8+
7	432	S	F	1 or BC	175	2	2–4	—	—	—	—	6–8	—	D	13+
7	432	S	F	1 or BC	175	2	2–4	—	—	—	—	17–21	—	D	12
7	432	S	F	1 or BC	175	2	2–4	—	—	—	—	10–13	—	D	12+
5	833	S	F	1 or BC	175	2	1–2	—	—	—	—	13–17	—	6.5	13+
9	248	S	F	2	42	—	2–4	—	—	—	—	17	—	.64	24
60	4	S	F	1	175	—	2–3	—	—	—	—	22	26+	D	16+
12	159	S	F	BC	175	4	1	3	1.5	111	3	16	—	D	26
9	248	S	F	BC	175	2	1–2	—	—	—	—	D	D	D	20
4	1,343	S	F	1	175	—	2	—	—	—	—	17	—	20.8	24
5	833	S	F	1 or BC	175	2	1–2	—	—	—	—	17	—	.6	24
5	833	S	F	1	175	—	2–3	—	—	—	—	17	—	Oil: "1.0"	17+
6	621	L	F	1	175	—	3	—	—	—	—	13–17	8	D	6+
Reg. type: 7 Broom type: 4	432 1,343	S	F	1 or BC	162	2	2–3	—	—	—	—	13	—	D	24
6	621	S	F	1	187	—	2	—	—	—	—	Green: 8–9 Dry: 16–17	2–4	All purposes: "467.4"	14
24 / 9	26 / 248	S	F	1	125+	—	2–3	—	—	—	—	12	—	D	10
5	833	S	F	1 or BC	175	2	1–2	—	—	—	—	16–18	—	See Wheat, Hard Red Spring	26
5	833	L	F	1 or BC	175	2	2–3	—	—	—	—	16–20	—	D	17+
5	833	S	F	1 or BC	175	2	1–2	—	—	—	—	16–18	—	All purposes: 911 Food products: 151.4	26
5	833	S	F	1 or BC	175	2	1–2	—	—	—	—	16–18	—		26
5	833	S	F	1 or BC	175	2	1–2					16–18	—		26

Letter codes on page 88, footnotes on page 116.

CALORIE, GRAIN, PROTEIN SOURCE, AND VEGETABLE OIL CROPS (continued)	FOOD NEEDED	MATERIALS NEEDED			
	BB	CC	DD	EE	FF
PLANT AA	Pounds You Select	Approx. No. Plants You Need [28]	Approx. Square Feet You Need [29]	Approx. No. Flats You Need [30]	Approx. Ounces Seed You Need [31]
1 Amaranth, Grain and Leaf					
2 Barley					
3 Beans, Fava, Cold-Weather					
4 Beans, Fava, Hot-Weather					
5 Beans, Kidney					
6 Beans, Mung					
7 Beans, Pinto					
8 Beans, Red Mexican and Black					
9 Beans, White					
10 Cassava					
11 Chickpea (Garbanzo)					
12 Corn, Flour, or Fodder, Dry					
13 Cowpea					
14 Lentils					
15 Millet, Japanese					
16 Millet, Pearl					
17 Millet, Proso					
18 Oats					
19 Peanuts					
20 Pigeon Pea					
21 Quinoa					
22 Rapeseed					
23 Rice					
24 Rye, Cereal					
25 Safflower					
26 Sesame					
27 Sorghum					
28 Soybeans					
29 Sunflowers					
30 Wheat, Durum					
31 Wheat, Early Stone Age					
32 Wheat, Hard Red Spring					
33 Wheat, Red Winter					
34 Wheat, White					

YIELDS		MISCELLANEOUS			NUTRITION			NOTES
GG	**HH**	**II**	**JJ**	**KK**	**LL**	**MM**	**NN**	**OO**
Your Actual Yield per 100 Square Feet	*Your Yield Compared with U.S. Average* [32]	*Heavy Giver (HG), Light Feeder (LF), Low Nitrogen User (LNU), Heavy Feeder (HF)*	*Especially Good Varieties, Possible Seed Sources, and Remarks* (see p. 145)	*Time of Year to Plant (SP, SU, FA, WI)*	*Protein Content per Pound in Grams (g) (454g per pound)* [33]	*Calorie Content per Pound* [33]	*Calcium Content per Pound in Milligrams (mg)* [33]	
		41	HF	SU	15.9 69.5	200 1,775	1,212 2,224	:Greens. Good calcium source. :Seed.
		Hull-less[41]	HF	SP, FA	37.2 43.5 3.2*	1,583 1,579 224	73 154 145	:Light. :Pearled or scotch. :Straw and chaff, dry. } Hulling of regular varieties difficult. Use hull-less varieties.
		Banner (to 10°F)[41]	HG	FA, SP	13.0 113.9	162 1,533	42 463	:In pods. 66% refuse. :Dry beans. } Excellent organic matter crop. For biomass only, harvest when plants begin to lose their maximum green. Fixes up to .16+ lb
		50	HG	SP	13.0 113.9	162 1,533	42 463	:In pods. 66% refuse. :Dry beans. nitrogen per 100 sq ft per year. Caution: Beans can be toxic to some people.
		51	HG	SU	102.1	1,556	499	
		51	HG	SU	109.8	1,542	535	
		51	HG	SU	103.9	1,583	612	} :Dry seeds, raw. Harvest sequentially when seeds bulge through pods.
		50	HG	SU	103.9 102.1	1,583 1,556	612 499	:Red Mexican. :Black.
		51	HG	SU	101.2	1,542	653	
		—	LF	—	5.5	677	309	:Raw. Transplant stem cuttings 12–18 inches long and 1–1.5 inches in diameter at beginning of rains. Some varieties take 104 weeks to mature.
		51	HG	SU	93.0	1,633	680	:Dry seeds, raw. Harvest like beans.
		50	HF	SP	40.4	1,579	100	:Dry seeds, raw. Also produces a lot of organic matter.
		50, 51	HG	SU	103.4	1,556	336	:Dry. Harvest sequentially when seeds bulge through pods. Can harvest up to ⅛ of leaves from 21–30 days until flowering.
		51	HG	SP, SU	112.0	1,542	538	:Dry seeds, raw. Harvest like beans.
		52	HF	SU	D	D	D	Use 45-day variety.
		—	HF	SU	19.0*	D	D	:Dry. Seeds form in about 45 days when days become shorter. Yields can be 3 times higher in hot climate and good soil.
		53	HF	SU	44.9	1,483	91	:Dry. High in iron.
		Hull-less[41]	HF	SP, FA	64.4 3.2*	1,769 233	240 86	:Grain, dry. :Straw and chaff, dry. } Hulling of regular varieties difficult. Use hull-less varieties.
		53	HG	SU	117.9	2,558	313	:Shelled, raw. Shells 27% of unshelled weight. Can be carcinogenic if not stored properly.
		—	HG	SU	92.5	1,551	485	:Dry. Hulls 61% of unhulled weight. Short-lived perennial in tropical climates.
		—	HF	SU	73.5	1,600	640	:Dry.
		53	HF	SP, SU, FA	D	1,960	D	:Dry. Helps eradicate weeds.
		—	HF	SU	34.0 30.4 2.7*	1,633 1,647 D	145 109 86	:Brown. :White. :Straw and chaff, dry.
		35	HF	FA	54.9	1,515 90	172 118	:Dry, whole grain. :Straw and chaff, dry. } 15% in wheat bread buffers phytates that otherwise tie up iron.
		54	HF	SU	86.6	2,790	—	:Dry, hulled. Source of organic matter and vegetable oil. Harvest when 98–100% of heads dry. Hulls 49% unhulled weight.
		—	HF*	SU	84.4	2,554	5,262	:Dry. Very high in calcium. Seed = 40% oil.
		41	HF	SU	49.9 15.0*	1,506 351	127 154	:Grain, dry. :Fodder, dry.
		35	HG	SU	49.9 154.7	608 1,828	304 1,025	:Green. :Hulled, dry.
		—	HF	SU	108.9	2,540	544	:Dry seeds without hulls. Hulls 46% of unhulled weight. Seed = approx. 20% oil.
		—	HF	FA	57.6 1.3*	1,506 100	168 95	:Grain, dry. :Straw and chaff, dry.
		41	HF	FA	83.0 D	D D	D D	:Grain, dry. :Straw and chaff, dry. } *Triticum monococcum* var. *Hornemanii*. Variety up to 12,000 years old. More difficult to thresh than other wheat.
		41	HF	FA	63.5 1.3*	1,497 100	163 95	:Grain, dry. :Straw and chaff, dry.
		—	HF	FA	55.8 46.3 1.3*	1,497 1,497 100	209 191 95	:Grain, dry, hard variety. :Grain, dry, soft variety. :Straw and chaff, dry.
		—	HF	FA	42.6 1.3*	1,520 100	163 95	:Grain, dry. :Straw and chaff, dry. } For milder, wetter climate, like the Pacific Northwest. Not widely used.

Letter codes on page 88, footnotes on page 116.

COMPOST, CARBON, ORGANIC MATTER, FODDER, AND COVER CROPS

For organic matter, also see: Artichoke, Jerusalem; Beans, Fava

A PLANT	B Approx. No. Seeds per Ounce [12] (range: larger–smaller seed)	C Minimum Legal Germination Rate [13]	D Ounces / Volume Seed per 100 Square Feet (adj. for germ. rate, offset spacing, and curv. surf.) [14,15,16]	E Possible GROW BIOINTENSIVE Yield in Pounds per 100-Square-Foot Planting [17]	F Possible GROW BIOINTENSIVE Yield in Pounds per Plant [18,19]	G Average U.S. Yield in Pounds per 100 Square Feet [20,21]
	SEED			YIELD		
1 Alfalfa	14,000	.70[A]	.085 / ¼ T	Biomass, air-dry: 44 / 82 / 123 Biomass, wet: 148 / 275 / 412, 5–6 cuttings	D	Biomass, air-dry: 16.0; Biomass, wet: "53.6"
2 Buckwheat	1,000	.70[A]	2.6 / ½ c	Biomass, air-dry: 2 / 4 / 6 Grain: 4 / 8 / 16+	D	D
3 Cardoon	688	.60	.04 / 1½ t	Biomass, air-dry: 20 / 40 / 80	Dry: 1.11–4.44	D
4 Clover, Alsike	44,875	.70[A]	.3–.55+ / ⅛ t	Biomass, air-dry: 12 / 25 / 38	.01–.05	Biomass, air-dry: "4.3"
5 Clover, Crimson	7,000	.70[A]	.6+ / 1¼ t	Biomass, air-dry: 12 / 25 / 38 Biomass, wet: 22 / 41 / 60 (6-mo. yield)	Dry: .01–.05	Biomass, air-dry: "4.3"
6 Clover, Sweet, Hubam	11,400	.70[A]	1.1 / ⅔ t	Biomass, air-dry: 12 / 25 / 38 Biomass, wet: 22 / 41 / 60 (6-mo. yield)	Dry: .01–.05	Biomass, air-dry: "4.3"
7 Clover, Medium Red	14,500	.70[A]	.08 for hay / .72 for green manure / 2 T / 1¹⁄₁₀ c	Biomass, air-dry: 25 / 50 / 75 Biomass, wet: 38 / 76 / 114 (6-mo. yield)	Dry: .03–.09	Biomass, air-dry: "8.7"
8 Clover, White	45,750	.70[A]	.03 / ¼ t	Biomass, air-dry: 12 / 25 / 38 Biomass, wet: 22 / 41 / 60 (6-mo. yield)	Dry: .01–.05	Biomass, air-dry: "4.3"
9 Comfrey, Russian	—	—	53 roots	Biomass, air-dry: 10 / 14 / 37 Biomass, wet: 92 / 184 / 176 (6-mo. yield)	Dry: .06–.23	Biomass, air-dry: "62.6" world high (12-mo. season)
10 Grass, Rye, Italian	16,875	.70[A]	3.6 / 1⅓ c	D	D	D
11 Kudzu	2,000	.70[A]	D / D	Biomass, air-dry: 13 / 26 / 53 Biomass, wet: 53 / 105 / 211	Propagated by seeds,	
12 Roots, General	An important hidden compost crop beneath the ground. Root matter in the soil can range from					
13 Sainfoin	In pods: 1,560 Cleaned: 2,040	.50[A]	.82 hulled / D	Biomass, air-dry: 12 / 25 / 38 (6-mo. yield)	Dry: .01–.05	D
14 Sunnhemp, Giant	D	.70[A]	D / D	Biomass, air-dry: 18 / 44 / 108 Biomass, wet: 79 / 198 / 475	Dry: .04–.25	D
15 Teosinte	440	.70[A]	.11 / ⅔ T	Grain: 2 / 4 / 6 Biomass, air-dry: 17 / 34 / 68 Biomass, wet: 88 / 166 / 232	Dry: .48–1.94	D
16 Timothy	82,500	.70[A]	.01 / ⅛ t	Biomass, air-dry: 12 / 25 / 38 Biomass, wet: 22 / 41 / 60 (6-mo. yield)	Dry: .01–.05	Biomass, air-dry: "4.3"
17 Vetch, Purple, Hairy, or Woolly Pod[BB]	800	.70[A]	5.5 (.63 if interplanted) / ¾ c (1½ T)	Biomass, air-dry: 5 / 9 / 18 Biomass, wet: 25 / 45 / 90 } Planted alone	D	D

	BEDS/FLATS											MATURITY		FOOD NEEDED	SEED YIELD
H	**I**	**J**	**K**	**L¹**	**L²**	**L³**	**L⁴**	**M¹**	**M²**	**M³**	**M⁴**	**N**	**O**	**P**	**Q**
				FIRST FLAT—3 INCHES DEEP				SECOND FLAT							
In-Bed Spacing (inches)	Maximum No. Plants per 100 Square Feet [15]	Short/Long/Extra-Long Germination Time	Plant Initially in Flats/Beds (in order of preference)	Spacing in First Flat (inches) or Broadcast (BC)	Approx. No. Plants per Flat (adj. for germ. rate) [22]	Division Factor to Determine Flats to Broadcast [23]	Approx. No. Weeks in First Flat [24]	Depth of Second Flat (inches)	Spacing in Second Flat (inches)	Approx. No. Plants per Flat [22]	Approx. No. Weeks in Second Flat [24]	Approx. No. Weeks to Maturity in Ground [25]	Approx. No. Weeks in Harvesting Period	Pounds Consumed per Year by Average Person in U.S. [21,26]	Approx. Maximum Pounds Seed Yield per 100 Square Feet [27]
5	833	S	F	BC	175	4	8	—	—	—	—	12 to first cutting, 5–9 thereafter	3–50+ years	611.9	1.8+
Broadcast	D	S	B	—	—	—	—	—	—	—	—	9–13	—	D	16+
36	18	S	F	1	150	—	2–3	6	2	60	3–4	Harvest when stalks mature	1 harvest	D	D
5	833	S	F	BC	175	4	8	—	—	—	—	17–26	1 cutting	}"547.5"	}2.2+
5	833	S	F	BC	175	4	8	—	—	—	—	17–26	1 cutting		
5	833	S	F	BC	175	4	8	—	—	—	—	17–26	1 cutting		
5	833	S	F	BC	175	4	8	—	—	—	—	17 to first cutting, 5–9 thereafter	2–3 years		
5	833	S	F	BC	175	4	8	—	—	—	—	17–26	3–5 years		
12	159	S	B	—	—	—	—	—	—	—	—	12–17 to first cutting	Years	D	D
Broadcast	D	S	B	—	—	—	—	—	—	—	—	D	D	D	6.9+

cuttings, and roots. More research needs to be performed. For some information see *Book of Kudzu,* by Bill Shurtleff, in the bibliography.

45–120% of aboveground biomass at the end of the growing season. (Brady and Weil, *The Nature and Properties of Soils,* 12th ed., p. 423.)

5	833	S	F	BC or 1	125	2	8	—	—	—	—	17 to first cutting, 9 thereafter	D	D	.46+
7	432	S	F	1	175	—	2–3	—	—	—	—	17+	D	D	D
21	35	S	F	1	175	—	2–3	—	—	—	—	D	D	D	D
5	833	S	F	BC	175	4	8	—	—	—	—	17	D	D	.46+
Broadcast	D	S	B	—	—	—	—	—	—	—	—	D	D	D	1.1+

COMPOST, CARBON, ORGANIC MATTER, FODDER, AND COVER CROPS (continued)	FOOD NEEDED	MATERIALS NEEDED				
PLANT AA	BB *Pounds You Select*	CC *Approx. No. Plants You Need* [28]	DD *Approx. Square Feet You Need* [29]	EE *Approx. No. Flats You Need* [30]	FF *Approx. Ounces Seed You Need* [31]
1 Alfalfa					
2 Buckwheat					
3 Cardoon					
4 Clover, Alsike					
5 Clover, Crimson					
6 Clover, Sweet, Hubam					
7 Clover, Medium Red					
8 Clover, White					
9 Comfrey, Russian					
10 Grass, Rye, Italian					
11 Kudzu					
12 Roots, General					
13 Sainfoin					
14 Sunnhemp, Giant					
15 Teosinte					
16 Timothy					
17 Vetch, Purple, Hairy, or Woolly Pod					

YIELDS		MISCELLANEOUS			NUTRITION			NOTES
GG	**HH**	**II**	**JJ**	**KK**	**LL**	**MM**	**NN**	**OO**
Your Actual Yield per 100 Square Feet	*Your Yield Compared with U.S. Average* [32]	*Especially Good Varieties, Possible Seed Sources, and Remarks*	*Heavy Giver (HG), Light Feeder (LF), Low Nitrogen User (LNU), Heavy Feeder (HF)* (see p. 145)	*Time of Year to Plant (SP, SU, FA, WI)*	*Protein Content per Pound in Grams (g) (454g per pound)* [33]	*Calorie Content per Pound* [33]	*Calcium Content per Pound in Milligrams (mg)* [33]	
		41, AC	HG	SP	Air dry: 53.1*	411	667	:Air dry at 10% bloom point. Transplant when seedling is 2–3 months old. Harvest when in 10–50% flowering range. Fixes .35–.57 lb nitrogen/100 sq ft/year.
		41	HF	SP, mid-SU	53.1	1,520	517	:Dry grain. Hulling difficult. Good honeybee plant. ½ lb honey/100 sq ft.
		—	HF	SP	—	—	—	Flower market potential. Can become a noxious weed; do not allow seeds to disperse.
		41, AC	HG	SP	36.7*	436	522	:Dry. Fixes up to .27 lb nitrogen/100 sq ft/year.
		41, AC	HG	SP	44.5*	391	558	:Dry. Fixes up to .21 lb nitrogen/100 sq ft/year.
		53, AC	HG	SP	42.6	355	567	:Dry.
		41, AC	HG	SP	51.3*	450	767	:Before bloom. Fixes up to .23–.3 lb nitrogen/100 sq ft/year.
		41, AC	HG	SP	42.6*	355	567	:Dry. Fixes up to .23–.3 lb nitrogen/100 sq ft/year.
		—	HF	SP	3.4	D	D	
		—	HF	SP	15.4*	D	—	Not good for soil.
		—	LF	D	13.3 / 11.3	D / D	D / D	:Dried root. Plus cloth can be made from the root. :Cured hay. Can be invasive.
		—	—	—	—	—	—	
		54	HG	SP	34.0*	D	—	:Dry. Does best in slightly dry climate.
		—	HG	SU	D	D	D	
		50, 54	HF	SU	22.2*	D		
		53	HF	SP	18.6*	D	186	:Dry, early bloom.
		41	HG	SP, FA	69.0*	D	513	:Dry. Fixes up to .25 lb nitrogen/100 sq ft/year.

See Voison books in the bibliography (under "Compost Crops") for ways to increase grazing yields significantly. Try 3–5 times the seeding rate for hay if growing crop seed. Roots can equal biomass weight above ground.

A PLANT	SEED			YIELD		
	B Approx. No. Seeds per Ounce [12] (range: larger–smaller seed)	C Minimum Legal Germination Rate [13]	D Ounces / Volume Seed per 100 Square Feet (adj. for germ. rate, offset spacing, and curv. surf.) [14, 15, 16]	E Possible *GROW BIOINTENSIVE* Yield in Pounds per 100-Square-Foot Planting [17]	F Possible *GROW BIOINTENSIVE* Yield in Pounds per Plant [18, 19]	G Average U.S. Yield in Pounds per 100 Square Feet [20, 21]
1 Bamboo, Paper	Under research.					General: "27.5"
2 Bamboo, Regular	Under research.					
3 Beets, Sugar	1,600	.65[A]	.4[AA]	91 / 182 / 364	.21–.84	102.8
4 Cheese	Approx. 1 lb per gallon of milk. Heat milk to 180°F. Add ½ cup vinegar per gallon of milk.					
5 Cotton, Regular	300	.70[A]	.76	1.2 / 2.4 / 4.8+	.007–.03+	1.4
6 Cotton, Tree	An African perennial variety. Under research.					
7 Eggs, Chicken	See Ecology Action's *Backyard Homestead, Mini-Farm and Garden Log Book.*					
8 Flax	6,000	.70[A]	Seed: .2 / ½ t Fiber: .6 / 1⅔ t	D	D	D
9 Gopher Plant	For automotive oil. Under research. Also, a toxic plant for gopher control. Not to be used around					
10 Gourds	150	.70[A]	.5	D	D	D
11 Guayule	For rubber. Under research.					
12 Jojoba	50	D	For oil. Under research.			
13 Kenaf	For newsprint, toilet paper, fiber, twine, rope.					
14 Milk, Cow	See Ecology Action's *Backyard Homestead, Mini-Farm and Garden Log Book.* A cow requires about twice the fodder as a goat and produces about twice the milk.					
15 Milk, Goat						
16 Sprouts, Alfalfa	To be developed. Nutritious, but a large area is required for the production of the seed.					
17 Sprouts, Wheat						

				BEDS/FLATS								MATURITY		FOOD NEEDED	SEED YIELD
H	**I**	**J**	**K**	**L¹**	**L²**	**L³**	**L⁴**	**M¹**	**M²**	**M³**	**M⁴**	**N**	**O**	**P**	**Q**
				FIRST FLAT—3 INCHES DEEP				SECOND FLAT							
In-Bed Spacing (inches)	Maximum No. Plants per 100 Square Feet [15]	Short/Long/Extra-Long Germination Time	Plant Initially in Flats/Beds (in order of preference)	Spacing in First Flat (inches) or Broadcast (BC)	Approx. No. Plants per Flat (adj. for germ. rate) [22]	Division Factor to Determine Flats to Broadcast [23]	Approx. No. Weeks in First Flat [24]	Depth of Second Flat (inches)	Spacing in Second Flat (inches)	Approx. No. Plants per Flat [22]	Approx. No. Weeks in Second Flat [24]	Approx. No. Weeks to Maturity in Ground [25]	Approx. No. Weeks in Harvesting Period	Pounds Consumed per Year by Average Person in U.S. [21, 26]	Approx. Maximum Pounds Seed Yield per 100 Square Feet [27]
														All paper and paperboard: "699"	
7	432	L	F	1	162	—	3–4	—	—	—	—	12	—	All sugars: 67.1 lbs All syrups: 10+ gal	"30.6"

Stir. Let sit for 5 minutes. Pour through cheesecloth lining a colander. Let drain until excess moisture is gone. Result: soft cheese.

H	I	J	K	L¹	L²	L³	L⁴	M¹	M²	M³	M⁴	N	O	P	Q
12	159	L	F	1	175	—	3–4	—	—	—	—	17–26	—	D	22.7
														Eggs: 240 (30 lbs)	
Seed: 5 Fiber: 3	833 2,507	S	F	1	175	—	2–3	—	—	—	—	12–14	—	D	D

young children.

H	I	J	K	L¹	L²	L³	L⁴	M¹	M²	M³	M⁴	N	O	P	Q
18	53	S	F	2	42	—	3–4	—	—	—	—	16	—	D	D

Grows up to 18 ft high. 8–10 tons of fiber yield per acre possible annually (5 times the pulp per acre compared with wood).

H	I	J	K	L¹	L²	L³	L⁴	M¹	M²	M³	M⁴	N	O	P	Q
														Fluid milk and cream: 218 lbs (27.2 gal)	
														D	

ENERGY, FIBER, PAPER, AND OTHER CROPS (continued)	FOOD NEEDED	MATERIALS NEEDED				
PLANT AA	BB *Pounds You Select*	CC *Approx. No. Plants You Need*[28]	DD *Approx. Square Feet You Need*[29]	EE *Approx. No. Flats You Need*[30]	FF *Approx. Ounces Seed You Need*[31]
1 Bamboo, Paper					
2 Bamboo, Regular					
3 Beets, Sugar					
4 Cheese					
5 Cotton, Regular					
6 Cotton, Tree					
7 Eggs, Chicken					
8 Flax					
9 Gopher Plant					
10 Gourds					
11 Guayule					
12 Jojoba					
13 Kenaf					
14 Milk, Cow					
15 Milk, Goat					
16 Sprouts, Alfalfa					
17 Sprouts, Wheat					

YIELDS		MISCELLANEOUS			NUTRITION			NOTES
GG	**HH**	**II**	**JJ**	**KK**	**LL**	**MM**	**NN**	**OO**
Your Actual Yield per 100 Square Feet	*Your Yield Compared with U.S. Average* [32]	*Especially Good Varieties, Possible Seed Sources, and Remarks*	*Heavy Giver (HG), Light Feeder (LF), Low Nitrogen User (LNU), Heavy Feeder (HF)* (see p. 145)	*Time of Year to Plant (SP, SU, FA, WI)*	*Protein Content per Pound in Grams (g) (454g per pound)* [33]	*Calorie Content per Pound* [33]	*Calcium Content per Pound in Milligrams (mg)* [33]	Δ Probably any abundant local species, reasonably priced, may be used. Better grades of paper are made from young and still leafless culms; older, mature culms are too lignified for easy processing, but can be used for coarse, dark-fibered paper. 40% paper yield. For wrapping, news, and book-quality paper. Paper can also be made from many fibrous plants, including cabbage.
								See above. Δ
								Building materials, piping.
		53	LF	SP, SU, FA	D	D	D	
				—	36.3	1,696	281	:Cream cheese. Add parsley, dill seeds, chives for flavor.
		50	HF	SU	—	—	—	Minimum clothes replacement rate per year: 2.5 lbs. Thousands of years ago in India, people placed a mineral in the soil with the cotton plants, and colored fibers resulted!
				SU	—	—	—	
				—	52.1	658	218	:11% refuse.
		54	HF	SP	—	—	—	
				—	—	—	—	
			HF	SU	—	—	—	
		—		—	—	—	—	
				—	—	—	—	For more information on kenaf, write for information packet: The Newspaper Mill Center, Box 17047, Dulles International Airport, Washington, DC 20041.
				—	15.9	299	531	:3.7% fat.
				—	14.5	304	585	Has only ⅓ the vitamin B$_{12}$ that cow milk has.
				All year				
				All year	} Nutritive amounts given for sprouts differ.			

TREE AND CANE CROPS

A PLANT	B Approx. No. Seeds per Ounce [12] (range: larger–smaller seed)	C Minimum Legal Germination Rate [13]	D Approx. No. Plants per Acre	E Possible GROW BIOINTENSIVE Yield in Pounds per 100-Square-Foot Planting [17]	F Possible GROW BIOINTENSIVE Yield in Pounds per Plant [18, 19]	G Average U.S. Yield in Pounds per 100 Square Feet [20, 21]
	SEED			YIELD		
1 Almond	12–15	D	160	In shell: 2.8 / 5.6 / 8.4+	7.6–22.8+	4.7
2 Apple, Dwarf	600–1,000	D	681	50 / 75 / 100	32–64	57.4
3 Apple, Regular	600–1,000	.65A	27	50 / 75 / 100	800–1,600	57.4
4 Apple, Semi-Dwarf	600–1,000	D	194	50 / 75 / 100	112–225	57.4
5 Apricot, Dwarf	18–20	D	681	25 / 50 / 100	25–100	25.4
6 Apricot, Regular	18–20	.90A	70	25 / 50 / 100	156–625	25.4
7 Apricot, Semi-Dwarf	18–20	D	303	25 / 50 / 100	36–144	25.4
8 Avocado, Tall Dwarf	D	D	302–193 / 681	9 / 18 / 36	13–81 / 6–23	10.9
9 Banana, Tall Dwarf	—	D	302–193 / 681	27 / 60 / 92+	39–208 / 12–59	34.0
10 Blackberries	10,000	—	2,723 propagated by cuttings	24 / 36 / 48+	3.8–7.6+	"23.8"
11 Blueberries, Low Bush High Bush	—	—	10,890 / 2,723 } propagated by softwood cuttings in late SP	19 / 37 / 75	.76–3.0 / 3.0–12.0	D
12 Boysenberries	—	—	681 propagated by cuttings	26 / 39 / 52+	16.6–33+	"25.7"
13 Cherry, Sour, Bush	D	D	4,840	8 / 17 / 34	.8–3.0	D
14 Cherry, Sour, Dwarf	200–250	.80A	681	17 / 34 / 51	11–32.6	19.8
15 Cherry, Sour, Regular	200–250	D	1,089	17 / 34 / 51	68–204	19.8
16 Cherry, Sweet, Bush	D	D	4,840	8 / 17 / 34	.8–3.0	D
17 Cherry, Sweet, Dwarf	150–160	D	681	17 / 34 / 51	11–32.6	16.9
18 Cherry, Sweet, Regular	150–160	.75A	481	17 / 34 / 51	153–459	16.9
19 Chestnut	1	.72A	27	In shell: 3.5 / 7 / 15	56–240	D
20 Coconut	—	D	48	3 / 6 / 13	27–118	D
21 Currants, Black	—	—	2,723 propagated by cuttings	D	D	D
22 Dates	40	—	48 propagated by cuttings	23 / 46 / 70	207–630	23.3
23 Filbert	10–20	—	194 propagated by cuttings	In shell: 13 / 27 / 55	29–123	2.4
24 Fig	—	—	194 propagated by cuttings	12 / 24 / 36++	27–81++	14.5
25 Grapefruit	150–200	D	76	63 / 95 / 126	362–724	69.3
26 Grapes, Raisin	—	—	681 propagated by cuttings	Raw, dried: 45 / 67 / 90	29–58	"45.4"
27 Grapes, Table	—	—	681 propagated by cuttings	45 / 67 / 90	28.8–57.6	31.2
28 Grapes, Wine	—	—	681 propagated by cuttings	32 / 48 / 64	20.5–41	"31.6"
29 Guava	D	D	303	D	D	47.3
30 Hickory	1–5 depends on variety.	.55–.80 J depends on variety	27	D	D	D

		BEDS/FLATS						MATURITY		FOOD NEEDED	SEED YIELD
H In-Bed Spacing (feet)	**I** Square Feet Required per Plant	**J** Short/Long/Extra-Long Germination Time	**K** Plant Initially in Flats/Beds (in order of preference)	**L** Flats Spacing for First Flat and Second Flat (inches)	**M** Approx. No. Plants per Flat (adj. for germ. rate)[22]	**N** Approx. No. Weeks in Flats[24]	**O** Approx. No. Years to Bearing / Approx. No. Years to Max. Bearing	**P** Approx. No. Weeks in Harvesting Period / Possible Bearing Years	**Q** Pounds Consumed per Year by Average Person in U.S.[21,26]	**R** Approx. Maximum Pounds Seed Yield per 100 Square Feet[27]
16.5	272	L	F	4 / I	D / —	D / D	3–4 / D	D / D	".4"	In shell: 8.4
8	64	EL	F	2 / I	D / —	D / D	3 / D	D / D	} ".16.0" → "16.0"	D
40	1,600	EL	F	2 / I	39 / —	D / D	5 / 10	D / 35–50		D
15	225	EL	F	2 / I	D / —	D / D	4 / 10	D / D		D
8	64	L	F	4 / I	D / —	D / D	2 / D	D / D	} ".17"	D
25	625	L	F	4 / I	14 / —	D / D	3 / D	D / D		D
12	144	L	F	4 / I	D / —	D / D	3 / D	D / D		D
12–15 / 8	144–225 / 64	D	F	4 / I	D / —	D / D	D / D	D / D	"1.3"	D
12–15 / 8	144–225 / 64	D	F	4 / I	D / —	D / D	D / D	D / D	D	—
4	16	D	Deep flat	6 / I	D / —	D / D	2 / 3	D / 6–25	D	—
2 / 4	4 / 16	D	D	— / —	D / —	D / D	3–4 / 8	6–7 / 10–15	".12"	—
8	64	D	Deep flat	6 / I	D / —	D / D	2 / D	D / 6–10	D	—
3	9	L	F	3 / I	D / —	D / D	3 / D	D / D	} ".62"	D
8	64	L	F	3 / I	22 / —	D / D	3 / D	D / D		D
20	400	L	F	3 / I	D / —	D / D	4 / 10–20	D / D		D
3	9	L	F	3 / I	D / —	D / D	3 / D	D / D		D
8	64	L	F	3 / I	D / —	D / D	3 / D	D / D		D
30	900	L	F	3 / I	20 / —	D / D	4 / 10–20	D / D		D
40	1,600	D	Deep flat	6 / I	5 / —	D / D	D / D	D / D	D	In shell: 15.0
30	900	D	F	4 / I	D / —	D / D	D / D	D / D	D	D
4	16	D	Deep flat	6 / I	D / —	D / D	3 / D	D / D	D	—
30	900	D	Deep flat	9 / I	D / —	D / D	5–6 / 10–15	D / D	D	D
15 (18–25)	225	D	Deep flat	9 / I	D / —	D / D	D / D	D / D	".07"	In shell: 55.0
15	225	D	Deep flat	9 / I	D / —	D / D	D / D	D / 17	D	D
24	576	L	F	3 / I	D / —	D / D	3 / D	D / D	"6.7"	D
8	64	D	F	6 / I	D / —	D / D	3 / D	D / D	Dry: "2.0"	D
8	64	D	F	6 / I	D / —	D / D	3 / D	D / D	"4.6"	D
8	64	D	F	6 / I	D / —	D / D	3 / D	D / D	"20.4"	D
12	144	D	F	1 / I	D / —	D / D	D / D	D / D	D	D
40	1,600	D	F	4 / I	8–12 / —	D / D	D / D	D / 25–350	D	D

TREE AND CANE CROPS (continued)	FOOD NEEDED	MATERIALS NEEDED				
	BB	CC	DD	EE	FF	
PLANT AA	*Pounds You Select*	*Approx. No. Plants You Need* [28]	*Approx. Square Feet You Need* [29]	*Approx. No. Flats You Need* [30]	*Approx. Ounces Seed You Need* [31]	
1 Almond						
2 Apple, Dwarf						
3 Apple, Regular						
4 Apple, Semi-Dwarf						
5 Apricot, Dwarf						
6 Apricot, Regular						
7 Apricot, Semi-Dwarf						
8 Avocado, Tall Dwarf						
9 Banana, Tall Dwarf						
10 Blackberries						
11 Blueberries, Low Bush High Bush						
12 Boysenberries						
13 Cherry, Sour, Bush						
14 Cherry, Sour, Dwarf						
15 Cherry, Sour, Regular						
16 Cherry, Sweet, Bush						
17 Cherry, Sweet, Dwarf						
18 Cherry, Sweet, Regular						
19 Chestnut						
20 Coconut						
21 Currants, Black						
22 Dates						
23 Filbert						
24 Fig						
25 Grapefruit						
26 Grapes, Raisin						
27 Grapes, Table						
28 Grapes, Wine						
29 Guava						
30 Hickory						

	YIELDS		MISCELLANEOUS			NUTRITION			NOTES
GG	**HH**	**II**	**JJ**	**KK**	**LL**	**MM**	**NN**	**OO**	
Your Actual Yield per 100 Square Feet	Your Yield Compared with U.S. Average [32]	Especially Good Varieties, Possible Seed Sources, and Remarks	Heavy Giver (HG), Light Feeder (LF), Low Nitrogen User (LNU), Heavy Feeder (HF) (see p. 145)	Time of Year to Plant (SP, SU, FA, WI)	Protein Content per Pound in Grams (g) (454g per pound) [33]	Calorie Content per Pound [33]	Calcium Content per Pound in Milligrams (mg) [33]		
		—	HF	Early SP	84.4	2,713	1,061	:Shelled. Shells 49% of unshelled weight.	
		—	HF	Early SP	.8	242	29	:Raw. 8% refuse. Spur-type yields higher.	
		—	HF	Early SP	.8	242	29	:Raw. 8% refuse.	
		—	HF	Early SP	.8	242	29	:Raw. 8% refuse.	
		—	HF	Early SP	4.3	217	72	:Raw. 6% refuse. A fall-yielding variety also exists.	
		Manchurian	HF	Early SP	4.3	217	72	:Raw. 6% refuse. 30 ft high.	
			HF	Early SP	4.3	217	72	:Raw. 6% refuse.	
		—	HF	Early SP	7.1	568	34	:25% refuse.	
		—	HF	Early SP	3.4 / 3.7	262 / 278	25 / 31	:Yellow. / :Red. 32% refuse.	
		—	HF	Early SP	5.3	264	145	:Raw. Beds 2–3 ft wide. Some people use 2–ft centers.	
		—	HF	Early SP	2.9	259	63	:8% refuse. Remove blossoms for first 2 years. Use bird netting.	
		—	HF	Early SP	3.2	163	86	:Canned. 8% refuse. 2–ft wide beds. 4–8 canes/center. Bearing season: Logan (midsummer); young (midsummer); Olallie (late summer).	
		2 varieties for pollination	HF	Early SP	5.0	242	92	:Raw. 8% refuse.	
			HF	Early SP	5.0	242	92	:Raw. 8% refuse.	
			HF	Early SP	5.0	242	92	:Raw. 8% refuse. Bear in 3–5 years.	
			HF	Early SP	3.6	195	68	:Canned, without pits.	
			HF	Early SP	3.6	195	68	:Canned, without pits. One self-pollinating variety exists.	
			HF	Early SP	3.6	195	68	:Canned, without pits.	
		—	HF	Early SP	30.4	1,710	236	:Dried and shelled: 18% of unshelled weight. Problems with blight.	
		—	HF	Early SP	8.3 / 15.9	816 / 1,569	31 / 59	:Fresh. 48% refuse. / :Meat.	
			HF	Early SP	7.6	240	267	:Raw. 2% refuse. 2-foot-wide beds.	
		—	HF	Early SP	10.0	1,243	268	:Dry and pitted. 1 male to 100 female plants for pollination. Pits: 13% of dried weight.	
		—	HF	Early SP	57.2	2,876	948	:Shelled: 54% of unshelled weight. 46% refuse.	
		—	HF	Early SP	5.4 / 19.5	363 / 1,243	159 / 572	:Raw. Drying ratio 3:1. / :Dried. 23% moisture.	
		—	HF	Early SP	1.0	84	33	:Raw. 55% refuse.	
		—	HF	Early SP	11.3	1,311	281	:Dry. 18% moisture. Drying ratio 4.3:1.	
		—	HF	Early SP	2.4	270	48	:Raw. 11% refuse.	
		—	HF	Early SP	3.7	197	46	:Raw. 37% refuse.	
		—	HF	Early SP	3.5	273	101	:Raw. 35% refuse. 15 ft high.	
		—	HF	Early SP	59.9	3,053	Trace	:Shelled: 65% of unshelled weight.	

PLANT A	SEED			YIELD		
	B Approx. No. Seeds per Ounce [12] (range: larger–smaller seed)	**C** Minimum Legal Germination Rate [13]	**D** Approx. No. Plants per Acre	**E** Possible GROW BIOINTENSIVE Yield in Pounds per 100-Square-Foot Planting [17]	**F** Possible GROW BIOINTENSIVE Yield in Pounds per Plant [18, 19]	**G** Average U.S. Yield in Pounds per 100 Square Feet [20, 21]
31 Honey Locust	180	.50 J	27	Pods and beans: 6 / 13 / 26+	128–320	D
32 Lemon	200–300	D	76	75 / 112 / 150	432–864	65.7
33 Lime	300–400	D	194	D	D	32.3
34 Mango	D	D	48 propagated by seed or grafting	D	D	D
35 Mesquite	D	D	109	Seed: D Pods: D	D D	D
36 Nectarine, Dwarf	D	D	681	40 / 60 / 80	25.6–51+	29.0
37 Nectarine, Regular	D	D	194	40 / 60 / 80	90–180+	29.0
38 Olive	D	D	27	8 / 17 / 35	129–564	11.7
39 Orange, Sweet	200–300	D	97 76	Navel: 32 / 48 / 64 Valencia: 42 / 63 / 84	155–310 242–484	75.8
40 Peach, Dwarf	610	D	681	Clingstone: 60 / 90 / 120	38–76	"60.3"
41 Peach, Regular	610	D	194	Clingstone: 60 / 90 / 120 Freestone: 39 / 59 / 78	135–270 88–176	"53.4" 34.6
42 Pear, Dwarf	750	D	681	36 / 72 / 108	23–70	66.1
43 Pear, Regular	750	D	170	36 / 72 / 108	92–276	66.1
44 Pecan	6	.50 J	27	In shell: 6 / 12 / 25+	96–400+	D
45 Persimmon	74	D	134	8 / 16 / 32+	26–103	D
46 Pistachio	In shell: 28	D	109	D	D	6.3
47 Plum, Bush	D	SED	4,840	9.5 / 19 / 38	.85–3.4	D
48 Plum, Regular	50–55	D	134	Regular: 19 / 38 / 57 Fresh prune: 11 / 22 / 33	61–184 36–107	20.6 18.2
49 Pomegranate	D	D	435	50 / 75 / 100	50–100	D
50 Raspberries	—	—	2,723 propagated by cuttings	12 / 18 / 24	.95–.38+	"12.3"
51 Strawberries	40,000	D	43,560 propagated by seed or runners	40 / 80 / 160	.4–1.6	83.1
52 Tangelo	200–300	D	109	D	D	48.2
53 Tangerine	300–400	D	109	D	D	39.8
54 Walnut, No. Calif. Black	3	.40 A	27	In shell: 5 / 7.5 / 10+	80–160+	5.4
55 Walnut, English (Persian)	2	.80 A	27	In shell: 5 / 7.5 / 10+	80–160+	5.4
56 Walnut, Eastern, Black	3	.50 A	27	In shell: 5 / 7.5 / 10+	80–160+	5.4

	BEDS/FLATS							MATURITY		FOOD NEEDED	SEED YIELD
H	**I**	**J**	**K**	**L**	**M**	**N**		**O**	**P**	**Q**	**R**
In-Bed Spacing (feet)	Square Feet Required per Plant	Short/Long/Extra-Long Germination Time	Plant Initially in Flats/Beds (in order of preference)	Flats Spacing for First Flat and Second Flat (inches)	Approx. No. Plants per Flat (adj. for germ. rate)[22]	Approx. No. Weeks in Flats[24]	Approx. No. Years to Bearing / Approx. No. Years to Max. Bearing	Approx. No. Weeks in Harvesting Period / Possible Bearing Years		Pounds Consumed per Year by Average Person in U.S.[21,26]	Approx. Maximum Pounds Seed Yield per 100 Square Feet[27]
40	1,600	D	F	4 / I	8 / —	D / D	D / D	D / 10–100		D	In shell: 13.0
24	576	D	F	2 / I	D / —	D / D	3 / D	D / 50+		"3.8"	D
15	225	D	F	2 / I	D / —	D / D	3 / D	D / D		".3"	D
30	900	D	F	2 / I	D / —	D / D	D / D	D / D		".02"	D
20	400	D	F	2 / I	D / —	D / D	D / D	D / D		D	D
8	64	D	Sapling: B	—	—	—	3–4 / 8–12	D / D		} "1.8"	D
15	225	D	F	4 / I	D / —	D / D	D / D	D / D			D
40	1,600	D	F	2 / I	D / —	D / D	D / D	D / D		D	D
22 / 24	448 / 576	D	F	2 / I	D / —	D / D	3 / D	D / 50+		"17.2"	D
8	64	D	Sapling: B	—	—	—	3 / D	D / D		} "2.6"	D
15	225	D	F	4 / I	D / —	D / D	3–4 / 8–12	D / 8–12			D
8	64	D	Sapling: B	—	D / —	D / D	3 / D	D / D		} "3.4"	D
16 (–20)	256	EL	F	1 / I	D / —	D / D	4 / D	D / 50–75			D
40 (–70)	1,600	L	F	4 / I	8 / —	D / D	D / D	D / up to 150		".4"	In shell: 25.0+
18	324	D	F	1 / I	D / —	D / D	2–3 / D	D / 20–300		D	D
20	400	D	F	2 / I	D / —	D / D	D / D	D / 30–50		D	D
3	9	D	Sapling: B	—	—	—	3 / D	D / D		} "2.0"	D
18 (–24)	324	D	F	4 / I	D / —	D / D	4 / D	D / 20–25			D
10	100	D	F	2 / I	D / —	D / D	D / D	D / D		D	D
4	16	D	Deep flat	6 / I	D / —	D / D	2 / D	D / 6–10		D	—
1	1	D	F	1 / 2	60	D / D	2 / D	D / 4		"3.3"	D
20	400	D	F	1 / I	D / —	D / D	3 / D	D / D		".34"	D
20	400	D	F	1 / I	D / —	D / D	3 / D	D / D		".7"	D
40	1,600	EL	F	4 / I	6 / —	D / D	D / D	D / D			In shell: 10.0+
40	1,600	L	F	4 / I	12 / —	D / D	D / D	D / D		} "4.6"	In shell: 10.0+
40	1,600	EL	F	4 / I	8 / —	D / D	D / D	D / D			In shell: 10.0+

TREE AND CANE CROPS (continued)	FOOD NEEDED	MATERIALS NEEDED				
PLANT AA	BB *Pounds You Select*	CC *Approx. No. Plants You Need* [28]	DD *Approx. Square Feet You Need* [29]	EE *Approx. No. Flats You Need* [30]	FF *Approx. Ounces Seed You Need* [31]	
31 Honey Locust						
32 Lemon						
33 Lime						
34 Mango						
35 Mesquite						
36 Nectarine, Dwarf						
37 Nectarine, Regular						
38 Olive						
39 Orange, Sweet						
40 Peach, Dwarf						
41 Peach, Regular						
42 Pear, Dwarf						
43 Pear, Regular						
44 Pecan						
45 Persimmon						
46 Pistachio						
47 Plum, Bush						
48 Plum, Regular						
49 Pomegranate						
50 Raspberries						
51 Strawberries						
52 Tangelo						
53 Tangerine						
54 Walnut, No. Calif. Black						
55 Walnut, English (Persian)						
56 Walnut, Eastern, Black						

YIELDS		MISCELLANEOUS			NUTRITION			NOTES
GG	HH	II	JJ	KK	LL	MM	NN	OO
Your Actual Yield per 100 Square Feet	Your Yield Compared with U.S. Average [32]	Especially Good Varieties, Possible Seed Sources, and Remarks	Heavy Giver (HG), Light Feeder (LF), Low Nitrogen User (LNU), Heavy Feeder (HF) (see p. 145)	Time of Year to Plant (SP, SU, FA, WI)	Protein Content per Pound in Grams (g) (454g per pound) [33]	Calorie Content per Pound [33]	Calcium Content per Pound in Milligrams (mg) [33]	
		—	HF	Early SP	72	D	D	Can make a flour from the beans. Pods and beans a good fodder. A very important tree. *Gleditsia trianconti.*
		—	HF	Early SP	3.3	82	79	:33% refuse.
		—	HF	Early SP	2.7	107	126	:16% refuse.
		—	HF	D	2.1	201	30	:33% refuse. 90 ft high at maturity.
		—	HF	Early SP	17.0 / 76.2	D / D	260 / D	:Seed. / :Pod.
		—	HF	Early SP	2.5	267	263	:8% refuse. 8 ft high.
		—	HF	Early SP	2.5	267	263	:8% refuse. 25 ft high.
		—	HF	Early SP	5.3 / 8.0	442 / 1,227	232 / —	:Green. 16% refuse. } Pasquale, up to 40% oil. / :Ripe. 20% refuse. } All other, 16.5–21.8% oil.
		—	HF	Early SP	4.0 / 4.1	157 / 174	123 / 136	:Navels (winter-bearing). 32% refuse. / :Valencia (summer-bearing). 25% refuse.
		—	HF	Early SP	2.4	150	36	:13% refuse. 8 ft high.
		—	HF	Early SP	2.4	150	36	:13% refuse. 25 ft high.
		—	HF	Early SP	2.9	252	33	:9% refuse. 8 ft high.
		—	HF	Early SP	2.9	252	33	:9% refuse. 30–40 ft high.
		—	HF	Early SP	41.7	3,116	331	:Shelled. 47% of unshelled weight.
		—	HF	Early SP	2.6	286	22	:18% refuse. 30 ft high.
		—	HF	Early SP	87.5	2,694	594	:Shelled. 50% of unshelled weight. 30 ft high.
		—	HF	Early SP	2.1	272	74	:9% refuse. 3 ft high.
		—	HF	Early SP	2.1 / 3.4	272 / 320	74 / 51	:Damson. 9% refuse. / :Prune. 6% refuse.
		—	HF	Early SP	1.3	160	8	:44% refuse.
		—	HF	Early SP	6.6 / 5.3	321 / 251	132 / 97	:Black. Prune to 2–8 canes/ft of row. Beds 2–3 ft wide. Some people plant on 2-ft centers. / :Red. Also yellow and purple varieties. } 3% refuse.
		—	HF	Early SP	3.0	161	91	:4% refuse. Bear well second through fourth year. Use new plants on end of runners to renew bed by fifth year. Plant initially in fall for a better first-year crop. Usually propagated by runner rather than seed, except for Alpine variety.
		—	HF	Early SP	1.3	104	—	:44% refuse. 30 ft high.
			HF	Early SP	2.7	154	134	:26% refuse. 30 ft high.
		—	HF	Early SP	D	D	D	30–60 ft high.
		—	HF	Early SP	93.0	2,849	449	:Shelled. 55% refuse. Up to 60 ft high.
		—	HF	Early SP	67.1	2,953	Trace	:Shelled. 78% refuse. Up to 150 ft high. A good tree to plant for your great-great-grandchildren!

FOOTNOTES

12. From Donald N. Maynard and George J. Hochmuth, *Knott's Handbook for Vegetable Growers* (New York: John Wiley & Sons, 1999), pp. 97–98; and other reference sources.

13. Ibid., p. 460; and other reference sources.

14. To determine amount divide Column I by Column B by Column C.

15. The number of plants you will need may vary. The rise of a curved bed surface (approximate 10-inch rise) adds up to 10% to the planting surface, and a "flat-topped" raised bed (see p. 58) adds up to 20% to the planting surface. Also, the hexagonal "offset" spacing uses up less space than spacing where plants are lined up opposite each other. Up to 159 plants fit in 120 square feet of curved surface on 12-inch (1-foot) centers, rather than fewer plants. You will probably have more plants ready than you need, when using Column I to plan so use the best plants first and save the rest for "spotting" areas that lose plants, or give the extras to friends. To calculate the distance between rows on offset spacing, multiply the spacing by 0.87. To calculate the number of plants on offset spacing in a *flat* bed, first calculate the number of plants on "square" spacing, then multiply by 1.13.

16. Less seed may be necessary if the seed of a given variety is particularly small and/or if there is not much rise to the bed.

17. Estimates based on our experience and research. Use lowest figure if you are a beginning gardener; middle if a good one; highest if an excellent gardener with a good soil and climate. (The testing and development process requires a long time and has involved many failures. Its direction, however, has been encouraging over the years, as the soil, our skills, and yields have improved, and as resource-consumption levels have decreased. There is still much left to be done.)

18. The approximate plant yield averages in some instances are much lower than one would expect. For example, a beginning gardener will get carrots much larger than the 2/3 ounce noted, but all of your carrots will probably not germinate as well as a good or excellent gardener's will and they will probably not be as large. Therefore, it is estimated that the average weight of each carrot would be 2/3 ounce, assuming the bed produces 2,507 carrots.

19. Column E ÷ Column I.

20. From U.S. Department of Agriculture, *Agricultural Statistics—2000,* 1998 data (Washington, DC: U.S. Government Printing Office, 2000), see the index at the end of the volume; and other reference sources.

21. Numbers in quotes are approximations from other data, because official data are not available for this crop.

22. Assumes flat with *internal* dimensions of 13 inches by 21 inches (or 273 square inches) for both 3-inch- and 6-inch-deep flats, in which at least 250 plants fit on 1-inch centers and 60 plants on 2-inch centers; *if half-sized flats are used,* 125 plants fit on 1-inch centers and 30 plants on 2-inch centers.

23. When seeds are broadcast into a flat, it is possible to reduce the number of flats used. To calculate the number of flats needed for broadcast seed, determine the number of plants you need, divide by the number in Column L2, then divide by the number in Column L3. Broadcast the needed amount of seed evenly into the number of flats just calculated.

24. From Donald N. Maynard and George J. Hochmuth, *Knott's Handbook for Vegetable Growers* (New York: John Wiley & Sons, 1999), p. 51; and from our experience and research.

25. The Approximate Weeks to Maturity in Ground generally remains the same whether seeds are started in a flat or in a bed because the number of weeks to maturity indicated on the seed packet assumes optimal growing conditions that are rarely present.

26. From U.S. Department of Agriculture, *Agricultural Statistics—2000,* 1998 data (Washington, DC: U.S. Government Printing Office, 2000), see the index at the end of the volume; and other sources.

27. Based in part on standard field figures from James Edward Knott, *Handbook for Vegetable Growers* (New York: John Wiley & Sons, 1975), pp. 198–199; in combination with a multiplier factor based on our research and experience, and other reference sources. The result, however, is preliminary, for your guidance, and very experimental. If growing seed, remember to adjust for the germination rate when determining the amount to grow for your use.

28. Column BB ÷ Column F.

29. Column BB ÷ Column E × 100. Use the lowest figure in Column E if you are a beginning gardener; middle if a good one working with good soil; highest if an excellent gardener working with excellent soil.

30. Column CC ÷ Column M.

31. Column DD × Column D × .01.

32. Column GG ÷ Column G.

33. From U.S. Department of Agriculture, *Composition of Foods* (Washington, DC: U.S. Government Printing Office, 1963); and other reference sources.

34. 6 to 8 weeks in warm weather and/or with a good mini-greenhouse; 9 to 12 weeks in cooler weather outdoors without a mini-greenhouse.

35. Johnny's Selected Seeds (see page 202).

36. Smaller secondary and tertiary heads may also be used and may double the yield.

37. The Redwood City Seed Company carries an interesting tropical variety, Snow Peak, which heads only in the summer. A good variety with small heads for out-of-season growing.

38. Produces 4 times the general protein (not amino acids) and 8 times the calcium (free of oxalic acid) per unit of area compared to the milk produced by a cow or a goat fed on an equal area of alfalfa.

39. Be sure to obtain "seed" Irish potatoes; many potatoes in stores have been treated to retard sprouting. Sprout without soil in a 3-inch-deep flat or box with small air spaces between the tubers in a warm, dry, airy location in indirect light for up to 1 month, until sprouts are about 1/4 inch long. Caution: Avoid conditions of 90% humidity and 70°F, or more, for a period of 24 hours; they can encourage blight. Use pieces of potato weighing at least 1.5 to 2 ounces. Each potato piece should optimally have 2 or 3 sprouted eyes. For planting purposes, tubers are in dormancy for 5 to 20 weeks after harvest. For planting procedure, see p. 15.

40. Be sure to obtain "seed" sweet potatoes; many potatoes in stores have been treated to retard sprouting. Sprout in wide-mouth canning jars with water. Insert toothpicks into sweet potatoes around their outside to hold the upper half out of the water. Roots form on the portion in the water, and small plantlets grow from the eyes on the upper portion. Each 8-ounce sweet potato will make 3 to 4 of these "starts." When a shoot is about 1 to 1½ inches long, nick it off along with a very small piece of the sweet potato where it is attached, and plant it in a 3-inch-deep flat on 2-inch centers so only the last set of leaves is above the surface of the flat soil. Whole sweet potatoes may also be sprouted side by side in a flat; approximately 4 to 8 flats are needed for a 100-square-foot bed. When the seedlings are 7 to 9 inches tall, transplant them into the growing bed so at least 6 inches of the stem is beneath the soil.

41. Bountiful Gardens (see page 201).

42. Use the French variety (Vilmorin's Cantalun—orange-fleshed) or the Israeli variety (Haogen—green-fleshed). Both have a smooth exterior without netting. This minimizes rotting.

43. Stokes Seeds (see page 204). Specify untreated seeds.

44. Try the Torpedo onion. Its long shape is particularly suited to intensive raised-bed gardening and farming, and it can produce twice the yield per unit of area.

45. Irish potatoes. Place your order for the entire year in January in order to ensure availability. Specify *untreated* seed and delivery date(s) desired (1 month before planting, so sprouts can develop properly). Irish Eyes (see page 202) is a good source.

46. Sweet potatoes: Jewel, Centennial, Garnett, and Jersey varieties. Order in September *untreated*, number 2 size, for the following summer in 40-pound boxes, to ensure availability. Joe Alvernaz, P.O. Box 474, Livingston, CA 95334 is a good source, although not organic. Ask for prices and include a stamped, self-addressed envelope.

47. Burpee's Triple Treat variety with hull-less seeds. No shelling of nutritious and tasty seeds!

48. Burpee's Sparkler variety: red top with white bottom half. Good looking.

49. Burpee's New Hampshire Midget variety.

50. Native Seeds/SEARCH (see page 203).

51. Vermont Bean Seed Co. (see page 204).

52. Fedco Seeds (see page 201).

53. R. H. Shumway Seed (see page 203).

54. J. L. Hudson, Seedsman (see page 202).

NOTES ON THE PLANNING CHARTS

FLOWER SPACING CHART

Spacings vary for flowers depending on the variety and how the flowers are used. The following will help you start out with the most common flowers.

Annuals—Replant each year in spring from seed

	Height	Inches Apart*		Height	Inches Apart*
African daisy	4–6"	12	Petunia	12–16"	12
Aster	1–3'	10–12	Phlox		
Calendula***	1½–2'	12	(P. drummondii)**	6–18"	9
California poppy***	9–12"	12	Portulaca	6"	6–9
Columbine	2–3'	12	Scabiosa		
Cosmos***	2–3'	12–18	(Salvia splendens)	2½–3'	12–18
Echinacea	12"	18–24	Scarlet sage	12–18"	12
Flowering tobacco	2–3'	18–24	Schizanthus	1½–2'	12–18
Hollyhock***	4–6'	12	Shirley poppy	1½–2'	12–18
Marigold, African	2–4'	12–24	Snapdragons	1½–3'	12
Marigold, French	6–18"	8–12	Stocks	12–30"	12
Nasturtium, climbing***	Trailing	10	Strawflower	2–3'	12–18
Nasturtium, dwarf***	12"	8	Sweet peas	Climbing	12
Pansy	6–9"	8–10	Zinnia	1–3'	12–18

Perennials—Need a permanent space in the garden

	Height	Inches Apart*		Height	Inches Apart*
Alyssum			Gazania	6–12"	10
(Lobularia maritima)	4–6"	10–12	Iceland poppy	1'	12
Aubrieta	Trailing	12–15	Jacob's ladder		
Baby's breath	3–4'	14–16	(Polemonium caeruleum)	6"–3'	12–15
Bachelor's button	2'	12	Marguerite	2½–3'	18–24
Carnation	1'	12	Oriental poppy	2½–3'	12–14
Chrysanthemum	2–3'	18–24	Painted daisy	3'	12
Coral bells			Peony	2'	14–16
(Heuchera sanguinea)	2'	12	Pinks (Dianthus)	1'	12
Coreopsis	2'	9–18	Scabiosa	2'	12
Delphinium	1–5'	24	Sea pink (Armeria)	4–6"	10–12
Foxglove	3'	12	Shasta daisy	2½–3'	12
Gaillardia	2–3'	12	Sweet William	1–2'	12

Note
Most flowers have long-germinating seeds (8 to 21 days).

*   Spacings for standard-sized plants. For smaller varieties, reduce the spacings in proportion to the reduced plant size.

**   Botanical Latin names prevent possible confusion.
*** Reseed themselves easily by dropping many seeds on ground.

HERB SPACING CHART

Annuals—Plant seed in spring for late summer harvest

	Height	Inches Apart*		Height	Inches Apart*
Anise	2'	8	Cilantro	1–1½'	5
Basil, sweet	1–2'	6	Coriander	1–1½'	6
Borage	1½'	15	Cumin	1'	18
Caraway	2½'	6	Dill	2½'	8
Chamomile			Fennel	3–5'	12
(*Matricaria vecutita*)	2½'	6–10	Parsley	2½'	5
Chervil	1½'	4	Savory, summer	1½'	6

*Perennials***—Need a permanent space in the garden

	Height	Inches Apart		Height	Inches Apart
Angelica	4–6'	36	Lovage	6'	3
Bee balm*	3'	30	Marjoram	1'	12
Burnet	15"	15	Oregano*	2'	18–24
Catnip	2–3'	15 (spreads)#	Peppermint	2½'	12 (spreads)#
Chamomile, Roman			Pineapple sage*	4'	24–36
(*Chamaemelum nobile*)*	3–12"	12	Rosemary	3–4'	18–24
Chives	10–24"	5	Rue	3'	18
Comfrey*	15–36"	15–36	Sage	2'	18
Costmary	2–6'	12	Santolina	2'	30
Feverfew	1–3'	10–15	Savory, winter	1'	12
Geraniums, scented*			Southernwood	3–5'	30
Apple	10"	18	Spearmint*	2–3'	15 (spreads)#
Coconut	8–12"	18	Stinging nettle	4–6'	24 (spreads)#
Lemon	2–3'	##	St. Johnswort	2'	8
Lime	2'	18	Tansy	4'	30
Peppermint	2'	48	Tarragon	2'	12–18
Rose	3'	30	Thyme	1'	6
Good King Henry	1'	16	Valerian	4'	18
Horehound	2'	9 (spreads)#	Woodruff*	6–10"	8–12 (spreads)#
Hyssop	2'	12	Wormwood	3–5'	12–24
Lavender	3'	18	Yarrow, common		
Lemon balm	3'	12 (spreads)#	(*Achillea millefolium*)	3–5'	12–18
Lemon verbena	10'	24	Yarrow, white-, red-, or pink-flowered*	2½–3'	12

Note
Many herbs have long-germinating seeds (22 to 28 days).

* Generally based on our experience. Others are from the *Herb Chart* by Evelyn Gregg, Biodynamic Farming and Gardening Association, Wyoming, Rhode Island.

** Normally started from cuttings or root divisions, they often take 1 to 4 years to reach full size from seed.

\# Spreads underground; keep it contained or plant where it can keep going.

\#\# Unknown.

Use this space to record your favorite flowers and herbs that are not included in the preceding spacing charts. *Use within-the-row spacings given on the back of the seed packets.*

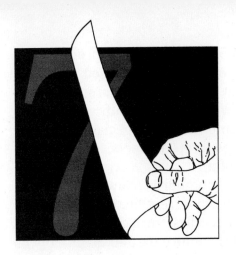

Making the Garden Plan

Goal: Maximize the quality and quantity of crops produced through good planning and timing while maintaining sustainable soil fertility

Now we come to the art of putting the theory into a garden plan. No book can make gardening foolproof. If growing plants did not involve real learning and *experimentation*, it would not be nearly so satisfying. The plants that follow illustrate some of the considerations that make a garden successful. They are based on what the average American consumes each year, but do not take the precise amounts too seriously. Everyone has different tastes and your "average American diet" will change rapidly when you have abundant fresh vegetables to eat. You will probably want to eat many more fresh fruits and vegetables than you do now.

Before you start, you will need some local information. Talk to your neighbors who garden, check with the county agricultural agent, or ask at the local nursery. You want to know:

Which vegetables grow well in your area?

When does the main planting season start?

When are your first and last frosts?

When are your periods with and without rains?

What are the special requirements of your specific soil?

Are there any special climatic conditions to be aware of, such as heavy winds, hot dry spells, or excessive rains?

How do people usually plan for this?

The first sample plan that follows is for a one-person mini-garden. Plans are included for each of the first four years. The first year includes the easiest crops to grow in 100 square feet based on yields expected of a good gardener. The second year, *the square footage doubles*, and more difficult crops are added. The third and fourth years, trees, herbs, strawberries, and asparagus are included—permanent plantings that are placed in soil that has now been worked and improved for 2 years—

and a third bed is added. After 3 or 4 years, with improved gardening skills, the vegetable crop can be condensed from 200 square feet to 100 square feet, leaving 100 square feet of improved soil for protein crops (wheat, rye, peanuts, lentils, soybeans, and rice), fibers (cotton or flax), or special interest crops (chicken, goat, or bee forage; grapes; blueberries; bamboo; herbs; nut trees; and so on).

Lastly, a garden plan for a family of four is shown. We recommend using a similar 3- to 4-year progression, starting with approximately 300 square feet for the first year, and adding 300 more square feet each year until the entire garden is developed. Buying seeds for a backyard garden easily runs up a $10 to $20+ bill. At our garden supply store in Palo Alto, we purchase seeds in bulk and sell them out in jars like penny candy using teaspoons and tablespoons to measure. You can easily buy seeds for 6 months of vegetables in our store for less than $2. You can take advantage of the same low prices by having your favorite local co-op grocery store order bulk seeds for you.

Consider spacing and maturation when you develop your plan. If you have extra plants, plant the best ones and give any extras to a friend or save them in case of damage to first transplants. Leaf lettuce matures sooner than head lettuce. Planting both ensures a continuous harvest. Similarly, half of the tomatoes should be an early variety (maturing in 65 days) for continuous harvesting. Save space by tying tomatoes up to stakes. Pumpkins take up a lot of space. Plant them at the edge of the garden where they can sprawl over uncultivated areas. Corn is pollinated by the wind; a square block of 4 corn plants in each direction (not a row), for a total of 16 plants, is the minimum for adequate pollination. In small plantings you may want to hand-pollinate corn so all the ears fill out optimally. (See Suzanne Ashworth's *Seed to Seed* on page 205 in the bibliography.)

When choosing a site for your garden, take into consideration the amount of available direct sunlight. *Optimally*, your garden area should have 11 hours of sunlight or more; 7 hours may allow plants to grow acceptably, and in some instances, 4 hours may work for cool season crops (see page 82). Experimentation will probably be needed if you plan to garden in soil that receives less than 11 hours of sun.

THE GARDEN YEAR

Winter

☐ Plan the garden.

☐ Order *open-pollinated*, untreated seeds (allow 2 months for delivery if ordering by mail).

☐ Make flats, trellises, mini-greenhouses, and shade-netting units.[1]

Spring

☐ Plant flats so seedlings can mature while the soil is being prepared.

☐ Start new compost piles with weeds, grass clippings, and compost crops.

☐ Harvest compost crops, dig garden beds, and spread cured fall/winter compost.

☐ Plant cool-weather crops in early spring and warm- and hot-weather crops in late spring and early summer.

Summer

☐ Plant summer crops.

☐ Keep the garden watered and weeded.

☐ Harvest and enjoy the fruits of your work.

☐ In mild-winter areas, plant fall gardens of cool-weather crops at the end of summer.

Fall

☐ Start additional compost piles with plentiful leaves and garden waste.

☐ Harvest summer crops.

☐ Plant fall/winter compost crops.

---

1. See Ecology Action's *Backyard Homestead, Mini-Farm and Garden Log Book* for miniature mini-greenhouse and shade-netting house plans.

SIMPLE MINI-GARDEN, 6-MONTH GROWING SEASON
100–140+ SQUARE FEET

As early as possible in spring, plant (optional):
bare root
  dwarf fruit tree — 1 tree 40.0+ sq ft

6 weeks before last spring frost _____
(date)

Start seedlings in flats:
head lettuce — 4 seeds⑤
leaf lettuce — 8 seeds⑤
parsley — 2 seeds

5 weeks before last frost _____
(date)

Start seedlings in flats:
carrots — 58 seeds

Prick out seedlings into flats:
head lettuce — 3 seedlings⑤
leaf lettuce — 6 seedlings⑤

4 weeks before last frost _____
(date)

Sprout:
potatoes
  (65 days to maturity) — 9.5 lbs tubers

Start seedlings in flat:
chard — 2 seeds

3 weeks before last frost _____
(date)

Start seedlings in flat in flat:
bush peas — 230 seeds

Prick out seedlings into flat:
parsley — 1 seedling

2 weeks before last frost _____
(date)

Start seedlings in flats:
bunching onions
  (60 days to maturity) — 10 seeds
cherry tomatoes — 10 seeds

Transplant:
bush peas — 184 seedlings 10.0 sq ft
carrots — 32 seedlings
head lettuce — 4 seedlings⑤ 2.0 sq ft
leaf lettuce (9″) — 2 seedlings⑤ 2.0 sq ft

Plant:
radishes — 10 seeds

On last frost _____
(date)

Start seedlings in flats:
cantaloupes — 10 seeds
cucumbers — 3 seeds
dwarf marigolds — 3 seeds
New Hampshire midget
  watermelons (12″) — 16 seeds
sunflowers — 4 seeds

Transplant:
potatoes** — 75 sprouted
              pieces 30.0 sq ft

1 week after last frost _____
(date)

Start seedlings in flat:
early corn — 20 seeds

2 weeks after last frost _____
(date)

Sprout:
potatoes — 9.5 lbs tubers

Start seedlings in flats:
acorn winter squash — 2 seeds
pumpkins — 3 seeds
zucchini — 2 seeds

Prick out seedlings into flat:
cherry tomatoes — 7+ seedlings

Transplant:
chard — 1 seedling①
early corn — 15 seedlings 20.0 sq ft
sunflowers — 2 seedlings①

3 weeks after last frost _____
(date)

Transplant:
cantaloupes — 7 seedlings 10.0 sq ft
cucumbers — 2 seedlings①
dwarf marigolds — 2 seedlings①
New Hampshire midget
  watermelons (12″) — 11 seedlings 10.0 sq ft

Notes
- Numbers given are for the approximate number of seeds and seedlings that should be required for each crop for the area involved.
- To improve the soil fertility and increase the sustainability of your garden/mini-farm, additionally grow 200 to 300 square feet of carbon-and-calorie crops, described on pages 31 and 32.

⑤ = Stagger planting for a more continuous harvest.
① = Transplant seedlings on edge of bed; see plan, opposite.
* = Spot additional seeds later where seeds do not germinate.
** = See potato planting instructions on page 15.

6 weeks after last frost _____
　　　　　　　　　　　　　　　　(date)

Transplant:
acorn winter squash — 1 seedling℗
bunching onions (3″) — 7 seedlings
cherry tomatoes (18″) — 7 seedlings　15.0 sq ft
pumpkins — 2 seedlings℗
zucchini — 1 seedling℗

8 weeks after last frost _____
　　　　　　　　　　　　　　　　(date)

Start seedlings in flats:
head lettuce — 3 seeds⑤
leaf lettuce — 11 seeds⑤

As first planting comes out, transplant:
parsley — 1 seedling℗
potatoes** — 75 sprouted
　　　　　　　　　pieces　30.0 sq ft

13 weeks before first fall frost _____
　　　　　　　　　　　　　　　　(date)

Start seedlings in flats:
bush beans — 65 seeds
carrots — 17 seeds

11 weeks before first frost _____
　　　　　　　　　　　　　　　　(date)

Start seedlings in flats:
early corn — 20 seeds

Prick out seedlings into flats:
head lettuce — 2+ seedlings
leaf lettuce — 9+ seedlings

Transplant:
bush beans — 46 seedlings　10.0 sq ft

10 weeks before first frost _____
　　　　　　　　　　　　　　　　(date)

Transplant:
carrots — 9 seedlings　.5 sq ft
early corn — 15 seedlings　20.0 sq ft

8 weeks before first frost _____
　　　　　　　　　　　　　　　　(date)

Transplant:
head lettuce — 2 seedlings⑤　2.0 sq ft
leaf lettuce (8″) — 9 seedlings⑤　2.0 sq ft

7 weeks before first frost _____
　　　　　　　　　　　　　　　　(date)

Plant:
radishes — 5 seeds　.125 sq ft

SIMPLE MINI-GARDEN

North

sunflowers

chard　corn (2 crops)

acorn winter squash

cherry tomatoes

dwarf marigold　　dwarf marigold

potatoes (2 crops)

bush peas, then bush beans

zucchini

watermelons

cantaloupe

cucumber　cucumber

lettuce

parsley　pumpkins (2)

bunching onions　carrots　radishes

Scale: 5/16 inch = 1 foot. Growing bed is 100 square feet (5 by 20 feet).

ONE-PERSON MINI-GARDEN, *FIRST* YEAR, 6-MONTH GROWING SEASON
100 SQUARE FEET

6 weeks before last spring frost _____
(date)

Start seedlings in flats:

broccoli	—	3 seeds
cabbage	—	6 seeds
cylindra beets	—	15 seeds
head lettuce	—	3 seeds⑤
leaf lettuce	—	8 seeds⑤

5 weeks before last frost _____
(date)

Prick out seedlings into flats:

head lettuce	—	2+ seedlings⑤
leaf lettuce	—	6+ seedlings⑤

4 weeks before last frost _____
(date)

Sprout:

potatoes (65 days to maturity)	—	10.9 lbs tubers

Start seedlings in flat:

carrots	—	100 seeds

3 weeks before last frost _____
(date)

Start seedlings in flat:

bush peas	—	215 seedlings

Prick out seedlings into flats:

broccoli	—	2+ seedlings
cabbage	—	4+ seedlings

2 weeks before last frost _____
(date)

Start seedlings in flats:

cucumbers	—	12 seeds
green peppers	—	12 seeds
regular tomatoes	—	10 seeds
sweet basil	—	2 seeds
zinnias	—	6 seeds

Transplant:

bush peas	—	172 seedlings	9.0 sq ft
carrots	—	55 seedlings	3.0 sq ft
cylindra beets	—	10 seedlings	1.0 sq ft
head lettuce	—	2 seedlings⑤	2.0 sq ft
leaf lettuce (9″)	—	6 seedlings⑤	3.0 sq ft

Plant:

onions (purchased)	—	95 sets	3.8 sq ft
radishes	—	10 seeds	.25 sq ft

On last frost _____
(date)

Start seedlings in flats:

pumpkins	—	2 seeds
zucchini	—	2 seeds

Prick out seedlings into flats:

green peppers	—	5+ seedlings
regular tomatoes	—	5+ seedlings

Transplant:

cucumbers	—	6 seedlings	4.0 sq ft
potatoes**	—	87 sprouted pieces	35.0 sq ft
sweet basil	—	1 seedling	1.0 sq ft
zinnias	—	3 seedlings	3.0 sq ft

1 week after last frost _____
(date)

Transplant:

broccoli	—	2 seedlings	3.2 sq ft
cabbage	—	4 seedlings	6.7 sq ft

Approx. 4 weeks after last frost _____
(date)

Start seedlings in flats:

cosmos	—	2 seeds

Transplant:

green peppers	—	4 seedlings	4.0 sq ft
pumpkins	—	2 seedlings	6.0 sq ft
regular tomatoes (24″)	—	4 seedlings	15.0 sq ft
zucchini	—	1 seedling	2.0 sq ft

Approx. 6 weeks after last frost _____
(date)

Start seedlings in flat:

bush lima beans	—	59 seeds

Approx. 7 weeks after last frost _____
(date)

Start seedlings in flat:

early corn (65 days to maturity)	—	20 seeds

Approx. 8 weeks after last frost _____
(date)

Transplant:

bush lima beans	—	41 seedlings	9.0 sq ft
cosmos	—	1 seedling⑪	1.0 sq ft
early corn	—	15 seedlings	20.0 sq ft

Note

Numbers given are for the approximate number of seeds and seedlings that should be required for each crop for the area involved.

⑤ = Stagger planting for a more continuous harvest.

⑪ = Transplant seedlings on edge of bed; see plan

* = Spot additional seeds later where seeds do not germinate.

** = See potato planting instructions on page 15.

12 weeks after last frost _____
(date)

Start seedlings in flat:
bush green beans — 55 seeds

13 weeks after last frost _____
(date)

Start seedlings in flat:
corn — 24 seeds

14 weeks after last frost _____
(date)

After potatoes come out, transplant:
corn — 18 seedlings 25.0 sq ft
bush green beans — 46 seedlings 10.0 sq ft

13 weeks before first fall frost _____
(date)

Start seedlings in flat:
broccoli — 2 seeds

12 weeks before first frost _____
(date)

Start seedlings in flats:
carrots — 112 seeds
head lettuce — 4 seeds Ⓢ
leaf lettuce — 17 seeds Ⓢ

11 weeks before first frost _____
(date)

Start seedlings in flats:
calendulas — 8 seeds
chard — 2 seeds
stocks — 8 seeds

Prick out seedlings in flats:
broccoli — 1 seedling
head lettuce — 3+ seedlings Ⓢ
leaf lettuce — 14+ seedlings Ⓢ

9 weeks before first frost _____
(date)

Start seedlings in flat:
bush peas — 156 seeds

8 weeks before first frost _____
(date)

As early corn and bush lima beans come out, transplant:
broccoli — 1 seedling 1.6 sq ft
calendulas — 6 seedlings 5.0 sq ft
carrots — 62 seedlings 2.7 sq ft
chard — 1 seedling .25 sq ft
head lettuce — 3 seedlings Ⓢ 2.7 sq ft
leaf lettuce — 14 seedlings Ⓢ 5.3 sq ft
bush peas — 125 seedlings 6.8 sq ft
stocks — 6 seedlings 5.0 sq ft

Plant:
radishes — 10 seeds .25 sq ft

See page 128 for plan of One-Person Mini-Garden, First Year.

Notes
- Numbers given are for the approximate number of seeds and seedlings that should be required for each crop for the area involved.
- To improve the soil fertility and increase the sustainability of your garden/mini-farm, additionally grow 200 to 300 square feet of carbon-and-calorie crops, described on pages 31 and 32.

Ⓢ = Stagger planting for a more continuous harvest.
Ⓣ = Transplant seedlings on edge of bed; see plan, page 128.
* = Spot additional seeds later where seeds do not germinate.
** = See potato planting instructions on page 15.

ONE-PERSON MINI-GARDEN, *FIRST* YEAR

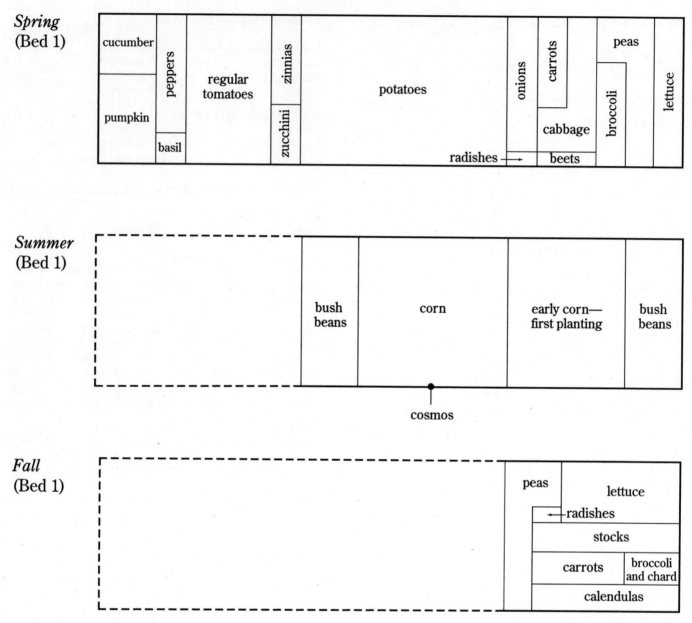

Spring
(Bed 1)

cucumber

pumpkin

peppers

basil

regular tomatoes

zinnias

zucchini

potatoes

radishes →

onions

carrots

cabbage

beets

peas

broccoli

lettuce

Summer
(Bed 1)

bush beans

corn

early corn— first planting

bush beans

cosmos

Fall
(Bed 1)

peas

lettuce

← radishes

stocks

carrots

broccoli and chard

calendulas

Scale: 5/16 inch = 1 foot. Growing bed is 100 square feet (5 by 20 feet).

ONE-PERSON MINI-GARDEN, *SECOND* YEAR, 6-MONTH GROWING SEASON
240 SQUARE FEET (including path)

6 weeks before last spring frost _____
(date)

Start seedlings in flats:

broccoli	—	3 seeds
brussels sprouts	—	2 seeds
cabbage	—	5 seeds
cauliflower	—	2 seeds
celery	—	20 seeds
head lettuce	—	3 seeds Ⓢ
leaf lettuce	—	15 seeds Ⓢ
parsley	—	2 seeds
regular tomatoes	—	10 seeds

5 weeks before last frost _____
(date)

Start seedlings in flats:

carrots	—	90 seeds
cylindra beets	—	16 seeds

Prick out seedlings into flats:

head lettuce	—	2+ seedlings
leaf lettuce	—	12+ seedlings

4 weeks before last frost _____
(date)

Sprout:

potatoes (65 days to maturity)	—	12.5 lbs tubers

Prick out seedlings into flat:

parsley	—	1+ seedlings

3 weeks before last frost _____
(date)

Start seedlings in flats:

bush peas	—	156 seeds
spinach	—	17 seeds

Prick out seedlings into flats:

broccoli	—	2+ seedlings
brussels sprouts	—	1+ seedlings
cabbage	—	4+ seedlings
cauliflower	—	1+ seedlings

2 weeks before last frost _____
(date)

Start seedlings in flats:

dill	—	2 seeds
eggplant	—	2 seeds
green peppers	—	10 seeds

Prick out seedlings into flat:

celery	—	12 seedlings

Transplant:

broccoli	—	2 seedlings	2.6 sq ft
brussels sprouts	—	1 seedling	2.3 sq ft
bush peas	—	125 seedlings	6.8 sq ft
cabbage	—	4 seedlings	5.2 sq ft
carrots	—	50 seedlings	2.7 sq ft
cauliflower	—	1 seedling	1.3 sq ft
cylindra beets	—	10 seedlings	1.0 sq ft
head lettuce	—	2 seedlings Ⓢ	2.0 sq ft
leaf lettuce (9″)	—	12 seedlings Ⓢ	6.0 sq ft
spinach	—	10 seedlings	2.2 sq ft

Plant:

garlic	—	3 cloves	.3 sq ft
onions (purchased)	—	39 sets	3.8 sq ft
radishes	—	25 seeds	.8 sq ft

On last frost _____
(date)

Sprout:

sweet potatoes	—	.5 lb tubers

Start seedlings in flats:

cantaloupes	—	7 seeds
cosmos	—	4 seeds
cucumbers	—	6 seeds
honeydew melons	—	7 seeds
New Hampshire midget watermelons	—	26 seeds
sweet basil	—	2 seeds

Prick out seedlings into flats:

celery	—	11+ seedlings
regular tomatoes	—	7+ seedlings

Transplant:

parsley	—	1 seedling	.2 sq ft
potatoes**	—	100 sprouted pieces	40.2 sq ft

2 weeks after last frost _____
(date)

Start seedlings in flats:

bush green beans	—	86 seeds
bush lima beans	—	59 seeds
early corn (65 days to maturity)	—	24 seeds

Prick out seedlings into flat:

celery	—	12 seedlings

3 weeks after last frost _____
(date)

Transplant:

early corn	—	18 seedlings	25.0 sq ft

Note

Numbers given are for the approximate number of seeds and seedlings that should be required for each crop for the area involved.

Ⓢ = Stagger planting for a more continuous harvest.
Ⓣ = Transplant seedlings on edge of bed; see plan, page 128.
* = Spot additional seeds later where seeds do not germinate.
** = See potato planting instructions on page 15.

4 weeks after last frost _____
(date)

Sprout:
potatoes
(65 days to maturity)— 12.5 lbs tubers

Start seedlings in flats:

pumpkins	—	2 seeds	
zucchini	—	2 seeds	

Transplant:

bush green beans	—	64 seedlings	14.0 sq ft
bush lima beans	—	41 seedlings	9.0 sq ft
cantaloupes	—	5 seedlings	7.0 sq ft
celery	—	11 seedlings	2.5 sq ft
cosmos	—	3 seedlings Ⓣ	3.0 sq ft
cucumbers	—	5 seedlings	4.0 sq ft
dill	—	1 seedling Ⓣ	.4 sq ft
honeydew melons	—	5 seedlings	7.0 sq ft
regular tomatoes (21″) —		7 seedlings	20.0 sq ft
New Hampshire midget watermelons —		18 seedlings	16.0 sq ft
sweet basil	—	1 seedling	1.0 sq ft
sweet potatoes	—	20 sprouted pieces	4.5 sq ft
zinnias	—	3 seedlings Ⓣ	3.0 sq ft

5 weeks after last frost _____
(date)

Prick out seedlings into flats:

eggplant	—	1+ seedlings
green peppers	—	5+ seedlings

6 weeks after last frost _____
(date)

Start seedlings in flat:

chard	—	5 seeds

Transplant:

celery	—	12 seedlings	2.5 sq ft
pumpkin	—	1 seedling	6.3 sq ft
zucchini	—	1 seedling	2.3 sq ft

8 weeks after last frost _____
(date)

As first planting comes out, transplant:

potatoes**	—	100 sprouted pieces	40.2 sq ft

9 weeks after last frost _____
(date)

Transplant:

eggplant	—	1 seedling	2.3 sq ft
green peppers	—	5 seedlings	4.0 sq ft

14 weeks before first fall frost _____
(date)

Start seedlings in flats:

broccoli	—	2 seeds
cabbage	—	5 seeds
calendulas	—	6 seeds
stocks	—	6 seeds

13 weeks before first frost _____
(date)

Start seedlings in flats:

corn (65 days to maturity)—		25 seeds
head lettuce	—	5 seeds Ⓢ
leaf lettuce	—	25 seeds Ⓢ

Transplant:

chard	—	3 seedlings	1.0 sq ft

12 weeks before first frost _____
(date)

Prick out seedlings into flats:

head lettuce	—	5+ seedlings Ⓢ
leaf lettuce	—	20+ seedlings Ⓢ

As first potatoes come out, transplant:

corn	—	18 seedlings	25.0 sq ft

11 weeks before first frost _____
(date)

Start seedlings in flats:

carrots	—	90 seeds
bush peas	—	156 seeds
spinach	—	17 seeds

Prick out seedlings into flats:

broccoli	—	1+ seedlings
cabbage	—	4+ seedlings

9 weeks before first frost _____
(date)

Transplant:

bush peas	—	125 seedlings	6.8 sq ft
chard	—	3 seedlings	1.0 sq ft

8 weeks before first frost _____
(date)

Transplant:

broccoli	—	1 seedling	1.3 sq ft
cabbage	—	4 seedlings	5.2 sq ft
calendulas	—	4 seedlings	4.0 sq ft
carrots	—	50 seedlings	2.7 sq ft
head lettuce	—	3 seedlings Ⓢ	2.7 sq ft
leaf lettuce (8″)	—	20 seedlings Ⓢ	7.8 sq ft
spinach	—	10 seedlings	2.2 sq ft
stocks	—	4 seedlings	4.0 sq ft

Plant:

radishes	—	10 seeds	.25 sq ft

Notes

- Numbers given are for the approximate number of seeds and seedlings that should be required for each crop for the area involved.
- To improve the soil fertility and increase the sustainability of your garden/mini-farm, additionally grow 475 square feet of carbon-and-calorie crops, described on pages 31 and 32.

Ⓢ = Stagger planting for a more continuous harvest.

Ⓣ = Transplant seedlings on edge of bed; see plan, page 128.

* = Spot additional seeds later where seeds do not germinate.

** = See potato planting instructions on page 15.

ONE-PERSON MINI-GARDEN, *SECOND* YEAR

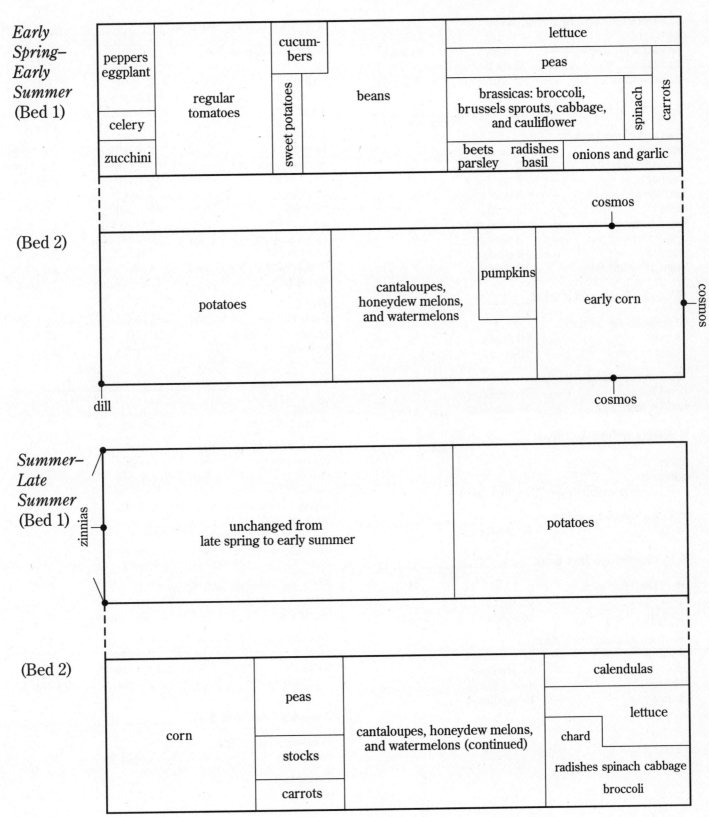

Scale: 5/16 inch = 1 foot. Growing bed is 100 square feet (5 by 20 feet).

Note
By the second year, the curved bed surface gives you up to 120 square feet of planting area in each 100 square feet of bed.

ONE-PERSON MINI-GARDEN, *THIRD* YEAR, 6-MONTH GROWING SEASON
380 SQUARE FEET (including path)

As early as possible in spring, plant:
bare root

dwarf fruit trees	—	1 tree	64.0 sq ft
asparagus	—	13 roots	8.0 sq ft
strawberries	—	32 seedlings	20.0 sq ft

6 weeks before last spring frost _____ (date)

Start seedlings in flats:

broccoli	—	3 seeds
brussels sprouts	—	2 seeds
cabbage	—	6 seeds
cauliflower	—	2 seeds
celery	—	18 seeds
head lettuce	—	3 seeds⑤
leaf lettuce	—	5 seeds⑤
parsley	—	2 seeds
regular tomatoes	—	10 seeds

5 weeks before last frost_____ (date)

Start seedlings in flats:

carrots	—	90 seeds
cylindra beets	—	16 seeds

Prick out seedlings into flats:

head lettuce	—	2+ seedlings⑤
leaf lettuce	—	4+ seedlings⑤

4 weeks before last frost_____ (date)

Sprout:
potatoes
(65 days to maturity)— 15.5 lbs tubers

Prick out seedlings into flat:

parsley	—	1+ seedlings

3 weeks before last frost_____ (date)

Start seedlings in flats:

bush peas	—	100 seeds
spinach	—	16 seeds

Prick out seedlings into flats:

broccoli	—	2+ seedlings
brussels sprouts	—	1+ seedlings
cabbage	—	4+ seedlings
cauliflower	—	1+ seedlings

2 weeks before last frost_____ (date)

Start seedlings in flats:

dill	—	2 seeds
eggplant	—	2 seeds
green peppers	—	10 seeds
tomatoes	—	14 seeds

Transplant:

broccoli	—	2 seedlings	2.6 sq ft
brussels sprouts	—	1 seedling	2.3 sq ft
bush peas	—	70 seedlings*	6.8 sq ft
cabbage	—	4 seedlings	5.2 sq ft
carrots	—	50 seedlings	2.7 sq ft
cauliflower	—	1 seedling	1.3 sq ft
cylindra beets	—	10 seedlings	1.0 sq ft
head lettuce	—	2 seedlings⑤	2.0 sq ft
leaf lettuce (9″)	—	4 seedlings⑤	2.0 sq ft
spinach	—	10 seedlings	2.2 sq ft

Plant:

garlic	—	3 cloves	.3 sq ft
onions (purchased)	—	39 sets	3.8 sq ft
radishes	—	10 seeds	.25 sq ft

On last frost _____ (date)

Sprout:
sweet potatoes — .5 lb tubers

Start seedlings in flats:

cantaloupes	—	6 seeds
cosmos	—	7 seeds
cucumbers	—	6 seeds
honeydew melons	—	7 seeds
New Hampshire midget watermelons	—	26 seeds
sweet basil	—	2 seeds
zinnias	—	7 seeds

Prick out seedlings into flats:

celery	—	10+ seedlings
tomatoes	—	7+ seedlings

Transplant:

parsley	—	1 seedling	.2 sq ft
potatoes	—	124 sprouted pieces	50.0 sq ft

2 weeks after last frost _____ (date)

Start seedlings in flats:
early corn — 49 seeds

Transplant:

dill	—	1 seed	.2 sq ft

Note

Numbers given are for the approximate number of seeds and seedlings that should be required for each crop for the area involved.

⑤ = Stagger planting for a more continuous harvest.

* = Spot additional seeds later where seeds do not germinate.

** = See potato planting instructions on page 15.

3 weeks after last frost _____
                                          (date)

Start seedlings in flats:
bush green beans   —   96 seeds
bush lima beans   —   62 seeds

4 weeks after last frost _____
                                          (date)

Sprout:
potatoes   —   9.3 lbs tubers

Prick out seedlings into flats:
bush green beans   —   96 seeds
bush lima beans   —   62 seeds
celery   —   10+ seedlings

Transplant:
bush green beans   —   68 seedlings*   14.0 sq ft
bush lima beans   —   43 seedlings*   9.0 sq ft
cantaloupes   —   4 seedlings   5.0 sq ft
celery   —   9 seedlings   2.0 sq ft
cosmos   —   5 seedlings   5.0 sq ft
cucumbers   —   5 seedlings   4.0 sq ft
honeydew melons   —   5 seedlings   7.5 sq ft
New Hampshire
   midget watermelons— 18 seedlings   16.0 sq ft
regular tomatoes (21″)— 7 seedlings   20.0 sq ft
sweet basil   —   1 seedling   1.0 sq ft
sweet potatoes   —   20 seedlings   4.5 sq ft
zinnias (12″)   —   5 seedlings   5.0 sq ft

Start seedlings in flats:
pumpkins   —   2 seeds
zucchini   —   2 seeds

5 weeks after last frost _____
                                          (date)

Prick out seedlings into flats:
eggplant   —   1+ seedlings
green peppers   —   5+ seedlings

6 weeks after last frost _____
                                          (date)

Transplant:
pumpkin   —   1 seedling   6.3 sq ft
zucchini   —   1 seedling   2.3 sq ft

8 weeks after last frost _____
                                          (date)

As first planting comes out, transplant:
potatoes**   —   75 sprouted
                         pieces   30.0 sq ft
celery   —   9 seedlings   2.0 sq ft

9 weeks after last frost _____
                                          (date)

Transplant:
eggplant   —   1 seedling   2.3 sq ft
green peppers   —   5 seedlings   4.0 sq ft

13 weeks before first fall frost _____
                                          (date)

Start seedlings in flats:
broccoli   —   2 seeds
cabbage   —   8 seeds

11 weeks before first frost _____
                                          (date)

Start seedlings in flats:
calendulas   —   6 seeds
carrots   —   90 seeds
chard   —   11 seeds
head lettuce   —   4 seeds⑤
leaf lettuce   —   25 seeds⑤
spinach   —   17 seeds
stocks   —   6 seeds

Prick out seedlings into flats:
broccoli   —   1+ seedlings
cabbage   —   4+ seedlings
head lettuce   —   3+ seedlings⑤
leaf lettuce   —   20+ seedlings⑤

9 weeks before first frost _____
                                          (date)

Start seedlings in flat:
bush peas   —   156 seeds

8 weeks before first frost _____
                                          (date)

As first potatoes come out, transplant:
broccoli   —   1 seedling   1.3 sq ft
bush peas   —   125 seedlings*   6.8 sq ft
cabbage   —   4 seedlings   5.2 sq ft
calendulas   —   4 seedlings   4.0 sq ft
carrots   —   49 seedlings   2.7 sq ft
chard   —   7 seedlings   2.7 sq ft
head lettuce   —   3 seedlings⑤   2.7 sq ft
leaf lettuce (8″)   —   20 seedlings⑤   7.8 sq ft
spinach   —   10 seedlings   2.2 sq ft
stocks   —   4 seedlings   4.0 sq ft

Plant:
radishes   —   10 seeds   .25 sq ft

*See page 134 for plan of One-Person Mini-Garden,
Third Year.*

Notes
- Numbers given are for the approximate number of seeds and seedlings that should be required for each crop for the area involved.
- To improve the soil fertility and increase the sustainability of your garden/mini-farm, additionally grow 665 square feet of carbon-and-calorie crops, described on pages 31 and 32.

⑤ = Stagger planting for a more continuous harvest.

* = Spot additional seeds later where seeds do not germinate.

** = See potato planting instructions on page 15.

ONE-PERSON MINI-GARDEN, *THIRD* YEAR

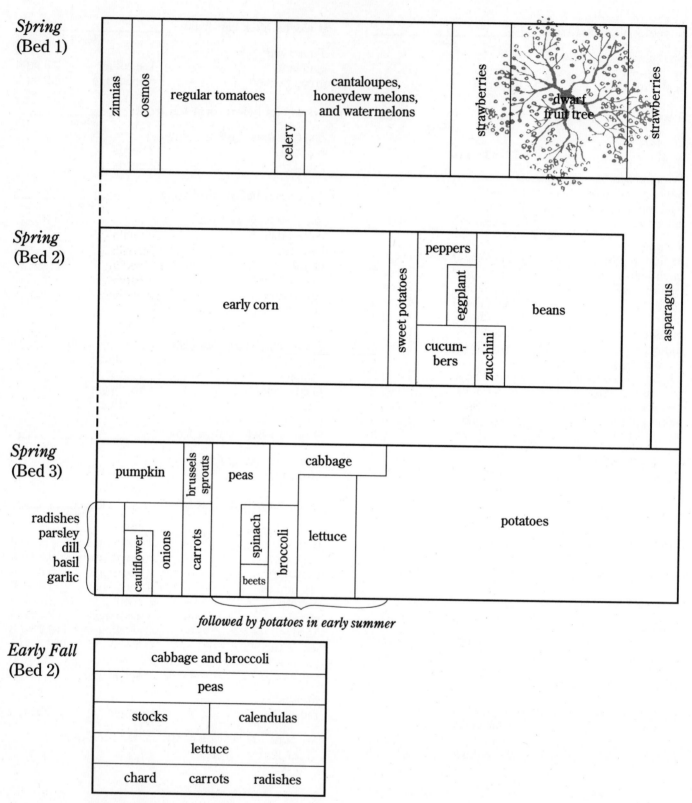

Spring
(Bed 1)

zinnias | cosmos | regular tomatoes | celery | cantaloupes, honeydew melons, and watermelons | strawberries | dwarf fruit tree | strawberries

Spring
(Bed 2)

early corn | sweet potatoes | peppers | eggplant | cucumbers | zucchini | beans | asparagus

Spring
(Bed 3)

radishes
parsley
dill
basil
garlic

pumpkin | brussels sprouts | peas | cabbage | cauliflower | onions | carrots | spinach | beets | broccoli | lettuce | potatoes

followed by potatoes in early summer

Early Fall
(Bed 2)

cabbage and broccoli	
peas	
stocks	calendulas
lettuce	
chard carrots radishes	

Scale: 5/16 inch = 1 foot. Growing beds are 100 square feet (5 by 20 feet).

ONE-PERSON MINI-GARDEN, *FOURTH* YEAR, 6-MONTH GROWING SEASON
380 SQUARE FEET (including paths)

As soon as possible in spring, plant:

chives (purchased)	—	3 seedlings	.5 sq ft
lavender (purchased)	—	1 seedling	4.0 sq ft
marjoram (purchased)	—	1 seedling	1.0 sq ft
sage (purchased)	—	1 seedling	2.3 sq ft
strawberries (relocated; see plan)	—	32 seedlings	20.0 sq ft
bare root dwarf fruit tree	—	1 tree	64.0 sq ft

or whatever herbs are desired

6 weeks before last spring frost _____
(date)

Start seedlings in flats:

broccoli	—	3 seeds
brussels sprouts	—	2 seeds
cabbage	—	5 seeds
cauliflower	—	2 seeds
celery	—	18 seeds
head lettuce	—	3 seeds Ⓢ
leaf lettuce	—	13 seeds Ⓢ
parsley	—	2 seeds
regular tomatoes	—	9 seeds

5 weeks before last frost_____
(date)

Start seedlings in flats:

cylindra beets	—	16 seeds
carrots	—	90 seeds

Prick out seedlings into flats:

head lettuce	—	2+ seedlings Ⓢ
leaf lettuce	—	10+ seedlings Ⓢ

4 weeks before last frost_____
(date)

Sprout:

potatoes	—	12.5 lbs tubers

Prick out seedlings into flat:

parsley	—	1+ seedlings

3 weeks before last frost_____
(date)

Start seedlings in flat:

bush peas	—	156 seeds

Prick out seedlings into flats:

broccoli	—	2+ seedlings
brussels sprouts	—	1+ seedlings
cabbage	—	4+ seedlings
cauliflower	—	1+ seedlings

2 weeks before last frost_____
(date)

Start seedlings in flats:

dill	—	2 seeds
eggplant	—	2 seeds
green peppers	—	8 seeds

Prick out seedlings into flat:

celery	—	9+ seedlings

Transplant:

broccoli	—	2 seedlings	2.6 sq ft
brussels sprouts	—	1 seedling	2.3 sq ft
bush peas	—	125 seedlings	6.8 sq ft
cabbage	—	4 seedlings	5.2 sq ft
carrots	—	50 seedlings	2.7 sq ft
cauliflower	—	1 seedling	1.3 sq ft
cylindra beets	—	10 seedlings	1.0 sq ft
head lettuce	—	2 seedlings Ⓢ	2.0 sq ft
leaf lettuce (9″)	—	10 seedlings Ⓢ	6.0 sq ft

Plant:

garlic	—	3 cloves	.3 sq ft
onions (purchased)	—	39 sets	3.8 sq ft
radishes	—	15 seeds	.25 sq ft

On last frost _____
(date)

Start seedlings in flats:

cantaloupes	—	4 seeds
cucumbers	—	6 seeds
honeydew melons	—	4 seeds
New Hampshire midget watermelons	—	41 seeds
pumpkins	—	3 seeds
sweet basil	—	2 seeds

Prick out seedlings into flats:

celery	—	9+ seedlings
tomatoes	—	7+ seedlings

Transplant:

parsley	—	1 seedling	.15 sq ft
potatoes	—	99 sprouted pieces	40.0 sq ft

2 weeks after last frost _____
(date)

Start seedlings in flats:

bush green beans	—	86 seeds *
bush lima beans	—	59 seeds *
early corn (65 days to maturity)	—	25 seeds

Prick out seedlings into flat:

celery	—	9+ seedlings

Note

Numbers given are for the approximate number of seeds and seedlings that should be required for each crop for the area involved.

Ⓢ = Stagger planting for a more continuous harvest.

* = Spot additional seeds later where seeds do not germinate.

** = See potato planting instructions on page 15.

3 weeks after last frost _____
(date)

Transplant:
early corn	—	18 seedlings	25.0 sq ft
tomatoes (21")	—	7 seedlings	20.0 sq ft

4 weeks after last frost _____
(date)

Transplant:
bush green beans	—	64 seedlings*	14.0 sq ft
bush lima beans	—	41 seedlings*	9.0 sq ft
cantaloupes	—	3 seedlings	5.0 sq ft
cucumbers	—	5 seedlings	4.0 sq ft
honeydew melons	—	3 seedlings	5.0 sq ft
New Hampshire midget watermelons	—	23 seedlings	20.0 sq ft
pumpkins	—	2 seedlings	6.3 sq ft
sweet basil	—	1 seedling	.25 sq ft

5 weeks after last frost _____
(date)

Prick out seedlings into flats:
eggplant	—	1+ seedlings
green peppers	—	5+ seedlings

6 weeks after last frost _____
(date)

Transplant:
celery	—	9 seedlings	2.0 sq ft

7 weeks after last frost _____
(date)

Sprout:
potatoes	—	12.5 lbs tubers

Transplant:
eggplant	—	1 seedling	2.3 sq ft
green peppers	—	5 seedlings	4.0 sq ft

8 weeks after last frost _____
(date)

As first planting comes out, transplant:
potatoes**	—	99 sprouted pieces	40.0 sq ft

16 weeks before first fall frost _____
(date)

Start seedlings in flat:
chard	—	3 seeds

14 weeks before first frost _____
(date)

Start seedlings in flats:
broccoli	—	2 seeds
cabbage	—	4 seeds
calendulas	—	7 seeds
head lettuce	—	4 seeds Ⓢ
leaf lettuce	—	25 seeds Ⓢ
stocks	—	7 seeds

13 weeks before first frost _____
(date)

Prick out seedlings into flats:
head lettuce	—	3+ seedlings Ⓢ
leaf lettuce	—	20+ seedlings Ⓢ

Transplant:
chard	—	2 seedlings	1.0 sq ft

11 weeks before first frost _____
(date)

Start seedlings in flats:
carrots	—	90 seeds
bush peas	—	156 seeds
spinach	—	17 seeds

Prick out seedlings in flats:
broccoli	—	1+ seedlings
cabbage	—	3+ seedlings

10 weeks before first frost _____
(date)

Transplant:
bush peas	—	125 seedlings	6.8 sq ft
head lettuce	—	3 seedlings Ⓢ	2.7 sq ft
leaf lettuce (8")	—	20 seedlings Ⓢ	7.8 sq ft

9 weeks before first frost _____
(date)

Start seedlings in flats:
bush peas	—	156 seeds
corn (65 days to maturity)	—	24 seeds

8 weeks before first frost _____
(date)

As first potatoes comes out, transplant:
broccoli	—	1 seedling	1.3 sq ft
bush peas	—	125 seedlings	6.8 sq ft
cabbage	—	3 seedlings	5.2 sq ft
calendulas	—	5 seedlings	5.0 sq ft
carrots	—	50 seedlings	2.7 sq ft
corn	—	18 seedlings	25.0 sq ft
spinach	—	10 seedlings	2.2 sq ft
stocks	—	5 seedlings	5.0 sq ft

Notes
- Numbers given are for the approximate number of seeds and seedlings that should be required for each crop for the area involved.
- To improve the soil fertility and increase the sustainability of your garden/mini-farm, additionally grow 570 square feet of carbon-and-calorie crops, described on pages 31 and 32.

Ⓢ = Stagger planting for a more continuous harvest.

* = Spot additional seeds later where seeds do not germinate.

** = See potato planting instructions on page 15.

ONE-PERSON MINI-GARDEN, *FOURTH* YEAR

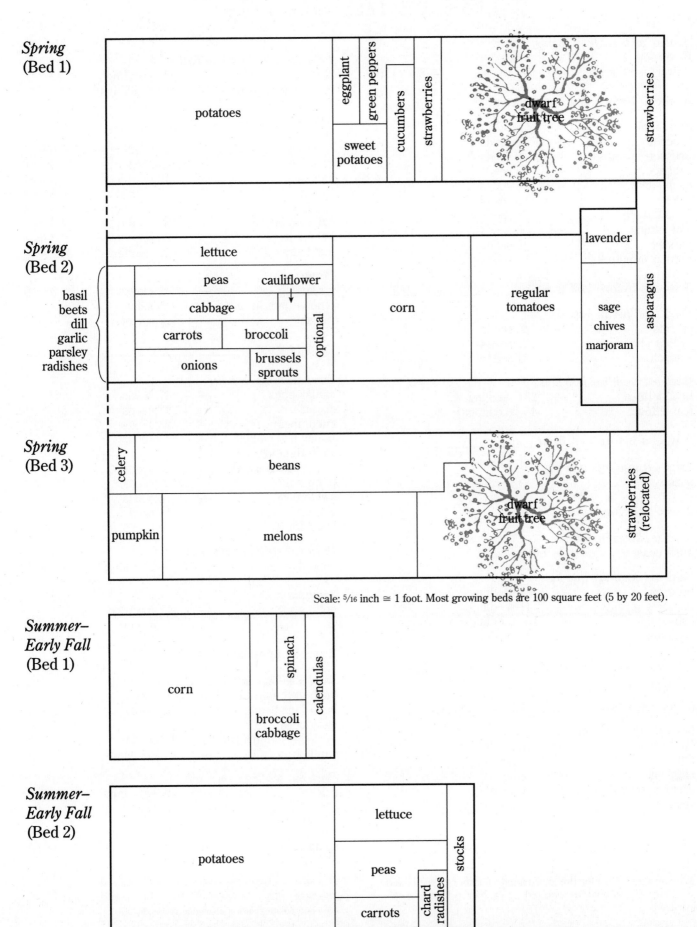

Spring
(Bed 1)

potatoes

eggplant

green peppers

sweet potatoes

cucumbers

strawberries

dwarf fruit tree

strawberries

Spring
(Bed 2)

basil
beets
dill
garlic
parsley
radishes

lettuce

peas

cauliflower

cabbage

carrots

broccoli

onions

brussels sprouts

optional

corn

regular tomatoes

lavender

sage
chives
marjoram

asparagus

Spring
(Bed 3)

celery

beans

pumpkin

melons

dwarf fruit tree

strawberries (relocated)

Scale: ⁵⁄₁₆ inch ≅ 1 foot. Most growing beds are 100 square feet (5 by 20 feet).

Summer–Early Fall
(Bed 1)

corn

spinach

broccoli cabbage

calendulas

Summer–Early Fall
(Bed 2)

potatoes

lettuce

peas

carrots

chard
radishes

stocks

FOUR-PERSON FAMILY FOOD GARDEN, 6-MONTH GROWING SEASON
1,302 SQUARE FEET (including paths)

As soon as possible in spring, plant:
bare root
   dwarf fruit trees   —   7 trees   448.0 sq ft

6 weeks before last spring frost _____
                                     (date)

Start seedlings in flats:
broccoli	—	16 seeds
brussels sprouts	—	8 seeds
cabbage	—	32 seeds
cauliflower	—	8 seeds
celery	—	96 seeds
head lettuce	—	56 seeds ⓢ
leaf lettuce	—	96 seeds ⓢ
parsley	—	16 seeds
regular tomatoes	—	35 seeds

5 weeks before last frost _____
                                     (date)

Start seedlings in flats:
carrots	—	86 seeds
cylindra beets	—	36 seeds
spinach	—	61 seeds

Prick out seedlings into flats:
head lettuce	—	28+ seedlings ⓢ
leaf lettuce	—	48+ seedlings ⓢ

4 weeks before last frost _____
                                     (date)

Prick out seedlings into flat:
parsley	—	4+ seedlings

3 weeks before last frost _____
                                     (date)

Start seedlings in flats:
bush peas	—	1,880 seeds

Prick out seedlings into flats:
broccoli	—	8+ seedlings
brussels sprouts	—	4+ seedlings
cabbage	—	16+ seedlings
cauliflower	—	4+ seedlings

2 weeks before last frost _____
                                     (date)

Sprout:
sweet potatoes	—	1.5 lbs tubers

Start seedlings in flats:
chard	—	16 seeds
dill	—	8 seeds
eggplant	—	8 seeds
green peppers	—	36 seeds
spinach	—	61 seeds

Prick out seedlings into flats:
celery	—	53+ seedlings
regular tomatoes	—	26+ seedlings

Transplant:
broccoli	—	8 seedlings	45.6 sq ft
brussels sprouts	—	4 seedlings	45.6 sq ft
bush peas	—	1,500 seedlings	68.0 sq ft
cabbage	—	16 seedlings	45.6 sq ft
carrots	—	43 seedlings	2.7 sq ft
cauliflower	—	4 seedlings	45.6 sq ft
cylindra beets	—	36 seedlings	4.0 sq ft
head lettuce	—	28 seedlings ⓢ	31.2 sq ft
leaf lettuce (9″)	—	48 seedlings ⓢ	31.2 sq ft

Plant:
garlic	—	3 cloves	.3 sq ft
onions (purchased)	—	39 sets	3.8 sq ft
radishes	—	10 seeds	.25 sq ft

On last frost _____
                                     (date)

Start seedlings in flats:
cantaloupes	—	17 seeds
cosmos	—	17 seeds
cucumbers	—	23 seeds
honeydew melons	—	17 seeds
New Hampshire midget watermelons	—	17 seeds
pumpkins	—	6 seeds
sweet basil	—	8 seeds
zinnias	—	14 seeds
zucchini	—	10 seeds

Prick out seedlings into flat:
parsley	—	9+ seedlings ⓢ	1.5 sq ft

Transplant:
potatoes**	—	546 sprouted pieces	220.0 sq ft

2 weeks after last frost _____
                                     (date)

Start seedlings in flats:
bush green beans	—	299 seeds
bush lima beans	—	206 seeds
early corn (65 days to maturity)	—	98 seeds
sunflowers	—	8 seedlings

Prick out seedlings into flat:
celery	—	53+ seedlings

Transplant:
chard	—	16 seedlings	4.0 sq ft
spinach	—	36 seedlings	9.0 sq ft

Note
Numbers given are for the approximate number of seeds and seedlings that should be required for each crop for the area involved.

ⓢ = Stagger planting for a more continuous harvest.
* = Spot additional seeds later where seeds do not germinate.
** = See potato planting instructions on page 15.

3 weeks after last frost _____
                                    (date)

Transplant:
early corn	—	73 seedlings	100.0 sq ft
regular tomatoes (21″)	—	28 seedlings	80.0 sq ft

4 weeks after last frost _____
                                    (date)

As early brassicas, onions, and lettuce come out, transplant:
bush green beans	—	224 seedlings	56.0 sq ft
bush lima beans	—	144 seedlings	36.0 sq ft
sweet potatoes	—	27 seedlings	6.0 sq ft

Transplant:
cosmos (*after potatoes are harvested*)	—	12 seedlings	10.0 sq ft
cucumbers	—	18 seedlings	16.0 sq ft
dill	—	4 seedlings	1.6 sq ft
pumpkins	—	4 seedlings	25.2 sq ft
sunflowers (24″)	—	4 seedlings	15.0 sq ft
sweet basil	—	4 seedlings	4.0 sq ft
zinnias (*after potatoes are harvested*)	—	10 seedlings	10.0 sq ft
zucchini	—	7 seedlings	9.2 sq ft

5 weeks after last frost _____
                                    (date)

Prick out seedlings into flats:
eggplant	—	4+ seedlings
green peppers	—	18+ seedlings

6 weeks after last frost _____
                                    (date)

Sprout:
potatoes	—	31 lbs tubers

Prick out seedlings into flat:
parsley	—	3+ seedlings

As peas and carrots come out, replant bed with:
cantaloupes	—	12 seedlings	
honeydew melons	—	12 seedlings	50.0 sq ft
New Hampshire midget watermelons (12″)	—	12 seedlings	

Transplant:
celery	—	50 seedlings	15.0 sq ft

7 weeks after last frost _____
                                    (date)

Transplant:
eggplant	—	4 seedlings	9.2 sq ft
green peppers	—	18 seedlings	16.0 sq ft

Notes
- Numbers given are for the approximate number of seeds and seedlings that should be required for each crop for the area involved.
- To improve the soil fertility and increase the sustainability of your garden/mini-farm, additionally grow 1,562 square feet of carbon-and-calorie crops, described on pages 31 and 32.

8 weeks after last frost _____
                                    (date)

Transplant:
parsley	—	3 seedlings

10 weeks after last frost _____
                                    (date)

As first corn planting comes out, transplant:
potatoes**	—	248 sprouted pieces	100.0 sq ft

13 weeks before first frost _____
                                    (date)

Start seedlings in flats:
broccoli	—	5 seeds
cabbage	—	20 seeds
calendulas	—	14 seeds
head lettuce	—	14 seeds$^{\text{Ⓢ}}$
leaf lettuce (8″)	—	69 seeds$^{\text{Ⓢ}}$
stocks	—	14 seeds

12 weeks before first frost _____
                                    (date)

Prick out seedlings in flats:
head lettuce	—	11+ seedlings$^{\text{Ⓢ}}$
leaf lettuce	—	55+ seedlings$^{\text{Ⓢ}}$

11 weeks before first frost _____
                                    (date)

Start seedlings into flats:
chard	—	15 seeds
spinach	—	61 seeds

Prick out seedlings into flats:
broccoli	—	1+ seedlings
cabbage	—	15+ seedlings

10 weeks before first frost _____
                                    (date)

Transplant:
head lettuce	—	11 seedlings$^{\text{Ⓢ}}$	10.0 sq ft
leaf lettuce	—	55 seedlings$^{\text{Ⓢ}}$	21.2 sq ft

8 weeks before first frost _____
                                    (date)

As last potatoes comes out, transplant:
broccoli	—	1 seedling	1.3 sq ft
cabbage	—	15 seedlings	20.8 sq ft
calendulas	—	10 seedlings	10.0 sq ft
chard	—	10 seedlings	4.0 sq ft
spinach	—	37 seedlings	8.0 sq ft
stocks	—	10 seedlings	10.0 sq ft

Plant:
radishes	—	41 seeds	1.0 sq ft

See pages 140 and 141 for plan of Four-Person Family Food Garden.

Ⓢ = Stagger planting for a more continuous harvest.

* = Spot additional seeds later where seeds do not germinate.

** = See potato planting instructions on page 15.

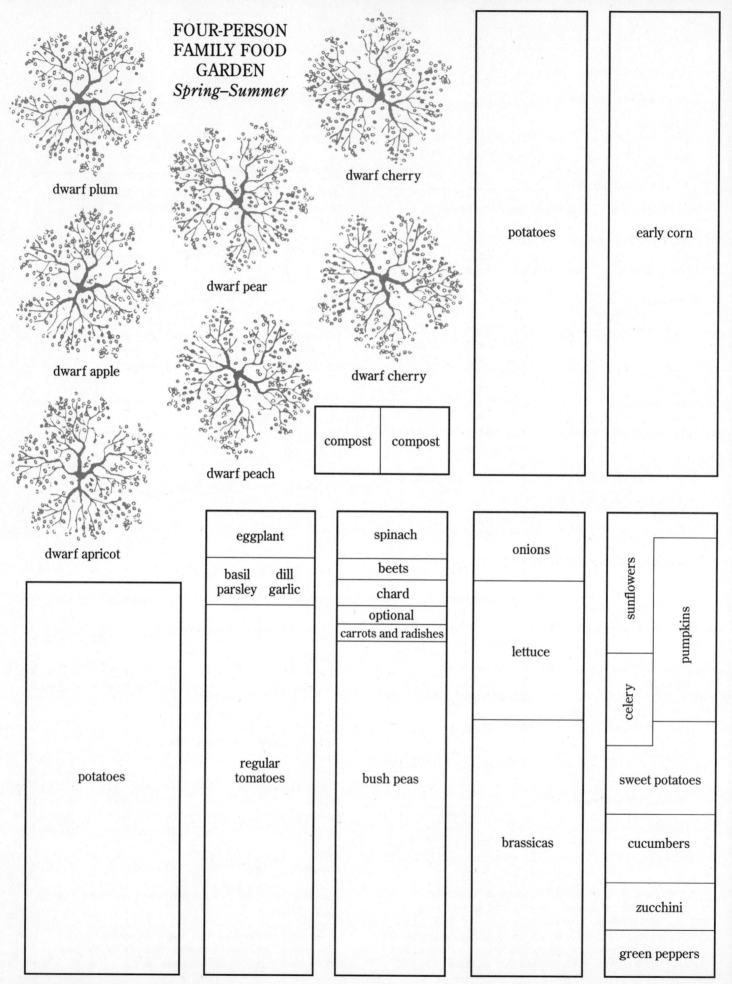

FOUR-PERSON
FAMILY FOOD
GARDEN
Spring–Summer

dwarf plum

dwarf cherry

dwarf pear

dwarf apple

dwarf cherry

dwarf peach

dwarf apricot

| compost | compost |

potatoes

early corn

eggplant

basil   dill
parsley garlic

regular
tomatoes

spinach

beets

chard

optional

carrots and radishes

bush peas

onions

lettuce

brassicas

potatoes

sunflowers

pumpkins

celery

sweet potatoes

cucumbers

zucchini

green peppers

Scale: ¼ inch ≅ 1 foot. Most growing beds are 100 square feet (5 by 20 feet).

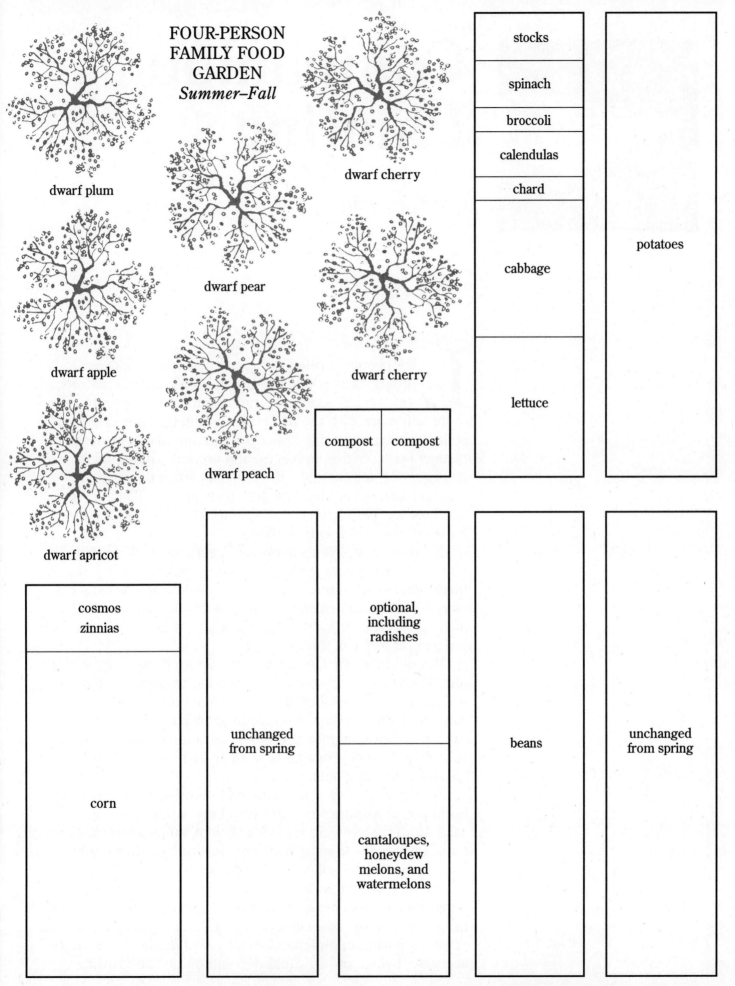

FOUR-PERSON
FAMILY FOOD
GARDEN
Summer–Fall

dwarf plum

dwarf pear

dwarf cherry

dwarf apple

dwarf cherry

dwarf peach

dwarf apricot

stocks

spinach

broccoli

calendulas

chard

cabbage

lettuce

potatoes

compost | compost

cosmos
zinnias

corn

unchanged
from spring

optional,
including
radishes

cantaloupes,
honeydew
melons, and
watermelons

beans

unchanged
from spring

Companion Planting

Goal: Grow a garden with thriving symbiotic genetic diversity

L ike people in relationships, certain plants like and dislike each other, depending on the specific natures involved. Seedlings of transplanting size begin to relate more and more with the plants around them. These relationships become especially important as adult plants develop distinct personalities, essences, and aromas. Green beans and strawberries, for example, thrive better when they are grown together than when they are grown separately. To get really good-tasting Bibb lettuce, one spinach plant should be grown for every four Bibb lettuce plants.

In contrast, no plants grow well near wormwood due to its toxic leaf and root excretions. However, wormwood tea repels black fleas, discourages slugs, keeps beetles and weevils out of grain, and combats aphids. So wormwood is not a totally noxious herb. Few plants are. Instead, they have their place in the natural order of things.

Weeds are often specialists and doctors in the plant community. They take very well to sick soil that needs to be built up and almost seem to seek it out. Where cultivated garden plants can not manage, weeds are able to draw phosphorus, potash, calcium, trace minerals, and other nutrients out of the soil and subsoil and concentrate them in their bodies. Plants seem to have uncanny instincts.

Weeds can be used to concentrate nutrients for future fertilization or to withdraw noxious elements, such as unwanted salts, from the growing area. A deficient soil is often enriched by adding weeds to man-made compost or by returning their dead bodies to the soil as nature does.

Companion planting is the constructive use of plant relationships by gardeners, horticulturists, and farmers. A scientific definition of companion planting is: "The placing together of plants having complementary physical demands." A more accurate, living, and spiritual description is "the growing together of all those elements and beings that encourage *life* and *growth*: the creation of a microcosm that includes vegetables, fruits, trees, bushes, wheat, flowers, weeds, birds, soil, microorganisms, water, nutrients, insects, toads, spiders, and chickens."

Companion planting is still an experimental field in which much more research needs to be performed. The age of the plants involved and the percentage of each of the types of plants grown together can be critical, as can be their relative proximity to one another. Companion planting should, therefore, be used with some caution and much observation. You may want to study the causes of some of these beneficial relationships. Are they due to root excretions, plant aroma, or the pollen of composite flowers that attracts certain beneficial insects? Companion planting is a fascinating field.

Some of the companion planting techniques you might try and experience are for: health; nutrition; physical complementarity; and weed, insect, and animal relationships.

Health

Better Growth—Growing green beans and strawberries together, and Bibb lettuce and spinach, has already been mentioned. On the other end of the spectrum, onions, garlic, chives, and shallots seriously inhibit the growth of peas and beans. In between the extremes, *bush* beans and beets may be grown together with no particular advantage or disadvantage to either plant. *Pole* beans and beets, however, do not get along well. The nuances are amazing. What is the difference between bush and pole beans? No one appears to know the scientific reason yet for this difference in behavior, but it can be observed.

Ehrenfreid Pfeiffer developed a method known as crystallization, from which one can predict whether or not plants will be good companions. In this technique, part of a plant is ground up and mixed with a chemical solution. After the solution dries, a crystalline pattern remains. Different plants have distinct, representative patterns. When two plant solutions are mixed, the patterns increase, decrease, or stay the same in strength and regularity. Sometimes both patterns improve, indicating a reciprocal, beneficial influence. Or both patterns may deteriorate in a reciprocal negative reaction. One pattern may improve while another deteriorates, indicating a one-sided advantage. Both patterns may remain the same, indicating no particular companion advantage or disadvantage. And one plant pattern may increase or decrease in quality while the other undergoes no change. Two plants that suffer a decrease in quality on a one-to-one basis may show an increase in strength in a one-to-ten ratio.

Stinging nettle and tomatoes are good garden companions.

Note

Lemon balm, marjoram, oregano, dandelion, chamomile, stinging nettle, and valerian are perennials. They are traditionally planted in a section along one end of the bed so they need not be disturbed when the bed is replanted.

Spacing for Better Companions—Using GROW BIOINTENSIVE spacing with the plant leaves barely touching allows good companions to be better friends.

All-Around Beneficial Influence—Certain herbs and one tree have a beneficial influence on all of the plant community. These plants and their characteristics are:[1]

- Lemon balm creates a beneficial atmosphere around itself and attracts bees. Part of the mint family.
- Marjoram has a "beneficial effect on surrounding plants."
- Oregano has a "beneficial effect on surrounding plants."
- Stinging nettle (*Urtica dioica*): "Helps neighboring plants to grow more resistant to spoiling." Increases the essential oil content in many herbs. "Stimulates humus formation." Helps stimulate fermentation in compost piles. As a tea, it promotes plant growth and helps strengthen plants. Concentrates sulfur, potassium, calcium, and iron in its body.
- Valerian (*Valeriana officinalis*): "Helps most vegetables." Stimulates phosphorus activity in its vicinity. Encourages health and disease resistance in plants.
- Chamomile (*Chamaemelum nobile*): A lime specialist. "Contains a growth hormone which . . . stimulates the growth of yeast." In a 1:100 ratio, it helps the growth of wheat. As a tea, it combats diseases such as damping off in young plants. Concentrates calcium, sulfur, and potash in its body.
- Dandelion (*Taraxacum officinale*): Increases the "aromatic quality of all herbs." "In small amounts" it helps most vegetables. Concentrates potash in its body.
- Oak tree: Concentrates calcium in its bark (bark ash is 77% calcium). In a special tea, it helps plants resist harmful diseases. The oak tree provides a beneficial influence around it that helps create excellent soil underneath its branches. This is a great place to build a compost pile for the same reason, but keep the pile at least 6 feet from the tree trunk so the environment near the tree will not be conducive to disease or attractive to harmful insects.

Soil Life Stimulation—Stinging nettle helps stimulate the microbial life, and this helps plant growth.

Soil Improvement—Sow thistle (*Sonchus oleraceus*) brings up nutrients from the subsoil to enrich a depleted topsoil. After years of dead sow thistle bodies have enriched the topsoil, heavier-feeding grasses return. This is part of nature's recycling program, in which leached-out nutrients are returned to the topsoil, and it is a natural method for raising new nutrients to

1. Helen Philbrick and Richard B. Gregg, *Companion Plants and How to Use Them* (Old Greenwich, CT: Devin-Adair Company, 1966), pp. 16, 57, 58, 60, 65, 84, 85, 86, 92; and Rudolf Steiner, *Agriculture—A Course of Eight Lectures* (London: Biodynamic Agricultural Association, 1958), pp. 93–95, 97, 99, 100.

the upper layers of the soil. It has been estimated that *one* rye plant grown in good soil produces an average of 3 miles of roots per day; that is 387 miles of roots and 6,603 miles of root hairs during a season. Plants are continuously providing their own composting program underground. In one year, plants put 800 to 1,500 pounds of roots per acre into the soil in a small garden, and red clover puts 1,200 to 3,850 pounds of roots into the soil in the same period of time.[2]

Nutrition

Over Time—Companion planting "over time" has been known for years as "crop rotation." After properly preparing the soil, heavy feeders are planted. These are followed by heavy givers and then by light feeders. This is a kind of *agricultural recycling* in which man and plants participate to return as much to the soil as has been taken out.

Heavy feeders—most of the vegetables we like and eat (including corn, tomatoes, squash, lettuce, and cabbage)—take large amounts of nutrients, especially nitrogen, from the soil. In the GROW BIOINTENSIVE method, after harvesting heavy feeders, you can return phosphorus and potassium to the soil in the form of compost. To return nitrogen to the soil, grow heavy givers. Heavy givers are nitrogen-fixing plants or legumes, such as peas, beans, alfalfa, clover, and vetch. Fava beans are also good for this purpose. Not only do they bring large amounts of nitrogen into the soil, they also excrete substances that help eradicate tomato wilt–causing organisms. (*Caution:* Some people of Mediterranean descent are *fatally allergic* to fava beans, even though the beans are very popular and widely eaten in that area. People on certain medications experience the same reaction. Check with your physician first.) After heavy givers, plant light feeders (all root crops) to give the soil a rest before the next heavy feeder onslaught. Three vegetables are low nitrogen lovers: turnips (a light feeder), sweet potatoes (a light feeder), and green peppers (a heavy feeder of nutrients other than nitrogen). The two light feeders would normally be planted after heavy givers, which put a lot of nitrogen into the soil. You may find it useful to have them follow a heavy feeder instead. It would also be good to have green peppers follow a heavy feeder. (They normally come after a heavy giver and a light feeder.)[3] You should experiment with these out-of-sequence plantings.

Plant root systems improve the topsoil by bringing up nutrients from the subsoil.

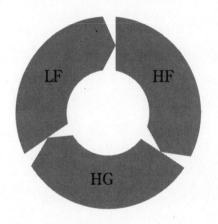

Agricultural recycling:
To preserve the soil's nutrients, plant heavy feeders, then heavy givers, then light feeders.

2. Helen Philbrick and Richard B. Gregg, *Companion Plants and How to Use Them* (Old Greenwich, CT: Devin-Adair Company, 1966), pp. 75–76.

3. This way of looking at crops was developed many years ago. It is based on how much nitrogen crops generally consume or produce. Actually, it is not always accurate. For example, potatoes, a root crop and, therefore, a light feeder, consume one of the largest amounts of nitrogen. As a result, they are functionally a heavy feeder. Nonetheless, this system can be a good way to organize crop rotation.

In Space—Companion planting of heavy feeders, heavy givers, and light feeders can be done in the same growing area, or space, at the same time. For example, corn, beans, and beets can be intermingled in the same bed. Just as with companion planting over time, you should proceed with care. In this combination, the beans must be bush beans, since pole beans and beets do not grow well together. Also, pole beans have been reported to pull the ears off corn stalks. Sometimes pole beans have been grown successfully with corn, however, and a vegetable such as carrots may be substituted for the beets so you can use the tall beans. When different plants are grown together, you sacrifice some of the *living mulch* advantage to companion planting "in space" because of the different plant heights. One way to determine the spacing for different plants grown together is to add their spacing together and divide by 2. If you grow corn and beets together, add 15 inches and 4 inches for a total of 19 inches. Divide by 2 and you get a per-plant spacing of 9.5 inches. The beets, then, would be 9.5 inches from each corn plant and vice versa. Each corn plant will be 19 inches from each corn plant and most beet plants will be 9.5 inches from the other beet plants nearest to them. In the drawing below, note that each corn plant gets the 7½ inches in each direction that it requires for a total growing area with a diameter of 15 inches. Each beet plant, at the same time, gets the 2 inches it requires in each direction for a growing space with a 4-inch diameter.

TWO-CROP COMPANION PLANTING
Circles show average root growth diameters.

C = Corn (15″ C)
B = Beets (4″ C)

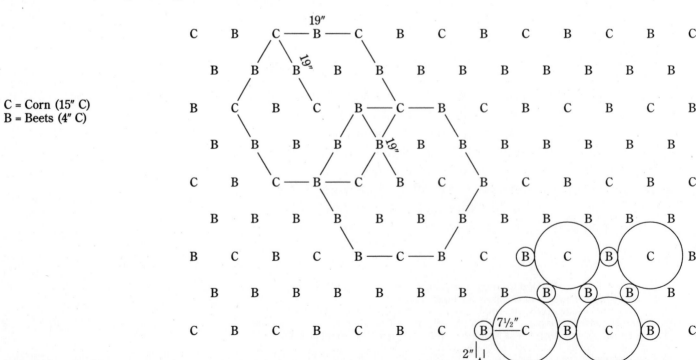

An easier, and probably just as effective, method of companion planting in space is to divide your planting bed into separate sections (or beds within a bed) for each vegetable. In this method, a grouping of corn plants would be next to a group of bush beans and a group of beets. In reality, this is a kind of companion planting over time, since there are heavy feeder, heavy giver, and light feeder sections within a bed. Roots extend 1 to 4 feet around each plant, so it is also companion planting in space. *We recommend you use this approach*. Additional spacing patterns no doubt exist and will be developed for companion planting "in space."

MULTI-CROP COMPANION PLANTING "IN SPACE"

corn	bush beans	beets	corn	bush beans	beets

A spacing example for 3 crops grown together—corn (a heavy feeder), bush beans (a heavy giver), and beets (a light feeder)—is given on page 148. You should note that this approach to companion planting in space uses more bush bean and beet plants than corn plants.

Compromise and Planning—You can see by now that companion planting involves selecting the combination of factors that works best in your soil and climate. Fortunately, the myriad of details fall into a pattern of simple guidelines. Within the guidelines, however, there are so many possible combinations that the planning process can become quite complex. Be easy on yourself. Do only as much companion planting as is reasonable for you and comes naturally. What you learn this year and become comfortable with can be applied next year, and so on. An easy place to start is with salad vegetables, since these are generally companions. Also, it is easier to companion plant over time rather than in space. Since you probably will not have enough area to use an entire bed for each crop, you might create several heavy feeder, heavy giver, and light feeder sections within each bed. You may want to grow a preponderance of crops from one group, such as the heavy feeders. (It is unlikely that you will want to grow ⅓ of each crop type.) Therefore, you will need to make adjustments, such as adding extra fertilizer and compost, when you follow one heavy feeder with another. Because of lack of space, you may have to grow some plants together that are not companions. If so, you may need to be satisfied with lower

THREE-CROP COMPANION PLANTING
Circles show average root growth diameters.

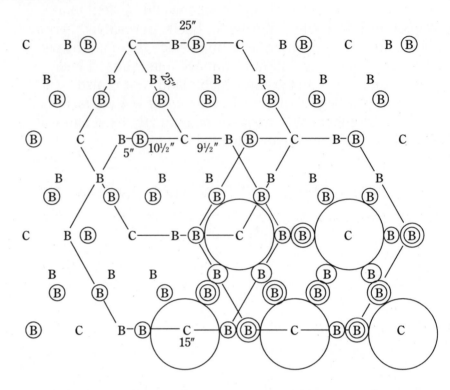

C = Corn (15″ C)
B = Beets (4″ C)
Ⓑ = Bush beans (6″ C)

Using the sun/shade technique is one way to make the most of your plants' physically complementary characteristics.

Lettuce plants can be nestled among other larger plants for the partial shade they need.

Corn can provide the shade that cucumbers enjoy.

yields, lower-quality vegetables, and less healthy plants. Or you might try to alter your diet to one that is still balanced but more in line with the balances of nature. At any rate, you can see it is useful to plan your garden in advance. You will need to know how many pounds of each vegetable you want during the year, how many plants are needed to grow the weight of vegetables you require, when to plant seeds in flats and in the ground, when and how to rotate your crops, and when to raise and transplant herbs so they will be at the peak of their own special influence. Use the Master Charts at the end of "Seed Propagation" to assist in this work. Herb plants should be reasonably mature when transplanted into a bed for insect control or general beneficial influence to have their optimum effect as companions. Try to plan your garden 12 months at a time, and always at least 3 months in advance.

Physical Complementarity

Sun/Shade—Many plants have special needs for sunlight or a lack of it. Cucumbers, for example, are very hard to please. They like heat, moisture, a well-drained soil, and some shade. One way to provide these conditions is to grow cucumbers with corn. The corn plants, which like heat and sun, can provide partial shade for the cucumber plants. Having lettuce or carrot plants nestle among other plants for partial shade is another example. Sunflowers, which are tall and like lots of sun, should be planted at the north side of the garden. There they will receive enough sun for themselves but will not shade other plants.

Shallow/Deep Rooting—One example is shallower-rooting beans interplanted with deeper-rooting corn. A dynamic process of improved soil structure occurs over time as plants with root systems of differing depths and breadths work different areas of soil in the planting bed.[4]

Fast/Slow Maturing—The French intensive gardeners were able to grow as many as 4 crops in a growing bed at one time due to the staggered growth and maturation rates of different vegetables. The fact that the edible portions of the plants appeared in different vertical locations also helped. Radishes, carrots, lettuce, and cauliflower were grown together in one combination used by the French to take advantage of these differences.

Vertical Location of the Plant's Edible Portion—See Fast/Slow Maturing.

Weed, Insect, and Animal Relationships

"Weed" Control—The growth of beets, members of the cabbage family, and alfalfa is slowed down significantly by the presence of weeds. To minimize the weed problem for sensitive plants, you can grow other plants during the previous season that discourage 'weed' growth in the soil in the current season. Two such plants are kale and rape. Another example is the *Tagetes minuta*, Mexican marigold.[5] "In many instances it has killed even couch grass, convolvulus (wild morning glory), ground ivy, ground elder, horsetail, and other persistent weeds that defy most poisons. Its lethal action works only on starch roots and has no effect on woody ones like roses, fruit bushes, and shrubs. Where it had grown, the soil was enriched as well as cleansed, its texture was refined and lumps of clay were broken up."[6] Some care should be taken when using this marigold, however, since it might also kill vegetable crops and it does give off toxic excretions. Tests need to be performed to determine how long the influence of these excretions stays with the soil. But to cleanse a soil of pernicious weeds and thereby get it ready for vegetables, *Tagetes minuta* appears to be a useful plant.

Insect and Pest Control—At least two elements are important in companion planting for insect control. One is the use of older plants with well-developed aroma and essential oil accumula-

Sow thistle grows with lettuce in one example of shallow/deep rooting symbiosis. Their roots do not compete with each other.

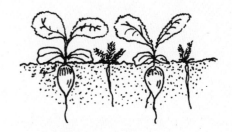

An example of using fast/slow maturing to advantage is to interplant carrots with radishes.

4. Also see Emanuel Epstein, "Roots," *Scientific American*, May 1973, pp. 48–58.

5. Illegal in California, where it is considered a noxious weed that aggressively takes over cattle lands and prevents fodder from growing. It is probably also toxic to cattle.

6. Audrey Wynne Hatfield, *How to Enjoy Your Weeds* (New York: Sterling Publishing, 1971). Copyright © 1969 by Audrey Wynne Hatfield.

tions. You want the insects to know the plant is there. Second, it is important to use a large variety of herbs. Five different herbs help discourage the cabbageworm butterfly, although one herb may work better than another in your area. Testing several herbs will help you determine the ones that work best for you. The more "unpleasant" plants there are in the garden, the sooner harmful insects will get the idea that your garden is not a pleasant place to eat and propagate. Using a large number of herbs also fits in with the diversity of plant life favored by nature. Much more research needs to be performed to determine the optimum ages for control plants and the number of control plants per bed. Too few plants will not control an insect problem, and too many may reduce your yields. Some insect controls are:

- Whiteflies: Marigolds—but not pot marigolds (calendula)— and flowering tobacco. The first are supposed to excrete substances from their roots that the other plants absorb. When the whiteflies suck on the other plants, they think they are on a strong-tasting marigold and leave. The flowering tobacco plant has a sticky substance on the underside of its leaves to which whiteflies stick and die when they come for a meal.

- Ants: Spearmint, tansy, and pennyroyal. Mint often attracts whiteflies so you may want to grow a few marigolds for control, but not so many as to possibly impair the taste of the mint and certainly not one of the more poisonous marigolds. This is another area for compromise. A few insects are probably less of a problem than mint with a strange taste.

- Nematodes and root pests: Mexican marigold (*Tagetes minuta*) "eliminates all kinds of destructive eelworms . . . wireworms, millipedes and various root-eating pests from its vicinity." The French marigold, *Tagetes patula*, eliminates some "plant-destroying nematodes . . . at up to a range of three feet . . . The beneficial . . . eelworms which do not feed on healthy roots were not affected."[7]

- Aphids: *Yellow* nasturtiums are a *decoy* for black aphids. They may be planted at the base of tomatoes for this purpose. Remove the plants and aphids before the insects begin to produce young with wings. Spearmint, stinging nettle, southernwood, and garlic help repel aphids.

- Tomato worms: Borage reportedly helps repel tomato worms and/or serves as a decoy. Its blue flowers also attract bees.

Gophers—Elderberry cuttings placed in gopher holes and runs reportedly repel these animals. Daffodils, castor beans, and gopher plant (*Euphorbia lathyrus*) are all poisonous to gophers. Be careful with the latter two, however, as they are also *very* toxic to children, especially infants.

7. Ibid., p. 17.

Birds, Bees, and Other Animals—Sow thistle attracts birds. Some birds are vegetarian, and some are omnivorous. The omnivorous birds may stay for a main course of insects after a seed snack. If you are having trouble with birds eating the berries in your berry patch, you could erect a wren house in the middle of it. Wrens are insectivores, and they will not bother the berries. But they will attack any bird, however large, that comes near their nest.

Hummingbirds are attracted to red flowers. They especially like the tiny, red, torchlike flowers of the pineapple sage in our garden. Bees may be attracted by hyssop, thyme, catnip, lemon balm, pot marjoram, sweet basil, summer savory, borage, mint, and *blue* flowers. Once in the garden they help pollinate.

Animals are good for the garden, too. Their manures can be used as fertilizers. Chickens are one of the few reliable controllers of earwigs, sowbugs, pill bugs, snails, grasshoppers, and maggots, though you may have to protect young seedlings from chickens pecking tasty plant morsels.

Companion planting in all its aspects can be a complex and often mind-boggling exercise—if you worry too much about the details. Nature is complex. We can only assist and approximate her in our creations. If we are gentle in relation to her forces and balances, she will correct our errors and fill in for our lack of understanding. As you gain more experience and develop a sensitivity and feeling for gardening, more companion planting details will become clear naturally. Do not let too much planning spoil the fun and excitement of working with nature!

Birds and plants can work together. The *Sonchus* plant seeds attract the finch, which afterwards eats aphids from the cabbage.

A LIST OF COMMON GARDEN VEGETABLES, THEIR COMPANIONS, AND THEIR ANTAGONISTS[8]

	Companions	Antagonists
Asparagus	Tomatoes, parsley, basil	
Beans	Potatoes, carrots, cucumbers, cauliflower, cabbage, summer savory, most other vegetables and herbs	Onions, garlic, gladiolus, chives
Beans, bush	Potatoes, cucumbers, corn, strawberries, celery, summer savory	Onions
Beans, pole	Corn, summer savory, sunflowers	Onions, beets, kohlrabi, cabbage
Beets	Onions, kohlrabi	Pole beans
Cabbage family (cabbage, cauliflower, kale, kohlrabi, broccoli)	Aromatic plants, potatoes, celery, dill, chamomile, sage, peppermint, rosemary, beets, onions	Strawberries, tomatoes, pole beans
Carrots	Peas, leaf lettuce, chives, onions, leeks, rosemary, sage, tomatoes	Dill
Celery	Leeks, tomatoes, bush beans, cauliflower, cabbage	
Chives	Carrots, tomatoes	Peas, beans
Corn	Potatoes, peas, beans, cucumbers, pumpkins, squash	
Cucumbers	Beans, corn, peas, radishes, sunflowers, lettuce	Potatoes, aromatic herbs
Eggplant	Beans, potatoes	
Leeks	Onions, celery, carrots	
Lettuce	Carrots and radishes (lettuce, carrots, and radishes make a strong team grown together), strawberries, cucumbers, onions	
Onions (and garlic)	Beets, strawberries, tomatoes, lettuce, summer savory, leeks, chamomile (sparsely)	Peas, beans

8. From *Organic Gardening and Farming*, February 1972, p. 54.

	Companions	**Antagonists**
Parsley	Tomatoes, asparagus	
Peas	Carrots, turnips, radishes, cucumbers, corn, beans, most vegetables and herbs	Onions, garlic, gladiolus, potatoes, chives
Potatoes	Beans, corn, cabbage, horse-radish (should be planted at the corners of the patch), marigolds, eggplant (as a lure for the Colorado potato beetle)	Pumpkins, squash, cucumbers, sunflowers, tomatoes, raspberries
Pumpkins	Corn	Potatoes
Radishes	Peas, nasturtiums, lettuce, cucumbers	
Soybeans	Grows with anything, helps everything	
Spinach	Strawberries	
Squash	Nasturtiums, corn	Potatoes
Strawberries	Bush beans, spinach, borage, lettuce (as a border), onions	Cabbage
Sunflowers	Cucumbers	Potatoes
Tomatoes	Chives, onions, parsley, asparagus, marigolds, nasturtiums, carrots	Kohlrabi, potatoes, fennel, cabbage
Turnips	Peas	

A COMPANIONATE HERBAL FOR THE ORGANIC GARDEN[9]

A list of herbs, their companions, and their uses, including some beneficial weeds and flowers.

Basil	Companion to tomatoes; dislikes rue intensely; improves growth and flavor; repels flies and mosquitoes.
Bee balm	Companion to tomatoes; improves growth and flavor.
Borage	Companion to tomatoes, squash, and strawberries; deters tomato worms; improves growth and flavor.
Caraway	Plant here and there; loosens soil.
Catnip	Plant in borders; deters flea beetles.

9. From *Organic Gardening and Farming*, February 1972, pp. 52–53.

Chamomile	Companion to cabbage and onions; improves growth and flavor.
Chervil	Companion to radishes; improves growth and flavor.
Chives	Companion to carrots; improves growth and flavor.
"Dead" nettle	Companion to potatoes; deters potato bugs; improves growth and flavor.
Dill	Companion to cabbage; dislikes carrots; improves the growth and health of cabbage.
Fennel	Plant away from gardens; most plants dislike it.
Flax	Companion to carrots and potatoes; deters potato bugs; improves growth and flavor.
Garlic	Plant near roses and raspberries; deters Japanese beetles; improves growth and health.
Henbit	General insect repellent.
Horseradish	Plant at the corners of a potato patch to deter potato bugs.
Hyssop	Deters cabbage moths; companion to cabbage and grapes. Keep away from radishes.
Lamb's quarters	This edible weed should be allowed to grow in moderate amounts in the garden, especially in corn.
Lemon balm	Sprinkle throughout the garden.
Lovage	Improves flavor and health of plants if planted here and there.
Marigolds	The workhorse of the pest deterrents. Plant throughout the garden; discourages Mexican bean beetles, nematodes, and other insects.
Marjoram	Here and there in the garden; improves flavor.
Mint	Companion to cabbage and tomatoes; improves health and flavor; deters white cabbage moths.
Mole plant	Deters moles and mice if planted here and there.
Nasturtium	Companion to radishes, cabbage, and cucurbits*; plant under fruit trees; deters aphids, squash bugs, and striped pumpkin beetles; improves growth and flavor.

* Plants in the gourd family.

Peppermint	Planted among cabbages, it repels white cabbage butterflies.
Petunia	Protects beans.
Pigweed	One of the best weeds for pumping nutrients from the subsoil; it is good for potatoes, onions, and corn; keep weeds thinned.
Pot marigold (Calendula)	Companion to tomatoes, but plant elsewhere in the garden, too; deters asparagus beetles, tomato worms, and general garden pests.
Purslane	This edible weed makes good ground cover in the corn.
Rosemary	Companion to cabbage, beans, carrots, and sage; deters cabbage moths, bean beetles, and carrot flies.
Rue	Keep it far away from sweet basil; plant near roses and raspberries; deters Japanese beetles.
Sage	Plant with rosemary, cabbage, and carrots; keep away from cucumbers; deters cabbage moth, carrot fly.
Southernwood	Plant here and there in garden; companion to cabbage; improves growth and flavor; deters cabbage moths.
Sow thistle	This weed in moderate amounts can help tomatoes, onions, and corn.
Summer savory	Plant with beans and onions; improves growth and flavor; deters bean beetles.
Tansy	Plant under fruit trees; companion to roses and raspberries; deters flying insects, Japanese beetles, striped cucumber beetles, squash bugs, and ants.
Tarragon	Good throughout the garden.
Thyme	Here and there in the garden; deters cabbage worms.
Valerian	Good anywhere in the garden.
Wild morning glory**	Allow it to grow in the corn.
Wormwood	As a border, it keeps animals from the garden.
Yarrow	Plant along borders, paths, and near aromatic herbs; enhances essential oil production.

** We discourage growing wild morning glory anywhere in your garden since it is a pernicious weed. Cultured morning glory is fine, however.
This information was collected from many sources, most notably the Bio-Dynamic Association and the Herb Society of America.

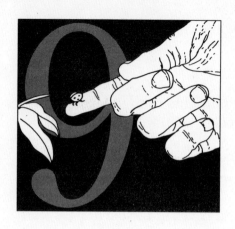

A Balanced Natural Backyard Ecosystem and Its Insect Life

Goal: Grow a mini-ecosystem thriving with life

Insects and people are only part of the complex, interrelated world of life. Both are important, integral parts of its living dynamism. Insects are an important part of the diet for many birds, toads, frogs, and for some insects in nature's complex food chain. The GROW BIOINTENSIVE method reminds you that every time you relate to an insect you are relating to the whole system of life, and that if you choose to dominate the insect population, rather than work in harmony with it, part of the system dies. For example, we depend on insects to pollinate many of our vegetables, fruits, flowers, herbs, fibers, and cover crops. When we choose dominating, death-oriented control, then the scope and depth of our lives become narrower and smaller. We are actually detracting from our lives rather than adding to them. In trying to isolate an insect and deal with it separately out of relation to the ecosystem in which it lives, we work against nature, which in turn works against us in counter-productive results.

When an excess of insects appears in a garden, nature is indicating that a problem exists in the life of that garden. In each case, we need to become sensitive to the source of the imbalance. Observation and gentle action will produce the best results. In contrast, when a heavy-handed approach is taken and poisons are used, beneficial predators are killed as well as the targeted harmful insects. Spraying trees to eliminate worms or beetles often results in a secondary outbreak of spider mites or aphids because ladybugs and other predators cannot reestablish themselves as quickly as the destructive species.

Paying attention to the soil and to plant health, planning a varied environment, and leaving a few wild spaces for unexpected benefactors minimize pest losses more effectively than the use of poison. Also, in order to have beneficial insects in your food-producing area, you must provide food for them—which may be some of the harmful insects! If there are no harmful insects to feed them, then there will be few, if any, beneficial insects around to act as friendly guardians for your garden. This seeming paradox—the need for both kinds of insects for the most healthy garden—is symbolic of nature's balances. Not too much moisture, but enough. Not too much aeration, but enough. Not too many harmful insects, but enough. You find the need for these balances everywhere—in the compost pile, in the soil, in the miniclimate, and in the backyard microcosm as a whole.

In a small backyard garden ecosystem or mini-farm, it is especially important to welcome all life-forms as much as possible. Ants destroy fruitfly and housefly larvae and keep the garden cleared of rotting debris. Have you ever squashed a snail and watched how the ants come to whisk the remains away almost within a day? Earwigs are carnivorous and prey on other insects. Tachinid flies parasitize caterpillars, earwigs, tomato worms, and grasshoppers by laying their eggs in them. We've found cabbage worms immobilized and bristling with cottony white torpedoes the size of a pinhead—larvae of the braconid wasp, which will hatch and go in search of more cabbage worms. Toads eat earwigs, slugs, and other pests. Chickens control earwigs, sowbugs, and flies. Even the ancient and fascinating snails have a natural predator: humans!

The first step in insect control is to cultivate strong, vigorous plants by cultivating a healthy place where they can grow. Normally (about 90% of the time), insects only attack unhealthy plants. Just as a healthy person who eats good food is less susceptible to disease, so are healthy plants on a good diet less susceptible to plant disease and insect attack. The insect is *not* the source of the problem, but rather an unhealthy soil is. The soil needs your energy, not the insect. The uninterrupted growth that the GROW BIOINTENSIVE method stresses is also important to maintaining plant health. We are shepherds providing the conditions our plants need for healthy, vigorous growth.

Here are some elements to consider when caring for your garden's health:

- Did you dig the soil properly?
- Are the proper plant nutrients available in the soil?
- Did you use enough compost?
- Is the soil pH within reasonable limits for the plant being grown?
- Did you transplant the seedlings properly?
- Are you watering the plants properly?

- Are you weeding effectively?
- Are you maintaining the soil in a way that will enable it to retain moisture and nutrients?
- Are the plants receiving enough sun?
- Are you growing the plants in season?

Another factor that aids plant health and minimizes insect and disease problems is keeping a correct balance of phosphorus and potash in the soil in relation to the amount of nitrogen present. The optimal ratio among these elements is still to be determined. Research also needs to be completed to determine the *minimum* amounts of these elements (in pounds per 100 square feet) that should be in the soil. (Smaller amounts of organic fertilizer elements are required in comparison with soluble synthetic chemical fertilizers, since they break down more slowly and remain available to the plants for a longer period of time.)

Properly planning the garden can eliminate many insect and disease problems!

- Use seeds that grow well in your climate and soil.
- Use plant varieties that are weather hardy, insect resistant, and disease resistant. New strains, especially hybrids (whether developed for higher yields, disease resistance, or other reasons), should usually be avoided. Some hybrids produce foods of lower nutritive value in comparison with older strains, and often use up nutrients from the soil at a more rapid rate than a living soil can sustain over time. Hybrids also tend to be very susceptible to a few diseases even when they are greatly resistant to many prevalent ones.
- Companion plant. Grow vegetables and flowers together that grow well with each other.
- Avoid putting the same vegetable in the same growing bed each year. This practice invites disease.
- Rotate your crops; follow heavy feeders with heavy givers and then light feeders.

Natural Predators

Encourage natural insect control by enlisting the aid of nature.

Birds—Some are vegetarians. Others are omnivorous. A bird that stops for a seed snack may remain for an insect dinner. A house wren feeds 500 spiders and caterpillars to her young in one afternoon; a brown thrasher consumes 6,000 insects a day; a chickadee eats 138,000 canker worm eggs in 25 days; and a pair of flickers eats 5,000 ants as a snack. A Baltimore oriole can consume 17 hairy caterpillars in a minute. You can encourage the presence of birds with moving water, by planting bushes for their protection, by planting sour berry bushes for food, and by growing plants that have seeds they like to eat.

Toads, Snakes, and Spiders—They also eat insects and other garden pests. Toads eat as many as 10,000 insects in 3 months, including cutworms, slugs, crickets, ants, caterpillars, and squash bugs.

Ladybugs—These beetles are good predators in your garden since they eat one particular pest, aphids, and do not eat beneficial insects. Ladybugs eat 40 to 50 insects per day, and their larvae eat even more.

Praying Mantids—These predators should only be used in infestation emergencies, since they eat beneficial as well as harmful insects. They are not selective and even eat each other.

Trichogramma Wasps—They lay their eggs in hosts, such as moth and butterfly larvae, that eat leaves. When they hatch, the wasp larvae parasitize the host larvae, which fail to reach maturity. Up to 98% of the hosts are rendered useless in this way.

Tachinid Flies—These parasites help control caterpillars, Japanese beetles, earwigs, gypsy moths, brown tail moths, tomato worms, and grasshoppers.

Syrphid Flies—These parasites prey upon aphids and help pollinate crops.[1]

After you have done everything possible to provide a healthy, balanced garden for your plants, you may still have insect problems. If so, you should approach the unwanted insects with the idea of *living control* rather than elimination. If there is a problem, identify the pest and try to determine whether an *environmental change* can solve the problem. In our research garden, we have minimized (not eliminated, though) gophers by introducing gopher snakes.

The pocket Golden Guides on *Insects* and *Insect Pests* are invaluable guides for getting to know the creatures that inhabit your garden. Out of the 86,000 species of insects in the United States, 76,000 are considered beneficial or friendly.[2] So, be careful! An insect that looks ugly or malicious may be a friend. If you can't seem to find an obvious culprit for your problem, try exploring at night with a flashlight. Many predators are active then.

Ask yourself whether the *damage* is *extensive* enough to warrant a "policing" effort. During 1972, we grew bush beans in one of our test beds. The primary leaves were almost entirely destroyed by the 12-spotted cucumber beetle. But in most cases the damage was not so rapid as to prevent the development of

---

1. Beatrice Trum Hunter, *Gardening Without Poisons* (New York: Berkeley Publishing Corp., 1971), pp. 31, 37, 42, 43,48. The Berkeley Edition was published by arrangement with Houghton Mifflin, who are the origional publishers of *Gardening Without Poisons*.
2. Ibid., p. 28.

healthy secondary leaves. The less tender secondary leaves were ultimately attacked and quite heavily eaten. About 80% of the secondary leaf area remained, however, and we harvested very tasty, unblemished beans. The yield in pounds was still 3.9 times the United States average! Recent tests have shown that leaf damage of up to 30% by insects can actually increase the yield in some crops. You may decide to sacrifice some yield for beauty; many destructive caterpillars become beautiful butterflies. To get the yield you want and/or to encourage the presence of butterflies, you can plant extra plants of the crops they like.

We often underestimate the ability of plants to take care of themselves. The damage done by insects often affects only a very small percentage of the edible crop. Because of this, many GROW BIOINTENSIVE gardeners plant a little extra for the insect world to eat. This practice is beautiful, mellow, and in keeping with life-giving forms of insect control. Furthermore, extensive research has shown that beneficial organisms found in soil and ocean environments can withstand stress, in the form of temperature, pressure, pH, and nutrient fluctuations, to a much greater degree in an organically fertilized medium than in a synthetically fertilized medium. I suspect researchers will come to a similar conclusion about plant resistance to insect attack.

Any time an insect or other pest invades your garden, there is an opportunity to learn more about nature's cycles and balances. Learn why they are there and find a *living control*. Look for controls that will affect only the one harmful insect. Protect new seedlings from birds and squirrels with netting or chicken wire, trap earwigs in dry dark places, wash aphids off with a strong spray of water, or block ants with a sticky barrier of Vaseline, Tanglefoot, or a tack trap. While you are doing this, continue to strive for a long-term natural balance in your growing area.

At our Common Ground Research Garden, only 3 pest problems have taken a lot of our energy: snails, slugs, and gophers. The first few years we primarily trapped gophers. A lot of time was spent checking and resetting traps and worrying about them, yet the gophers probably only damaged about 5% of our crop. We later found that, in addition to gopher snakes, they really do not like certain things placed in their holes (sardines, garlic juice, fish heads, male urine, and dead gophers). The gophers may also be blocked with strips of daffodils. Daffodils contain arsenic in their bulbs and can discourage them. Gopher snakes, of course, prevent a population explosion. A combination of approaches and gentle persistence paid off.

We have a simple routine for snails and slugs. At the end of the spring rains we go out at night with flashlights and collect gallons of them. We drop the snails in buckets of soapy water, which kills them. If you use soap that is quick to degrade, you can dump them on the compost pile the next day. We catch most of them in the first 3 nights. Going out occasionally over the next 2 weeks, you can catch new ones that were too small to get in the first sweep or that have just hatched from eggs laid in the soil. Such a concentrated cleanup can be effective for several months. The red-bellied snake (*Storeria occipitomacu-lata*) in Canada eats large numbers of slugs. A sorghum mulch is reported to repel slugs as well.

Another kind of problem has been solved through observation. For example, one year a cherry tomato bed was wilting. Several people, including a graduate student studying insects, told us it was caused by nematodes. When we dug down into the soil to look for the damage, we discovered the real source. The soil was bone dry below the upper 8 inches. A good soaking took care of the problem, and we learned not to take gardening advice on faith, but to always check it out for ourselves— as we hope you will.

Other Initiatives

Some other living control approaches to try are:

Hand-picking—You can pick the insects from plants once you are certain the insect involved is *harmful* and is the source of the problem. Consult a book such as *Insect Pests* (see page 194 of the bibliography), which has color drawings of insects in their several stages (nymph, larva, and adult). Some insects are only harmful in one stage and can even be beneficial in other stages.

Spraying—In general, insects may be divided into two categories—those that chew and bite plants and those that suck juices from them. *Chewing or biting insects* include caterpillars, flea beetles, potato bugs, cankerworms, cutworms, and grasshoppers. *Aromatic and distasteful* substances such as garlic, onion, and pepper sprays can discourage them. *Sucking insects* include aphids, thrips, squash bug nymphs, flies, and scale insects. Soap solutions (not detergents, which would damage the plant and soil as well as the insects), clear miscible oil solutions, and other solutions that asphyxiate the insects by coating their tender bodies and preventing respiration through body spiracles or breathing holes help control these insects.

Traps—Some traps, such as shredded newspaper in clay pots turned upside down on sticks in the garden, will attract earwigs during daylight hours. Snails and slugs can be trapped under damp boards. They retreat to these places in the heat and light of the day.

Barriers—The sticky commercial Tanglefoot substance will catch some insects crawling along tree trunks during part of their life cycle. Catching insects in this manner often prevents infestation of the tree in a later season. (Tanglefoot barriers must be applied to apple tree trunks in July to catch codling

moth larvae leaving the tree. This will minimize codling moth infestation the following spring. Plan ahead!) You can also use plant barriers and decoys. Grow a vegetable or flower preferred by a particular insect away from the garden to attract it to another location. Place repellent plants near a vegetable or flower that needs protection.

Companion Plants—You may also wish to plant some herbs in your bed for insect control. The age and number of plants used per 100 square feet determine the herb's effectiveness. A young plant does not have an aroma or root exudate strong enough to discourage harmful insects or to attract beneficial ones. Similarly, too few herbs will not control a pest or attract a needed predator. But too many herbs may retard vegetable growth and yield. Composite flowers, such as pot marigolds (calendulas) and sunflowers, are excellent attractants for predatory insects because their large supplies of pollen serve as predator food sources. A few (2 to 4) plants per 100-square-foot bed will probably suffice. We have not done many experiments with them yet, since accurate testing can take 2 to 3 years for one herb grown with one food plant to control one insect. You may wish to try some of these biodynamic observations, though. It's a lot of fun to try and see for yourself!

Probably the most important form of insect control with plants is just diverse cropping. The GROW BIOINTENSIVE method we use utilizes diverse cropping, and we have only experienced 5% to 10% crop loss due to pests. Biodynamic gardeners and farmers also use diverse cropping and have suggested planting 10% more area to make up for crop losses. In contrast, the monocropped acreage of today's commercial agriculture provides an ideal uniform habitat for widespread attack by pests that favor a single crop. Pesticides have been used to counteract the problem inherent in monocropping. Yet the Environmental Protection Agency estimated that in 1940, "American farmers used 50 million pounds of pesticides and lost 7 percent of their crop before harvest," and that by 1970, 12 times more pesticides were used, "yet the percentage of crops lost before harvest has almost doubled."[3] Today, about 30 times more pesticides are used than in 1940, and the percentage of crops lost to insects has been estimated to be as high as 37 percent. In fact, many pesticides targeted for one-pest species actually cause increases in numbers of nontargeted pests. By their action on the physiology of the plant, pesticides can make a plant more nutritionally favorable to insects, thereby increasing the fertility and longevity of feeding pests.[4]

3. James S. Turner, *A Chemical Feast: Report on the Food and Drug Administration* (Ralph Nader Study Group Reports) (New York: Grossman, 1970). Cited in Frances Moore Lappe and Joseph Collins, *Food First* (Boston: Houghton Mifflin Company, 1977), p. 49.

4. Francis Chaboussou, "The Role of Potassium and of Cation Equilibrium in the Resistance of the Plant." Chaboussou is the Director of Research at the French National Institute for Agricultural Research, Agricultural Zoology Station of the South-West, 22 Pont de la Maye, France.

INSECT PESTS AND PLANT CONTROLS[5]

Insect Pest	Plant Control
Ants	Spearmint, tansy, pennyroyal
Aphids	Nasturtium, spearmint, stinging nettle, southernwood, garlic
Black flea beetle	Wormwood, mint
Black fly	Intercropping, stinging nettle
Cabbageworm butterfly	Sage, rosemary, hyssop, thyme, mint, wormwood, southernwood
Colorado potato beetle	Eggplant, flax, green beans
Cutworm	Oak leaf mulch, tanbark
Flies	Nut trees, rue, tansy, spray of wormwood and/or tomato
Japanese beetle	White geranium, datura
June bug grub	Oak leaf mulch, tanbark
Malaria mosquito	Wormwood, southernwood, rosemary
Mexican bean beetle	Potatoes
Mosquito	Legumes
Moths	Sage, santolina, lavender, mint, stinging nettle, herbs
Plant lice	Castor bean, sassafras, pennyroyal
Potato bugs	Flax, eggplant
Slugs	Oak leaf mulch, tanbark
Squash bugs	Nasturtium
Striped cucumber beetle	Radish
Weevils	Garlic
Woolly aphids	Nasturtium
Worms in goats	Carrots
Worms in horses	Tansy leaves, mulberry leaves

It is evident that pesticides are not an effective solution for crop losses due to pests. *Diverse* cropping without pesticides may be able to reduce total pest losses more than monocropping with pesticides, even in large-scale agriculture. Using standard agricultural practices, Cornell University researchers, in a 5-year study

5. Helen Philbrick and Richard B. Gregg, *Companion Plants and How to Use Them* (Old Greenwich, CT: Devon-Adair Company, 1966), pp. 52–53. This book and others should be consulted for the proper use and application rates of these plant remedies. Improper use or application can cause problems and could be harmful to you, your plants, and animals.

completed in 1970, found that without pesticides the insect population could be cut in half when only 2 crops were grown together.[6] You can do this when you grow a diversity of plants in your backyard with life-giving techniques!

This introduction to insect control has emphasized philosophy and general approaches. *Companion Plants and How to Use Them, Gardening Without Poisons,* and *The Bug Book* (see pages 172, 194, and 195 of the bibliography) have already vigorously explored the spectrum of organic insect control in detail. These books provide companion planting combinations, recipes for insect control solutions, and addresses for buying predatory insects.

I hope each person who reads this book will plant at least one small, 3-foot-by-3-foot GROW BIOINTENSIVE bed. You will find the experience fun and exciting beyond your wildest expectations!

6. See Jeff Cox, "The Technique That Halves Your Insect Population," *Organic Gardening and Farming,* May 1973, pp. 103–104.

Bibliography

Ecology Action's Bountiful Gardens Mail Order Service offers numerous books. You can write to them at 18001 Shafer Ranch Rd., Willits, CA 95490 for a free catalog for current prices, and to inquire about other titles. Ecology Action has numerous publications on the GROW BIOINTENSIVE® method as well as books, booklets, and information on gardening, mini-farming, and related topics. You can use the books listed here to develop your own mini-course(s) for study of those areas that interest you most. Publications followed by "BL," "IL," or "AL" are particularly recommended for, respectively, a Basic-Level, Intermediate-Level, or Advanced-Level Library. Publications preceded with an asterisk (*) are particularly recommended for a given topic. See the table of contents for a list of the bibliography topics.

Alan Chadwick

*Bronson, William. "The Lesson of a Garden." *Cry California,* Winter 1970–71, 4–17.

Cuthbertson, Tom. *Alan Chadwick's Enchanted Garden.* New York: Dutton, 1978. 199 pp. Captures the flavor of working with Alan Chadwick.

Mulligan, Jim, and John de Graaf. *Gardensong.* Oley, PA: Bullfrog Films (Box 149, Oley PA 19547). Video.

National Video Portrait Library (1869 Kirby Rd., McLean, VA 22101). 55-minute, black-and-white, ¾-inch videocassette of a spontaneous philosophical interview with the late Alan Chadwick. Send 2 stamps for a response when inquiring.

Singh, Tara. *Awakening a Child from Within.* Los Angeles: Life Action Press (P.O. Box 48932, Los Angeles, CA 90048), 1991, 333–334.

Animals

Bement, C. U. *The American Poulterer's Companion.* New York: Harper, 1871. 304 pp.

Booth, Barbara. "Birds in the Farm." *Biodynamics,* Fall 1992, 6–33.

Bull and Carroll, *Principles of Feeding Farm Animals.* New York: Macmillan, 1937. 395 pp.

Calf Rearing. Zero Grazing Series. Vol. 3. Nairobi, Kenya: Ministry of Livestock Development, National Dairy Development Project (P.O. Box 34188, Nairobi, Kenya). 16 pp.

Craig, John A., and F. R. Marshall. *Sheep Farming.* New York: Macmillan, 1913. 302 pp.

Cuthbertson, Sir David (Chairman). *The Nutrient Requirements of Farm Livestock—No. 2 Ruminants.* London: Agricultural Research Council, 1965. 264 pp.

de Baïracle Levi, Juliette. *Herbal Handbook for Farm and Stable.* Emmaus, PA: Rodale Press, 1976. 320 pp. **BL**

Devendra, C., and Marcia Burns. *Goat Production in the Tropics.* Farnham, Royal, Bucks, England: Commonwealth Agricultural Bureaux, 1970. 177 pp.

The Feeding of the Dairy Cow. Zero Grazing Series. Vol. 5. Nairobi, Kenya: Ministry of Livestock Development, National Dairy Development Project (P.O. Box 34188, Nairobi, Kenya). 15 pp.

The Fertility of the Dairy Cow. Zero Grazing Series. Vol. 4. Nairobi, Kenya: Ministry of Livestock Development, National Dairy Development Project (P.O. Box 34188, Nairobi, Kenya). 12 pp.

Jordan, Whitman H. *The Feeding of Animals.* New York: Macmillan, 1903. 450 pp.

Juhre, Robert G. *Preventing Deer Damage.* Kettle Falls, WA: Robert G. Juhre, 1996. 54 pp.

Laurie, Duncan Forbes. *Poultry Foods and Feeding.* New York: Cassell and Co., 1912. 188 pp.

Luttmann, Rick and Gail. *Chickens in Your Backyard.* Emmaus, PA: Rodale Press, 1976. 157 pp.

Mackenzie, David. *Goat Husbandry.* London: Faber and Faber, 1970. 336 pp. **BL**

Oxen Culture Demonstration Farm (Tillers International, 5239 S. 24th St., Kalamazoo, MI 49002).

Rollin, Bernard E. *The Frankenstein Syndrome—Ethical and Social Issues in the Genetic Engineering of Animals.* New York: Cambridge University Press, 1995. 241 pp.

Savory, Allan. *The Complete Holistic Management™ Planning and Monitoring Guide.* Albuquerque, NM: The Allan Savory Center for Holistic Management (1010 Tijeras NW), 2000. Looseleaf binder. 158 pp.

———. *Holistic Management in Practice.* The Allan Savory Center for Holistic Management. Bimonthly publication.

————. *Grazing Plan & Control Chart. (Livestock/Wildlife/Crops/Other Uses)*. The Allan Savory Center for Holistic Management, 1997.

————. *Holistic Management: A New Framework for Decision Making*. Covelo, CA: Island Press, 1999. 616 pp.

Sibley, David Allen. *National Audubon Society: The Sibley Guide to Birds*. New York: Knopf, 2000. 544 pp.

Sunset Editors. *Attracting Birds to Your Garden*. Menlo Park, CA: Sunset Books, 1974. 96 pp.

Watson, George C. *Farm Poultry*. New York: Macmillan. 1901.

*Wolf, Tom. "Bucking Tradition: Moving toward Sustainable Ranching—The Gospel According to Pete Tatschl—An Environmentalist Questions Whether Cows Belong in the Southwest, and Gets in Response a Healthy Dose of Holistic Range Management." *High Country News* (P.O. Box 1090, Paonia, CO 81428), March 1990, 25–27.

Woll, F. W. *Lippincott's Farm Manuals: Productive Feeding of Farm Animals*. Philadelphia, PA: J. B. Lippincott, The Washington Square Press, 1916. 385 pp.

Appropriate Technologies

101 Technologies from the South for the South. Ottawa, Canada: International Development Research Centre (P.O. Box 8500, Ottawa, ON K1G 3H9, Canada), 1992. 231 pp.

Allen, Hugh. *The Kenya Ceramic Jiko: A Manual for Stovemakers*. Croton-on-Hudson, NY: International Technology Development Group of North America (The Bootstrap Press, P.O. Box 337, Croton-on-Hudson, NY 10520), 1991. 99 pp.

Appropriate Technology Project. *Volunteers in Asia*. P.O. Box 4543, Stanford, CA 94309. A nonprofit research organization that makes information about key appropriate technology publications available to others.

Ap-Tech. Gandhi Bhawan, India: Appropriate Technology Development Association (P.O. Box 311, Gandhi Bhawan, Lucknow-226001, U.P. India). Occasional papers on topics telated to appropriate technology.

Bielenberg, Carl, and Allen, Hugh. *How to Make and Use the Treadle Irrigation Pump*. London: Intermediate Technology Publications, 1995. 77 pp.

Brace Research Institute, Faculty of Engineering (P.O. Box 900, Macdonald College of McGill University, Ste. Anne de Bellevue, Quebec H9X 3V9, Canada). Appropriate technology publications focusing on small communities in rural areas.

"Building the Outdoor Oven." *Countryside and Small Stock Journal*. Vol. 78, No. 4. July/August 1994.

*Darrow, Ken. *Appropriate Technology Source Book*. Stanford, CA: Volunteers in Asia (Box 4543, Stanford, CA 94305), 1986. 799 pp. **BL**

*Evans, Ianto. *Lorena Stoves*. Stanford, CA: Volunteers in Asia (Box 4543, Stanford, CA 94305), 1981. 144 pp.

The Hay Box—The Energy Saving Cooker. Eugene, OR: The Aprovecho Institute (359 Polk St., Eugene, OR 97402). 20 pp.

Joseph, Stephen, et al. *Wood-Conserving Cookstoves: A Design Guide*. Mount Rainer, MD: Volunteers in Technical Assistance, 1981. 111 pp.

Kaufman, Marcus. *From Lorena to a Mountain of Fire—A case study of Yayasan Dian Desa's fuel efficient stove program (1978–1983)*. (Yayasan Dian Desa, P.O. Box 19 Bulaksumer, Yogyadarta, Indonesia), 1983. 52 pp.

*Rohde, Eleanour S. *Haybox Cookery*. London: George Routledge & Sons (Broadway House, 68–74 Carter Ln., E.C., England), 1939. 108 pp.

Schaeffer, John, ed. *Alternative Energy Sourcebook*. Hopland, CA: Real Goods Trading Corp. (13771 S. Hwy. 101, Hopland, CA), 1992. 518 pp.

Village Technology Handbook. Volunteers in Technical Assistance (1815 N. Lynn St., Arlington, VA 22209), 1988. 422 pp.

Arid Regions/Dryland Farming

Adams, L. H. and E. S. Goff. "Reports on Oats, Barley, and Potatoes for 1889." *Bulletin No. 22*. Madison, WI: University of Wisconsin, January 1890. 12 pp.

Anderson, Edward F. *The Cactus Family*. Portland, OR: Timber Press, 2001.

Appropriate Technology Development Association. "Water Harvesting," *ApTech Newsletter* (Box 311, Gandhi Bhawan, Lucknow-226001, U.P. India). 776 pp.

Arid Land Newsletter. Center for People, Food, and Environment (344 S. 3rd Ave., Tucson, AZ 85701).

Arnon, I. *Crop Production in Dry Regions*. Vols. 1 and 2. London: Leonard Hill, 1972. Vol. 1: 649 pp.; Vol. 2: 682 pp.

Atkinson, Alfred. "Crop Growing Suggestions to Dry-Land Farmers." *Circular 45*. Bozeman, MT: Montana Agricultural College Experiment Station, February 1915, 121–140.

Atkinson, Alfred, and N. C. Donaldson. "Dry Farm Grain Tests in Montana." *Bulletin No. 110*. Bozeman, MT: Montana Agricultural College Experiment Station, February 1916, 167–218.

Atkinson, Alfred, and J. B. Nelson. "Dry Farming Investigations in Montana." *Bulletin No. 74*. Bozeman, MT: Montana Agricultural College Experiment Station, December 1908, 63–89.

Aune, Beyer. "Suggestions to Settlers on the Belle Fourche Irrigation Project." *Circular No. 83*. Washington, DC: USDA Bureau of Plant Industry, July 24, 1911. 14 pp.

Bainbridge, David A. "Using Trees to Maintain Groundwater," *Drylander*, Vol. I, No. 2, 1987, 3.

————. "Pitcher Irrigation," *Drylander*. Vol. II, No. 1, 1988, 3.

Baylor, Byrd. *The Desert Is Theirs*. New York: Macmillan, 1975.

Briggs, Lyman J., and J. O. Belz. "Dry Farming in Relation to Rainfall and Evaporation." *Bulletin No. 188*. Washington, DC: USDA Bureau of Plant Industry, November 5, 1910. 71 pp.

Bromfield, Louis. *Malabar Farm*. New York: Harper & Row, 1948, 10–17, 252, 257–261. 405 pp. **BL**

Brookbank, George. *Desert Gardening: The Complete Guide*. Tucson, AZ: Fisher Books, 1991. 282 pp.

Buffum, B. C. "Crop Report for 1893. Cost and Profit of Growing Wheat, Sugar Beets, Garden Vegetables and Tobacco. Progress Report on Fruits and Trees. Meteorology for 1893. Notes on Climate." *Bulletin No. 17*. Laramie, WY: University of Wyoming, March 1894. 45 pp.

Buffum, B. C. and Aven Nelson. "Growing and Preparing Agricultural Crops for Exhibition." *Bulletin No. 58*. Laramie, WY: University of Wyoming, April 1903. 12 pp.

Cardon, P. V. "Minor Dry Land Crops at the Nephi Experiment Farm." *Bulletin 132*. Logan, UT: Utah Agricultural College Experiment Station, March 1914, 349–378.

*Cleveland, David A., and Daniela Soleri. *Food from Dryland Gardens: An Ecological, Nutritional and Social Approach to Small-Scale Household Food Production*. Tucson, AZ: Center for People, Food, and Environment (344 S. 3rd Ave., Tucson, AZ 85701), 1991. 387 pp. **BL**

Clothier, R. W. "Dry-Farming in the Arid Southwest." *Bulletin No. 70*. Tucson, AZ: University of Arizona Agricultural Experiment Station, February 1, 1913, 725–798.

Connell, J. H., et al. "Field Experiments at College Station with Corn, Cotton, and Forage Plants." *Bulletin No. 40*. College Station, TX: Texas Agricultural Experiment Station, September 1896, 851–874.

———. "Field Experiments at McKinnley Sub-Station and Wichita Falls Sub-Station with Wheat, Corn, Cotton, Grasses and Manures." *Bulletin No. 34*. College Station, TX: Texas Agricultural Experiment Station, February 1895, 523–592.

Cook, O. F. "Vegetation Affected by Agriculture in Central America." *Bulletin No. 145*. Washington, DC: USDA Bureau of Plant Industry, April 10, 1909. 30 pp.

Cooley, F. S. "Suggestions to the Dry Farmer." *Circular 19*. Bozeman, MT: Montana Agricultural College Experiment Station, May 1912. 52 pp.

Cottrell, H. M. "Dry Land Farming in Eastern Colorado." *Bulletin 145*. Fort Collins, CO: Colorado Agricultural College Experiment Station, December 1909. 32 pp.

Critchley, Will. *Looking After Our Land: New Approaches to Soil and Water Conservation in Dryland Africa*. Oxford, U.K.: OXFAM, 1991. 84 pp.

Critchley, Will, et al. *Water Harvesting for Plant Production, Vol. II*. Washington, DC: World Bank, 1992. 134 pp.

Cromell, Cathy, Linda A. Guy, and Lucy K. Bradley. *Desert Gardening for Beginners*. Phoenix, AZ: Master Gardener Press, 1999. 100 pp.

"Crop Management in the Semi-Arid Tropics." Silang, Cavite, Philippines and Indian Rural Reconstruction Movement, Bangalore, India: International Institute of Rural Reconstruction. 14 pp.

"Cross Ridging Holds Precious Rainwater on the Land." *Developing Countries Farm Radio*, Package No. 14. Toronto, Canada: Developing Countries Farm Radio (c/o Massey Ferguson, 595 Bay St., Toronto, Canada), 1988. 5 pp.

Dillman, Arthur C. "Breeding Drought-Resistant Forage Plants for the Great Plains Area." *Bulletin No. 196*. Washington, DC: USDA Bureau of Plant Industry, December 1910. 40 pp.

Ebeling, Walter. *Handbook of Indian Foods and Fiber of Arid America*. Berkeley, CA: University of California Press, 1986. 971 pp.

Ellison, A. D., et al. "Dry-Farming in Utah." *Circular No. 21*. Lehi Sun Print, 1916, 2–35.

Fargher, John. "Arid Landwater Harvesting." Orange, MA: John Fargher, 1985. 8 pp.

Foaden, George P. "Notes on Egyptian Agriculture." *Bulletin No. 62*. Washington, DC: USDA Bureau of Plant Industry, July 9, 1904. 61 pp.

Forbes, R. H. "Agriculture of Sulphur Spring Valley Arizona." *Bulletin No. 72*. University of Arizona, June 30, 1913, 214–224.

Fraps, G. S. "Observations of European Agriculture." *Bulletin No. 143*. College Station, TX: Texas Agricultural Experiment Station, December 1911. 35 pp.

Friends of the Arboretum. *Desert Plants*. Tucson, AZ: Friends of the Arboretum (P.O. Box 3607, Tucson, AZ 85722).

Goldstein, Walter A., and Douglas L. Young. "An Agronomic and Economic Comparison of a Conventional and a Low-Input Cropping System in the Palouse." *American Journal of Alternative Agriculture*, Spring 1987, 51–56.

Goldstein, W. *Alternative Crops, Rotations and Management Systems for the Palouse*. Pullman, WA: Washington State University, 1986. 333 pp.

Gore, Rick. "No Way to Run a Desert." *National Geographic*, June 1985, 694–719.

Granatstein, David. *Dryland Farming in the Northwestern United States*. Pullman, WA: College of Agriculture and Home Economics Research Center, Washington State University, 1992. 31 pp.

Hall, A. E. *Agriculture in Semi-Arid Environments*. New York: Springer-Verlag, 1979. 340 pp.

Harrington, H. H. "Grasses and Forage Plants: A Study of Composition and Value. Texas Grains-Composition. Ash Analyses, Grasses and Grains." *Bulletin No. 20*. College Station, TX: Texas Agricultural Experiment Station, 1892, 170–190.

Harris, Frank S., et al. "Variety Tests of Field Crops in Utah." *Bulletin 131*. Logan, UT: Utah Agricultural College, March 1914, 317–346.

Harsch, Jonathon. "Dryland Farming May Return as Ground Water Levels Drop." *Christian Science Monitor*, July 19, 1980, 10.

Hartley, Carl. "Injury by Disinfectants to Seeds and Roots in Sandy Soils." *Bulletin No. 169*. Washington, DC: USDA Bureau of Plant Industry, February 20, 1915, 2–35.

Hilgard, E. W., et al. "The Conservation of Soil Moisture and Economy in the Use of Irrigation Water." *Bulletin 121*. Berkeley, CA: University of California Agricultural Experiment Station, August 1898. 15 pp.

Hugalle, N. R. "Tied Ridges Improve Semi-Arid Crop Yields." *International Ag-Sieve* 1, No. 2 (1988), 4.

Hutchison, C. B., et al. "Experiments with Farm Crops in Southwest Missouri." *Bulletin No. 123*. Columbia, MO: University of Missouri, January 1915, 163–185.

Indian Agricultural Research Institute. *A New Technology for Dryland Farming*. New Delhi: Indian Agricultural Research Institute, 1970. 189 pp.

Kezer, Alvin. "Dry Farming in Colorado." *Bulletin 227*. Fort Collins, CO: Colorado Agricultural College Experiment Station, April 1917. 40 pp.

Letteer, C. R. "Experiments in Crop Production of Fallow Land at San Antonio." *Bulletin No. 151*. Washington, DC: USDA Bureau of Plant Industry, September 19, 1914. 10 pp.

McClelland, C. K. "Variety Work with Corn and Cotton." *Bulletin 113*. Experiment, GA: Georgia Experiment Station, January 1915, 252–256.

Merriam, Hart C. "Life Zones and Crop Zones of the United States." *Bulletin No. 10*. Washington, DC: USDA Division of Biological Survey, June 20, 1898. 79 pp.

Mooers, Charles. "Experiments with Fertilizers and Field Crops on Important Soil Types of Middle Tennessee." *Bulletin No. 92*. Knoxville, TN: University of Tennessee, June 1911, 27–95.

———. "Experiments with Soils, Fertilizers, and Farm Crops." *Bulletin No. 86*. Knoxville, TN: University of Tennessee, April 1909, 35–88.

Nehrling, Arno, et al. *Easy Gardening with Drought-Resistant Plants*. New York: Dover, 1968. 320 pp.

Nyhuis, Jane. *Desert Harvest*. Tuscon, AZ: Meals for Millions (Box 42622, Tucson, AZ 85733), 1982. 63 pp.

Oklahoma Agricultural Experiment Station. "Field Crops, 1899." *Bulletin No. 44*. Stillwater, OK: Oklahoma Agricultural Experiment Station, December 1899. 12 pp.

Paddock, Wendell, and Orville B. Whipple. *Fruit Growing in Arid Regions*. Boston, MA: Macmillan, 1913. 395 pp.

Payne, J. E. "The Plains." *Bulletin 123*. Fort Collins, CO: Colorado Agricultural College Experiment Station, January 1908, 4–32.

"Quantitative phenology of warm desert legumes: Seasonal growth of six Prosopis species at the same site." *Journal of Arid Environments*, 1991, 299–311.

Reij, Chris, et al. *Water Harvesting for Plant Production, Vol. 1*, Washington, DC: World Bank, 1988. 123 pp.

Riddle, R. "Drought-Resistant Fruit and Nuts for the Water-Efficient Landscape." *CFRG Journal*, 1989, 8–19.

Rodale, J. I. *Stone Mulching in the Garden*. Emmaus, PA: Rodale Press, 1949. 164 pp.

Saunders, D. A. "Drought Resistant Forage Experiments." *Bulletin 74*. Brookings, SD: South Dakota Agricultural College Experiment Station, March 1902. 16 pp.

———. "Drought Resistant Forage Experiments at Highmore, South Dakota, 1900." *Bulletin 70*. Brookings, SD: South Dakota Agricultural College Experiment Station, February 1901, 57–73.

Shepard, James H. "Drought-Resisting Forage Plants at the Co-Operative Range Experiment Station, Highmore, South Dakota." *Bulletin 66*. Brookings, SD: South Dakota Agricultural College Experiment Station, March 1900, 35–52.

Snyder, W. P. "Crop Production in Western Nebraska. Principles of Cultivation." *Bulletin No. 109*. Lincoln, NE: University of Nebraska Agricultural Experiment Station, 56 pp.

Snyder, W. P., and W. W. Burr. "Growing Crops in Western Nebraska." *Bulletin No. 7*. Lincoln, NE: University of Nebraska Agricultural Experiment Station, February 15, 1911. 69 pp.

Snyder, W. P., and W. M. Osborn. "Rotations and Tillage Methods in Western Nebraska." *Bulletin No. 155*. Lincoln, NE: University of Nebraska Agricultural Experiment Station, June 1, 1916. 48 pp.

Soule, Andrew M., and John R. Fain. "Crops for the Silo." *Bulletin No. 1*. Knoxville, TN: University of Tennessee, January 1904. 24 pp.

Stephens, D. E., and C. E. Hill. "Dry Farming Investigations at the Sherman County Branch Experiment Station." *Station Bulletin 144*. Moro, OR: Oregon Agriculture College Experiment Station, April 1917. 48 pp.

Stewart, Robert. "The Nitrogen and Humus Problem in Dry-Land Farming." *Bulletin No. 109*. Logan, UT: Utah Agricultural College Experiment Station, August 1910. 73 pp.

Sunset Editors. *Desert Gardening*. Menlo Park, CA: Sunset Books, 1967. 96 pp.

———. *Waterwise Gardening: Landscaping Ideas, Watering Systems and Unthirsty Plants*. Menlo Park, CA: Sunset Books, 1989. 96 pp.

"Sustainable Living in Drylands," *Journal of Arid Lands Permaculture*. Southwest Regional Permaculture Institute (P.O. Box 27371, Tucson, AZ 85726-7371), Fall 1989.

Swingle, Walter T. A., et al. "Miscellaneous Papers." *Circular No. 129.* Washington, DC: USDA Bureau of Plant Industry, June 17, 1913. 32 pp.

Thatcher, R. W. "The Nitrogen and Humus Problem in Dry Farming." *Bulletin No. 105.* Pullman, WA: State College of Washington Agricultural Experiment Station, June 1912. 16 pp.

Thom, C. C., and H. F. Holz. "Dry Farming in Washington." *Popular Bulletin No. 69,* Pullman, WA: State College of Washington Agricultural Experiment Station, April 1, 1914. 31 pp.

Thysell, John, et al. "Dry Farming Investigations in Western North Dakota." *Bulletin No. 110.* Agricultural College, ND: North Dakota Agricultural Experiment Station, February 1915, 159–207.

Tonge, Peter. "Twice the Yield, Half the Work." *Christian Science Monitor,* January 12, 1988, 23.

Towar, J. D. "Dry Farming in Wyoming." *Bulletin No. 80.* Laramie, WA: University of Wyoming Agricultural College Department, March 1909. 29 pp.

"Trench Composting: A Model for Africa." *Organic Gardening and Farming,* January 1976, 149–150.

"Trench Composting for Arid Regions." International Federation of Organic Agricultural Movements (R.D. 1, Box 323, Kutztown, PA 19530), June 1976. Newsletter.

UNICEF. "Some Sources of Nutrition from the Dry Season Garden." New York: UNICEF. 1 p.

University of Arizona. "Timely Hints for Farmers." *Bulletin No. 57.* Tuscon, AZ: June 20, 1908, 247–287.

Voorhees, J. F. "Relation of Temperature and Rainfall to Crop Systems and Production." *Bulletin No. 91.* Knoxville, TN: University of Tennessee, January 1911, 3–23.

"What an Inch of Rain Is Worth." *Successful Farming,* January 1974, 79.

Whitney, Milton. "Fertilizers on Soils Used for Oats, Hay, and Miscellaneous Crops." *Bulletin No. 67.* Washington, DC: USDA Bureau of Soils, June 8, 1910. 73 pp.

*Widtsoe, John A. *Dry Farming.* New York: Macmillan, 1919. 445 pp. An important basic work. **BL**

———. "The Nature of the Dry Farm Soils of Utah." *Bulletin No. 122.* Salt Lake City, UT: Utah Agricultural College Experiment Station, January 1913, 270–288.

———. "The Storage of Winter Precipitation in Soils." *Bulletin No. 104.* Logan, UT: Agricultural College of Utah Experiment Station, October 1908, 282–316.

Bamboo

Bell, Michael. *The Gardener's Guide to Growing Temperate Bamboos.* Portland, OR: Timber Press, 2000. 159 pp.

Cusack, Victor. *Bamboo Rediscovered.* Trentham, Victoria, Australia: Earth Garden Books, 1997. 95 pp.

Guardiani, Nunzia. *Construccion de Viviendas Con Bambu.* Santo Domingo: ENDA-Caribe, 1991. 47 pp.

Judziewicz, Emmet J., Lynn G. Clark, Ximena Londono, and Margaret J. Stern. *American Bamboos.* Washington, DC: Smithsonian Institution Press, 1999. 392 pp.

Meeker, John. "Backyard Bamboo." *Organic Gardening,* October 1980, 88–99.

Ueda, Dr. Koichiro. *Studies on the Physiology of Bamboo.* Japan: Resources Bureau, Science and Technics Agency, Prime Minister's Office, 1960. 167 pp.

van den Heuvel, Kick. *Wood and Bamboo for Rural Water Supply.* Delft, The Netherlands: Delft University Press, 1981. 76 pp.

Biodynamic

Bio-Dynamic Gardening: A How-To Guide. Canoga Park, CA: Rudolf Steiner Research Foundation (BOKAJO Enterprises, 20959 Elkwood St., Canoga Park, CA 91304), 1988. 58:30 mins.

Biodynamic Farming and Gardening Association. Bldg. 1002B, Thoreau Center, The Presidio, San Francisco, CA 94120.

Biodynamics: Farming and Gardening for the 21st Century. Biodynamic Farming and Gardening Association . Bimonthly journal.

Bockemuhl, Jochen. *In Partnership with Nature.* Wyoming, RI: Bio-Dynamic Literature, 1981. 84 pp.

Booth, Barbara. "Birds in the Farm." *Biodynamics,* Fall 1992, 6–33.

Brinton, William F., Jr. "Living Compost, Living Carbon." *Biodynamics: Farming and Gardening for the 21st Century,* January/February 1998. 1–3.

———. "The End of Reductionism: Science and the 21st Century." *Biodynamics: Farming and Gardening for the 21st Century,* March/April 1997, 20–23.

Carpenter-Boggs, Lynne A. *Effects of Biodynamic Preparations on Compost, Crop, and Soil Quality.* Washington State University Doctoral Dissertation, 1997. 164 pp.

Childs, Gilbert. *Rudolf Steiner: His Life and Work.* Hudson, NY: Anthroposophic Press, 1995. 94 pp.

Ehrenfried Pfeiffer Himself. Metairie, LA: Acres U.S.A. Masters of Eco-Agriculture Series (P.O. Box 8800, Metairie, LA 70011). 8 audiotapes.

Gregg, Evelyn S. *Herb Chart.* Wyoming, RI: Biodynamic Farming and Gardening Association. Detailed cultural notes. Available from BDFGA.

Groh, Trauger, M., and Steven S. H. McFadden. *Farms of Tomorrow—Community-Supported Farms, Farm-Supported Communities.* Kimberton, PA: Biodynamic Farming and Gardening Association, 1990. 169 pp.

Heckel, Alice, ed. *The Pfeiffer Garden Book: Biodynamics in the Home Garden.* Stroudsburg, PA: Biodynamic Farming and Gardening Association, 1967. 199 pp. **IL**

Joly, Nicolas. *Wine, from Sky to Earth Growing & Appreciating Biodynamic Wine.* Austin, TX: Acres U.S.A., 1999. 168 pp.

*Koepf, Herbert H. *Compost.* Wyoming, RI: Biodynamic Farming and Gardening Association, 1966. 18 pp. Short, detailed pamphlet. Available from BDFGA. **AL**

———. *The Biodynamic Farm.* Hudson, NY: Anthroposophic Press, 1989. 245 pp. Available from BDFGA.

———. *Ehrenfried Pfeiffer: Pioneer in Agriculture and Natural Science.* Kimberton, PA: Biodynamic Farming and Gardening Association, 1991. 31 pp. Available from BDFGA.

———. *Research in Biodynamic Agriculture Methods and Results.* Kimberton, PA: Biodynamic Farming and Gardening Assoc., 1993. 78 pp. Available from BDFGA.

*Koepf, Herbert H., B. D. Peterson, and Wolfgang Schauman. *Biodynamic Agriculture: An Introduction.* Spring Valley, NY: Anthroposophic Press, 1976. 429 pp. **IL**

Lovel, Hugh. *A Biodynamic Farm for Growing Wholesome Food.* Kansas City, MO: Acres U.S.A., 1994. 215 pp. Available from BDFGA.

Pauli, F. W. *Soil Fertility: A Biodynamic Approach.* London: Adarn Hilger (98 St. Pancras Way, London NW1, England), 1976. 204 pp.

Pfeiffer, Ehrenfried. "Applied Biodynamics." *Newsletter of the Josephine Porter Institute,* Spring 1999, 122–136.

———. *Biodynamic Farming and Gardening: Soil Fertility Renewal and Preservation.* New York: Anthroposophic Press, 1943. 240 pp.

———. *Biodynamic Farming—Articles 1942–1962.* Wyoming, RI: Biodynamic Farming and Gardening Association. 150 pp.

———. *Chromatography Applied to Quality Testing.* Wyoming, RI: Bio-Dynamic Literature, 1984. 44 pp. Available from BDFGA.

———. *The Compost Manufacturer's Manual.* Philadelphia, PA: The Pfeiffer Foundation, 1956. 137 pp.

*———. *Sensitive Crystallization Processes.* Spring Valley, NY: Anthroposophic Press, 1936. 59 pp.

*Philbrick, John, and Helen Philbrick. *Gardening for Health and Nutrition.* Blauvelt, NY: Rudolf Steiner Publications, 1971. 93 pp. **BL**

Podolinksy, Alex. *Bio-Dynamic Agriculture: Introductory Lectures, Vol. 1* and *Vol. 2.* Sydney, Australia: Gavemer, 1988. 190 pp. Available from BDFGA.

Sattler, Friedrich, and Eckard V. Wistinghausen. *Bio-Dynamic Farming Practice.* Sturbridge, England: Bio-Dynamic Agricultural Association, 1989. 333 pp.

Soper, John. *Studying the Agriculture Course.* London: Bio-Dynamic Agricultural Association, 1976. 88 pp. **AL**

*Steiner, Rudolf. *Agriculture—A Course of Eight Lectures.* London: Bio-Dynamic Agricultural Association, 1958. 175 pp. The basis of the biodynamic movement. **AL**

*Storl, Wolf. *Culture and Horticulture.* Wyoming, RI: Biodynamic Farming and Gardening Association, 1979. Biodynamics and organic agricultural history simply explained. Available from BDFGA.

The Voice of Demeter—Newsletter of the Demeter Association for Certification of Biodynamic Agriculture. Aurora, NY: The Demeter Association for Certification of Agriculture. Newsletter.

Biointensive

(see also GROW BIOINTENSIVE*)*

Agricultura Bio-Intensiva Sostenible en el Minifundio Mexicano. Universidad Autonoma Chapingo (Departmento de Suelos, Chapingo, Texcoco, Mexico).

B.I.G. Biointensive Gardening Cebuano. Silang, Cavite, Philippines: International Institute of Rural Reconstruction. Vol. III, No. 5.

B.I.G. Biointensive Gardening Tagalog. Silang, Cavite, Philippines: International Institute of

Rural Reconstruction. 32 pp. (2 languages)

The Biointensive Approach to Family Food Gardens. International Institute of Rural Reconstruction (1775 Broadway, New York, NY 10019). Information packet.

The Biointensive Approach to Small-Scale Household Food Production. Silang, Cavite, Philippines: The International Institute of Rural Reconstruction.

Biointensive Mini-Farming Information—Mexico. Ecopol. Av. Centenario, Edif. H10-1-2, Col. Lomas de Plateros, D.F. C.P. 01480, Mexico. Specializes in training. Excellent.

*Burck, Doug, and Sandra Mardigian. *A Journey in Kenya—Visiting Biointensive Farmers and Manor House Agricultural Centre.* Video.

Centre for Biointensive Agriculture. *Training and Demonstration Syllabus.* Kitale, Kenya: Manor House Agricultural Centre, 1996. 49 pp.

International Institute of Tropical Agriculture, 133 Dharmapala Mawatha, Columbo 7, Sri Lanka.

Martinez Valdez, Juan Manuel, and Dr. Francisco Alarcón Navarro. *Huertos Familiares.* Mexico: Academia de Investigacion en Demografía Médica (Edif H10-1-2, Col. Lomas de Plateros, D.F. C.P. 01480, Mexico), 1988. 116 pp. plus 24 slides. Very good.

*Seshadri, C. V. *Biodynamic Gardening: Monograph Series on Engineering of Photosynthetic Systems.* Vol. 4. Tharamani, Madras, India: Shri AMM Murugappa Chettier Research Center, 1980. 38 pp. Available from Ecology Action.

Sunset Editors. "Getting Started with the French Intensive Method." *Sunset,* September 1972, 168.

Calorie/Diet Crops

Beard, Benjamin H. "The Sunflower Crop." *Scientific American,* May 1981, 150–161.

Cox, Jeff. "The Sunflower Seed Huller and Oil Press." *Organic Gardening,* April 1979, 58–61.

Eames-Sheavly, Marcia. *The Great American Peanut.* Ithaca, NY: Cornell University Cooperative Extension, 1994. 20 pp.

Eames-Sheavly, Marcia and Tracy Farrell. *The Humble Potato—Underground Gold.* Cornell University Cooperative Extension, 1995. 40 pp.

Flores, Barbara. *The Great Sunflower Book.* Berkeley, CA: Ten Speed Press, 1997. 130 pp.

Graff, E. *Beet-Root Sugar and Cultivation of the Beet.* New York: Cornhill Press, 1880. 158 pp.

Harris. *The Sugar Beet in America.* New York: Macmillan.

Heiser, Charles B., Jr. *The Sunflower.* Norman, OK: University of Oklahoma Press, 1976. 198 pp.

Hurt, E. F. *Sunflower for Food, Fodder and Fertility.* London: Faber and Faber, 1946. 155 pp.

Kay, Daisy K. *Food Legumes.* Kent, U.K.: Natural Resource Institute (Central Ave., Chatherm, Maritime, Kent ME4 4TB, U.K.), 1979. 435 pp.

Pustovoit, V. S. *Handbook of Selection and Seed Growing of Oil Plants.* Jerusalem: Israel Program for Scientific Translations, 1973. 304 pp. Translated from Russian.

Willis, Dr. Harold. *How to Grow Super Soybeans.* Austin, TX: Acres U.S.A. (P.O. Box 91299, Austin, TX 78709), 1989. 48 pp.

Children's Books

Barrett, Judith. *Old MacDonald Had an Apartment House.* Atheneum, 1969.

Begley, Evelyn M. *The Little Red Hen.* Racine, WI: Golden Press, 1974.

Fryer, Lee, and Leigh Bradford. *A Child's Organic Garden.* Washington, DC: Acropolis Books, 1989. 88 pp.

*Ichikawa, Satomi and Elizabeth Laird. *Rosy's Garden—A Child's Keepsake of Flowers.* New York: Putnam and Grosset, 1990. 48 pp. Excellent.

Katzen, Mollie, and Ann Henderson.

Pretend Soup and Other Real Recipes. Berkeley, CA: Tricycle Press, 1994. 95 pp. Cookbook for preschoolers and up.

Krauss, Ruth. *The Carrot Seed.* New York: Harper Festival, 1993. 22 pp.

Main, Jody. *The Children's Garden (An organic gardening primer).* Woodside, CA: The Woodside School (3195 Woodside Rd.) and Jody Main (333 B Albion, Woodside, CA 94602), 1996. 53 pp.

Ocone, Lynne. *Guide to Kids' Gardening.* New York: John Wiley & Sons. 148 pp.

Paladino, Catherine. *One Good Apple—Growing Our Food for the Sake of the Earth.* Boston, MA: Houghton Mifflin, 1999. 48 pp.

Partridge, Jenny. *Lop Ear.* New York: Holt Rinehart and Winston, 1981.

Seymour, John. *John Seymour's Gardening Book (for Children).* London: G. Whizzard (105 Great Russell St., London WC1, England), 1978. 61 pp.

Climate

Thompson, Tim. "Where Have All the Clouds Gone?" *Southern Hemisphere*, Fall 1992, 40–43.

Communities

1995 National Directory of Conservational Land Trusts. Washington DC: Land Trust Alliance, 1995. 238 pp.

Bouvard, Marguerite. *The Intentional Community Movement: Building a New Moral World.* Port Washington, NY: National University Publications, Kennikat Press, 1975. 207 pp.

Caneff, Denny. *Sustaining Land, People, Animals, and Communities.* Washington, DC: Midwest Sustainable Agriculture Working Group (110 Maryland Ave., NE, Box 76, Washington, DC 20020), 1993. 26 pp.

"Cohousing." *Communities,* Spring 2000.

Communities. FIC (Rte. 1, Box 155-CM, Rutledge MO 63563). Magazine.

Communities Directory: A Guide to Intentional Communities and Cooperative Living, 2000 Edition. Rutledge, MO: Fellowship for International Community. (R.R. 1, Box 156-D, Rutledge, MO 63563), 2000. 456 pp.

Exchange. Washington, DC: The Land Trust Alliance (900 17th St. NW, Ste. 410, Washington, DC 20006-2596).

Gaia Trust and Context Institute. *Eco-Villages & Sustainable Communities.* Bainbridge Island, Washington: Context Institute (P.O. Box 11470, Bainbridge Island, WA 98110), 1991. 213 pp.

Gaia Trust and Findhorn Foundation. *Eco-Villages and Sustainable Communities.* Scotland: Findhorn Press, 1996. 95 pp.

Hanson, Chris. *The Cohousing Handbook.* Pt. Roberts, WA: Hartley and Marks Publishers (P.O. Box 147, Pt. Roberts, WA 98281), 1996. 278 pp.

Kinkade, Kathleen. *A Walden Two Experiment: The First Five Years of Twin Oaks Community.* New York: William Morrow, 1973. 271 pp.

Malakoff, David. "What Good Is Community Greening?" Philadelphia: American Community Gardening Association (100 N. 20th St., 5th Floor, Philadelphia, PA), 1995. 23 pp.

*McCamant, Kathryn, and Charles Durrett. *Cohousing.* Berkeley, CA: Ten Speed Press, 1988. 208 pp.

Morehouse, Ward, ed. *Building Sustainable Communities.* New York: The Bootstrap Press (Intermediate Technology Development Group of North America, Ste. 3C, 777 United Nations Plaza, New York, NY), 1997. 218 pp.

Norwood, Ken, and Kathleen Smith. *Rebuilding Community in America: Housing for Ecological Living, Personal Empowerment, and the New Extended Family.* Berkeley, CA: Shared Living Resource Center (2375 Shattuck Ave., Berkeley, CA 94704), 1995. 432 pp.

Payne, Karen, and Deborah Fryman. *Cultivating Community: Principles and Practices for Community Gardening as a Community-Building Tool.* Philadelphia: American Community Gardening Association (100 N. 20th St., 5th Floor, Philadelphia, PA), 2001. 56 pp.

Powell, G. Harold. *Co-Operation in Agriculture.* New York: Macmillan, 1918. 327 pp.

Starting a Land Trust. Washington, DC: The Land Trust Alliance, 1990. 175 pp.

Companion Planting

Allardice, Pamela. *A–Z of Companion Planting.* Pymble, Australia: Angus and Robertson, 1993. 208 pp.

*Carr, Anna. *Good Neighbors: Companion Planting for Gardeners.* Emmaus, PA: Rodale Press, 1985. 379 pp. A useful compilation of tradition, research, and practical gardening advice. Out of print. **BL**

Eames-Sheavly, Marcia. *The Three Sisters: Exploring an Iroquois Garden.* Ithaca, NY: Media Services (Cornell University), 1993. 20 pp.

Flowerdew, Bob. *Good Companions: A Guide to Gardening with Plants That Help Each Other.* New York: Summit Books, 1991. 96 pp.

Franck, Gertrud. *Companion Planting—Successful Gardening the Organic Way.* Wellingborough, Northamptonshire, England: Thorsons, 1983. 128 pp. Interesting systematic approach.

*Philbrick, Helen, and Richard B. Gregg. *Companion Plants and How to Use Them.* Old Greenwich, CT: Devin-Adair, 1966. 113 pp. **BL**

Ruttle, Jack. "The Tomato and Vetch Connection." *National Gardening,* July/August 1994, 44–47.

University of California Agriculture and Natural Resources. *Overseeding and Companion Cropping in Alfalfa.* Oakland, CA: Communication Services. (6701 San Pablo Ave., 2nd Floor, Oakland, CA), 2000. 31 pp.

Watts, Mag T. *Reading the Landscape of America.* New York: Collins Books, 1975. 354 pp.

Compost/Carbon/Fodder/ Organic Matter/Cover Crops

Ahlgren, Gilbert H. *Forage Crops.* New York: McGraw-Hill, 1942. 418 pp.

Anderson, Simon, et al. *Cover Crops in Smallholder Agriculture—Lessons from Latin America.* Southampton Row, London: ITDG, 2001. 136 pp.

Awang, Dr. D. V. C. "Herb Report: Comfrey." *American Herb Association Newsletter,* 1989, 6–7.

Ball, Carleton R. *The History and Distribution of Sorghum.* Washington, DC: Government Printing Office, 1910. 63 pp.

Biological Sciences Communication Project of the George Washington University. *Sorghum: A Bibliography of the World Literature.* Metuchen, NJ: The Scarecrow Press, 1967. 301 pp.

Buckles, D., et al., eds. *Cover Crops in West Africa Contributing to Sustainable Agriculture.* Ottawa, Canada: International Development Research Centre (P.O. Box 8500, Ottawa, ON, Canada), 1998. 291 pp.

Buckles, Daniel, Bernard Triomphe, and Gustavo Sain. *Cover Crops in Hillside Agriculture—Farmer Innovation with Mucuna.* Ottawa, Canada: International Development Research Centre, 1998. 218 pp.

Bunch, Roland. *The Use of Green Manures by Villager Farmers: What We Have Learned to Date.* CIDICCO Technical Report, July 1995. 8 pp.

CIDICCO. *Cover Crops News.* Tegucigalpa, Honduras: Centro Internacional de Informacion sobre Cultivos de Cobertura (Apartado Postal 3385, Tegucigalpa, M.D.C., Honduras C.A.). Quarterly newsletter. Miscellaneous articles. No. 3, n.d. 4 pp.

———. "Lablab Bean Use." No. 4, n.d. 4 pp.

———. "Management Practices to Work with Velvetbean." No. 5, n.d. 6 pp.

———. "The Utilization of Legumes in Traditional High Altitude Farming Systems." No. 6. August 1993. 8 pp.

———. "The Use of Legume Cover Crops in Orchards." No. 7. February 1994. 6 pp.

Clark, George. H., and M. Oscar Malte. *Fodder and Pasture Plants.* Ottawa, Canada: Department of Agriculture, 1913. 143 pp.

Clark, Wilson. "China's Green Manure Revolution." *Science 80,* September/October 1980.

Clover vs. Alfalfa for Milk Production. Bulletin 327. Wooster, Ohio: Ohio Agricultural Experiment Station, July 1918. 36 pp.

Coburn, F. D. *The Book of Alfalfa.* New York: Orange Judd, 1907. 344 pp.

"Cover Crops as Miracle Workers," *Sunset Magazine,* October 1989, 196-D.

Dickinson's Alfalfa Facts: Useful Guide for Growing Alfalfa. Chicago: Albert Dickinson Co., 1913. 48 pp.

Duggar, John. *Southern Forage Crops.* New York: Macmillan, 1925. 283 pp.

Evans, Ianto. *A Gardener's Guide to Fava Beans.* Eugene, Oregon: Fava Project/Gardeners Guide (549 Van Buren St.), 1992–1999. 58 pp.

Folmer, H. D. *Alfalfa on Wildwood Farm.* Columbus, OH: Nitschke Brothers, Printers. 1911. 105 pp.

Foster, Steven. "Comfrey—A Fading Romance." *The Herbal Companion,* February/March 1992, 50–55.

Grain Sorghum Date of Planting and Spacing Experiments. College Station, TX: Texas Agricultural Experiment Station, 1931. 71 pp.

Graves, Walter. *Legumes, Inoculation and Nitrogen Fixation: Understanding the Relationship.* San Diego: Cooperative Extension (University of California, Bldg. 4, 5555 Overland Ave., San Diego, CA 92123), July 1986.

Graves, Walter L., William A. Williams, and Craig D. Thomsen. *Berseem Clover: A Winter Annual Forage for California Agriculture.* Oakland, CA: Publication 21536,

University of California Communication Services—Publications, Division of Agriculture and Natural Resources (6701 San Pablo Ave., 2nd Floor), 1996. 12 pp.

Henry, W. A. *Feeds and Feeding: A Hand-Book for the Student and Stockman.* Madison, WI: Published by the author, 1910. 613 pp.

Hills, Lawrence D. *Comfrey.* New York: Universe, 1976. 253 pp.

Hitchcock, A. S. *Rape as a Forage Crop.* Washington, DC: U.S. Department of Agriculture, Farmers' Bulletin No. 164, Government Printing Office, 1903. 16 pp.

Hodgson, Harlow J. "Forage Crops." *Scientific American,* February 1976, 60–75.

Howard, Albert, and Yeshwant D. Wad. *The Waste Products of Agriculture.* NY: Humphrey Milford Oxford University Press, 1931. 167 pp.

Hughes, H. D., Maurice E. Heath, and Darrel Metcalfe. *Forages.* Ames, IA: Iowa State College Press, 1951. 724 pp.

Hunter, Peter J. P. *Hunters Guide to Grasses, Clovers, and Weeds.* Chester, England: James Hunter, 80 pp.

Jeavons, John, and Bill Bruneau. "Green Manure Crops." *Mother Earth News,* September/October 1986, 42–45.

Knowles, Paul F., and Milton D. Miller. *Safflower.* Circular 532. Davis, CA: California Agricultural Extension Services, 1965. 51 pp.

Koepf, Herbert H., Scott M. Schreiber, and Michael Fields Agricultural Institute. "Forage Based Farming, Manure Handling and Farm Composting." *Bulletin No. 4.* East Troy, WI: Michael Fields Agricultural Institute (W2493 County Rd. ES, East Troy, WI 53120), 1993. 48 pp.

Kuepper, George. *Sweet Sorghum—Production and Processing.* Poteau, OK: Kerr Center for Sustainable Agriculture, 1994. 95 pp.

Lewis, Rebecca, et al. *Making Pastures Produce.* Emmaus, PA: Rodale Press, 1980. 43 pp.

The Management of Napier Grass. Zero Grazing Series Vol. 3. Nairobi, Kenya: Ministry of Livestock Development, National Dairy Development Project (P.O. Box 34188, Nairobi, Kenya). 18 pp.

Managing Cover Crops Profitably. Beltsville, MD: Sustainable Agriculture Network, 1998. 212 pp.

McLeod, Edwin. *Feed the Soil.* Graton, CA: Organic Agriculture Research Institute, 1982. 209 pp.

*Morrison, Frank B. *Feeds and Feeding*, 22nd edition. Ithaca, NY: Morrison, 1957. 1,165 pp.

*Murphy, Bill. *Greener Pastures on Your Side of the Fence—Better Farming with Voisin Grazing Management.* Colchester, VT: Arriba, 1991. 298 pp.

Orloff, Steve B., and Harry L. Carlson, eds. *Intermountain Alfalfa Management.* Oakland, CA: Publication 3366, University of California Communication Services—Publications, Division of Agriculture and Natural Resources (6701 San Pablo Ave., 2nd Floor, Oakland, CA), 1997. 138 pp.

Piper, Charles V. *Forage Plants and Their Culture.* New York: Macmillan, 1924. 671 pp.

Rather, Howard C. *Field Crops.* New York: McGraw-Hill, 1942. 454 pp.

Sarrantonio, Marianne. *Soil-Improving Legumes, Methodologies for Screening.* Kutztown, PA: Rodale Institute, 1991. 312 pp.

Schmid, Otto, et al. *Green Manuring, Principles and Practice.* Mt. Vernon, ME: Woods End Agricultural Institute (RFD 1, Box 4040, Mt. Vernon, ME 04357), 1984. 50 pp.

Shaw, Thomas. *Clovers and How to Grow Them.* New York: Orange Judd, 1922. 349 pp.

Sheaffer, Craig, et al. *Forage Legumes: Clovers, Birdsfoot Trefoil, Cicer Milkvetch, Crownvetch, Sainfoin, and Alfalfa.* St. Paul, MN: University of Minnesota Agricultural Experiment Station, 1993. 40 pp.

Shurtleff, William, and Akiko Aoyagi. *The Book of Kudzu—A Culinary and Healing Guide.* Wayne, NJ: Avery, 1985. 102 pp.

Snook, Laurence C. *Tagasaste (Tree Lucerne): High Production Fodder Crop.* Shepparton, New Zealand: Night Owl, 1986. 102 pp. Temperate "living terracing" crop.

U.S. Department of Agriculture. *Farmers' Bulletin No. 1731, Alfalfa Varieties in the United States.* Washington, DC: U.S. Government Printing Office, 1940. 13 pp.

———. *Farmers' Bulletin No. 1539, High-Grade Alfalfa Hay.* Washington, DC: U.S. Government Printing Office, 1939. 29 pp.

———. *Farmers' Bulletin No. 1770, High-Grade Timothy and Clover Hay.* Washington, DC: U.S. Government Printing Office, 1937. 16 pp.

———. *Farmers' Bulletin No. 1126, Sudan Grass.* Washington, DC: U.S. Government Printing Office, 1940. 24 pp.

———. *Technical Bulletin No. 352, Sudan Grass as Hay, Silage, and Pasture for Dairy Cattle.* Washington, DC: U.S. Government Printing Office, 1933. 28 pp.

———. *Technical Bulletin No. 506, Identification, History, and Distribution of Common Sorghum Varieties.* Washington, DC: U.S. Government Printing Office, 1936. 102 pp.

Vinall, H. N., J. C. Stephens, and J. H. Martin. *U.S. Department of Agriculture Technical Bulletin No. 506. Identification, History, and Distribution of Common Sorghum Varieties,* July 1936.

*Voisin, Andre. *Better Grassland Sward.* London: Crosby Lockwood & Son (26 Old Brompton Rd., London SW7, England), 1960. 340 pp. A unique approach to greatly increased fodder production. **IL**

*———. *Grass Productivity.* New York: Philosophical Library (15 E. 40th St., New York, NY 10016), 1959. 353 pp. **IL**

Willis, Dr. Harold. *How to Grow Great Alfalfa.* Madison, WI: A-R Editions, 1983. 42 pp.

Wrightson, John. *Fallow and Fodder Crops.* London: Chapman & Hall, Limited, 1989. 276 pp.

Composting

Alther, Richard, and Richard O. Raymond. *Improving Garden Soil with Green Manures.* Charlotte, VT: Garden Way, 1974. 44 pp. Contains a good 2-page chart.

Cox, Jeff. "What You Should Know about Nitrogen." *Organic Gardening and Farming,* June 1972, 69–94. See also insert on page 68.

Darwin, Charles. *Darwin on Humus and the Earthworm.* London: Faber and Faber, 1945. 153 pp.

*Denison, William C. "Life in Tall Trees." *Scientific American,* June 1973, 75–80.

Golueke, Clarence G. *Composting: A Study of the Process and Its Principles.* Emmaus, PA: Rodale Press, 1972. 110 pp. For those with an advanced interest.

Gotaas, Harold B. *Composting, Sanitary Disposal and Reclamation of Organic Wastes.* Geneva, Switzerland: World Health Organization, 1956. 205 pp.

*"Is Too Much Compost Harmful?" in *The Complete Book of Composting.* Emmaus, PA: Rodale Press, 1960, 386–392. **BL**

Martin, Deborah L., and Grace Gershuny, eds. *The Rodale Book of Composting—Easy Methods for Every Gardener.* Emmaus, PA: Rodale Press, 1992. 278 pp.

McGarey, Michael G., and Jill Stainforth, eds. *Compost, Fertilizer, and Biogas Production from Human and Farm Wastes in the People's Republic of China.* Ottawa, Canada: International Development Research Centre, 1978. 94 pp.

Minnich, Jerry, et al. *The Rodale Guide to Composting.* Emmaus, PA: Rodale Press, 1979. 405 pp.

Raabe, Robert D. *The Rapid Composting Method.* Berkeley, CA: California Cooperative Extension Service, 1981. 4 pp.

Rynk, Robert, et al. *On Farm Composting Handbook.* Ithaca, NY: Northeast Regional Agricultural Engineering Service (152 Riley-Robb Hall, Cooperative Extension, Ithaca, NY 14853-5701), 1992. 186 pp.

Soucie, Gary. "How You Gonna Keep It Down on the Farm." *Audubon,* September 1972, 112–115.

Urban Home Composing, Rodent-Resistant Bins, and Environmental Health Standards. City Farmer. Vancouver, Canada: Canada's Office of Urban Agriculture (318 Homer St., Ste. 801, Vancouver, BC V6B 2V3, Canada), 1991. 36 pp.

Container Gardening

*Newcomb, Duane. *The Apartment Farmer: The Hassle-Free Way to Grow Vegetables Indoors, on Balconies, Patios, Roofs, and in Small Yards.* New York: Avon Books, 1976. 154 pp. Excellent. **BL**

Stevens, Elaine. *The Creative Container Gardener.* Berkeley, CA: Ten Speed Press, 1995. 216 pp.

Cookbooks

Adams, Margaret Byrd. *American Wood Heat Cookery.* Seattle, WA: Pacific Search Press, 1984. 250 pp.

Brown, Edward Espe. *The Tassajara Bread Book.* Boston: Shambhala Books, 1986. 146 pp.

Costenbader, Carol W. *Mustards, Ketchups and Vinegars.* Pownal, VT: Storey, 1996. 96 pp.

Courter, Gay. *The Beansprout Book.* New York: Simon & Schuster, 1973. 96 pp.

Creasy, Rosalind. *Cooking from the Garden.* San Francisco: Sierra Club Books, 1988. 547 pp.

Crowhurst, Adrienne. *The Weed Cookbook.* New Jersey: Lancer Books, 1973. 198 pp.

———. *The Flower Cookbook.* New York: Lancer Books, 1973. 198 pp.

Diamond, Marilyn. *The American Vegetarian Cookbook.* New York: Warner Books, 1990. 422 pp.

Drückler, Sabine. *Grain Food for Sustainable Living Power.* Kaiwaka, New Zealand: Pukahukahu Press (Otamatea Eco Village RD 2, Kaiwaka, Northland, New Zealand). 63 pp. Good beginning for grain-based diets.

Fabricant, Florence. *Elizabeth Berry's Great Bean Book.* Berkeley, CA: Ten Speed Press, 1999. 129 pp.

Gerras, Charles, ed. *Rodale's Basic Natural Foods Cookbook.* New York: Simon & Schuster, 1989. 899 pp.

Graf, Emma. *Cooking with Grains.* Stroud, U.K.: InterActions, 1996. 128 pp.

Greene, Bert. *The Grains Cookbook.* New York: Workman, 1988. 410 pp.

Hagler, Louise, and Dorothy R. Bates. *The New Farm Vegetarian Cookbook.* Summertown, TN: Book Publishing Co., 1988. 219 pp.

———. *The Farm Vegetarian Cookbook.* Summertown, TN: Book Publishing Co., 1978. 219 pp.

Haynes, Linda. *The Vegetarian Lunchbasket.* Willow Springs, MO: Nucleus Publications, 1990. 198 pp.

Hewitt, Jean. *The New York Times Natural Foods Cookbook.* New York: Avon Books, 1971. 434 pp.

Homemade Olive Oil. University of California: Division of Agricultural Sciences, 1977. Leaflet #2789.

Hurd, Frank J. *Ten Talents.* Collegedale, TN: College Press, 1985. 368 pp.

Jason, Dan, and Paul Ingraham. *Salt Spring Seeds Garlic Book.* Salt Spring Island, BC: Lightning Press, 1996. 87 pp.

Katzen, Mollie. *The Moosewood Cookbook.* Berkeley, CA: Ten Speed Press, 1977. 240 pp. Tasty recipes for lots of fresh vegetables.

———. *The Enchanted Broccoli Forest.* Berkeley, CA: Ten Speed Press, 1982. 320 pp.

———. *Still Life with Menu.* Berkeley, CA: Ten Speed Press, 1988. 350 pp.

McCarty, Meredith. *Fresh: From a Vegetarian Kitchen.* Eureka, CA: Turning Point Publications, 1989. Unique cookbook of vegetarian whole foods.

*McDougall, John A., and Mary A. McDougall. *The McDougall Plan*. Clinton, NJ: New Win (P.O. Box 5159, Clinton, NJ 08809), 1983. 340 pp.

McKay, G. L., and C. Larsen. *Principles and Practice of Butter-Making*. New York: John Wiley & Sons, 1908. 351 pp.

Moosewood Staff. *New Recipes from Moosewood Restaurant*. Berkeley, CA: Ten Speed Press, 1987. 302 pp.

Morash, Marian. *The Victory Garden Cookbook*. New York: Knopf, 1982. 374 pp. **IL**

Munroe, Esther. *Sprouts to Grow and Eat*. Brattleboro, VT: The Stephen Greene Press, 1974. 119 pp.

Nearing, Helen. *Simple Food for the Good Life*. White River Junction, VT: Chelsea Green, 1999. 309 pp.

Niethammer, Carolyn J. *The Tumbleweed Gourmet: Cooking with Wild Southwestern Plants*. Tucson, AZ: The University of Arizona Press, 1987. 229 pp.

Pickarski, Brother Ron. *Friendly Foods*. Berkeley, CA: Ten Speed Press, 1991. 277 pp.

Proulx, Annie, and Lew Nichols. *Cider: Making, Using & Enjoying Sweet & Hard Cider*. Pownal, VT: Storey, 1997. 219 pp.

Robertson, Laurel, et al. *New Laurel's Kitchen*. Berkeley, CA: Ten Speed Press, 1986. 512 pp. **BL**

———. *The Laurel's Kitchen Bread Book*. New York: Random House, 1984. 447 pp. **BL**

Saltzman, Joanne. *Amazing Grains—Creating Vegetarian Main Dishes with Whole Grains*. Novato, CA: New World Library (14 Pamaron Way, Novato, CA 94948), 1990. 202 pp.

Santa Clara County Planned Parenthood. *Zucchini Cookbook*. Santa Cruz, CA: Planned Parenthood (421 Ocean St., Santa Cruz, CA 95060).

*Sass, Lorna J. *Recipes from an Ecological Kitchen*. New York: William Morrow, 1992. 492 pp.

Sibbett, G. Steven and Joseph Connell. *Producing Olive Oil in California*. Butte & Tulare Co. Farm Advisors, 1991. 19 pp.

Simmons, Paula. *Zucchini Cookbook*. Seattle, WA: Pacific Search, 1974. 127 pp.

Stepaniak, Joanne. *The Nutritional Yeast Cookbook*. Summertown, TN: Book Publishing Co., 1997. 143 pp.

Stowe, Sally and Martin. *The Brilliant Bean*. New York: Bantam, 1988. 276 pp.

Turner, Kristina. *The Self Healing Cookbook*, 4th edition. Vashon Island, WA: Earthtones Press (P.O. Box 411, Vashon Island, WA 98070), 1989. Excellent, simple introduction to natural foods cooking and healing.

Wagner, Lindsey, and Ariane Spade. *The High Road to Health*. New York: Simon & Schuster, 1994. 287 pp.

Wasserman, Debra. *Simply Vegan—Quick Vegetarian Meals*. Baltimore: The Vegetarian Resource Group (P.O. Box 1463, Baltimore, MD 21203), 1991. 224 pp.

Wing, Daniel, and Alan Scott. *The Bread Builders—Hearth Loaves and Masonry Ovens*. White River Junction, VT: Chelsea Green, 1999. 253 pp.

Woodruff, Sandra. *Secrets of Fat-Free Baking*. Garden City Park, NY: Avery, 1994. 232 pp.

Crafts

Ben Hunt's Big Indiancraft Book. New York: Bruce Publishing, 1945.

Bliss, Anne. *North American Dye Plants*. Boulder, CO: Juniper House, 1986. 288 pp.

Brill, Edith. *Cotswald Crafts*. Exeter, Great Britain: A. Wheaton, 1977. 184 pp.

Buchanan, Rita. *A Dyer's Garden—From Plant to Pot, Growing Dyes for Natural Fibers*. Loveland, CO: Interweave Press, 1995. 112 pp.

Cary, Mara. *Useful Baskets*. Boston: Houghton Mifflin, 1977. 132 pp.

Daugherty, Robin Taylor. *Splint-woven Basketry*. Loveland, CO: Interweave Press, 1986. 160 pp.

Dyer, Anne, Lettice Sandford, and Zena Edwards. *Country Crafts*. London: Book Club Associates, 1979. 133 pp.

Editors of *The American Agriculturist*. *Broom-Corn and Brooms*. New York: Orange Judd, 1906. 59 pp.

Hiebert, Helen. *Papermaking with Plants*. Pownal, VT: Storey, 1998. 107 pp.

———. *The Papermaker's Companion: The Ultimate Guide to Making and Using Handmade Paper*. Pownal, VT: Storey, 2000. 219 pp.

Jenkins, J. Geraint. *Traditional Country Craftsmen*. Boston, MA: Routledge & Kegan Paul, 1978. 253 pp.

———. *Traditional Country Craftsmen*. London: Routledge & Kegan Paul Limited (Broadway House, 68–74 Carter Ln., E.C., England), 1965. 236 pp.

Jensen, Elizabeth. *Baskets from Nature's Bounty*. Loveland, OR: Interweave Press, 1991. 197 pp.

Keville, Kathi. "Soap—What It Is and How to Make It." *Vegetarian Times/Well-Being Magazine*, 1981. Issue #52.

———. "How to Make Tooth Powder, Toothpaste and Mouthwash." *Vegetarian Times/Well-Being Magazine*, 1981. Issue #53.

Langsner, Drew. *Country Woodcraft*. Emmaus, PA: Rodale Press, 1978. 304 pp.

———. *Green Woodworking*. Asheville, NC: Lark Books, 1995. 176 pp.

Langsner, Drew and Louise. *Handmade*. New York: Harmony Books, 1974. 192 pp.

Long, Jim. *Making Bent Wood Trellises, Arbors, Gates and Fences*. Pownal, VT: Storey, 1998. 155 pp.

Mack, Daniel. *Making Rustic Furniture*. New York: Sterling, 1992. 160 pp.

Newsholme, Christopher. *Willows: The Genus Salix*. London: B. T. Batsford (4 Fitzhardinge St., London W1H OAH, England), 1992. 224 pp.

Oppenheimer, Betty. *Gifts for Herb Lovers*. Pownal, VT: Storey, 1997. 123 pp.

Rudge, Geraldine. *Garden Crafts—A Practical Guide to Creating Hand-Crafted Features for Your Garden*. New York: The Lyons Press, 1999. 144 pp.

Ruoff, Abby. *Making Twig Furniture*. Roberts, WA: Hartley & Marks Publishers, 1991. 243 pp.

Seymour, John. *The Forgotten Crafts: A Practical Guide to Traditional Skills*. New York: Random House, 1984. 192 pp.

Stiles, David and Jeanie. *Garden Retreats—A Build-It-Yourself Guide*. Pownal, VT: Storey, 1999. 155 pp.

Van Straten, Trudy. *Indigo, Madder, and Marigold—A Portfolio of Colors from Natural Dyes*. Loveland, CO: Interweave Press, 1993. 127 pp.

Verdet-Fierz, Bernard and Regula. *Willow Basketry*. Loveland, CO: Interweave Press, 1993. 355 pp.

White, Elaine C. *Super Formulas Arts and Crafts*. Brandon, MS: Quail Ridge Press (P.O. Box 1223, Brandon, MS), 1993. 114 pp.

Woodwork Magazine. 42 Digital Dr., #5, Novato, CA 94949.

Development

Alternatives to the Peace Corps, A Directory of Third World and U.S. Volunteer Opportunities, 9th edition. Oakland, CA: Food First Books, 2000. 116 pp. **BL**

Altieri, Miguel A. *Latin American Institutions Conducting Research, Training, and Development Activities in Sustainable Agriculture*. Albany, CA: University of California (Division of Biological Control, 1050 San Pablo Ave., Albany, CA 94706). 46 pp.

Amigos Handbook. Houston, TX: Amigos de las Americas (5618 Star Ln., Houston TX 77057), 1970s.

Arbab, Farzam. *Rural University, Learning about Education and Development*. Ottawa, Canada: International Development Research Center (Box 8500, Ottawa, Canada), 1984. 71 pp.

Benor, Daniel, and James Q. Harrison. *Agricultural Extension: The Training and Visit System*. Washington, DC: World Bank, 1977. 55 pp.

Bradfield, D. J. *Guide to Extension Training*. Rome, Italy: Food and Agriculture Organization of the United Nations, 1966. 176 pp.

Brusko, Michael, ed. *Proceedings of Workshop on Resource-Efficient Farming Methods for Tanzania*. Emmaus, PA: Rodale Press, 1983. 128 pp.

*Bunch, Roland. *Two Ears of Corn—A Guide to People-Centered Agricultural Improvement*. Oklahoma City: World Neighbors (5116 N. Portland, Oklahoma City, OK 73112), 1982. 251 pp. **BL**

Clark, Colin, and Margaret Haswell. *The Economics of Subsistence Agriculture*. Glasgow, U.K.: The University Press, 1970. 267 pp.

CODEL. *Integration of Programs for Managing Renewable Natural Resources for Human Development, Report on Workshop Seminar San Jose de Ocoa, D.R. Jan. 29–Feb. 3, 1984*. Environment and Development Program, 1984. 47 pp. Also available in Spanish.

———. *People's Participation in Development and the Management of Natural Resources, Report on the Caribbean Regional Workshop in Vieux Fort, St. Lucia April 15–19, 1985*. Environment and Development Program, 1985. 42 pp.

*Darrow, Ken, et al. *Trans-Cultural Study Guide*. Stanford, CA: Volunteers in Asia (Box 4543, Stanford, CA 94305), 1981. 155 pp. **BL**

*Edwards, Michael. *Arriving Where We Started*. London: Voluntary Service Overseas (9 Belgrave Square, London, England), 1983. 208 pp. **BL**

*Fantini, Alvino E., ed. *Cross-Cultural Orientation*. Brattleboro, VT: The Experiment in International Living (P.O. Box 676, Brattleboro, VT 05301), 1984. 115 pp. **BL**

Gliessman, Stephen, and Robert Grantham. "Agroecology—Reshaping Agricultural Development," from Head, Suzanne and Robert Heinzman, eds., *Lessons of the Rainforest*, Sierra Club Books, 1990, 196–207 and 266.

IMSS. *Catálogo de actividades de acción comunitaria*. Mexico City, Mexico: Instituto Mexicano del Seguro Social (Paseo de la Reforma 476, D.F. C.P. 0600, Mexico), 1984. 386 pp.

Kann, Peter R. "The Food Crisis." *The Wall Street Journal*. November 18, 1974, 1, 14.

Kohr, Leopold. *Development Without Aid: The Translucent Society*. New York: Schocken, 1973. 226 pp.

Office of Technology Assessment Workshop November 24–25, 1980. *Background Papers for Innovative Biological Technologies for Lesser Developed Countries*. Washington, DC: U.S. Government Printing Office, 1981. 511 pp.

Pradervand, Pierre. *Listening to Africa: Developing Africa from the Grassroots*. New York: Praeger Publishers (One Madison Ave., New York, NY 10010), 1989. 229 pp.

Roberts, Glyn. *Handbook for Development Workers Overseas*. Alverstoke, Hampshire: The Alver Press, 1978. 43 pp.

Rosset, Peter, and Medea Benjamin, eds. *Greening of the Revolution: Cuba's Experiment with Organic Agriculture*. San Francisco: Global Exchange (2017 Mission St., Rm. 303, San Francisco, CA 94110).

Sachs, Wolfgang, ed. *The Development Dictionary: A Guide to Knowledge as Power*. Atlantic Highlands, NJ: Zed Books, 1992. 306 pp.

Seymour, John. *La Vida en al Campo y e Horticultur Autosuficiente*. Libro Blume, 1976. 256 pp.

Slider, Ronald J. *Rich Christians in an Age of Hunger*. Downers Grove, IL: Inter-Varsity Press, 1980. 249 pp.

Smith, Marney. *Growing Your Own Food.* Westport, CT: Save the Children Federation (48 Wilton Rd., Westport, CT 06880), 1980. 35 pp.

Toledo, Victor Manuel. *Ecologia y Autosuficiencia Alimentaria.* Mexico Espana Argentina Colombia: Siglo Veintiuno Editores, 1985. 118 pp.

United Nations Development Programme. *Human Development Report—1990.* New York: Oxford University Press, 1990. 189 pp.

———. *Sustainable Human Development and Agriculture.* New York: UNDP Bureau for Program Policy and Evaluation, 1994. 92 pp.

*van den Bor, Wout. *The Art of Beginning.* Pudoc, Wageningen: Centre for Agricultural Publishing and Documentation, 1983. 174 pp. **BL**

Volunteers in Technical Assistance. *Village Technology Handbook.* Mt. Rainier, MD: VITA, 1977. 387 pp.

*Wade, Isabel. *City Food: Crop Selection in Third World Cities.* San Francisco: Urban Resource Systems (783 Buena Vista W., San Francisco, CA 94117), 1986. 54 pp.

*"Wasteful North," *World View Magazine,* Spring 1992, 17.

Weisman, Alan. *Gaviotas: A Village to Reinvent the World.* White River Junction, VT: Chelsea Green, 1998. 227 pp.

Winblad, Uno. *The Productive Homestead: A Report of a Study Tour.* Sweden: Winblad Konsult AB (Pataholm 5503, 384 92 ALEM, Sweden), 1992. 16 pp.

World Neighbors. Oklahoma City: World Neighbors (54127 NW 122 St., Oklahoma City, OK 73120-8869).

Energy

Center for Renewable Energy and Sustainable Technology. *Energy Stories* CD-ROM. Washington, DC: Crest, 1999.

Clark, Wilson. "U.S. Agriculture Is Growing Trouble as Well as Crops." *Smithsonian,* January 1975. **BL**

Dazhong, W., and D. Pimental. *Energy Flow through an Organic Agro-ecosystem in China.* 1984, 145–160.

———. "Energy Use in Crop Systems in Northeastern China," in *Food and Energy Resources,* D. Pimentel and C. W. Hall, eds. New York: Academic Press, 1984, 91–120.

MacPherson, George. *Home-Grown Energy from Short-Rotation Coppice.* Ipswich, U.K.: Farming Press, 1995. 214 pp.

*Odum, Howard T., and Elisabeth C. Odum. *Energy Basis for Man and Nature.* New York: McGraw-Hill, 1976. 297 pp. **IL**

*Perelman, Michael J. "Efficiency and Agriculture." Economics Department, Chico State College, Chico, CA.

*———. "Farming with Nature." *Environment,* Vol. 14, No. 8, 1972. **BL**

*———. "Farming with Petroleum." *Environment,* October 1972, 8–13. **BL**

*Perelman, Michael J., and Kevin P. Shea. "The Big Farm." *Environment,* December 1972, 10–15. **BL**

Pimentel, David, et al. "Energy and Land Constraints in Food Protein Production." *Science,* Vol. 190, November 1975, 754–761.

Pimentel, David, and E. Heichel. "Energy Efficiency and Sustainability of Farming Systems," in *Soil Management for Sustainability,* R. Lal and F. J. Pierce, eds. Ankeny, IA: Ankeny, IA: Soil and Water Conservation Society (7515 NE Ankeny Rd., Ankeny, IA 50021), 1991, 113–123.

———. "Energy Flow in Agroecosystems," in *Agricultural Ecosystems Unifying Concepts,* R. Lawrance, et al., eds. New York: John Wiley & Sons, 1984, 121–132.

———. "Energy Flow in the Food System," in *Food and Energy Resources,* D. Pimentel and C. W. Hall, eds. New York: Academic Press, 1984, 1–24.

———. "Energy Use in Cereal Grain Production," in *Energy Use Management Vol. 1,* R. A. Fazzoare and C. B. Smith, eds. New York: Permagon Press, 1977, 759–767.

Pimentel, David, and E. C. Terhune. "Energy Use in Food Production."

———. "Energy and Food." *Annual Review of Energy,* 1977, 171–195.

Farming

Ableman, Michael. *On Good Land: The Autobiography of an Urban Farm.* San Francisco: Chronicle Books, 1998. 144 pp.

Ashley, John. *Food Crops and Drought.* London and Basingstoke, U.K.:, 1999. 133 pp.

Bailey, L. H. *Principles of Agriculture.* New York: Macmillan, 1909. 336 pp.

Bromfield, Louis. *Malabar Farm.* New York: Ballantine Books, 1970. 470 pp.

Cavigelli, M. A., et al., eds. *Michigan Field Crop Ecology: Managing Biological Processes for Productivity and Environmental Quality.* Michigan State University Extension Bulletin E-2646, 1998. 92 pp.

Cocannouer, Joseph A. *Farming with Nature.* Norman, OK: University of Oklahoma Press, 1954. 147 pp.

Cox, Joseph F., and Lyman Jackson. *Field Crops and Land Use.* New York: John Wiley & Sons, 1942. 473 pp.

Dorf, P. *Liberty Hyde Bailey: An Informal Biography.* Ithaca, NY: Cornell University Press, 1956. 257 pp.

"Facing the Farm Crisis." *The Ecologist, Special Supplement.* June 2000.

Gliessman, Stephen R., et al. *Agroecology.* New York: Springer-Verlag (175 5th Ave., New York, NY 10010), 1990. 380 pp.

Gregson, Bob and Bonnie. *Rebirth of the Small Family Farm: A Handbook for Starting a Successful Organic Farm Based on the Community Supported Agriculture Concept.* Vashon Island, WA: IMF Associates (P.O. Box 2542, Vashon Island, WA 98070), 1996. 63 pp.

Hainsworth, P. H. *Agriculture— The Only Right Approach.* Pauma Valley, CA: Bargyla and Gylver Rateaver, 1976. 238 pp.

Hallberg, Milton C. *Economic Trends in U.S. Agriculture and Food Systems Since World War II.* Ames, Iowa: Iowa State University Press, 2001. 179 pp.

Kinsey, Neal. *Hands-On Agronomy.* Austin, TX: Acres U.S.A. (P.O. Box 91299, Austin, TX 78709), 1993. 352 pp.

Lampkin, Nicolas. *Organic Farming.* Ipswich, U.K.: Farming Press, 1998. 715 pp.

Logsdon, Gene. *The Contrary Farmer.* White River Junction, VT: Chelsea Green, 1994. 237 pp.

Masumoto, David Mas. *Harvest Son.* New York: W. W. Norton, 1998. 302 pp.

Medvedev, Zhores. *Soviet Agriculture.* New York: W. W. Norton, 1987. 464 pp.

Multiple Cropping Systems. Groenken, The Netherlands: AME Foundation (Groenekanseweg 90, 3737 AH Groenken, The Netherlands), 1985. 19 pp.

Mutsaers, H. J. W., et al. *A Field Guide for On-Farm Experimentation.* International Institute of Tropical Agriculture, 1997. 235 pp.

Myase, Ann D. *Sustainable Farming Systems: A Guide to the Transition.* Davis, CA: Sustainable Agriculture Research and Education Program (1 Shields Ave., University of CA, Davis, CA), 1997. 81 pp.

Nearing, Helen. *Loving and Living the Good Life.* White River Junction, VT: Chelsea Green, 1992. 194 pp.

Organic Farming in Kenya. Nairobi, Kenya: Kenya Institute of Organic Farming (P.O. Box 34972, Nairobi, Kenya) and CODEL, 1990. 80 pp.

Pimentel, David. *Agriculture and EcoTechnology.* Ithaca, NY: Department of Entomology, Cornell University, 1989.

———. *Agriculture, Technology, and Natural Resources.* Ithaca, NY: Department of Entomology, Cornell University.

Pretty, Jules N. *Regenerating Agriculture.* Washington, DC: Joseph Henry Press, 1995. 320 pp.

Reijntjes, Coen, Bertus Haverkort, and Ann Waters-Bayer. *Farming for the Future.* Leusden, The Netherlands: ILEIA (P.O. Box 64, NL-3830 AB Leusden, The Netherlands), 1992. 250 pp.

*Revelle, Roger. "The Resources Available for Agriculture." *Scientific American,* September 1976, 165–176.

Schafer, Kristin S., ed. *Learning from the BIOS Approach.* Davis, CA: World Resources Institute. 35 pp.

Singles in Agriculture. P.O. Box 7, Pearl City, IL 61062.

Soule, Judith D., and Jon K. Piper. *Farming in Nature's Image.* Covelo, CA: Island Press (P.O. Box 7, Covelo, CA 95428), 1992. 286 pp.

Strange, Marty. *Family Farming: A New Economic Vision.* Lincoln, NE: University of Nebraska Press, 1988. 311 pp.

Sykes, Friend. *Humus and the Farmer.* Emmaus, PA: Rodale Press, 1949. 392 pp.

———. *Food, Farming and the Future.* Emmaus, PA: Rodale Press, 1951. 293 pp.

U.S. Department of Agriculture National Commission on Small Farms. *A Time to Act.* Washington, DC: USDA, 1998. 121 pp.

U.S. Department of Agriculture. *Report and Recommendations on Organic Farming.* Washington, DC: Office of Governmental and Public Affairs, USDA (Washington, DC 20205), 1980. 94 pp.

Volin, Lazar. *A Survey of Soviet Russian Agriculture.* Washington, DC: U.S. Department of Agriculture, 1951. 194 pp.

Walters, Charles, Jr., and C. J. Fenzau. *Eco-Farm: An Acres U.S.A. Primer.* Austin, TX: Acres U.S.A. (P.O. Box 91299, Austin, TX 78709), 1996. 447 pp.

Warren, G. F. *Farm Management.* New York: Macmillan, 1922. 590 pp.

Wilken, Gene C. *Good Farmers.* London: University of California Press, 1987. 302 pp.

Williams, Allan N., and Neville Graham, *The Small Farmers' Guide to Alternative Farming Techniques.* Belmont, Port of Spain, Trinidad and Tobago, and Roseau, Commonwealth of Dominica: ACT Press, 1998. 61 pp.

Wittwer, Sylvan, et al. *Feeding a Billion—Frontiers of Chinese Agriculture.* East Lansing, MI: Michigan State University Press, 1987. 462 pp.

Wortman, Sterling. "Food and Agriculture." *Scientific American,* September 1976, 31–39.

Zimmer, Gary F. *The Biological Farmer.* Austin, TX: Acres U.S.A., 2000. 352 pp.

Fertilizer

Chemical Periodic Table, Permachart. Concord, Canada: Papertech Marketing Group (163 Buttermill Ave., Unit 12, Concord, ON L4K 3X8, Canada). Helpful for better understanding of soil nutrient exchange.

Ingham, Elaine R. "Brewing Compost Tea." *Kitchen Gardener,* October/November 2000, 16–19.

The New Farm Staff, eds. *The Farmer's Fertilizer Handbook.* Emmaus, PA: Rodale Institute, 1986. 208 pp.

Norman, Cynthia, "Dung Ho." *National Gardening,* May 1987, 28–30.

Organic Soil Amendments and Fertilizers. Publications Division of Agriculture and Natural Resources, University of California (6701 San Pablo Ave., Oakland, CA 94608-1239), 1992. 36 pp.

Pettersson, B. D., and E. V. Wistinghausen. *Effects of Organic and Inorganic Fertilizers on Soils and Crops.* Temple, ME: Woods End Agricultural Institute (Orchard Hill Rd., Temple, ME 04984), 1979. 44 pp. **AL**

Shirley, Christopher, and The New Farm Staff, eds. *What Really Happens When You Cut Chemicals?* Emmaus, PA: Rodale Institute, 1993. 156 pp.

Tandon, Dr. H. L. S. *Fertilizer Management in Rainfed Dryland Agriculture—A Guidebook.* New Delhi: Fertiliser Development and Consultation Organisation (204-204A Bhanot Corner, 1-2 Pamposh Enclave, New Delhi-110048, India), 1993. 103 pp.

Tisdale, Samuel L., and Werner L. Nelson. *Soil Fertility and Fertilizers.* New York: Macmillan, 1956. 634 pp.

Van Slyke, Lucius. *Fertilizers and Crop Production.* New York: Orange Judd, 1932. 193 pp.

Fiber Crops

Baines, Patricia. *Linen: Hand Spinning and Weaving.* London: B. T. Batsford, 1989. 208 pp.

Buchanan, Rita. *A Weaver's Garden.* Loveland, CO: Interweave Press, 1987. 230 pp. **IL**

Chandler, Deborah. *Learning to Weave.* Loveland, CO: Interweave Press, 1995.

Davidson, Marguerite Porter. *A Handweaver's Pattern Book.* Swarthmore, PA: Marguerite P. Davison (Box 263, Swarthmore, PA 19081), 1944.

Dempsey, James M. *Fiber Crops.* Gainesville, FL: The University Presses of Florida, 1975. 457 pp.

Eaton, Frank M. "Early Defloration as a Method of Increasing Cotton Yields and the Relation of Fruitfulness to Fiber and Boll Characters." *Journal of Agricultural Research,* April 15, 1931, 447–462.

Fryxell, Paul A. *The Natural History of the Cotton Tribe.* College Station, TX: Texas A & M University Press.

Jarman, Cyril. *Plant Fibre Processing: A Handbook.* London: Intermediate Technology Publications, 1998. 52 pp.

Linder, Olive and Harry. *Handspinning Flax.* Phoenix, AZ: Bizarre Butterfly, 1986.

Myers, Dorothy, and Sue Stolton. *Organic Cotton: From Field to Final Product.* London: Intermediate Technology Publications, 1999. 267 pp.

Flowers

Anderson, E. B., et al. *The Oxford Book of Garden Flowers.* New York: Oxford University Press, 1963. 207 pp.

Armitage, Allan M. *Specialty Cut Flowers.* Portland, OR: Timber Press, 1995. 372 pp.

Arnosky, Pamela and Frank. "Specialty Cut Flowers: How to get long stems and high-quality flowers." *Growing for Market,* September 1998, 15–17.

Arranging Cut Flowers. San Francisco: Ortho Books, 1985. 96 pp.

Babcock, Mary Reynolds. *First Aid for Flowers.* New York: Farrar, Straus, & Giroux, 1954. 55 pp.

Ball, Jeff. *Rodale's Flower Garden Problem Solver.* Emmaus, PA: Rodale Press, 1990. 422 pp.

Black, Penny. *The Book of Pressed Flowers.* New York: Simon & Schuster, 1988. 120 pp. Excellent ideas, plants, and colors. Good information on tools, equipment, and how to press flowers.

Blamey, Marjorie. *Flowers of the Countryside.* New York: William Morrow, 1980. 224 pp.

Brennan Georgeanne, and Kathryn Kleinman. *Flowerkeeping: The Time-Honored Art of Preserving Flowers.* Berkeley, CA: Ten Speed Press, 1999. 142 pp.

Byczynski, Lynn. *The Flower Farmer.* White River Junction, VT: Chelsea Green, 1997. 208 pp.

Cavagnaro, David. "A Seed Saver's Guide to Flowers." *National Gardening,* August 1988, 39–45.

Christopher, Thomas. *In Search of Lost Roses.* New York: Summit Books, 1989.

Crockett, James U. *Crockett's Flower Garden.* New York: Little, Brown, 1981. 311 pp.

Curless, Chris. "Renovating a Perennial Bed: How to Give an Old Border a New Lease on Life." *Fine Gardening,* Vol. 37.

DeWolf, Gordon P., Jr., et al. *Taylor's Guide to Bulbs.* New York: Houghton Mifflin, 1961. 463 pp.

Duthie, Pam. *Continuous Bloom.* Batavia, IL: Ball Publishing, 2000. 328 pp.

Easton, Valerie. "A Cutting Garden for All Seasons." *Fine Gardening,* May/June 1998,

*Foster, Catharine O. *Organic Flower Gardening.* Emmaus, PA: Rodale Press, 1975. 305 pp. Excellent!

Gips, Kathleen M. *Flora's Dictionary: The Victorian Language of Herbs and Flowers.* Chagrin Falls, OH: Village Herb Shop (26 S. Main St., Chagrin Falls, OH 44022), 1990. 199 pp.

Hatfield, Audrey W. *Flowers to Know and Grow.* New York: Scribner's, 1950. 174 pp.

Hawks, Kim. "Starting Native Perennials from Seeds: Tips on Collection, Storage, and Germination." *Fine Gardening,* July/August 1991.

Hillier, Malcolm. *The Book of Fresh Flowers.* New York: Simon & Schuster, 1986. 252 pp.

Hillier, Malcolm, et al. *The Book of Dried Flowers.* New York: Simon & Schuster, 1986. 192 pp.

Horn, Elizabeth L. *Sierra Nevada Wildflowers.* Missoula, MT: Mountain Press, 1998. 215 pp.

*Huxley, Anthony, ed. *Garden Annuals and Bulbs.* New York: Macmillan, 1971. 208 pp.

*———. *Garden Perennials and Water Plants.* New York: Macmillan, 1971. 216 pp.

Jacobs, Betty E. M. *Flowers That Last Forever.* Pownal, VT: Storey, 1988. 222 pp.

James, Theodore, Jr. *The Potpourri Gardener.* New York: Macmillan, 1990. 148 pp.

Karel, Leonard. *Dried Flowers: From Antiquity to the Present.* Metuchen, NJ: Scarecrow Press, 1973.

*Kasperski, Victoria R. *How to Make Cut Flowers Last.* New York: William Morris, 1975. 191 pp. **IL**

Kramer, Jack. *The Old-Fashioned Cutting Garden.* New York: Macmillan, 1979. 160 pp.

Larson, Roy A., ed. *Introduction to Floriculture.* San Diego, CA: Academic Press, 1992. 636 pp.

Lovejoy, Ann. *The Year in Bloom.* Seattle, WA: Sasquatch Books (615 2nd Ave., Ste. 260, Seattle, WA 98104), 1987. 264 pp.

MacNicol, Mary. *Flower Cookery.* New York: Collier Books, 1967. 262 pp.

Madison, Mike. *Growing Flowers for Market.* Winters, CA: Yolo Press, 1998. 257 pp.

Martin, Laura C. *Wildflower Meadow Book—A Gardener's Guide.* Chester, CT: The Globe Pequot Press, 1990. 320 pp.

Nowak, Joanna, and Ryszard M. Rudnicki. *Postharvest Handling and Storage of Cut Flowers, Florist Greens, and Potted Plants.* Portland, OR: Timber Press, 1990. 210 pp. **IL**

Perennials, Eyewitness Garden Handbooks. New York: DK Publishing, 1996. 352 pp. A reference guide to more than 1,000 plants.

Phillips, Ellen and C. Colston Burrell. *Illustrated Encyclopedia of Perennials.* Emmaus, PA: Rodale Press, 1993. 533 pp.

Sanchez, Janet H. *Perennials.* Menlo Park, CA: Sunset Books, 2000. 128 pp.

*Schneider, Alfred F. *Parks Success with Bulbs.* Greenwood, SC: George W. Park Seed Co., 1981. 173 pp. **IL**

Squires, M. *The Art of Drying Plants and Flowers.* New York: Bonanza, 1958. 258 pp.

Stevenson, Violet. *Successful Flower Marketing.* London: W. H. & L. Collingridge, 1952. 164 pp.

Sturdivant, Lee. *Flowers for Sale.* Friday Harbor, WA: San Juan Naturals (P.O. Box 642, Friday Harbor, WA 98250), 1992. 197 pp.

Sunset Editors. *Garden Colors: Annuals and Perennials.* Menlo Park, CA: Sunset Books, 1981. 96 pp.

Taylor, Ronald J. *Desert Wildflowers of North America.* Missoula, MT: Mountain Press , 1998. 349 pp.

Thorpe, Patricia. *Everlastings: The Complete Book of Dried Flowers.* New York: Facts on File Publications, 1985. 144 pp.

Verey, Rosemary. *The Flower Arranger's Garden.* New York: Little, Brown, and Co., 1989. 144 pp.

Verner, Yvette. *The Blooming Lawn: Creating a Flower Meadow.* White River Junction, VT: Chelsea Green, 1998. 144 pp.

White, Edward A. *The Principles of Floriculture.* New York: Macmillan, 1931. 467 pp.

Whitelaw, Mark. "Growing Roses the Natural Way." *National Gardening,* May/June 1996, 62–65.

Wilder, Louise B. *The Fragrant Garden.* New York: Dover, 1974. 407 pp.

Food and Nutrition
(*see also* Solar Cooking)

*Agricultural Research Service, U.S. Department of Agriculture. *Composition of Foods.* Agriculture Handbook No. 8. Washington, DC: U.S. Government Printing Office, 1963. 190 pp. **BL**

Aihara, Herman. *Basic Macrobiotics.* Tokyo, Japan: Japan Publications, 1985. Introduction to holistic living with good details.

———. *Acid and Alkaline.* Oroville, CA: George Ohsawa Macrobiotic Foundation (1511 Robinson St., Oroville, CA 95965), 1986. 121 pp.

Alamgir, Mohiuddin, and Poonam Arora. *Providing Food Security for All.* New York: University Press, 1990. 269 pp.

Balch, James F., and Phyllis A. Balch. *Prescription for Nutritional Healing.* Garden City Park, NY: Avery, 1990. 368 pp.

Board of Directors. "Position Paper on the Vegetarian Approach to Eating." *The American Dietetic Association Reports*, July 1980, 61–69.

Comité Interdepartmental de Nutrición para la Defensa Nacional, et

al. *Tabla de Composicion de Alimentos Para Uso en America Latina.* Bethesda, MD: National Institutes of Health, 1961. 157 pp. Also available in English.

de Selincourt, Kate. *Local Harvest.* London: Lawrence & Wishart, 1997. 229 pp.

*Duhon, David, and Cindy Gebhard. *One Circle: How to Grow a Complete Diet in Less Than 1000 Square Feet.* Willits, CA: Ecology Action, 1984. 200 pp. Excellent. **BL/IL/AL**

Elliot, Rose. *Vegetarian Mother Baby Book.* New York: Pantheon Books, 1986. 261 pp.

*Flores, Marina, et al. *Valor Nutrivo de los Alimentos para Centro America y Panama.* Guatemala: Investigaciones Dietaticas— Nutrición Aplicada, 1971. 15 pp.

Food Composition Table for Use in Africa. U.S. Department of Health, Education, and Welfare, Public Health Service, Health Services and Mental Health Administration. Bethesda, MD: National Center for Chronic Disease Control, Nutrition Program, 1968. 306 pp.

Food Composition Table for Use in East Asia. Rome: Food and Agriculture Organization of the United Nations, 1972. 334 pp.

Freeman, John A. *Survival Gardening.* Rock Hill, SC: John's Press (Mt. Gallant Rd., P.O. Box 3405 CRS, Rock Hill, SC 29731), 1982. 84 pp.

Glenn, E., et al. *Sustainable Food Production for a Complete Diet.* Tucson, AZ: Environmental Research Laboratory, 1989. 25 pp.

Gussow, Joan. *The Feeding Web.* Palo Alto, CA: Bull Publishing, 1978. 457 pp.

*Heritage, Ford. *Composition and Facts about Foods.* Mokelumne Hill, CA: Health Research (70 LaFayette St., Mokelumne Hill, CA 95245), 1971. 121 pp. Very useful!

The Hunger Project. *Ending Hunger: An Idea Whose Time Has Come.* New York: Praeger, 1985. 430 pp.

Hur, Robin. *Food Reform: Our Desperate Need.* Austin, TX: Heidelberg Publishers (3707 Kerbey Ln., Austin, TX 78731), 1975. 260 pp.

*Kirschmann, John D. *Nutrition Almanac.* New York: McGraw-Hill, 1979. 313 pp.

Knight, Jonathan. "The Nutrition Garden Project." *The Cultivar,* Newsletter of the Center for Agroecology and Sustainable Food Systems, University of California at Santa Cruz, Winter 1997. 7 pp.

Kushi, Michio. *The Macrobiotic Way.* Wayne, NJ: Avery, 1985. Introduction to holistic living.

Lappé, Frances M. *Diet for a Small Planet.* New York: Ballantine Books, 1984. 496 pp.

Linder, Maria C. "A Review of the Evidence for Food Quality." *Biodynamics,* Summer 1973, 1–11.

Lockeretz, William, ed. *Agricultural Production and Nutrition: Proceedings of an International Conference, Boston, Massachusetts, March 19–21, 1997.* Medford, MA: School of Nutrition Science and Policy, Tufts University, 1997. 213 pp.

Metz, Edwin T., ed. *Quality Protein Maize.* St. Paul, MN: American Association of Cereal Chemists, 1992. 294 pp.

Minnich, Jerry. *Gardening for Maximum Nutrition.* Emmaus, PA: Rodale Press, 1983. 220 pp.

Muñoz de Chávez, et al. *Tablas de valor nutritivo de los alimentos de mahor consumo en México.* Mexico: Editorial Pax México. (Libreria Carlos Césarman, S.A., Av. Cuauhtémoc 1430, Col. Sta. Cruz Atoyac, Mexico), 1996. 330 pp.

*National Academy of Sciences. *Recommended Dietary Allowances,* 8th edition. Washington, DC: NAS, 1974. 129 pp. **IL**

Peavy, William, and Warren Peary Peavy. *Super Nutrition Gardening: How to Grow Your Own Powercharged Foods.* Garden City Park, NY: Avery, 1993. 236 pp.

*Pennington, Jean A. T. *Bowes and Church's Food Values of Portions Commonly Used.* Philadelphia, PA: Lippincott-Raven, 1998. 481 pp.

Postharvest Food Losses in Developing Countries. Washington, DC: National Academy of Sciences, 1978. 205 pp.

Programa de Autosuficiencia Alimentaria a Nivel Familiar (Ecoalimentacion) y Conservacion de Alimentos. IMSS, Mexico: Promotoras Voluntarias, 1992.

Robbins, John. *Diet for a New America.* Walpole, NH: Stillpoint Publishing, 1987. 423 pp.

———. *Diet for a New World.* New York: Avon Books, 1992. 415 pp.

Rodale, J. I., and staff, eds. *The Complete Book of Food and Nutrition.* Emmaus, PA: Rodale Books, 1961. 1,054 pp.

*Root, Waverly. *Food—An Authoritative and Visual History and Dictionary of the Foods of the World.* New York: Simon & Schuster, 1980. 602 pp. **BL**

Schmidt, Gerhard. *The Dynamics of Nutrition.* Wyoming, RI: Bio-Dynamic Literature, 1980. 243 pp.

Smith, Bob. "Organic Foods vs. Supermarket Foods: Element Levels." *Journal of Applied Nutrition,* Vol. 45, No. 1, 1993, 35–39.

Szekely, Edmond Bordeaux. *Scientific Vegetarianism.* International Biogenic Society, 1991. 48 pp.

United States Department of Agriculture. *Organically Produced Foods: Nutritive Content.* Beltsville, MD: Agriculture Research Service, National Agricultural Library, Alternative Farming Systems Information Center, 2000. 21 pp. Bibliography.

Walford, Roy L. *The 120-Year Diet.* New York: Simon & Schuster, 1986. 432 pp.

———. *How to Double Your Vital Years.* New York: Simon & Schuster, 1986. 432 pp.

Yepsen, Roger B., Jr., ed. *Home Food Systems.* Emmaus, PA: Rodale Press, 1981. 475 pp.

Food Preservation and Storage

Axtell, Barrie and Alex Bush. *Case Study—Try Drying It!* London: Intermediate Technology Publications (103/105 Southampton Row, London WC1B 4HH, England), 1991. 63 pp.

Bachmann, Janet. "Small-Scale Oilseed Processing." Fayetteville, AR: Appropriate Technology Transfer for Rural Areas (National Center for Appropriate Technology, University of Arkansas, Fayetteville), 1998. 9 pp.

*Bubel, Mike and Nancy. *Root Cellaring—Natural Cold Storage of Fruit and Vegetables.* Pownal, VT: Storey, 1991. 304 pp.

Cornell Extension Bulletin No. 22. *Construction and Management of Root Storage Cellars.* Ithaca, NY: New York State College of Agriculture at Cornell University, 1917.

Costenbader, Carol W. *The Big Book of Preserving the Harvest.* Pownal, VT: Storey, 1997. 348 pp.

———. *Preserving Fruits and Vegetables.* Pownal, VT: Storey, 1996. 96 pp.

De Long, Deanna. *How to Dry Foods.* Tucson, AZ: H. P. Books (P.O. Box 5367, Tucson, AZ 85703), 1979. 160 pp.

Gardeners and Farmers of Terre Vivante. *Keeping Food Fresh.* White River Junction, VT: Chelsea Green, 1999. 197 pp.

Hertzberg, Ruth, et al. *Putting Food By.* New York: Bantam Books, 1973. 565 pp.

Hobson, Phyllis. *Making and Using Dried Foods.* Pownal, VT: Storey, 1994. 82 pp.

*Hupping, Carol, and staff of the Rodale Food Center. *Stocking Up III.* Emmaus, PA: Rodale Press, 1986. 627 pp.

Kline, Jeff. *How to Sun Dry Your Food.* Las Trampas, NM: Self-Reliance Foundation (Box 1, Las Trampas, NM 87576), 1983. 100 pp.

Macmaniman, Gen. *Dry It.* Fall City, WA: Living Food Dehydrators, 1973. 58 pp.

McClure, Susan. *Preserving Summer's Bounty.* Emmaus, PA: Rodale Press, 1998. 372 pp.

Root Cellars. Mt. Vernon, KY: ASPI Publications (50 Lair St., Mt. Vernon, KY). Video.

Shaffer, Marcella. "Build a Stacked-Timber Root Cellar." *BackHome*, September/October 1998, 24–27.

*Twelve Months' Harvest. San Francisco: Ortho Books Division (Chevron Chemical Co., San Francisco, CA), 1975. 96 pp. Covers canning, freezing, smoking, drying, cheese, cider, soap, and grinding grains. Many good tips.

Vaughn, Reese. *Home Pickling of Olives.* Publication 2758. Oakland, CA: University of California, Division of Agriculture and Natural Resources. 11 pp.

Walk, Larisa. *A Pantry Full of Sunshine.* Winona, MN: Seldom Scene Productions (Rte. 3, Box 163A), 1997. 61 pp.

Yurk, George K. *Homemade Olive Oil.* Publication 2789. Oakland, CA: University of California, Division of Agriculture and Natural Resources.

Fruits, Berries, and Nuts

Agroforestry News—Peaches. Devon, U.K.: Agroforestry Research Trust (46 Hunters Moon, Dartington, Totnes, Devon, TQ96JT, U.K.).

Bailey, L. H., Jr. *Field Notes on Apple Culture.* New York: Orange Judd, 1906. 90 pp.

———. *The Principles of Fruit-Growing.* New York: Macmillan, 1897. 516 pp.

———. *The Apple Tree.* New York: Macmillan, 1922. 117 pp.

Bowling, Barbara L. *The Berry Grower's Companion.* Portland, OR: Timber Press, 2000. 284 pp.

Brickell, Christopher. *Fruit.* New York: Simon & Schuster, 1980. 96 pp.

Brooks, Reid, and Claron Hesse. *Western Fruit Gardening.* Berkeley, CA: University of California Press, 1953. 287 pp. Old but still good.

Chaplin, Lois Trigg. "Sing a Song of Blueberries." *Organic Gardening,* March 1992, 83–89.

Childers, Norman F., and Paul Eck. *Blueberry Culture.* New Brunswick, NJ: Rutgers University Press, 1966. 378 pp.

Christensen, L. Peter, ed. *Raisin Production Manual.* Oakland, CA: University of California Division of Agriculture and Natural Resources, 2000. 295 pp.

Coit, J. Eliot. *Citrus Fruits.* New York: Macmillan, 1917. 520 pp.

Cord, Fred W. *Bush Fruits.* New York: Macmillan, 1909. 537 pp.

Cox, Jeff. *From Vines to Wines: The Complete Guide to Growing Grapes and Making Your Own Wine.* Pownal, VT: Storey, 1999. 235 pp.

Crandall, Perry C. *Bramble Production: The Management and Marketing of Raspberries and Blackberries.* Binghamton, NY: Food Products Press, an imprint of the Haworth Press, 1995. 213 pp.

Downing, A. J. *The Fruits and Fruit Trees of America.* New York: John Wiley & Sons, 1862. 760 pp.

Edwards, Linda. *Organic Tree Fruit Management.* Keremeos, Canada: Similkameen Okanagan Organic Producers Association (SOOPA, formerly Certified Organic Associations of British Columbia, Box 577, Keremeos, BC V0H 1NO, Canada), 1998. 240 pp.

Eisen, Gustav, Ph.D. *The Fig: Its History, Culture, and Curing.* Washington, DC: Government Printing Office, 1901. 317 pp.

Ferguson, Louise, et al., eds. *Olive Production Manual.* Oakland, CA: University of California, Division of Agriculture and Natural Resources, 1994. 156 pp.

Flores, Barbara Jeanne. *The Great Book of Pears.* Berkeley, CA: Ten Speed Press, 2000. 163 pp.

Fraser, Samuel. *The Strawberry.* New York: Orange Judd, 1926. 120 pp.

Garner, R. J. *The Grafter's Handbook.* New York: Oxford University Press, 1979. 319 pp.

Gould, H. P. *Peach-Growing.* New York: Macmillan, 1918. 426 pp.

Hartmann, Hudson T., et al. *Propagation of Temperate-Zone Fruit Plants.* Davis, CA: University of California Cooperative Extension Service, 1979. 63 pp.

Hendrickson, A. H. *Prune Growing in California, Bulletin 328.*

Berkeley, CA: University of California Press, 1923. 38 pp.

Hendrickson, Robert. *The Berry Book.* Garden City, NY: Doubleday, 1981. 259 pp.

Hessayon, D. G. *The Fruit Expert.* London: Transworld Publishers, 1995. 128 pp.

Hume, H. H. *The Cultivation of Citrus Fruits.* New York: Macmillan, 1954. 561 pp.

*James, Theodore, Jr. *How to Select, Grow and Enjoy Fruit, Berries and Nuts in the East and Midwest.* Tucson, AZ: H. P. Books, 1983. 144 pp. Out of print.

Kiwifruit Enthusiasts Journal. Tonasket, WA: Friends of the Trees (P.O. Box 1064, Tonasket, WA 98855), 1992.

Koch, Frank D. *Avocado Grower's Handbook.* Bonsall, CA: Bonsall Publications, 1983. 273 pp.

Kourik, Robert. "Fabulous Figs." *National Gardening,* July/August 1996, 35–40.

Kraft, Ken, and Pat Kraft. *Fruits for the Home Garden.* New York: Morrow, 1968. 287 pp.

———. *Grow Your Own Dwarf Fruit Trees.* New York: Walker, 1974. 218 pp.

Krautwurst, Terry. "Overwintering Fruit Trees." *BackHome,* Winter 1996–1997, 62–63.

La Rue, James H., and R. Scott Johnson, eds. *Peaches, Plums and Nectarines: Growing and Handling for Fresh Market.* Oakland, CA: University of California, Division of Agriculture and Natural Resources, 1989. 246 pp.

Logsdon, Gene. *Organic Orcharding: A Grove of Trees to Live In.* Emmaus, PA: Rodale Press, 1981. 415 pp.

Martin, R. Sanford. *How to Prune Fruit Trees.* Published by the author (10535 Las Lunitas Ave., Tujunga, CA 91042), 1978. 90 pp. Best and simplest book on pruning for West Coast gardeners.

McEachern, George, and Larry Stein. *Planting and Establishing Pecan Trees.* College Station, TX: Texas Agricultural Extension

Service, Texas A&M University System, n.d.

Micke, Warren C., ed. *Almond Production Manual.* Oakland, CA: University of California Division of Agriculture and Natural Resources, 1996. 289 pp.

Miller, G. "Grape Growing Under Glass." *Journal of the Royal Horticultural Society,* Vincent Square, London, England, February 1963, 85–91.

Moore, S. W. *Practical Orcharding on Rough Lands.* Akron, OH: New Werner, 1911. 289 pp.

North American Fruit Explorer's Quarterly. (Henry Converse, 2317 Seneca Ln., Paducah, KY 42001.)

Ocean, Suellen. *Acorns and Eat 'em.* Willits, CA: Ocean-House (28970 Sherwood Rd., Willits, CA 95490), 1993. 86 pp.

Ortho Books Editorial Staff. *All about Citrus and Subtropical Fruits.* Des Moines, IA: Meredith Corporation Ortho Books, 1985. 96 pp.

Otto, Stella. *The Backyard Orchardist: A Complete Guide to Growing Fruit Trees in the Home Garden.* Grawn, MI: Otto Graphics (6893 Sullivan Rd., Grawn, MI 49637), 1993. 250 pp.

Paddock, Whipple. *Fruit Growing in Arid Regions.* New York: Macmillan, 1913. 395 pp.

Phillips, Michael. *The Apple Grower.* White River Junction, VT: Chelsea Green, 1998. 242 pp.

———. "Growing Apples… Naturally." *National Gardening,* March/April 1999, 46–50.

Ramos, David E., ed. *Walnut Production Manual.* Oakland, CA: University of California Division of Agriculture and Natural Resources, 1998. 317 pp.

*Ray, Richard, and Lance Walheim. *Citrus—How to Select, Grow, and Enjoy.* Tucson, AZ: H. P. Books (P.O. Box 5367, Tucson, AZ 85703), 1980. 176 pp.

Rivers, Thomas. *The Miniature Fruit Garden.* New York: Orange Judd, 1866. 133 pp.

Robinson, J. C. *Bananas and Plantains.* Wallingford, Oxon, U.K.: CAB International, 1996. 238 pp.

Sanders, Rosanne. *The Apple Book.* New York: Philosophical Library, 1988. 142 pp.

Sunset Books Editorial Staff. *Citrus.* Menlo Park, CA: Sunset Books, 1996. 96 pp.

Swezey, Sean L., et al. *Organic Apple Production Manual.* Oakland, CA: University of Californa Agriculture and Natural Resources, 2000. 72 pp.

Taylor, Judith M., M.D. *The Olive in California: History of an Immigrant Tree.* Berkeley, CA: Ten Speed Press, 2000. 316 pp.

Thompson, Bruce. *Black Walnuts for Fun and Profit.* Beaverton, OR: Timber Press, 1976. 285 pp.

Tufts, Warren P. *Pruning Deciduous Fruit Trees.* Circular 112. California Agricultural Ext. Service, 1941. 63 pp.

Tukey, Harold Bradford. *Dwarfed Fruit Trees.* Ithaca, NY: Cornell University Press, 1964. 562 pp. Definitive work on the subject.

University of California Extension Service. *Avocado Care in the Home Orchard.* 1975. 3 pp.

Waldo, George F., and Cecil O. Rawlings. *Black Raspberry Growing.* Extension Bulletin 750. Corvallis, OR: Federal Cooperative Extension Service, Oregon State College, 1955. 21 pp.

*Walheim, Lance, and Robert L. Stebbins. *Western Fruit, Berries and Nuts—How to Select, Grow and Enjoy.* Tucson, AZ: H. P. Books (P.O. Box 5367, Tucson, AZ 85703), 1981. 192 pp. Excellent. Worth several lifetimes of experience. Good for all tree raisers—not just Western ones.

Waugh, F. A. *Plums and Plum Culture.* New York: Orange Judd, 1910. 371 pp.

*Whealy, Kent, ed. *Fruit, Berry and Nut Inventory,* 3rd edition. Decorah, IA: Seed Savers Exchange, 2001. 560 pp.

Williams, S. R. *Compost Fruit Growing.* London: W. Foulsham, 1961. 126 pp.

Wilson, C. P. H. *Bush Peaches.* Forest Hill, NY: Transatlantic Arts, 1958. 140 pp.

Yepsen, Roger. *Apples.* New York: W. W. Norton, 1994. 255 pp.

Fukuoka Culture

*Fukuoka, Masanoubu. *The One-Straw Revolution.* Emmaus, PA: Rodale Press, 1978. 181 pp. Natural farming from a Japanese philosopher/farmer. One of the few to address a sustainable grain culture.

———. *The Natural Way of Farming: The Theory and Practice of Green Philosophy.* Tokyo and New York: Japan Publications, 1985. 280 pp.

———. *The Road Back to Nature.* Tokyo and New York: Japan Publications, 1987. 377 pp.

Gardening

(*see also* Container Gardening)

Abraham, Doc and Katy. *Green Thumb Wisdom, Garden Myths Revealed!* Pownal, VT: Storey, 1996. 152 pp.

Agate, Elizabeth. *Footpaths.* The Eastern Press, 1994. 192 pp.

Bailey, Liberty H. *The Garden Lover.* Norwood, MA: Macmillan, 1928. 154 pp.

———. *The Horticulturist's Rule-Book.* New York: Macmillan, 1909. 312 pp.

———. *Manual of Gardening.* New York: Macmillan, 1914. 541 pp.

Beard, Henry, et al. *Gardening, A Gardener's Dictionary.* New York: Workman, 1982. 95 pp.

Bieny, D. R. *The Why and How of Home Horticulture.* San Francisco: W. H. Freeman, 1980. 513 pp.

Bradley, Fern Marshall, and Barbara W. Ellis. *Rodale's All-New Encyclopedia of Organic Gardening.* Emmaus, PA: Rodale Press, 1992. 690 pp.

Brenzel, Kathleen Norris, ed. *Sunset Western Garden Book.* Menlo Park, CA: Sunset Books, 2001. 768 pp. Indispensable descriptions and cultural directions for flowering plants, trees, and landscaping. For West Coast gardeners. Not organic.

Brown, Marc. *Your First Garden Book.* Boston, MA: Little, Brown, and Co., 1991. 48 pp.

Bubel, Nancy. *52 Weekend Garden Projects.* Emmaus, PA: Rodale Press, 1992. 354 pp.

Campbell, Stu. *Mulch It! A Practical Guide to Using Mulch in the Garden and Landscape.* Pownal, VT: Storey, 2001. 123 pp.

Carr, Anna, et al. *Rodale's Chemical-Free Yard and Lawn.* Emmaus, PA: Rodale Press, 1991. 456 pp.

Creasy, Rosalind. *The Edible French Garden.* Boston, MA: Periplus Editions (HK), 1999. 106 pp.

———. *The Edible Asian Garden.* Boston, MA: Periplus Editions (HK), 2000. 106 pp.

———. *The Complete Book of Edible Landscaping.* San Francisco: Sierra Club Books, 1982. 379 pp.

Denckla, Tanya. *Gardening at a Glance.* Franklin, WV: Wooden Angel Publishing (Wooden Angel Farm, Bldg. 1-A, P.O. Box 869, Franklin, WV 26807), 1991. 272 pp.

———. *The Organic Gardener's Home Reference: A Plant-by-Plant Guide to Growing Fresh, Healthy Food.* Pownal, VT: Garden Way, 1994. 273 pp.

DiSabato-Aust, Tracy. *The Well-Tended Perennial Garden: Planting and Pruning Techniques.* Portland, OR: Timber Press, 1998. 269 pp.

Faust, Joan Lee. *The New York Times Book of Vegetable Gardening.* New York: Quadrangle/The New York Times Book Co., 1975. 282 pp.

Fine Gardening. Rodale Press (33 E. Minor St., Emmaus, PA 18049). Magazine.

Fisher, Joe and Dennis. *The Homebrewer's Garden.* Pownal, VT: Storey, 1998. 187 pp.

Foster, Catharine Osgood. *Building Healthy Gardens.* Pownal, VT: Storey, 1989. 279 pp.

*———. *The Organic Gardener.* New York: Random House, 1972. 234 pp. Excellent, chatty, experienced. New England area especially.

Gibson, Eric. *The Grower's Green Book.* Carmichael, CA: New World, 1992. 224 pp.

Greenprints. (P.O. Box 1355, Fairview, NC 28730.) Quarterly publication about gardening experiences.

Growth Point Magazine. (Horticultural Therapy, Goulds Ground, Vallis Way, Frome, Somerset BA11 3DW, England.) Gardening magazine for the physically handicapped.

Hale, Gill. *The Feng Shui Garden.* Pownal, VT: Storey, 1998. 128 pp.

Hill, Lewis. *Successful Cold-Climate Gardening.* Pownal, VT: Storey, 1987. 308 pp.

*HortIdeas. (750 Black Lick Rd., Gravel Switch, KY 40328.) A monthly report on the latest gardening research, methods, tools, plants, books, and so on. Excellent.

Horticulture. (Horticulture Association, 755 Boyleston St., Boston, MA 02116.) Magazine.

Jobb, Jamie. *My Garden Companion.* San Francisco: Sierra Club Books, 1977. 35 pp. Especially for beginners.

Kraft, Ken, and P. Kraft. *Growing Food the Natural Way.* New York: Doubleday, 1973. 292 pp. California-area orientation.

Langer, Richard W. *Grow It!* New York: Saturday Review Press, 1972. 395 pp.

Loewer, Peter. *Tough Plants for Tough Places.* Emmaus, PA: Rodale Press, 1992. 247 pp.

Marshall, Fern, et al. *The Experts' Book of Garden Hints.* Emmaus, PA: Rodale Press, 1993. 346 pp.

Merrill, Richard, and Joe Ortiz. *The Gardeners' Table: A Guide to Natural Vegetable Growing and Cooking.* Berkeley, CA: Ten Speed Press, 2000. 468 pp.

Neal, Bill. *Gardener's Latin.* Chapel Hill, NC: Algonquin Books (P.O. Box 2225, Chapel Hill, NC 27515).

Nuñez, Vera K. *Household Gardens: Theoretical Considerations on an Old Survival Strategy.* Report 1. Potatoes in Food Systems Research Series. Lima, Peru: International Potato Center, Training and Communications Department), 1985. 41 pp.

Olwell, Carol. *Gardening from the Heart—Why Gardeners Garden.* Berkeley, CA: Antelope Island Press, 1990, 144–152.

Organic Gardening. (Rodale Press, 33 E. Minor St., Emmaus, PA 18049.) Magazine.

OG. (Wiveliscombe, Taunton, U.K.) Magazine.

Patent, Dorothy Hinshaw, and Diane Bilderback. *The Harrowsmith Country Life Book of Garden Secrets.* Charlotte, VT: Camden House, 1991. 349 pp.

Peplow, Elizabeth and Reginald. *In a Monastery Garden.* North Pomfret, VT: David & Charles, 1988. 182 pp.

Perry, Robert L. *Basic Gardening in Florida Sand.* Largo, FL: Florida Gardening Companion (P.O. Box 896, Largo, FL 33540), 1977. 72 pp.

Pleasant, Barbara. *Warm-Climate Gardening.* Pownal, VT: Storey, 1993. 204 pp.

Rahn, James J. *Making the Weather Work for You—A Practical Guide for Gardener and Farmer.* Charlotte, VT: Garden Way, 1979. 205 pp.

Rateaver, Bargyla, and Gylver Rateaver. *The Organic Method Primer Update,* special edition. Published by the authors (P.O. Box 26567, San Diego, CA 92196-0567), 1993. 257 pp. Packed with detailed information, much of it very good.

Reader's Digest. *Ideas for Your Garden.* Pleasantville, NY: The Reader's Digest Association, 1995. 335 pp.

Rickett, Harold W. *Botany for Gardeners.* New York: Macmillan Co., 1957. 236 pp.

Rodale, Robert, ed. *The Basic Book of Organic Gardening.* New York: Ballantine Books, 1971. 377 pp. Condensed information includes 14-day compost and nationwide planting dates.

*———, ed. *The Encyclopedia of Organic Gardening.* Emmaus, PA: Rodale Press, 1959. 1,145 pp.

*———. *How to Grow Fruits and Vegetables by the Organic Method.*

Emmaus, PA: Rodale Press. 1961. 926 pp. Two excellent references. Many prefer the encyclopedia format, but we find the second to be more complete.

*Salisbury, E. J. *The Living Garden (or The How and Why of Garden Life)*. London: G. Bell & Sons, 1946. 232 pp. An excellent book.

*Seymour, John. *The Self-Sufficient Gardener*. London: Faber and Faber, 1978. 256 pp. Coffee-table size. Seymour has long been a popular back-to-the-land advocate in England, both doing it and writing about it in his own humorous style. His new "productions" are gorgeously illustrated, accurate, and uncluttered.

Smith, Edward C. *The Vegetable Gardener's Bible*. Pownal, VT: Storey, 2000. 309 pp.

Smith and Hawken Books. *The Book of Outdoor Gardening*. New York: Workman, 1996. 513 pp.

Smith, Marney. *Gardening with Conscience*. New York: Seabury Press, 1981. 86 pp.

Solomon, Steve. *Growing Vegetables West of the Cascades: The Complete Guide to Natural Gardening*. Seattle, WA: Sasquatch Books, 2000. 356 pp.

Sperry, Neil. *Neil Sperry's Complete Guide to Texas Gardening*. Dallas, TX: Taylor, 1991. 388 pp.

Sunset Editors. *Vegetable Gardening*. Menlo Park, CA: Sunset Books, 1998. 128 pp.

Tenenbaum, Frances, ed. *Taylor's Guide to Shade Gardening*. Boston: Houghton Mifflin, 1994. 501 pp.

Tiedjens, Victor A. *The Vegetable Encyclopedia and Gardener's Guide*. New York: New Home Library, 1943. 215 pp. Important cultural detailings.

Vasil'yev, I. M. *Wintering of Plants*. Washington, DC: Royer and Royer, 1961. 300 pp.

Vickery, Deborah and James. *Intensive Vegetable Gardening for Profit and Self-Sufficiency*. Washington, DC: U.S. Peace Corps, Information Collection and Exchange, 1981. 158 pp. In English and Spanish.

Wasowski, Sally and Andy. *Native Gardens for Dry Climates*. New York: Clarkson Potter, 1995. 176 pp.

Watkins, Norma. *How to Grow More Vegetables Organically in South Florida*. Miami, FL: Environmental Demonstration Center, Life Lab Division (Miami Dade Community College, 300 NE 2nd Ave., Miami, FL 33131), 1979. 8 pp. Visit www.mdcc.edu/wolfson/departments/environethics/eehomepage.html and click on Resources.

Year-Round Gardening. Mt. Vernon, KY: ASPI Publications (50 Lair St., Mt. Vernon, KY 40456). Video.

Young, Carol L. *What Grows Where?* Carol Young (229 Peninsula Dr., Lake Almanor, CA 96137), 1987. 187 pp.

Global Perspective

Akin, Wallace E. *Global Patterns—Climate, Vegetation and Soils*. Norman, OK: University of Oklahoma Press, 1991. 370 pp.

Anderson, Sarah, ed. *Views from the South: The Effects of Globalization and the WTO on Third World Countries*. Chicago: Food First Books, 2000. 195 pp.

Bennett, Charles F., Jr. *Man and Earth's Ecosystems*. New York: John Wiley & Sons, 1975. 331 pp.

*Brown, Lester R. *State of the World—1990*. New York: W. W. Norton, 1990. 253 pp. Excellent resource tool. Also see this publication for other years. Excellent. **AL**

———. *The Twenty-Ninth Day*. New York: W. W. Norton, 1978. 363 pp.

Carley, Michael, and Philippe Spapens. *Sharing the World, Sustainable Living and Global Equity in the 21st Century*. New York: St. Martin's Press, 1998. 208 pp.

Carson, Rachel. *Silent Spring*. Boston: Houghton Mifflin. 1962.

Cox, George W., and Michael D. Atkins. *Agricultural Ecology—An Analysis of World Food Production Systems*. San Francisco: W. H. Freeman, 1964. 72 pp.

Dahlberg, Kenneth A. *Beyond the Green Revolution—The Ecology and Politics of Global Agricultural Development*. New York: Plenum Press, 1979. 256 pp.

"Farming a Shrinking Planet." *Christian Science Monitor,* October 28, 1992, 9–12.

*Food and Agriculture Organization of the United Nations. *FAO Production Yearbook—1994*. Rome: FAO, 1995. 243 pp.

Gelbspan, Ross. *The Heat Is On—The Climate Crisis/The Cover-Up/The Prescription*. Cambridge, MA: Perseus Books, 1997, 1998. 278 pp.

Johnson, D. Gale. *World Agriculture in Disarray*. London: Fontana, 1973. 304 pp.

Kendall, Henry, and David Pimentel. *Constraints on the Expansion of the Global Food Supply*. Vol. 23, No. 3, 1994, 198–205.

Knickerbocker, Brad. "Living with the Planet in Mind." *The Christian Science Monitor,* March 3, 1992.

Meadows, Donella H. "Population, Poverty, and Planet Earth." *In Context,* Spring 1992, No. 31, 32–35.

*Meadows, Donella H., Dennis L. Meadows, and Jorgen Randers. *Beyond the Limits*. Post Mills, VT: Chelsea Green, 1992. 300 pp.

Nixon, Will. "Can Talking Heads Save an Ailing Planet?" *E Magazine,* May/June 1992, 37–42.

Pimentel, David. *Competition for Land: Development, Food and Fuel*. Boca Raton, FL: Technologies for a Greenhouse-Constrained Society, 1992, 325–348.

———. *Food and the Energy Crisis*. Vol. 54, No. 12, 1973, 11.

———. *Food, Energy, and Climate Change*. 1981, 303–323.

———. *Food, Energy and the Environment*. Vol. 31, 1981, 85–100.

———. *World Food, Energy, Man and Environment*. 1975, 5–16.

———. "Perspectives on Ecological Integrity." *The Global Population, Food, and the Environment,* Chap 15. Kluwer Academic Publishers, 1995, 239–253.

Rodale, Robert, and Mike McGrath. *Save Three Lives—A Plan for Famine Prevention.* San Francisco: Sierra Club Books, 1991.

Shiva, Vandana. *Monocultures of the Mind: Perspectives on Biodiversity and Biotechnology.* New York and London: Zed Books, 1993. 184 pp.

———. *Stolen Harvest: The Hijacking of the Global Food Supply.* Cambridge, MA: South End Press, 2000. 146 pp.

———. *Biopiracy: The Plunder of Nature and Knowlege.* Boston, MA: South End Press, 1997. 148 pp.

The Sierra Club. *The Case Against the Global Economy.* San Francisco: Sierra Club, 1996. 549 pp.

Stopping the Coming Ice Age. Berkeley, CA: Institute for a Future (2000 Center St., Berkeley, CA 94704). 60-minute video.

Timeline. Palo Alto, CA: The Foundation for Global Community (222 High St., Palo Alto, CA 94301). Bimonthly publication.

Vogtmann, Hartmut, Engelhard Boehncke, and Inka Frick, eds. *The Importance of Biological Agriculture in a World of Diminishing Resources: Proceedings of the 5th IFOAM International Scientific Conference at the University of Kassel (Germany) August 27–30, 1984.* Witzenhausen, Germany: Verlagsgruppe Weiland, Happ, Burkhard, 1986. 448 pp.

World Resources Institute. *World Resources—1990–91.* New York: Oxford University Press, 1990. 383 pp. Also see this publication for other years.

WSSA. *For All Generations: Making World Agriculture More Sustainable.* Glendale, CA: OM Publishing, 1997. 642 pp.

Gourds

Bailey, L. H. *The Garden of Gourds.* New York: Macmillan, 1937. 134 pp.

Bubel, Nancy. "Hordes of Gourds." *Horticulture*, November 1993, 59–64.

Consumer Tips. Cooperative Extension, University of California, November/December 1985, Vol. 1, No. 4.

The Gourd Book. Mt. Gilead, OH: Ohio Gourd Society (Box 274, Mt. Gilead, OH 43338).

Heiser, Charles. *The Gourd Book.* Norman, OK: University of Oklahoma Press, 1979. 248 pp.

Pleasant, Barbara. "Goodness! Gracious! Great Gobs of Gourds!" *Organic Gardening*, March 1992, 32–36.

Rood, Mary Ann. "Growing and Crafting Gourds." *Fine Gardening*, November/December 1991.

Grains

Bailey, Liberty H., ed. *The Small Grains.* Norwood, MA: Macmillan, 1920. 699 pp.

Beaven, E. S. *Barley—Fifty Years of Observation and Experiment.* London: Duckworth, 1947. 394 pp.

Board on Science and Technology for International Development, National Research Council. *Lost Crops of Africa, Vol. 1, Grains.* Washington, DC: National Academy Press, 1996. 383 pp.

Cavagnaro, David. "Amaranths: Ancient and Modern." *National Gardening*, May/June 1998, 36–40, 74.

Cole, John N. *Amaranth.* Emmaus, PA: Rodale Press, 1979. 311 pp.

Creasy, Rosalind. "The Bread Garden." *Harrowsmith*, September/October 1986, 89–90, 92–96.

Dondlinger, Peter Tracy. *The Book of Wheat: An Economic History and Practical Manual of the Wheat Industry.* New York: Orange Judd, 1919. 369 pp.

Gorman, Marion. "Gardener's Bread." *Organic Gardening*, December 1988, 53–54.

Granatstein, David. *Amber Waves.* Pullman, WA: College of Agriculture and Home Economics Research Center, Washington State University, 1992. 82 pp.

Hunt, Thomas F. *The Cereals in America.* New York: Orange Judd, 1912. 421 pp.

Jarde, Auguste. *Les Céréales dans l'Antiquité Grecque.* Paris: E. De Boccard, 1925. 237 pp.

Leonard, Thom. "Staff of Life." *Organic Gardening*, December 1988, 46–51.

*Leonard, Warren H., and John H. Martin. *Cereal Crops.* New York: Macmillan, 1963. 824 pp. **AL**

*Logsdon, Gene. *Small-Scale Grain Raising.* Emmaus, PA: Rodale Press, 1977. 305 pp. **BL**

Mangelsdorf, Paul C. *Corn—Its Origin, Evolution and Improvement.* Cambridge, MA: The Belknap Press of Harvard University Press, 1974. 262 pp.

Mangelsdorf, P. C., and R. G. Reeves. *The Origin of Indian Corn and Its Relatives.* College Station, TX: Texas Agricultural Experiment Station, 1939. 315 pp.

Montgomery, E. G. *The Corn Crops.* New York: Macmillan, 1916. 347 pp.

Piper, Jon K., ed. *The Land Institute Research Report, Summary of work to develop mixtures of perennial seed crops using the prairie ecosystem as standard.* Salina, KS: The Land Institute (2440 E. Water Well Rd., Salina, KS 67401). 39 pp.

———. "Soil Water and Nutrient Change in Stands of Three Perennial Crops." *Soil Science Society of America Journal* (677 S. Segoe Rd., Madison, WI 53711), Vol. 57, No. 2, March–April 1993.

———. "A Grain Agriculture Fashioned in Nature's Image: The Work of the Land Institute." *Great Plains Research,* Vol. 3, No. 2 (Salina, KS), 1993, 249–272.

Rachie, Kenneth, and J. V. Majmudar. *Pearl Millet.* University Park, PA: Pennsylvania State University Press, 1980. 307 pp.

Rodale, Robert. *Amaranth Round-Up.* Emmaus, PA: Rodale Press, 1977. 48 pp.

Schaller, Lorenz K. *What's Up with Triticale?* Ojai, CA: Kusa Seed Research Foundation (P.O. Box 761, Ojai, CA), 2000. 9 pp.

Swezey, Lauren Bonar. "From Seed to Bread." *Sunset*, November 1993, 88–91.

Wallace, Henry A., and Earl N. Bressman. *Corn and Corn Growing*. New York: John Wiley & Sons, 1937. 436 pp.

Willis, Harold. *How to Grow Top Quality Corn*. Madison, WI: A-R Editions, 1984. 58 pp.

Grasses

California Native Grass Association. *Techniques and Strategies for Using Native Grasses and Graminoids in Restoration Projects, A CNGA Training Workshop*. Davis, CA: CNGA (P.O. Box 72405, Davis, CA 95617), 2000.

Fe, John. *The Encyclopedia of Ornamental Grasses*. Emmaus, PA: Rodale Press, 1992. 186 pp.

Hitchcock, A. S. *Manual of the Grasses of the United States*. Washington, DC: U.S. Department of Agriculture, Government Printing Office, 1935. 1,040 pp.

Hopkins, Alan, ed. *Grass, Its Production and Utilization*. Oxford, England: Blackwell Science, 2000. 440 pp.

Packard, Stephen, and Cornelia Mutel, eds. *The Tallgrass Restoration Handbook*. Covelo, CA: Island Press, 1997. 463 pp.

Shaw, Thomas. *Grasses and How to Grow Them*. St. Paul, MN: Webb Publishing Co., 1903.

Shirley, Shirley. *Restoring the Tallgrass Prairie: An Illustrated Manual for Iowa and the Upper Midwest*. Iowa City, IA: University of Iowa Press, 1994. 330 pp.

Soil Conservation Society of America. *Warm-Season Grasses: Balancing Forage Programs in the Northeast and Southern Corn Belt*. Ankeny, IA: Soil and Water Conservation Society (7515 NE Ankeny Rd., Ankeny, IA 50021), 1986. 35 pp.

Staten, H. W. *Grasses and Grassland Farming*. New York: Devin-Adir, 1958. 319 pp.

*U.S. Department of Agriculture. *Grass—The Yearbook of Agriculture 1948*. Washington, DC: U.S. Government Printing Office, 1948. 892 pp.

Greenhouse Culture

Abraham, George and Katy. *Organic Gardening Under Glass*. Emmaus, PA: Rodale Press, 1975. 308 pp.

Anderson, Phyllis. "Gardening Under a Roomy Tent You Make with Shadecloth or Plastic over PVC Pipe." *Sunset*, Southern California edition. March 1980, 200–201.

*Antill, David. *Gardening Under Protection*. Wakefield, England: EP Publishing, 1978. 72 pp.

Aquatias, A. *Intensive Culture of Vegetables*. Harrisville, NH: Solar Survival Press (Harrisville, NH 03450), 1978. 129 pp. Reprint from 1913 on raising food under glass.

Bailey, L. H. *The Forcing Book*. New York: Macmillan, 1903. 259 pp.

———. *The Nursery Manual*. New York: Macmillan, 1923. 456 pp.

Chase, J. L. H. *Cloche Gardening*. London: Faber and Faber, 1948. 195 pp. A classic.

Colebrook, Binda. *Winter Gardening in the Maritime Northwest*. Arlington, WA: Tilth Association (Rte. 2, Box 190-A, Arlington, WA 98223), 1977. 128 pp.

Coleman, Eliot. *Four-Season Harvest*. White River Junction, VT: Chelsea Green, 1999. 234 pp.

———. *The New Organic Grower's Four Season Harvest*. Post Mills, VT: Chelsea Green, 1992. 212 pp.

Fisher, Rick, and Bill Yanda. *The Food and Heat Producing Solar Greenhouse*. Santa Fe, NM: John Muir Publications, 1976. 161 pp. Detailed.

Frazier, Jack. *Green Winters—The Solar-Heated Walk-In Season Extender Construction Manual*. Theodosia, MO: Ozark Exotica (Rte. 3, Box 500, Theodosia, MO 65761), 1990. 13 pp.

Hodgson, Larry. "The Greenhouse Effect." *Organic Gardening*, January/February 2001, 40–48.

Lawrence, William J. C. *Better Glasshouse Crops*. London: Allen & Unwin, 1949. 57 pp.

———. *Science and the Glasshouse*. London: Oliver & Boyd, 1950. 175 pp.

McCullagh, James C., ed. *The Solar Greenhouse Book*. Emmaus, PA: Rodale Press, 1978. 328 pp.

Moore, Steve and Carol. "Inside a passive solar greenhouse, crops thrive both winter and summer." *Growing for Market*, December 1999, 10–12.

*Nearing, Helen and Scott. *Building and Using Our Sun-Heated Greenhouse: Grow Vegetables All Year Round*. Charlotte, VT: Garden Way, 1977. 148 pp.

Nelson, Kennard S. *Flower and Plant Production in the Greenhouse*. Danville, IL: Interstate Publishers, 1991. 220 pp.

Poisson, Leandre, and Gretchen Vogel. *Solar Gardening: Growing Vegetables Year-Round the American Intensive Way*. White River Junction, VT: Chelsea Green, 1994. 267 pp.

Rieke, Paul E., and Warncke, Darryl D. *Greenhouse Soils*. Chestertown, MD: LaMotte Chemical Products Co,, 1975. 36 pp.

Smith, Shane. *Greenhouse Gardener's Companion*. Golden, CO: Fulcrum (350 Indiana St., Ste. 350, Golden, CO 80401-5093), 1992. 531 pp.

GROW BIOINTENSIVE
(*see also* Biointensive)

Belsie, Laurent, "Future Farms: Bigger, and possibly better, food suppliers. Intensive 'micro-farming' may help fill tables in third world." *The Christian Science Monitor*, October 16, 1987.

"Griffin, J. M., et al. *Growing and Gathering Your Own Fertilizers*. Willits, CA: Ecology Action, 1988. 140 pp. See Appendix D for information on night soil composting.

Jeavons, John C. "New Ways from Old." *Cry California*, Winter 1973–74.

MacFadyne, J. Tevere, "The Call to Dig." *Horticulture*, March 1985, 38.

"Mulching, Living Mulch and Double Digging." Willits, CA: Ecology Action. Information sheet. 2 pp. **BL**

"Roots in the Soil." Willits, CA: Ecology Action. Information sheet. **BL**

Stone, Pat. "John Jeavons: Digging Up the Future." *Mother Earth News*, January/February 1990, 45.

Tonge, Peter. "Feeding the World." *The Christian Science Monitor*, October 16, 1987.

Health

Balch, James F., and Phyllis A. *Prescription for Nutritional Healing*. Garden City, NY: Avery, 1990. 368 pp.

Batmanghelidj, F. *Your Body's Many Cries for Water*. Falls Church, VA: Global Health Solutions, 1995. 182 pp.

Burns, A. August, et al. *Donde no hay doctor para mujeres: un manual para la salud de la mujer*. Berkeley, CA: The Hesperian Foundation, 1999. 581 pp.

Burns, A. August, et al. *Where Women Have No Doctor: A health guide for women*. Berkeley, CA: The Hesperian Foundation, 1997. 583 pp.

Chevallier, Andrew. *The Encyclopedia of Medicinal Plants*. New York: DK Publishing, 1996. 336.

*Dickson, Murray. *Where There Is No Dentist*. Berkeley, CA: The Hesperian Foundation, 1983. 195 pp.

Finnegan, John. *The Facts about Fats*. Berkeley, CA: Celestial Arts, 1993. 130 pp.

The Gerson Therapy. Bonita, CA: The Gerson Institute (P.O. Box 430, Bonita, CA 91908). Information brochure.

Haas, Elson M. *Staying Healthy with Nutrition*. Berkeley, CA: Celestial Arts, 1992. 1,140 pp.

———. *Staying Healthy with the Seasons*. Berkeley, CA: Celestial Arts, 1981. 242 pp.

Haas, Elson M., and Eleonora Manzolini. *A Diet for All Seasons*. Berkeley, CA: Celestial Arts, 1995. 251 pp.

Healing Newsletter. Bonita, CA: The Gerson Institute (P.O. Box 430, Bonita, CA 91908), 1989. Vol. 5, No. 2.

The Hesperian Foundation, P.O. Box 11577, Berkeley, CA 94712-2577. Publications on self-help medical approaches.

How to Be Your Own Doctor . . . Sometimes. New York: Putnam, 1985.

Howard, Albert. *Farming and Gardening for Health or Disease*. London: Faber and Faber, 1945. 282 pp.

Keville, Kathi. "How to Make Poultices and Compresses." *Vegetarian Times/Well-Being Magazine*, Issue 48.

Klein, Susan. *A Book for Midwives: A manual for traditional birth attendants and community midwives*. Berkeley, CA: The Hesperian Foundation, 1995. 520 pp.

———. *Un libro para parteras: Una guia para comadronas y parteras tradicionales*. Berkeley, CA: The Hesperian Foundation, 1998. 508 pp.

Kneipp, Sebastian. *The Kneipp Cure*. New York: The Nature Cure Publishing Co., 1949.

The Life Science Health System—Part XIV: Common Illnesses and Diseases and How Hygienic Living Can Help. Austin, TX: Life Science Institute, 1986, 1,509–1,524.

Ogren, Thomas Leo. *Allergy-Free Gardening: The Revolutionary Guide to Healthy Landscaping*. Berkeley, CA: Ten Speed Press, 2000. 267 pp.

Pitchford, Paul. *Healing with Whole Foods: Oriental Traditions and Modern Nutrition*. Berkeley, CA: North Atlantic, 1993. 705 pp.

Pizzorno, Joseph, *Total Wellness*. Rocklin, CA: Prima, 1996. 419 pp.

Poxiletik, Syunal. *Plantas Medicinales*. Instituto Mexicano del Seguro Social, 1992. 73 pp.

Prevention Magazine Health Books. *The Complete Book of Cancer Prevention*. Emmaus, PA: Rodale Press, 1988. 562 pp.

Roberts, Wayne, Rod MacRae, and Lori Stahlbrand. *Real Food for a Change*. Random House of Canada, 1999. 243 pp.

Sears, Barry. *Enter the Zone: A Dietary Road Map*. New York: Regan Books, 1995. 286 pp.

Simpson, Harold N. *Unhealthy Food = Unhealthy People*. Chicago: Peter Jon Simpson, 1994. 117 pp.

Szekely, Edmond Bordeaux. *Search for the Ageless, Vol. 1: My Unusual Adventures on the Five Continents in Search for the Ageless*. Nelson, Canada: International Biogenic Society (P.O. Box 849, Nelson, BC ViL 6A5, Canada), 1977. 211 pp.

———. *The Essene Way: Biogenic Living*. Matsqui, Canada: I.B.S. Internacional, 1989. 184 pp.

Tourles, Stephanie. *Natural Foot Care*. Pownal, VT: Storey, 1998. 187 pp.

Voisin, André. *Soil, Grass and Cancer*. Austin, TX: Acres U.S.A., 1999 (originally published, 1959). 370 pp.

Walker, N. W. *Fresh Vegetable and Fruit Juices*. Prescott, AZ: Norwalk Press (P.O. Box 12260, Prescott, AZ 86304-2260), 1970. 118 pp.

*Werner, David. *Where There Is No Doctor: A village health care handbook*. Berkeley, CA: The Hesperian Foundation, 1992. 446 pp. **BL**

———. *Donde no hay doctor: Una guia para los campesinos que viven lejos do los centros médicos*. Berkeley, CA: The Hesperian Foundation, 1995. 455 pp.

*———. *Helping Health Workers Learn*. Palo Alto, CA: The Hesperian Foundation (Box 1692, Palo Alto, CA 94302), 1982. 573 pp. **BL**

Hedges

*Brooks, Alan. *Hedging: A Practical Handbook,* 3rd edition. Wallingford, U.K.: British Trust for Conservation Volunteers, 1988. 120 pp. Excellent book on the practical techniques needed to establish living fences.

Dowdeswell, W. H. *Hedgerows and Verges.* London: Allen and Unwin, 1987. 190 pp.

Elliott, Charles. "The Age of Hedges." *Horticulture,* August/ September 1993.

Hart, Edward. *Hedge Laying and Fencing—The Countryman's Art Explained.* Wellingborough, Northamptonshire, England: Thorsons, 1981. 128 pp.

Kuchelmeister, Guido. *Hedges for Resource-Poor Land Users in Developing Countries.* Deutsche Gesellschaft für Technische Zusammenarbeit (GTZ) GmbH (Postfach 5180, D-65726 Eschborn), 1989. 256 pp.

*White, John T. *Hedgerow.* New York: William Morrow, 1980. 46 pp.

Herbs

Barclay, Gwen, and Madalene Hill. "Hold That Flavor." *The Herb Companion,* October/November 2000, 34–37.

Bass, Ruth. *Herbal Breads.* Pownal, VT: Storey, 1996. 63 pp.

———. *Herbal Salads.* Pownal, VT: Storey, 1996. 63 pp.

———. *Herbal Soups.* Pownal, VT: Storey, 1996. 63 pp.

———. *Herbal Sweets.* Pownal, VT: Storey, 1996. 63 pp.

———. *Mushrooms Love Herbs.* Pownal, VT: Storey, 1996. 63 pp.

———. *Onions Love Herbs.* Pownal, VT: Storey, 1996. 63 pp.

———. *Peppers Love Herbs.* Pownal, VT: Storey, 1996. 63 pp.

———. *Tomatoes Love Herbs.* Pownal, VT: Storey, 1996. 63 pp.

Bender, Richard W. *Herbal Bonsai—Practicing the Art with Fast-Growing Herbs.* Mechanicsburg, PA: Stackpole Books, 1996. 100 pp.

Blose, Nora, and Dawn Cusick. *Herb Drying Handbook.* New York: Sterling, 1993. 96 pp.

Bremness, Lesley. *Herbs: The Visual Guide to More Than 700 Herb Species from around the World.* New York: DK Publishing, 1994. 304 pp.

Byers, Dorie. *Herbal Remedy Gardens.* Pownal, VT: Storey, 1999. 219 pp.

Castleman, Michael. *The Healing Herbs: The Ultimate Guide to the Curative Power of Nature's Medicines.* Emmaus, PA: Rodale Press, 1991. 436 pp.

Davies, Jill Rosemary. *Milk Thistle.* Boston, MA: Element Books, 2000. 57 pp.

DeBaggio, Thomas. "Growing Herbs from Seed." *The Herb Companion,* October/November 1988, 9–13.

*Foster, Gertrude B., et al. *Park's Success with Herbs.* Greenwood, SC: George W. Park Seed Co., 1980. 192 pp.

Foster, Steven. *Echinacea—Nature's Immune Enhancer.* Rochester, VT: Healing Arts Press (1 Park St., Rochester, VT 05767), 1991. 150 pp.

———. *Herbs for Your Health.* Loveland, CO: Interweave Press, 1996. 121 pp.

Foster, Steven, and Varro E. Tyler. *Tyler's Honest Herbal.* New York: Haworth Press, 1999. 442 pp.

Grieve, M. *A Modern Herbal.* London: Tiger, 1994. 912 pp.

Hartung, Tammi. *Growing 101 Herbs That Heal.* Pownal, VT: Storey, 2000. 250 pp.

The Herb Companion. (243 E. 4th St., Loveland, CO 80537.) Magazine.

Herzberger, Heidi. "Liquid Herbs." *The Herb Companion,* April/May 1998. 52–54.

Hobbs, Christopher. *Ginkgo: Elixir of Youth.* Santa Cruz, CA: Botanica Press, 1995. 80 pp.

———. *Valerian: The Relaxing and Sleep Herb.* Capitola, CA: Botanica Press, 1993. 71 pp.

———. *St. John's Wort: The Mood Enhancing Herb.* Loveland, CO: Botanica Press, 1997. 176 pp.

———. *Milk Thistle: The Liver Herb.* Loveland, CO: Botanica Press, 1984. 32 pp.

Hoffmann, David L. *The Herb User's Guide.* Rochester, VT: Thorsons, 1987. 240 pp.

———. *The New Holistic Herbal.* Rockport, MA: Element, 1992. 284 pp.

Hollis, Joe. "Chinese Medicinal Herbs." *The Permaculture Activist,* June 1996, 22–24.

Hylton, William H., ed. *The Rodale Herb Book.* Emmaus, PA: Rodale Press, 1974. 653 pp.

Keville, Kathy. *The Illustrated Herb Encyclopedia.* Mallard Press, 1991. 224 pp.

———. "A Guide to Harvesting." Part 2 in *The Herbal Craftsman.* Herb Farm (14648 Pear Tree Ln., Nevada City, CA 95959). 3 pp.

———. "Herbal Tinctures, Everything You Wanted to Know . . ." *Vegetarian Times—Well Being,* No. 49.

———. "Salves—Making and Keeping Your Own." *Vegetarian Times—Well Being,* No. 47. (Or write to Herb Farm, 14684 Pear Tree Ln., Nevada City, CA 95959).

———. "Make Your Herbal First Aid Kit." *Well-Being Magazine,* No. 30, 1978.

———. "Herbal Help for the Respiratory Tract." *Vegetarian Times Magazine,* February 1988.

———. "Say Goodbye to Colds and Flu." *Vegetarian Times Magazine,* February 1988.

———. "Herbs for the Immune System." *Herbs! Magazine,* 13–16.

Kowalchick, Claire, et al. *Rodale's Encyclopedia of Herbs.* Emmaus, PA: Rodale Press, 1987. 545 pp.

Lima, Patrick. *Harrowsmith's Illustrated Book of Herbs.* Ontario, Canada: Camden House, 1986. 175 pp.

Mabey, Richard. *The New Age Herbalist.* New York: Collier Books, 1988. 288 pp.

Mackin, Jeanne. *The Cornell Book of Herbs and Edible Flowers.* Ithaca, NY: Cornell Cooperative Extension, 1993. 104 pp.

Maine, Sandy. *Creating an Herbal Bodycare Business.* Pownal, VT: Storey, 1999. 155 pp.

Marcin, Marietta Marshall. *Herbal Tea Gardens, 22 Plans for Your Enjoyment and Well-Being.* Pownal, VT: Storey, 1999. 187 pp.

McClure, Susan. *The Herb Gardener.* Pownal, VT: Storey, 1996. 236 pp.

McLeod, Judith A. *Lavender, Sweet Lavender.* Kenthurst, Australia: Kangaroo Press, 1989. 120 pp.

Miller, Amy Bess. *Shaker Medicinal Herbs.* Pownal, VT: Storey, 1998. 215 pp.

Mowrey, Daniel B. *Proven Herbal Blends, A Rational Approach to Prevention and Remedy.* Lehi, UT: Cormorant Books (P.O. Box 386, Lehi, UT 84043), 1986. 46 pp.

Nuzzi, Debra. *Pocket Herbal Reference Guide.* Santa Cruz, CA: The Crossing Press, 1992. 138 pp.

Ody, Penelope. *Healing with Herbs,* Pownal, VT: Storey, 1999. 160 pp.

Oppenheimer, Betty. *Gifts for Herb Lovers.* Pownal, VT: Storey, 1997. 123 pp.

Oster, Maggie. *Herb Mixtures and Spicey Blends.* Pownal, VT: Storey, 1996. 156 pp.

Phillips, Harriet Flannery. "Herbal Ground Covers: Useful plants for problem areas." *The Herb Companion,* June/July 1997, 36–41.

Phillips, Roger, and Nicky Foy. *The Random House Book of Herbs— How to Grow or Gather Herbal Plants and Use Them for Cooking.* New York: Random House, 1990. 192 pp.

Pilarski, Michael. *Resource Guide to Sustainable Wildcrafting and Medicinal Herbs in the Pacific Northwest.* Bellingham, WA: Friends of the Trees Society, 2000. 82 pp.

Proctor, Peter. *Grasp the Nettle.* New Zealand: Random House New Zealand, 1997. 176 pp.

Shores, Sandie. *Growing and Selling Fresh-Cut Herbs.* Pownal, VT: Storey, 1999. 453 pp.

Smith, Ed. *Therapeutic Herb Manual: The Therapeutic Administration of Medicinal Herb Compounds.* Williams, OR: Herb Farm (20260 Williams Hwy, Williams, OR), 1997. 65 pp.

St. Clare, Debra. *The Herbal Medicine Cabinet—Preparing Natural Remedies At Home.* Berkeley, CA: Celestial Arts, 1997. 150 pp.

Sturdivant, Lee, and Tim Blakley. *Medicinal Herbs in the Garden, Field and Marketplace,* Friday Harbor, WA: San Juan Naturals, 1999. 323 pp.

Sunset Editors. *How to Grow Herbs.* Menlo Park, CA: Sunset Books, 1974. 80 pp.

Tierra, Lesley. *The Herbs of Life: Health and Healing Using Western and Chinese Techniques.* Freedom, CA: The Crossing Press, 1992. Food as medicine, natural living, and herbs from East and West.

Tierra, Michael. *The Way of Herbs.* New York: Pocket Books, 1990. Excellent guide to herbal health and lifestyle.

———. *Planetary Herbology.* Santa Fe, NM: Lotus Press, 1988. 485 pp.

———. *The Way of Herbs.* New York: Washington Square Press, 1983. 288 pp.

Tolley, Emelie, et al. *Herbs, Gardens, Decorations and Recipes.* New York: Crown, 1985. 244 pp.

Tourles, Stephanie. *The Herbal Body Book.* Pownal, VT: Storey, 1994. 122 pp.

Tyler, Varro E., and James E. Robbers. *Tyler's Herbs of Choice.* New York: Haworth Press, 1999. 287 pp.

Vickers, Lois. *The Scented Lavender Book.* Dawsonville, GA: Little Brown, 1991. 80 pp.

Wallis, Gail. "Herbal Skin Care." *The Herb Companion,* April/May 1992.

Wright, Robert R. "Ginseng and Goldenseal." *Countryside and Small Stock Journal,* March/April 1996, 28–29.

High-Altitude Food Raising

Allen, Judy. "Mountain Top Gardening." *National Gardening,* September 1985, 14–18.

———. "Undercover Report." *National Gardening,* September 1986, 18–19.

———. "Seedlings Under Snow." *National Gardening,* November 1986, 12–13.

———. "A Mountain Legend." *National Gardening,* November 1987, 24–27.

———. "Endless Summer." *National Gardening,* October 1989, 36–39, 50–51.

Jodha, N. S., M. Banskota, and Teg Partap. *Sustainable Mountain Agriculture—Vol. 1, Perspectives and Issues.* Mohan Primlani for Oxford & IBH (Pvt. Ltd., 66 Janpath, New Delhi 110 001), 1992. 389 pp.

———. *Sustainable Mountain Agriculture—Vol. 2, Farmers' Strategies and Innovative Approaches.* New Delhi, India: Mohan Primlani for Oxford and IBH , 1992. 389 pp.

Mountain Agriculture. Vol. 4, No. 1 (March 1988). Information for Low External Input Agriculture (P.O. Box 64, 3830 AB Leusden, The Netherlands). An excellent magazine. 24 pp.

Rocky Mountain Gardener. (403 N. Pine, Gunnison, CO 81230.) Quarterly.

Weinberg, July. *Growing Food in the High Desert.* Santa Fe, NM: Sunstone Press, 1985. 91 pp.

History

Bender, Barbara. *Farming in Prehistory.* London: John Baker, 1975.

Buchanan, Keith. *Transformation of the Chinese Earth.* New York: Praeger, 1970. 335 pp.

Dazhong, Wen, and David Pimental. "Seventeenth Century Organic Agriculture in China: I. Cropping Systems in Jiaxing Region." Vol. 14, No. 1, 1986, 1–14.

———. "Seventeenth Century Organic Agriculture in China: II Energy Flows through an Agroecosystem in Jiaxing Region." Vol. 14, No. 1, 1986, 15–28.

Doherty, Catherine de Hueck. *Apostolic Farming.* Combermere, Canada: Madonna House Publications (Combermere, ON K0J 1L0, Canada), n.d. 22 pp.

Fenton, Carroll Lane, and Herminie B. Kitchen. *Plants That Feed Us:*

The Story of Grains and Vegetables. New York: John Day, 1956. 95 pp.

Huxley, Anthony. *An Illustrated History of Gardening.* New York: Paddington Press, 1978. 352 pp.

*King, F. H. *Farmers of Forty Centuries.* Emmaus, PA: Rodale Press, 1972. 441 pp. Out of print. **IL**

Mann, Albert Russell. *Beginnings in Agriculture.* New York: Macmillan, 1926.

Matheny, Ray T., and Deanne L. Gurr. "Variation in Prehistorical Agricultural Systems of the New World." *Ann. Rev. Anthropol.* 12, 1983, 79–103.

Miller, Naomi, and Kathryn Gleason. *The Archaeology of Garden and Field.* Philadelphia: University of Pennsylvania Press, 1994. 221 pp.

Needham, Joseph. *Science and Civilization in China. Vol. VI:2— Biology and Biological Technology: Agriculture.* Cambridge, U.K.: Cambridge University Press, 1984. 724 pp.

Ponting, Clive. *A Green History of the World: The Environment and the Collapse of Great Civilizations.* New York: Penguin, 1991. 430 pp.

Reed, Charles A., ed. *Origins of Agriculture.* The Hague, The Netherlands: Mouton, 1977. 1,013 pp.

*Steinbeck, John. *The Grapes of Wrath.* New York: Penguin, 1992. 619 pp.

Strueur, Stuart. *Prehistoric Agriculture.* Garden City, NY: Natural History Press, 1971. 733 pp.

Weatherford, Jack. *Indian Givers.* New York: Random House, 1988. 272 pp.

Wilson, Gilbert L. *Buffalo Bird Woman's Garden.* St. Paul, MN: Minnesota Historical Society, 1987. 129 pp.

Homesteading

BackHome Magazine. (P.O. Box 370, Mountain Home, NC 28758.) Excellent urban and rural "homesteading" skills periodical.

Bacon, R. M. *The Yankee Magazine Book of Forgotten Arts.* New York: Simon & Schuster, 1978. 219 pp.

Bakule, Paula Dreifus, ed. *Rodale's Book of Practical Formulas: Easy-to-Make, Easy-to-Use Recipes for Hundreds of Everyday Activities and Tasks.* Emmaus, PA: Rodale Press, 1991. 456 pp.

Blankenship, Bart and Robin. *Earth Knack: Stone Age Skills for the 21st Century.* Layton, UT: Gibbs-Smith, 1996. 192 pp.

Burns, Deborah, ed. *Storey's Basic Country Skills.* Pownal, VT: Storey, 1999. 564 pp.

Burns, Scott. *The Household Economy.* Boston: Beacon House, 1974.

Byler, Emma (Jonas Em). *Plain and Happy Living: Amish Recipes and Remedies.* Cleveland, Ohio: Goosefoot Acres Press, 1991. 156 pp.

Cameron, Brenda and Brian. *Making Bent Willow Furniture.* Pownal, VT: Storey, 1998. 139 pp.

Dry Stone Walling. London: British Trust for Conservation Volunteers (Zoological Gardens, Regents Park, London NW1 4RY, England), 1977. 120 pp.

Dwyer, C. P. *The Homestead Builder: Practical Hints for Handy-Men: A Classic Guide to Building Cabins and Houses from Scratch,* 10th edition. New York, New York: The Lyons Press, 1998. 145 pp.

Emery, Carla. *The Encyclopedia of Country Living: An Old-Fashioned Recipe Book.* Seattle: Sasquatch, 1994. 858 pp.

Emptor, C. "Buying Country Property." *BackHome,* September/ October 1997, 18–19.

Farm Conveniences and How to Make Them. New York: The Lyons Press, 1998. 256 pp.

Gussow, Joan Dye. *This Organic Life: Confessions of a Suburban Homesteader.* White River Junction, VT: Chelsea Green, 2001. 273 pp.

Higginbothan, Pearl, and Mary Ellen Pinkham. *Mary Ellen's Best of Helpful Hints: Fast/Easy/Fun Ways of Solving Household Problems.* New York: Warner, 1979. 119 pp.

The Home Workplace. Compiled by the editors of *Organic Gardening* and *Farming.* Emmaus, PA: Rodale Press, 1979. 127 pp.

Jason, Dan. *Living Lightly on the Land: Self-Reliance in Food and Medicine.* Salt Spring Island, Canada: Barnyard Grafix (Box 444, Ganges, Salt Spring Island, BC V8K 2W1, Canada), 1998. 142 pp.

Lyle, David. *The Book of Masonry Stoves.* White River Junction, VT: Chelsea Green, 1997. 192 pp.

Mack, Norman, ed. *Back to Basics: How to Learn and Enjoy Traditional American Skills.* Pleasantville, NY: Reader's Digest, 1981. 456 pp.

Marks, Vic, and Michael Kovacsics, eds. *The Farmstead Book.* Seattle, WA: Cloudburst, 1978. 258 pp.

Martin, George A. *Fences, Gates, and Bridges and How to Build Them.* New York: The Lyons Press, 1999. 192 pp.

McRaven, Charles. *Stonework Techniques and Projects.* Pownal, VT: Storey, 1997. 183 pp.

*Nearing, Helen, and Scott Nearing. *Continuing the Good Life.* New York: Schocken, 1979. 194 pp.

*———. *Living the Good Life.* New York: Schocken, 1970. 213 pp.

Preston, Edward. *How to Buy Land Cheap.* Port Townsend, WA: Loompanics Unlimited (P.O. Box 1197, Port Townsend, WA 98368), 1977, 1981, 1984, 1991. 141 pp.

Proulx, Earl. *Make It Last.* Dublin, NH: Yankee, 1997. 394 pp.

Roy, Rob. *Mortgage Free! Radical Strategies for Home Ownership.* White River Junction, VT: Chelsea Green, 1998. 353 pp.

*Scher, Les, and Carol Scher. *Finding and Buying Your Place in the Country,* 4th edition. Chicago: Real Estate Education Co., 1996. 414 pp.

*Seymour, John. *The Complete Book of Self-Sufficiency.* London: Faber and Faber, 1976. 256 pp. Coffee-table size. Includes grains, livestock, energy, and skills such as spinning, metalwork, and thatching. **IL**

Stein, Matthew. *When Technology Fails.* Santa Fe, NM: Clear Light Publishers, 2000. 405 pp.

Tresemer, David. *Splitting Firewood.* Brattleboro, VT: Hand and Foot, 1981. 142 pp.

United Country Magazine. United National Real Estate (4700 Belleview, Ste. 200, Kansas City, MO 64112). Good source for farm real estate listings.

Vivian, John. *Building Stone Walls.* Charlotte, VT: Garden Way, 1978. 109 pp.

———. *Wood Heat.* Emmaus, PA: Rodale Press, 1978. 428 pp.

*Wells, Kenneth McNeil. *The Owl Pen Reader.* New York: Doubleday, 1969. 445 pp.

Zwinger, Ann. *Beyond the Aspen Grove.* New York: Random House, 1970. 368 pp.

Housing

Alexander, Christopher, Sara Ishikawa, and Murray Silverstein. *A Pattern Language.* New York: Oxford University Press, 1977. 1,171 pp.

Bainbridge, David. *Plastered Straw Bale Construction.* Canelo, AZ: The Canelo Project (HCR Box 324, Canelo, AZ 85611), 1989, 1990, 1992. 44 pp.

Beard, D. C. *Shelters, Shacks and Shanties.* Berkeley, CA: Ten Speed Press, 1992. 243 pp.

Beaudoin, Edna. "The Stenman Paper House." *BackHome,* November/December 2000, 45.

Bee, Becky. *The Cob Builder's Handbook.* Murphy, OR: Groundworks (P.O. Box 381, Murphy, OR 97553), 1997. 173 pp.

Billett, Michael. *Thatching and Thatched Buildings.* London: Robert Hale Limited, 1979. 208 pp.

Broadstreet, Jim. *Building with Junk and Other Good Stuff: A Guide to Home Building and Remodeling Using Recycled Materials.* Port Townsend, WA: Loompanics Unlimited (P.O. Box 1197, Port Townsend, WA 98368), 1990. 162 pp.

Burnham, Richard. *Housing Ourselves: Creating Affordable, Sustainable Shelter.* New York: McGraw Hill, 1998. 196 pp.

Chiras, Daniel D. *The Natural House.* White River Junction, VT: Chelsea Green, 2000. 468 pp.

Easton, David. *The Rammed Earth Experience.* Wilseyville, CA: Blue Mountain Press, 1982. 71 pp.

Eccli, Eugene, ed. *Low-Cost, Energy-Efficient Shelter for the Owner and Builder.* Emmaus, PA: Rodale, 1976. 408 pp.

Hunton, Linda Mason. *The Natural Home Handbook.* Emmaus, PA: Rodale Press, 1991. 39 pp.

Kern, Ken. *The Owner-Built Home.* Oakhurst, CA: Ken Kern Drafting (P.O. Box 550, Oakhurst, CA 93644), 1972. 274 pp.

Khalili, Nader. *Ceramic Houses: How to Build Your Own.* San Francisco: Harper & Row, 1986. 221.

The Last Straw: The Grass Roots Journal of Straw-Bale and Natural Building (HC 66, Box 9, Hillsboro, NM 88042), 1993. 27 pp.

MacDonald, S. O. *A Visual Primer to Straw-Bale Construction.* Gila, NM: Appropriate Development Project, UGWA (P.O. Box 383, Gila, NM), 1999. 22 pp.

Myhrman, Matts. *Build It with Bales: Version 2.* Tucson, AZ: Out On Bale, (un)limited, 1997. Previous edition: MacDonald, S. O., and Orien MacDonald. *A Straw-Bale Primer.* Gila, NM: S. O. MacDonald and Orien MacDonald (P.O. Box 58, Gila, NM 88038), 1992.

Niemeir, Randy and Donna. *Montana Log Cabin, Rugged and Rustic, $12,000.* Helmville, MT: Randy and Donna Niemeir (P.O. Box 69, Helmville, Montana 59843). 37 pp.

Norton, John. *Building with Earth: A Handbook.* Rugby, U.K.: Intermediate Technology Development Group (Myson House, Railway Terrace, Rugby CV21 3HT, U.K.), 1986. 68 pp.

Oehler, Mike. *The $50 and Up Underground House Book.* Bonners Ferry, ID: Mole, 1997. 115 pp.

Pearson, David. *The Natural House Book.* New York: Simon & Schuster, 1989. 287 pp.

Roy, Rob. *Mortgage Free! Radical Strategies for Home Ownership.* White River Junction, VT: Chelsea Green, 1998. 353 pp.

Smith, Michael G. *The Cobber's Companion: How to Build Your Own Earthen Home.* Cottage Grove, OR: Cob Cottage Co., 2000. 134 pp.

Solberg, Gordon. "Papercrete and Fibrous Adobe." *BackHome,* November/December 2000, 40–44.

VITRA, *Grow Your Own House, Simón Vélez and Bamboo Architecture.* Weil am Rhein, Germany: Vitra Design Museum, 2000. 255 pp. Available from Chelsea Green.

Walker, Lester. *Tiny, Tiny Houses.* Woodstock, NY: The Overlook Press, 1986. 220 pp.

Wells, Malcolm. *How to Build an Underground House.* Brewster, MA: Malcolm Wells (673 Satucket Rd., Brewster, MA 02631), 1991. 96 pp.

Human Waste

Beeby, John. *Future Fertility: Transforming Human Waste into Human Wealth.* Willits, CA: Ecology Action, 1995, 1998. 164 pp.

Chy, Viet. *Human Faeces, Urine and Their Utilization.* Bangkok, Thailand: Environmental Sanitation Information Center (Asian Institute of Technology, P.O. Box 2754, Bangkok, Thailand), 1978.

Clayton, Doug, and Dave Jacke. *The Gap Mountain Permaculture Mouldering Toilet.* Jaffrey, NH: Gap Mountain Permaculture, 1992. 32 pp.

Del Porto, David, and Carol Steinfeld. *The Composting Toilet System Book.* Concord, MA: The Center for Ecological Pollution Prevention (CEPP) (P.O. Box 1330, Concord, MA), 1999. 234 pp.

Feachem, R. G., et al. *Appropriate Technology for Water Supply and Sanitation, Vol. 3: Health Aspects of Excreta and Sullae Management—A State of the Art Review.* Washington, DC: World Bank, 1981. 80 pp.

Fertile Waste: Dealing Ecologically with Your Domestic Sewage. Machynlleth, U.K.: The Center for Alternative Technology, 1994. 26 pp.

Harper, Peter, and Louise Halestrap. *Lifting the Lid: An Ecological Approach to Toilet Systems.* Machynlleth, U.K.: The Centre for Alternative Technology, 1999. 153 pp.

Huggins, Geoffrey. "Building and Using a Composting Privy." *Back-Home,* May/June 1999, 41–43.

Jenkins, J. C. *The Humanure Handbook—A Guide to Composting Human Manure.* Grove City, PA: Jenkins Publishing (P.O. Box 607, Grove City, PA 16127), 1994. 198 pp. **AL**

Jenkins, Joseph. *The Humanure Handbook,* 2nd edition. White River Junction, VT: Chelsea Green, 1999. 302 pp.

Kahn, Lloyd, Blair Allen, and Julie Jones. *The Septic System Owner's Manual.* Bolinas, CA: Shelter Publications, 2000. 161 pp.

Shuval, H. L., et al. *Appropriate Technology for Water Supply and Sanitation, Vol. 10: Nightsoil Composting.* Washington, DC: World Bank, 1981. 81 pp.

*Stoner, C. H., ed. *Goodbye to the Flush Toilet.* Emmaus, PA: Rodale Press, 1977. Out of print.

*Van der Ryn, Sim. *The Toilet Papers.* Santa Barbara, CA: Capra Press, 1978. 124 pp.

Hydroponics

Grotzke, Heinz. "Can Food Plants Grown Hydroponically be Considered Organically Grown?" *The Voice of Demeter, Newsletter of the Demeter Association, Inc. for Certification of Biodynamic Agriculture,* Summer 1999, 10.

Income

Byczynski, Lynn. *Marketing Your Produce: Ideas for Small-Scale Farmers.* U.S.: Fairplan Publications, 1997. 112 pp.

DeVault, George. "City Farm Grosses $238,000 on ½ Acre." *The New Farm,* July/August 1990, 12–15.

Gibson, Eric. "Big Bucks from Small Acres." *Income Opportunities,* July/August 1988, 54–56.
———. *Sell What You Sow!* Carmichael, CA: New World, 1994. 302 pp.

Harlan, Michael and Linda. *Growing Profits: How to Start and Operate a Backyard Nursery.* Citrus Heights, CA: Moneta, 1997. 205 pp.

Henderson, Peter. *Gardening for Profit.* Chillicothe, IL: American Botanist, Booksellers (P.O. Box 532, Chillicothe, IL 61523). 243 pp.

Lee, Andrew. *Backyard Market Gardening: The Entrepreneur's Guide to Selling What You Grow.* Burlington, VT: Good Earth Publications (P.O. Box 4352, Burlington, VT 05406-4352), 1993. 351 pp.

Olson, Michael. *MetroFarm: The Guide to Growing for Big Profit on a Small Parcel of Land.* Santa Cruz, CA: TS Books (P.O. Box 1244, Santa Cruz, CA 95061), 1994. 498 pp.

Platt, Ellen Spector. *How to Profit from Flower and Herb Crafts.* Mechanicsburg, PA: Stackpole Books, 1996. 202 pp.

Profitable Farming Now! Emmaus, PA: Regenerative Agriculture Association, 1985. 100 pp.

"Salad: Fresh from 4th Street." *Berkeley Ecology Center Newsletter,* March 1986, 2.

Specialty and Minor Crops Handbook, 2nd edition. Oakland, CA: University of California, Division of Agriculture and Natural Resources, 1998. 184 pp. Useful for economic mini-farming.

Spring Newsletter. Kona Kai Farms (1824 5th St., Berkeley, CA 94710), March 1988. 4 pp.

Sturdivant, Lee. *Profits from Your Backyard Herb Garden.* Friday Harbor, WA: San Juan Naturals (P.O. Box 642, Friday Harbor, WA 98250), 1988. 118 pp.

Taylor, T. M. *Secrets to a Successful Greenhouse and Business.* Melbourne, FL: Green Earth, 1998. 279 pp.

Van En, Robyn. *Basic Formula to Create Community-Supported Agriculture.* Great Barrington, MA: CSA Indian Line Farm (R.R. 3, Box 85, Great Barrington, MA 02130), 1988. 80 pp.

Whatley, Booker. *How to Make $100,000 Farming 25 Acres.* Chillicothe, IL: The American Botanist, 1987. 180 pp.

Yepsen, Roger B., Jr. *Growing for Market.* Emmaus, PA: Rodale Press, 1978. 301 pp. New ideas for market gardeners.

Insect Life and Balance/ Plant Health

Attracting Butterflies to Your Garden. Emmaus, PA: Rodale Press, 1992. 32 pp.

Ball, Jeff. *Rodale's Garden Problem Solver.* Emmaus, PA: Rodale Press, 1988. 556 pp.

Barclay, Leslie W., et al. *Insect and Disease Management in the Home Orchard.* Berkeley, CA: California Cooperative Extension Service, 1981. 39 pp.

Brinton, William F. "The Control of Plant Pathogenic Fungi by Use of Compost Teas." *Biodynamics,* January/February 1995, 12–15.

Buchmann, Stephen L., and Gary Paul Nabhan. *The Forgotten Pollinators.* Washington, DC: Island Press, 1996. 292 pp.

Carr, Anna. *Rodale's Color Handbook of Garden Insects.* Emmaus, PA: Rodale Press, 1979. 241 pp.

Cavigelli, M. A., et al., eds. *Michigan Field Crop Pest Ecology and Management.* Michigan State University Extension Bulletin E-2704, 2000. 108 pp.

Christie, Jesse R. *Plant Nematodes, Their Bionomics and Control.* Jacksonville, FL: H. & W. B. Drew, 1959. 256 pp.

Dean, Molly. "Butterflies: Invite Them into Your Garden with These Easy-Care Shrubs." *National Gardening,* July/August 1994, 38–41.

*Ellis, Barbara W., and Fern Bradley, eds. *The Organic Gardener's Handbook of Natural Insect and Disease Control.* Emmaus, PA: Rodale Press, 1996. 534 pp. Good color insect photos.

Fichter, George S. *Insect Pests.* New York: Golden Press, 1966. 160 pp.

Fish and Wildlife Service, U.S. Department of the Interior. *Attracting and Feeding Birds.* Conservation Bulletin No. 1. Washington, DC: U.S. Government Printing Office, revised 1973. 10 pp.

Flint, Mary Louise. *Pests of the Garden and Small Farm.* University of California Publications, 1990.

Flint, Mary Louise, and Steve H. Dreistadt. *Natural Enemies Handbook: The Illustrated Guide to Biological Pest Control.* Berkeley, CA: University of California Press, 1998. 154 pp.

Free, J. B. *Insect Pollination of Crops.* New York: Academic Press, 1970. 544 pp.

Gilkeson, Linda, Pam Peirce, and Miranda Smith. *Rodale's Pest and Disease Problem Solver.* Emmaus, PA: Rodale Press, 1996. 384 pp.

Gordon, David George. *The Western Society of Malacologists: Field Guide to the Slug.* Seattle, WA: Sasquatch Books (1008 Western Ave., Seattle, WA 98104), 1994. 48 pp.

Grainger, Janette and Connie Moore. *Natural Insect Repellents.* Austin, TX: The Herb Bar (200 W. Mary, Austin, TX 78704), 1991. 152 pp.

Griffin, Brian L. *The Orchard Mason Bee.* Bellingham, WA: Knox Cellars Publishing, 1993. 69 pp.

Hart, Rhonda Massingham. *Squirrel Proofing Your Home and Garden.* Pownal, VT: Storey, 1999. 153 pp.
———. *Bugs, Slugs and Other Thugs.* Pownal, VT: Storey, 1991. 214 pp.

Hess, Lilo. *The Amazing Earthworm.* New York: Charles Scribner's Sons, 1979. 48 pp.

Hoffmann, Michael P. *Natural Enemies of Vegetable Insect Pests.* Ithaca, NY: Resource Center (7 Business/Technology Park, Cornell University, Ithaca, NY 14850), 1993. 63 pp.

Howes, F. N. *Plants and Beekeeping.* London: Faber and Faber, 1945. 224 pp.

*Hunter, Beatrice Trum. *Gardening without Poisons.* New York: Berkeley Publishing, 1971. 352 pp. Comprehensive survey of insect control methods.

Hunter, Charles D. *Suppliers of Beneficial Organisms in North America.* Sacramento, CA: California Environmental Protection Agency (Department of Pesticide Regulation, Environmental Monitoring and Pest Management, 0011 I St., Sacramento, CA 95814), 1992. 31 pp.

Insect Life. San Francisco: Pesticide Action Network (49 Powell St., Ste. 500, San Francisco, CA 94102). Computer disk (TAPP database).

Insect Pest Management Guidelines for California Landscape Ornamentals. University of California Pub. No. 3317, 1987.

The IPM Practitioner. Berkeley, CA: Bio-Integral Resource Center (P.O. Box 7414, Berkeley, CA 94707). 32 pp.

Keville, Kathi. "Herbal Bug Repellents." *Well-Being Magazine,* July 1982.

Khambata, S. R., and J. V. Bhat. "A Contribution to the Study of the Intestinal Microflora of Indian Earthworms." *Archiv für Mikrobiologie,* Bd. 28, S., 1957. 69–80.

Klein, Hilary Dole, and Adrian M. Wenner. *Tiny Game Hunting.* New York: Bantam, 1991. 278 pp.

Larch, W. *Physiological Plant Ecology.* Berlin-Heidelberg: Springer-Verlag, 1980. 303 pp.

Least-Toxic Pest Management Publications Catalog. Berkeley, CA: The Bio-Integral Resource Center (P.O. Box 7414, Berkeley, CA 94707), April 1990. 11 pp.

Levi, Herbert W. *Spiders.* New York: Golden Press, 1968. 160 pp.

Maeterlinck, Maurice. *The Life of the Bee.* New York: Dodd, Mead, 1916. 427 pp.

Maltas, Michael. *Orchard Pest Management and Spray Schedule.* Kimberton, PA: Biodynamic Farming and Gardening, 1987. 27 pp. Available from BDFGA.

*McGregor, S. E. *Insect Pollination of Cultivated Crop Plants.* Washington, DC: Agricultural Research Service, U.S. Department of Agriculture, 1976. 411 pp. Excellent.

Metcalf, C. L., and W. Flint, revised by R. L. Metcalf. *Destructive and Useful Insects—Their Habits and Control.* New York: McGraw-Hill, 1951.

Milne, Lorus, and Margery Milne. *The Audubon Society Field Guide to North American Insects and Spiders.* New York: Knopf, 1980. 1,008 pp. Small format. Excellent color photographs!

Minnich, Jerry. *The Earthworm Book.* Emmaus, PA: Rodale Press, 1977. 372 pp.

*Mitchell, Robert T. *Butterflies and Moths.* New York: Golden Press, 1962. 160 pp. **BL**

Newman, L. Hugh. *Create a Butterfly Garden.* Kingswood, England: World's Work (Kingswood, Fodworth, Surrey, England), 1969. 115 pp.

*Pesticide Action Network (49 Powell St., Ste. 500, San Francisco, CA 94102). World-wide information clearinghouse on pesticide dangers.

Pesticide Perspectives. Santa Cruz, CA: Agroecology Program, University of California, 1990. 11 pp. Information brochure.

Philbrick, John, and Helen Philbrick. *The Bug Book.* Charlotte, VT: Garden Way, 1963. 126 pp. **BL**
———. *The Bug Book.* Charlotte, VT: Garden Way, 1974. 126 pp. **BL**

Pimentel, David. "Reducing Pesticide Use through Alternative Agricultural Practices: Fungicides and Herbicides," in *Pesticide Interactions in Crop Production: Beneficial and Deleterious Effects,* J. Altman, ed. Boca Raton, FL: CRC Press, 1993, 435–448.
———, et al. "Environmental and Economic Costs of Pesticide Use." *BioScience,* November 1992, 750–760.

Proctor, Michael, Peter Yeo, and Andrew Lack. *The Natural History of Pollination.* Portland, OR:

Timber Press, 1996. 479 pp.

Rincon-Vitova Insectories (P.O. Box 95, Oak View, CA 93022). Predatory insect source.

Rodale's Successful Organic Gardening: Controlling of Pests and Diseases. Emmaus, PA: Rodale Press, 1992.

Schwartz, P. H., Jr. *Control of Insects on Deciduous Fruits and Tree Gnats in the Home Orchard—Without Insecticides.* Hyattsville, MD: U.S. Department of Agriculture Research Service, 1975. 36 pp.

Smith, Miranda, et al. *Rodale's Garden Insect, Disease and Weed Identification Guide.* Emmaus, PA: Rodale Press, 1979. 328 pp.

Starcher, Allison Mia. *Good Bugs for Your Garden.* Chapel Hill, NC: Algonquin, 1995. 54 pp.

Stein, Dan. *Least Toxic Home Pest Control.* Eugene, OR: Hulogosi, 1991. 88 pp.

Tanem, Bob. *Deer List: 1982 Update.* San Rafael, CA: Santa Venetia Nursery (273 N. San Pedro Rd., San Rafael, CA 94903). 2 pp.

———. *Deer Resistant Plant Books.* Brochure.

Thurston, H. David. *Sustainable Practices for Plant Disease Management in Traditional Farming Systems.* Ithaca, NY: Cornell University (Department of Plant Pathology, 330 Plant Sciences Bldg., Ithaca, NY 14853), 1991. 300 pp.

Thurston, H. David, and Jeanne M. Parker. *Raised Field and Plant Disease Management.* Ithaca, NY: Department of Plant Pathology, Cornell University. 21 pp.

Tompkins, Peter. *The Secret Life of Plants.* New York: Harper & Row, 1972. 402 pp. Fascinating.

Tompkins, Peter, and Christopher Bird. "Love Among the Cabbages." *Harper's*, November 1972.

Van Den Bosch, Robert. *The Pesticide Conspiracy.* Berkeley, CA: University of California Press, 1978. 223 pp.

Vivian, John. *Keeping Bees.* Charlotte, VT: Williamson, 1986. 238 pp.

Wiles, Richard and Christopher Campbell. *Washed, Peeled, Contaminated: Pesticide Residues in Ready-to-Eat Fruits and Vegetables.* Washington, DC: Environmental Working Group, 1994. 32 pp.

Yarborough, Alice. "Gardening for Butterflies." *National Gardening*, July/August 1996, 30–33.

Yepson, Roger B., Jr. *Organic Plant Protection.* Emmaus, PA: Rodale Press, 1976. 688 pp.

———. *The Encyclopedia of Natural Insect and Disease Control.* Emmaus, PA: Rodale Press, 1984. 490 pp.

Zim, Herbert S. *Insects.* New York: Golden Press, 1956. 160 pp.

Intensive Gardening

Bonnefons, Nicholas de. *The French Gardener: Instructing How to Cultivate All Sorts of Fruit Trees and Herbs for the Garden: Together with Directions to Dry and Conserve Them in Their Natural.* St. Paul's Church-Yard, England: John Crooke, 1658. 294 pp.

Borie, Victor. "The Parisian Market-Gardeners." *Revue Horticole*, Series IV, Vol. 5, 1956, 374–376.

Broad, William J. "Too Rich a Soil: Scientists Find the Flaw That Undid the Biosphere." *New York Times*, October 5, 1993, Section B.

Bronson, William. "The Lesson of a Garden." *Cry California*, Winter 1970–71, 4–6.

Coe, Michael D. "The Chinampas of Mexico." *Scientific American* 211, July 1964, 90–98, 144.

*Courtois-Gérard, M. *Manuel Pratique de Culture Maraîchère.* Paris: J. Hetzel et Cie, 1845. 336 pp.

Crews, Timothy E., and Stephen R. Gliessman. "Raised Field Agriculture in Tlaxcala, Mexico: An Ecosystem Perspective on Maintenance of Soil Fertility." *American Journal of Alternative Agriculture*, November 1991, 9–16.

Doscher, Paul, et al. History chapter in *Intensive Gardening Round the Year.* Brattleboro, VT: Stephen Greene Press, 1981. 144 pp.

*Duhon, David. *A History of Intensive Food Gardening.* Willits, CA: Ecology Action, 1984. 136 pp.

Erickson, Clark L. *An Archeological Investigation in the Lake Titicaca Basin of Peru.* Unpublished Ph.D. dissertation, Department of Anthropology, University of Illinois, Champagne-Urbana, 1988. See Chapter 4: "Experiments in Raised Field Agriculture," 205–221.

———. "Raised Field Agriculture in the Lake Titicaca Basin: Putting Ancient Agriculture Back to Work." *Expedition*, Vol. 30, No. 3, 1989.

Erickson, Clark L., and Kay L. Candler. "Raised Fields and Sustainable Agriculture in the Lake Titicaca Basin of Peru," from *Fragile Lands of Latin America—Strategies for Sustainable Development*, edited by John O. Browder. Boulder, CO: Westview Press (5500 Central Ave., Boulder, CO 80806), 1988.

Ferrell, J. E. "Andes Indians Use Agricultural Methods of Their Ancestors." *The Plain Dealer*, February 20, 1992, 6-C.

———. "A Return to Ancient Ways." *The Plain Dealer*, February 20, 1992.

Macself, A. J. *French Intensive Gardening on Money-Making Lines.* London: W. H. & L. Collingridge, n.d., circa 1930. 128 pp.

Marx, Gary. "Bolivia Sows Ancient Fruits." *Chicago Tribune*, September 2, 1990, Section 1, 5.

McKay, C. D. *The French Garden—A Diary and Manual of Intensive Cultivation.* London: Associated Newspapers, Carmelite House, 1908. 62 pp.

Moseley, Michael E. *Archeology and the Quest for Higher Yields.* Chicago: Field Museum of Natural History, n.d. 9 pp.

Mullen, William. "Secrets of Tiwanaku—How Ingenious Farmers Built an Empire That Inspired the Incas and Rivaled Rome." *Chicago Tribune Magazine*, November 23, 1986, 1–19, 23–27, and 29–32.

*O'Brien, R. Dalziel. *Intensive Gardening*. London: Faber and Faber, 1956. 183 pp. Useful for potential mini-farmers. Veganic approach. **BL/IL**

Painter, James. "Archeology Makes Edible Impact—Revival of Ancient Agricultural Techniques Make Bolivian Raised Bed Potato Project Pay." *Christian Science Monitor*, October 9, 1991, 12–13.

Pigorsch, Susan S. "Lost Horizons." *Wisconsin Alumni*, May/June 1988, 12–17.

Quarrell, C. P. *Intensive Salad Production*. London: Crosby Lockwood & Sons, 1945. 250 pp.

Robineau, Maryvonne and Bruno. "The Bolivian Andes: Farming on the Roof of the World," *Maine Organic Farmer and Gardener*, January/February 1994, 16–17.

Smith, Thomas. *French Gardening*. London: Utopia Press, 1909. 128 pp.

Stanhill, G. "An Urban Agro-Ecosystem: The Example of Nineteenth Century Paris." *Agro-Ecosystems,* 3, 1977, 269–284.

Stevens, William K. "Scientists Revive a Lost Secret of Farming—Ancient Peruvian Fields Yield Inexpensive Technology." *New York Times*, C-1, C-15.

Weathers, John. *French Market Gardening*. London: John Murray, 1909. 225 pp. Out of print.

———. *Commercial Gardening*. Vols. I–IV. London: Gresham, 1913. 230 pp., 235 pp., 240 pp., 239 pp. Out of print.

Language and Travel

Amery, Heather, et al. *The First 1,000 Words in Spanish*. London: Usborne Publishing, 1979. 62 pp.

Bourke, Desmond O'Donnell. *French-English Horicultural Dictionary with English-French Index*. Wallingford, U.K.: C. A. B. International, 1989. 240 pp.

———. *Spanish-English Horticultural Dictionary*. Wallingford, U.K.: C. A. B. International, 1987. 148 pp.

Cody, Anna. *Latin American Spanish Phrasebook*. Oakland, CA: Lonely Planet, 1991. 173 pp.

Hamilton, Gevase. *A Health Handbook for the Tropics*. London: Voluntary Service Overseas (9 Belgrave Square, London SW1X 8PW, England), 1982. 111 pp.

Harpstrite, Pat, and Georgia Montrouil. *Spanish/English Glossary of Terms Used in "How to Grow More Vegetables."* Willits, CA: Ecology Action, 1987. 30 pp.

MacKay, Susan E. *Field Glossary of Agriculture Terms in French and English—Emphasis: West Africa*. Lafayette, IN: Purdue Research Foundation, 1984. 197 pp.

Pavick, Alan M. *First Travel: Meds for Injuries and Illness*. Timonium, MD: Publishing Corporation of America, 1986. 138 pp. Compact.

Peace Corps. *A Glossary of Agricultural Terms: Spanish/English–English/Spanish*. Washington, DC: American Language Center, The American University, 1976. 107 pp.

Rice, Robert P., Jr. *Thomson's English/Spanish–Spanish/English Illustrated Agricultural Dictionary*. Fresno, CA: Thomson Publications (P.O. Box 9335, Fresno, CA 93791), 1993. 160 pp.

Schroeder, Dirk. *Staying Healthy in Asia, Africa and Latin America*. Stanford, CA: Volunteers in Asia, 1988. 168 pp.

The Sybervision Foreign Language Series. (7133 Koll Center Parkway, Pleasanton, CA 94566.) 647 pp. Excellent audio learning tapes with manual.

Wilkes, Angela. *Spanish for Beginners*. Lincolnwood, IL: National Textbook Co., 1988. 50 pp.

Learning/Teaching

Bailey, Liberty H. *The Nature Study Idea*. New York: Doubleday, Page, 1903. 159 pp.

Bailey, L. H., ed. *Cornell Nature Study Leaflets*. Albany, NY: J. B. Lyon, 1904. 607 pp.

———. *The Training of Farmers*. New York: Macmillan, 1909. 263 pp.

———. *The Outlook to Nature*. Norwood, MA: Macmillan, 1915. 195 pp.

Brown, Marc. *Your First Garden Book*. Boston, MA: Little, Brown, 1981. 48 pp.

Call, Leland E., and E. G. Schafer. *A Laboratory Manual of Agriculture for Secondary Schools*. New York: Macmillan, 1920. 344 pp.

Center for Ecoliteracy. *The Edible Schoolyard*. Berkeley, CA: Learning in the Real World (2522 San Pablo Ave., Berkeley, CA 94702), 1999. 90 pp.

The Common Roots Program: Education So Real You Can See It Growing. Montpelier, VT: Food Works (64 Main St., Montpelier, VT 05602). Excellent innovative hands-on teaching/learning program for kindergarten through grade 6.

Composite Growing Systems. (P.O. Box 343, Skyline Blvd., La Honda, CA 94020.) La Honda, CA: Learning Boxes. Four-tiered microcosm of garden beds for teachers.

Gibson, William G. *Eye Spy*. New York: Harper, 1899. 264 pp.

Guy, Linda A., Cathy Cromell, and Lucy K. Bradley. *Success with School Gardens—How to Create a Learning Oasis in the Desert*. Phoenix, AZ: Arizona Master Gardener Press, 1996. 140 pp.

Hayes, Marion. *Project Management from Idea to Implementation*. Oakville, Canada: Reid Publishing (P.O. Box 7267, Oakville, ON L6J 6L6, Canada), 1989. 85 pp.

Hilgard, E. W., and W. J. V. Osterhout. *Agriculture for Schools of the Pacific Slope*. New York: Macmillan, 1927. 428 pp.

Jeetze, Hartmut von. "In Defense of Old-Fashioned Training." *Biodynamics*. Kimberton, PA: Biodynamic Farming and Gardening Association (P.O. Box 550, Kimberton, PA 19442), Vol. 122 (Spring 1977): 7–11; Vol. 123 (Summer 1977): 23–26.

Jurenka, Nancy Allen, and Rosanne Blass. *Beyond the Bean Seed: Gardening Activities for Grades*

K–6. Englewood, CO: Teacher Ideas Press, 1996. 195 pp.

Kiefer, Joseph, and Martin Kemple. *Digging Deeper: Integrating Youth Gardens Into Schools and Communities.* Montpelier, VT: Food Works Common Roots Press, 1998. 141 pp.

Life Lab Science Curriculum. (1156 High St., Santa Cruz, CA 95060.) A good curriculum for high school students.

Lovejoy, Ann. *Sunflower Houses.* Loveland, CO: Interweave Press, 1991. 144 pp.

MacLatchie, Sharon. *Gardening with Kids.* Emmaus, PA: Rodale Press, 1977. 207 pp.

Ocone, Lynn and Eve Pranis. *The National Gardening Association Guide to Kid's Gardening: A Complete Guide for Teachers, Parents and Youth Leaders.* New York: John Wiley & Sons, 1990.

Osterhout, W. J. V. *Experiments with Plants.* New York: Macmillan, 1911. 492 pp.

Raftery, Kevin, and Kim Gilbert. *Kids Gardening.* Palo Alto, CA: Klutz Press, 1989. 92 pp., plus seeds for 13 kinds of crops.

Resources for Teaching Sustainable Agriculture. Mt. Horeb, WI: WRDC/CIAS Resource Guide, 1992. 26 pp.

Rivera, William M., and Daniel J. Gustafson. *Agriculture Extension: Worldwide Institutional Evolution and Forces for Change.* New York: Elsevier Science, 1991. 312 pp.

Sampson, H. O. *Effective Farming: A Text-Book for American Schools.* New York: Macmillan, 1919. 490 pp.

Smith, Marny, and June Plecan. *School Garden Manual.* Westport, CT: Save the Children (54 Wilton Rd., Westport, CT 06880), 1989. 84 pp.

Teaching Peace through Gardening. Seattle, WA: Seattle Tilth (4649 Sunnyside Ave. N., Rm. 1, Seattle, WA). Children's education.

Toward a Sustainable Agriculture: A Teacher's Guide. Madison, WI: The Sustainable Agriculture Curriculum Project, University of Wisconsin Center for Integrated Agriculture Systems (240 Ag Hall, Madison, WI 53706), 1991. 151 pp.

Wooliever, Mary Avery. *Tres Semillas para Una Mejor Alimentacion, Un Manual de Agricultura Familiar.* San Ysidro, CA: Los Ninos (7065 Marconi Dr., Ste. 105, San Ysidro, CA 92703), 1990. 171 pp.

"Living Farm" Museums

The Accokeek Foundation, 3400 Bryant Point Rd., Accokeek, MD 20607.

Howell Living Farm, Titusville, NJ.

Mushrooms

Arora, David. *Mushrooms Demystified.* Berkeley, CA: Ten Speed Press, 1979. 668 pp.

Stamets, Paul. *Growing Gourmet and Medicinal Mushrooms.* Berkeley, CA: Ten Speed Press, 2000. 574 pp. Excellent and thorough, for those with serious interest.

Native Americans

Bingham, Sam and Janet. *Navajo Farming.* Logan, UT: Utah State University, 1979. 122 pp.

Bruchac, Joseph, and Michael J. Caduto. *Native American Gardening: Stories, Projects and Recipes for Families.* Golden, CO: Fulcrum, 1996. 158 pp.

Buchanan, Carol. *Brother Crow, Sister Corn.* Berkeley, CA: Ten Speed Press, 1997. 124 pp.

Grant, Bruce. *Concise Encyclopedia of the American Indian.* New York: Wings Books, 1994. 352 pp.

Sturtevant, William C., and Alfonso Ortiz, eds. *Handbook of North American Indians, Southwest.* Washington, DC: Smithsonian Institution, 1983. 868 pp.

Sturtevant, William C., and Robert F. Heizer, eds. *Handbook of North American Indians, California.* Washington, DC: Smithsonian Institution, 1978. 800 pp.

Out-of-Print Book Sources

The American Botanist. P.O. Box 532, Chillicothe, IL 61523.

Calendula Horticultural Books. 160 SW Alfred St., Chehalis, WA 98532.

Fertile Ground Books. 3912 Vale Ave., Oakland, CA 94619-2222, (530) 298-2060, books@agribooks.com.

Hortulus. 101 Scollard St., Toronto, ON M5R 1G4, Canada.

Hurley Books. R.R. 1, Box 160, Westmoreland, NH 03467.

Interloc, P.O. Box 5, Southworth, WA 98386.

Old Library Shop. (610) 838-2790.

Robert Gear. Box 1137, Greenfield, MA 01302.

Permaculture

Baxter, Kay. *Design Your Own Orchard: Bringing Permaculture Design to the Ground in Aotearoa.* Maungaturoto, New Zealand: Koanga Gardens, n.d. 80 pp.

Bell, Graham. *The Permaculture Way.* London: HarperCollins, 1992. 240 pp.

"Cities and Their Regions." *The Permaculture Activist,* December 1995.

*Mollison, Bill. *Permaculture: A Practical Guide for a Sustainable Future.* Covelo, CA: Island Press, 1990. 579 pp.

Mollison, Bill, and David Holmgren. *Permaculture One.* Ealing, England: Corgi Books (Trans-World Publishers, Century House, 61–61 Uxbridge Rd., Ealing W5 5SA, England), 1978. 128 pp.

———. *Permaculture Two.* Tasmania: Tagari Books (P.O. Box 96, Stanley, Tasmania 7331, Australia).

Mollison, Bill, with Remy Mia Slay. *Introduction to Permaculture.* Tyalgum, Australia: Tagari Publications, 1994. 213 pp.

The Permaculture Activist. (Rte. 1, Box 38, Primm Springs, TN 38476.) Magazine.

Permaculture Resources. (56 Farmersville Rd., Caliton, NJ 07830, (800) 832-6285.) Magazine.

Weber, Don. Coppicing Workshops. (Box 1322, Mendocino, CA 95460.)

Whitefield, Patrick. *Permaculture in a Nutshell.* Hampshire, England: Permanent Publications, 2000. Distributed in the United States by Chelsea Green. 84 pp.

Philosophy

Adams, George, and Olive Whicher. *The Plant Between Sun and Earth.* Boulder, CO: Shambhala, 1980. 224 pp.

Agriculture, Food and Human Values. 100 E. Normal St., Kirksville, MO 63501-4211. Quarterly journal.

All-Consuming Passion: Waking Up from the American Dream. Seattle, WA: New Road Map Foundation (P.O. Box 15981, Seattle, WA 98115), 1993. 23 pp.

Amidon, Elias, and Elizabeth Roberts, eds. *Earth Prayers from around the World: 365 Prayers, Poems, and Invocations for Honoring the Earth.* New York: Harper Collins, 1991. 451 pp.

Bailey, L. H. *The Harvest of the Year to the Tiller of the Soil.* New York: Macmillan, 1927.

———. *The Holy Earth.* New York: New York State College of Agriculture and Life Sciences, 1980. 112 pp.

Berry, Thomas. *The Dream of the Earth.* San Francisco: Sierra Club Books, 1988. 247 pp.

*Berry, Wendell. *The Unsettling of America: Culture and Agriculture.* San Francisco: Sierra Club Books, 1977. 226 pp. Eloquent and passionate view of the sociological aspects of farming.

Blix, Jacqueline, and David Heitmiller. *Getting a Life.* New York: Viking, 1997. 363 pp.

Boice, Judith L. *At One with All Life.* Moray, Scotland: Findhorn Press, 1989. 273 pp.

Boldt, Laurence G. *Zen and the Art of Making a Living.* New York: Penguin, 1999. 640 pp.

Bortoft, Henri. *The Wholeness of Nature.* Hudson, NY: Lindisfarne Press, 1996. 407 pp.

Bullfrog Films. *Sowing for Need or Sowing for Greed?* Oley, PA: Bullfrog Films (Oley, PA 19547). 58-minute video.

Burch, Mark A. *Simplicity.* Philadelphia, PA: New Society Publishers, 1995. 130 pp.

Calder, Ritchie. *After the Seventh Day.* New York: Simon & Schuster, 1961. 448 pp.

Capra, Fritjof. *The Turning Point—Science, Society, and the Rising Culture.* New York: Bantam Books, 1982. 464 pp.

*Christensen, Carl. *The Green Bible.* Ben Lomond, CA: Johnny Publishing (P.O. Box 624, Ben Lomond, CA 95005), 1990. 81 pp. Excellent.

deGraaf, John, David Wann, and Thomas H. Naylor. *Affluenza: The All-Consuming Epidemic.* San Francisco: Berrett-Koehler Publishers, 2001. 268 pp.

DeVault, George, ed. *Return to Pleasant Valley: Louis Bromfield's Best from Malabar Farm and His Other Country Classics.* Chillicothe, IL: The American Botanist, 1996. 318 pp.

*Dominguez, Joe, and Vicki Robin. *Your Money or Your Life—Transforming Your Relationship with Money and Achieving Financial Independence.* New York: Penguin, 1992. 350 pp.

Duesing, Bill and Suzanne. *Living on the Earth: Eclectic Essays for a Sustainable and Joyful Future.* East Haven, CT: Long River Books (140 Commerce St., East Haven, CT 06512), 1993. 222 pp.

Dull, Christine and Ralph. *Soviet Laughter, Soviet Tears.* Englewood, OH: Stillmore Press (7000 Stillmore Dr., Englewood, OH 45322), 1992. 370 pp.

Durning, Alan. *How Much Is Enough?* New York: W. W. Norton, 1992. 200 pp.

The Earth Summit. San Francisco: U.S. Citizens Network on UNCED (300 Broadway, Ste. 39, San Francisco, CA 94133), 1991. 44 pp. An introductory guide to the Earth Summit (June 1–12, 1992; Rio de Janeiro, Brazil).

Ehrlich, Gretel. *John Muir: Nature's Visionary.* Washington, DC: National Geographic Society, 2000. 240 pp.

*Faulkner, Edward H. *Plowman's Folly.* Norman, OK: University of Oklahoma Press, 1943. 155 pp.

*Goering, Peter, Helena Norberg Hodge, and John Page. *From the Ground Up: Rethinking Industrial Agriculture.* Atlantic Highlands, NJ: Zed Books/International Society for Ecology and Culture, 1993. 130 pp.

Gowdy, John, ed. *Limited Wants, Unlimited Means: A Reader on Hunter-Gatherer Economics and the Environment.* Washington, DC: Island Press, 1998. 342 pp.

*Gray, Charles. *Toward a Nonviolent Economics.* Eugene, OR: Charles Gray (888 Almaden, Eugene, OR 97402), 1989. 143 pp.

Gussow, Joan Dye. *Chicken Little, Tomato Sauce and Agriculture.* New York: Bookstrap Press, 1991. 150 pp.

Harlan, Jack R. *Crops and Man.* Madison, WI: American Society of Agronomy, Crop Science Society of America (677 S. Segoe Rd., Madison, WI 53711), 1992. 284 pp.

Hillel, Daniel. *Out of the Earth.* Berkeley, CA: University of California Press, 1992. 321 pp.

Howard, Louise E. *The Earth's Green Carpet.* Emmaus, PA: Rodale Press, 1947. 258 pp.

Hudson, Lois Phillips. *The Bones of Plenty.* St. Paul, MN: Minnesota Historical Press, 1984. 439 pp.

Kotke, Wm. H. *The Final Empire: The Collapse of Civilization.* Portland, OR: Arrow Point Press, 1993. 401 pp.

Luhrs, Janet. *The Simple Living Guide.* New York: Broadway Books, 1997. 444 pp.

*Mander, Jerry. *In the Absence of the Sacred.* San Francisco: Sierra Club (730 Polk St., San Francisco, CA 94109), 1992. 446 pp.

Maté, Ferenc. *A Reasonable Life: Toward a Simpler, Secure, More Humane Existence.* New York: W. W. Norton, 1993. 259 pp.

McRobie, George. *Small Is Possible.* New York: Harper & Row, 1980. 331 pp.

Merrill, Richard, ed. *Radical Agriculture.* New York: Harper & Row, 1976. 459 pp. Philosophical and political aspects of food production.

*Millman, Don. *Way of the Peaceful Warrior—A Book That Changes Lives.* Tiburon, CA: H. J. Kramer (P.O. Box 1082, Tiburon, CA 94920), 1984. 210 pp.

Quinn, Daniel. *Ishmael.* New York: Bantam, 1992. 262 pp.

Return to the Earth. Penang, Malaysia: The Third World Network (87 Cantonment Rd., 10250 Penang, Malaysia), 1990. 570 pp.

Rifkin, Jeremy. *Entropy.* New York: Bantam Books, 1981. 302 pp.

Rodale, Robert. *Sane Living in a Mad World: A Guide to the Organic Way of Life.* Emmaus, PA: Rodale Press, 1972. 270 pp.

Rosset, Peter, and Medea Benjamin, et al. *Two Steps Backward, One Step Forward.* San Francisco: Global Exchange (2017 Mission St., Rm. 303, San Francisco, CA 94110), 1993. 67 pp.

Sahlins, Marshall. *Stone Age Economics.* New York: Aldine de Gruyter, 1972. 348 pp.

Sampson, R. Niel. *Farmland or Wasteland.* Emmaus, PA: Rodale Press, 1981. 422 pp.

Savage, Scott. *The Plain Reader.* New York: Ballantine, 1998. 241 pp.

Schumacher, E. F., et al. *The Collected Writings of Hazel Henderson—Creating Alternative Futures.* New York: Berkeley Publishing (200 Madison Ave., New York, NY 10016), 1978. 403 pp.

*———. *Small Is Beautiful.* New York: Harper & Row, 1973. 305 pp.

*———. *Good Work.* New York: Harper & Row, 1979. 223 pp.

Seymour, John. *I'm a Stranger Here Myself.* London: Faber and Faber, 1978. 140 pp. Absorbing personal account.

Teale, Edward Way, ed. *The Wilderness World of John Muir.* Boston: Houghton Mifflin, 1964. 332 pp.

Thomas, William L., Jr. *Man's Role in Changing the Face of the Earth.* Vols. 1 and 2. Chicago: University of Chicago Press, 1956. 1,193 pp.

Thompson, Paul B. *The Spirit of the Soil: Agriculture and Environmental Ethics.* New York: Routledge, 1995. 196 pp.

Vandenbroeck, Goldian. *Less Is More.* Rochester, VT: Inner Traditions (One Park St., Rochester, VT 05767), 1991. 316 pp.

Willers, Bill. *Learning to Listen to the Land.* Washington, DC: Island Press, 1991. 283 pp.

Plant Names

Bailey, L. H. *How Plants Got Their Names.* New York: Dover, 1963. 181 pp.

Healey, B. J. *A Gardener's Guide to Plant Names.* New York: Scribner's, 1972. 284 pp.

Johnson, A. F., and H. A. Smith. *Plant Names Simplified.* Bromyard, England: Landsman Bookshop (Buckenhill, Bromyard, Herefordshire, England), 1972. 120 pp.

Plant Nutrient Indicators

Bear, Firman E. *Hunger Signs in Crops.* Washington, DC: The American Society of Agronomy and the National Fertilizer Assoc., 1949. 390 pp.

Clement, Frederic. *Plant Indicators: The Relation of Plant Communities to Process and Practice.* Stanford, CA: Carnegie Institute of Washington, 1920. 388 pp.

Dale, Hugh M. "Weed Complexes on Abandoned Pastures as Indicators of Site Characteristics." *Canadian Journal of Botany,* Vol. 44, 11–17.

Dale, Hugh M., P. J. Harrison, and G. W. Thomson. "Weeds as Indicators of Physical Site Characteristics in Abandoned Pastures." *Canadian Journal of Botany,* Vol. 43, 1,319–1,327.

Gershuny, Grace, and Joseph Smillie. *The Soul of Soil.* St. Johnsbury, VT: Gaia Services, 1986. 174 pp.

Hill, Stuart, and Jennifer Ramsey. "Weeds as Indicators of Soil Conditions." *Macdonald Journal,* Vol. 38, No. 3, March 1939.

Pfeiffer, Ehrenfried. *Weeds and What They Tell.* Stroudsburg, PA: Biodynamic Farming and Gardening Assn., 1970. 96 pp. Reading soil conditions by weeds.

Sampson, Arthur W. "Plant Indicators—Concept and Status." *Botanical Review,* Vol. 5, No. 3, March 1939.

Shantz, Homer Leroy. *Natural Vegetation as an Indicator of the Capabilities of Land for Crop Production in the Great Plains Area.* Washington, DC: U.S. Department of Agriculture, 1911. 100 pp.

Pruning

Bailey, L. H. *The Pruning Manual.* New York: Macmillan, 1954. 320 pp. Constantly revised for 50 years and now out of print.

Brickell, Christopher. *Fruit.* New York: Simon & Schuster, 1980. 96 pp.

*———. *Pruning.* New York: Simon & Schuster, 1980. 96 pp.

Brickell, Christopher, and David Joyce. *Pruning and Training.* New York: DK, 1996. 336 pp.

DiSabato-Aust, Tracy. "Pruning Perennials in Midseason." *Fine Gardening,* May/June 1998, 55–59.

Hill, Lewis. *Pruning Simplified.* Pownal, VT: Storey, 1986. 208 pp.

Lorette, Louis. *The Lorette System of Pruning.* London: Martin Hopkinson, 1925. 164 pp. Practiced by Alan Chadwick. Fruit trees are gently pinched and trained during summer.

Stebbins, Robert L., and Michael MacCaskey. *Pruning: How-To Guide for Gardeners.* Los Angeles: HP Books, 1983. 160 pp.

Sunset Editors. *Pruning Handbook.* Menlo Park, CA: Sunset Books, 1976. 96 pp.

Reference

*Bailey, L. H. *Cyclopedia of American Agriculture in Four Volumes.* New York: Macmillan, 1907. 2,675 pp., including many illustrations. Excellent. See Vol. II, *Crops,* especially.

———. *The Farm and Garden Rule-Book.* New York: Macmillan, 1915. 586 pp.

———. *The Standard Cyclopedia of Horticulture in Three Volumes.* New York: Macmillan, 1944. 4,056 pp., including 4,000+ engravings and other illustrations.

Bailey, Liberty Hyde, and Ethel Zoe. *Hortus Third, A Concise Dictionary of Plants Cultivated in the United States and Canada.* New York: Macmillan, 1976. 1,290 pp.

Bullfrog Films. (Department F., Oley, PA 19547.) Good selection of films on food, farming, land use, and the environment, including *Gardensong,* a PBS special on Alan Chadwick and the Biointensive method, and *Circle of Plenty,* a PBS-TV special on Ecology Action's work and a key Biointensive mini-farming project in Mexico. Send 2 stamps for catalog.

Chittenden, Fred J., ed. *Dictionary of Gardening in Three Volumes,* 2nd edition. Oxford, England: Royal Horticulture Society, Clarendon Press, 1977. 2,316 pp.

Creasy, Rosalind. *Van Patten's Organic Gardener's Edible Plants.* Chicago, IL: Login Publishers Consortium (1436 W. Randolph St., Chicago, IL 60607), 1993. 222 pp.

DeMuth, Suzanne. *Vegetables and Fruits: A Guide to Heirloom Varieties and Community-Based Stewardship.* 3 vols.: *Annotated Bibliography, Resource Organizations, Historical Supplement.* Beltsville, MD: U.S. Department of Agriculture, Special Reference Briefs Series 98–05, 1998. 135 pp., 72 pp., 78 pp.

Department of Agronomy and Range Science, University of California, Davis, CA. *Bulletins, Crop Production, 80 B.* Various bulletins from 1890s through early 1900s.

*Erichsen-Brown, Charlotte. *Medicinal and Other Uses of North American Plants.* New York: Dover, 1989. 512 pp. Originally called *The Use of Plants for the Past 500 Years.*

Fern, Ken. *Plants for a Future: Edible and Useful Plants for a Healthier World.* East Meon, Hampshire, England: Permanent Publications, Hyden House, The Sustainability Centre (distributed in the United States by Chelsea Green, White River Junction, VT), 2000. 300 pp.

Hickman, James C. ed., *The Jepson Manual: Higher Plants of California.* Berkeley, CA: University of California Press, 1993. 1,400 pp.

Montgomery, E. G. *Lippincott's Farm Manuals: Productive Farm Crops.* Philadelphia, PA: J. B. Lippincott, 1916. 501 pp.

Past Worlds: The Times Atlas of Archeology. Maplewood, NJ: Hammond, 1988. 319 pp.

Pratt, Anne. *Flowering Plants, Grasses, Sedges and Ferns of Great Britain.* 4 vols. London: Frederick Warne, 1905. 215 pp., 279 pp., 269 pp., 258 pp.

Raven, Peter H., Ray F. Evert, and Susan E. Eichhorn. *Biology of Plants.* New York: Worth, 1992. 791 pp.

*Seagfer, Joni, ed. *The State of the Earth Atlas.* New York: Simon & Schuster, 1990. 127 pp.

Source Book of Sustainable Agriculture. Burlington, VT: University of Vermont, Sustainable Agriculture Publications, 1997. 136 pp. A guide to books, newsletters, conference proceedings, bulletins, videos, and more.

Sustainable Agriculture Directory of Expertise—1993. Burlington, VA: Sustainable Agriculture Publications (Hills Bldg., Rm. 12, University of Vermont, Burlington, VT 05405-0082), 1993.

Synge, Patrick M., ed. *Dictionary of Gardening,* 2nd edition supplement. Oxford, England: Royal Horticultural Society, Clarendon Press, 1979. 554 pp.

Roots

Epstein, Emanuel. "Roots." *Scientific American,* May 1973, 48–58.

*Weaver, John E. *Prairie Plants and Their Environment.* Lincoln, NE: University of Nebraska Press, 1968. 276 pp. **IL**

*———. *Root Development of Field Crops.* New York: McGraw-Hill, 1926. 291 pp. **IL**

*———. *Root Development of Vegetable Crops.* New York: McGraw-Hill, 1927. 351 pp. Excellent diagrams of root systems. **IL**

*Wilson, Charles M. *Roots: Miracles Below.* New York: Doubleday, 1968. 234 pp.

Seed Catalogs

Abundant Life Catalog. P.O. Box 772, Port Townsend, WA 98368. Open-pollinated and heirloom seeds; books.

AgroForester Tropical Seeds. P.O. Box 428, Holualoa, HI 96725.

A High Country Garden. 2909 Rufina St., Santa Fe, NM 87505-2929. Drought hardy, perennial plants for Western gardens.

American Bamboo Co. 345 W. 2nd St., Dayton, OH 45402.

American Willow Growers Network. RFD Box 124-A, S. New Berlin, NY 13843.

Anderson Valley Nursery. P.O. Box 504, Boonville, CA 95415. Perennials, shrubs, and trees.

The Antique Rose Emporium. Rte. 5, Box 143, Brenham, TX 77833. Excellent. $5 for catalog.

Applesource. Rte. 1, Chapin, IL 62628. Apple trees.

Archia's Seed. 106-108 E. Main St., Sedalia, MO 65301. Seeds; garden and greenhouse supplies.

Baker Creek Heirloom Seeds, 2278 Baker Creek Rd., Mansfield, MO 65704.

Bakker of Holland. U.S. Bulb Reservation Center, Louisiana, MO 63350. Bulbs and perennials.

The Banana Tree. 715 Northampton St., Easton, PA 18042. Rare seeds.

Bear Creek Nursery. P.O. Box 411, Northport, WA 99157. Trees, tools, and books.

Biologische Tuinzaden. 83 De Bolster, 9605 PL, Kielwindeweer, Germany. Vegetable seeds.

Books, Seeds and Plants—1996/7. Agroforestry Research Trust, Dartington, Totnes, Devon, U.K., 1996. 26 pp.

*Bountiful Gardens. 18001 Shafer Ranch Rd., Willits, CA 95490. Ecology Action's international mail order service for vegetable, grain, compost crop, flower, and herb seeds in growing area–sized packets; key gardening books and supplies; and all Ecology Action publications.

Breck's. 6523 N. Galena Rd., Peoria, IL 61632. Bulbs, wildflowers, and lilies.

Brittingham's Plant Farms. P.O. Box 2538, Salisbury, MD 21801. Berries, grapes, and asparagus.

Burgess Seed and Plant Co. 905 Four Seasons Rd., Bloomington, IL 61701. Seeds, bulbs, plants, and supplies.

Burpee Seed Co. Warminster, PA 18974 . Large, well-known company with wide selection of vegetables and flowers. Separate catalog of heirloom seeds.

California Conservation Corps. P.O. Box 329, Yountville Center, Yountville, CA 94599. Trees.

California Gardener's Seed Co. 904 Silver Spur Rd., Ste. 414, Rolling Hills Estates, CA 90274. Seeds and garden supplies.

Caprilands Herb Farm. 534 Silver St., Coventry, CT 06238.

Carroll Gardens. P.O. Box 310, Westminster, MD 21158. Seeds.

Catnip Acres Farm. Christian St., Oxford, CT 06483. Herbs and flowers.

Charles H. Mueller. River Rd., New Hope, PA 18938. Flowers, lilies, and bulbs.

Cherfas, Jeremy. *The Fruit and Veg Finder.* Coventry, England: Henry Doubleday Research Association, 1995. 367 pp.

Chestnut Hill Nursery. 15105 NW 94 Ave., Alachua, FL 32615. Chestnuts, persimmons, and figs.

Clyde Robin Seed Co. P.O. Box 2366, Castro Valley, CA 94546. Wildflower seeds.

Companion Plants. 7247 N. Coolville Ridge Rd., Athens, OH 45701. Herbs.

Comstock. 263 Main St., Wethersfield, CT 06109. Seeds and supplies.

Cook's Garden. P.O. Box 535, Londonderry, VT 05148. Seeds and supplies.

Country Heritage Nursery. P.O. Box 5, Hartford, MI 49057. Berries, grapes, roots, and hedges; fruit, nut, ornamental shade, and evergreen trees.

Country Hills Greenhouse. Rte. 2, Corning, OH 43710. Plants.

Crocket Seed Co. P.O. Box 327, Metamora, OH 43540. Seeds.

Cruikshank's. 1015 Mount Pleasant Rd., Toronto, ON M4P 2M1, Canada. Seeds, bulbs, books, and supplies.

Dave Wilson Nursery. 19701 Lake Rd., Hickman, CA 95323. Good fruit trees. Wholesale only.

Davidson-Wilson Greenhouses. R.R. 2, Crawfordsville, IN 47933. Familiar, flowering, and exotic tropical house plants, and mini and standard violets.

De Giorgi Co. 6011 N St., Omaha, NE 68117-1634.

De Grandchamp's Nursery. 15575 77th St., South Haven, MI 49090. Blueberries.

Dean Swift Seed Co. P.O. Box B, Jaroso, CO 81138. Bulk tree seeds.

*Deep Diversity. P.O. Box 15700, Santa Fe, NM 87506-5700. Wide variety of organically grown, open-pollinated seeds and related publications. Excellent.

Di Giorgi Co. 1411 3rd St., Council Bluffs, IA 51501. Forage crops, old-fashioned lettuce and other vegetables, and open-pollinated corn.

Dr. Yoo Farm. P.O. Box 90, College Park, MD 20740. Oriental vegetable seeds.

Earl May Seed and Nursery. Shenandoah, IA 51603. Fertilizers, berries, grapes, vines, hedges, shrubs, roses, and seeds;

fruit and nut trees.

Early Seed and Garden Center. 2615 Lorne Ave., Saskatoon, Saskatchewan S7J 0S5, Canada. Grain, fodder, and cover crops.

Ed Hume Seeds. P.O. Box 1450, Kent, WA 98035. Seeds and tools.

Edible Landscapes. P.O. Box 77, Afton, VA 22920. Trees, berries, grapes, and vines.

Elixir Farm Botanicals. Brixey, MO 65618. Chinese and indigenous medicinal plants, seeds, and garlic.

Environmental Seed. P.O. Box 5904, El Monte, CA 91734. Wildflower seeds.

Epicure Seeds. Avon, NY 14414. Choice varieties from gourmet seed houses of Europe.

Essence of Old Gardeners. P.O. Box 407, Redkey, IN 47373. Seeds.

Evergreen Y. H. Enterprises. P.O. Box 17538, Anaheim CA 92817. An extensive selection of oriental vegetable seeds.

Exotica Seed Company and Rare Fruit Nursery. P.O. Box 160, Vista, CA 92083. Rare fruits, vegetables, and vines; nuts, palms, and flowering trees.

Facciola, Stephen. *Cornucopia II— A Source Book of Edible Plants.* Vista, CA: Kampong Publications (1870 Sunrise Dr., Vista, CA 92084), 1998. 713 pp. A listing of seeds carried by many catalogs and sources in the United States and other countries.

Farmer's Seed and Nursery. 1706 Morrissey Dr., Bloomington, IL 61704. Seeds, cover crops, potatoes, berries, vines, grapes, hedges, shrubs, and roses; fruit and nut trees; and supplies.

Fedco Seeds. P.O. Box 520, Waterville, ME 04903-0520. A growers' cooperative with an extensive listing, including Japanese millet (not food quality).

Filaree Farm. 182 Conconully Hwy., Okanogan, WA 98840. Lots of garlic varieties organically grown.

Forest Farm. 990 Tethrow Rd., Williams, OR 97544-9599. Plants, trees, and books.

Fox Hill Farm. 440 W. Michigan Ave., Box 9, Parma, MI 49269. Flowers and herbs.

Fox Hollow Herb and Heirloom Seed Co. P.O. Box 148, McGrann, PA 16236.

Frey Nurseries. 14000 Tomki Rd., Redwood Valley, CA 95470. Plants.

*Friends of the Trees Society. P.O. Box 1064, Tonasket, WA 98855. Books. Excellent.

Fungi Perfecti. P.O. Box 7634, Olympia, WA 98507. Mushroom-growing supplies and books.

Future Forests Nursery and Design. P.O. Box 428, Holualoa, HI 96725. Sustainable reforestation and agroforestry.

Garlic King Farms. Dean and Mary Sue Sedinger, 833 Baxter Rd., Vineland, CO 81006.

The Gourmet Gardener. 8650 College Blvd., Oakland Park, KS 66210. Imported and domestic herb, vegetable, and flower seed.

Great Northern Botanicals Association. P.O. Box 362, Helena, MT 59624. Northern Rockies specialty crops and plant information.

G. S. Grimes Seeds. 201 W. Main St., Smethport, PA 16749. Seeds, bulbs, and perennials.

Gurney's Seed and Nursery. 110 Capital St., Yankton, SD 57079. Seeds, vines, berries, ground covers, hedges, shrubs, bulbs, perennials, roses, and house plants; fruit, nut, shade, and flowering trees; and supplies.

Harmony Farm Supply. P.O. Box 460, Graton, CA 95444. Plants, berries, fruit and nut trees.

Harris Seeds. P.O. Box 22960, Rochester, NY 14692-2960. Seeds, tools, and supplies.

Hart Seed Co. P.O. Box 9169, Wethersfield, CT 06109. Largest selection of old-fashioned and non-hybrid vegetables. Many hard-to-find varieties available on request.

Hartmann's Nursery. P.O. Box 100, Lacota, MI 49063-0100.

Heirloom Seed Project. 2451 Kissel Hill Rd., Lancaster, PA 17601. Seeds.

*Henry Doubleday Research Association—Ryton Gardens—The National Centre for Organic Gardening. Ryton-on-Dunsmore, Coventry CV8 3LG, England. Vegetable, flower, herb, and green manure seeds, organic fertilizer, safe pesticides, comfrey products, educational materials, books, and attractant plants. Excellent group.

Henry Field's Seed and Nursery. 415 N. Burnett, Shenandoah, IA 51602. Seeds, ground cover, vines, berries, roses, lilies, perennials, and oriental grasses; fruit, nut, and flowering trees; and supplies.

Herbst Brothers. 1000 N. Main St., Brewster, NY 10509. Seeds, annuals, perennials, trees, and bulbs; greenhouse and nursery supplies.

Heritage Roses. 40340 Wilderness Rd., Branscomb, CA 95417. Roses.

Hidden Springs Nursery. Rte. 14, Box 159, Cookeville, TN 38501. Edible landscaping plants, herbs, and tree crops.

High Altitude Gardens. P.O. Box 4619, Ketchum, ID 83340. Vegetable, wildflower, and herb seeds; native grasses and supplies.

High Mowing Seeds. 813 Brook Rd., Wolcott, VT 05680. Open-pollinated and heirloom varieties for the Northeast.

Hillier Nurseries, Ltd. Ampfield, Ramsey, Hants S05 9PA, England. Excellent tree and plant supplier.

Hilltop Herb Farm. Box 866, Cleveland, TX 77327. Herb plants.

Holland Bulb Farms. P.O. Box 220, Tatamy, PA 18085-0220. Bulbs.

Horizon Herbs. P.O. Box 69, Williams, OR 97544-0069. 62 pp.

Horus Botanicals. 341 Mulberry, Salem, AR 72576. Heirloom grains and other seeds from all over the world.

Hurov's Tropical Seeds. P.O. Box 1596, Chula Vista, CA 92012. Tropical seeds and indoor exotics.

Indiana Berry and Plant Company. 5218 West 500 South, Huntingburg, IN 47542.

Irish Eyes. P.O. Box 307, Ellensburg, WA 98926. Potatoes and garlic.

Johnny's Selected Seeds. Foss Hill Rd., R.R. 1, Box 2580, Albion, ME 04910-9731. Small seed company with integrity. Carries native American crops, select oriental vegetables, grains, short-maturing soybeans, and supplies.

J. H. Judkins and Sons Tree Nursery. Rte. 4, Smithville, TN 37166. Hedges, shrubs, ground cover, vines, and fruit trees.

*J. L. Hudson, Seedsman. Star Rte. 2, Box 337, LaHonda, CA 94020. Vegetable, flower, and herb seeds; books. Excellent selection.

Kester's Wild Game Nurseries. Box 516, Omro, WI 54963. Grain, vegetable, and grass seeds; publications.

*KUSA Seed Foundation. Box 761, Ojai, CA 93023. Key seed crop seeds and literature. Excellent.

Larner Seeds. P.O. Box 60143, 445 Monroe Dr., Palo Alto, CA 94306. Vegetable, flower, grass, shrub, vine, and tree seeds. Specializes in California and New England native seeds.

Legume Seed Source Directory. Kutztown, PA: Rodale Institute Research Center (611 Siegfriedale Rd., Kutztown, PA 19530), 1992. 23 pp.

Henry Leuthardt. Montauk Hwy., East Moriches, Long Island, NY 11940. Specializes in old-fashioned varieties of apple trees, pear trees, and grapes.

Henry Morton—Old Fashioned Apples. Rte. 1, Box 203, Gatlinburg, TN 37738. Old Appalachian Mountain varieties.

Living Tree Center. P.O. Box 797, Bolinas, CA 94924. Seeds and trees.

Lockhart Seeds. P.O. Box 1361, Stockton, CA 95205. Vegetable seeds.

Lost Prairie Herb Farm. 805 Kienas Rd., Kalispell, MT 59901. Plants, supplies, and books.

Machado Farms. P.O. Box 655, Sun City, CA 92586. Comfrey roots. Send a self-addressed, stamped envelope for more information.

Maine Seed Saving Network. P.O. Box 126, Penobscot, ME 04476.

McClure and Zimmerman. P.O. Box 368, 108 W. Winnebago, Friesland, WI 53935. Bulbs and books.

Mellinger's. 2310 W. South Range Rd., North Lima, OH 44452-9731. Unusual imported vegetable, herb, flower, and grass seeds; berries and vines. Wide variety of familiar and unusual trees, plants, and roses. Mushrooms, tools, supplies, books, and greenhouse equipment.

Messelaar Bulb Co. P.O. Box 269, Ipswich, MA 01938. Bulbs.

Michigan Bulb Co. 1950 Waldorf, Grand Rapids, MI 49550. Grapes, berries, roses, plants, flowers, and fruit trees.

Mongold, Susan and Rex. HCR 15, Dyer, NV 89010. Seed potatoes.

Moon Mountain. P.O. Box 34, Morro Bay, CA 93442. Wildflower seeds.

Moose Grower's Supply. P.O. Box 520, Waterville, ME 04903. Seed potatoes, onion sets, Jerusalem artichokes, cover crop seeds, organic fertilizers, and books.

Mountain Maples. 5901 Spy Rock Rd., Laytonville, CA 95454-1329. Variety of maples, bonsai, and dwarf conifers.

Native Seeds and Plants. Ankeny, IA: Soil and Water Conservation Society (7515 NE Ankeny Rd., Ankeny, IA 50021). 36 pp.

*Native Seeds/SEARCH. 526 N. 4th Ave., Tucson, AZ 85705. Herbs, books, dyes, and baskets. Excellent cotton and tobacco seeds, drought-tolerant corn, beans, and vegetables.

New England Strawberry Nursery. S. Deerfield, MA 01373. Strawberries.

Nichols Garden Nursery. 1190 Old Salem Rd. NE, Albany, OR 97321-4580. Unusual specialties: elephant garlic, luffa sponge, winemaking supplies, and herbs.

North Central Comfrey Products. P.O. Box 195, Glidden, WI 54527. Comfrey and comfrey products.

North Star Gardens. 19060 Manning Trail N., Marine-on-St. Croix, MN 55047-9723. Raspberries—northern, western, and southern stock.

Nourse Farms, Inc. 41 River Rd., South Deerfield, MA 01373. Strawberry, raspberry, asparagus, and rhubarb starts.

One Green World. 28696 S. Cramer Rd., Molalla, OR 97038-8576. Fruit trees and ornamentals.

Oregon Exotics Nursery. 1065 Messinger Rd., Grants Pass, OR 97527.

P. de Jager and Sons. P.O. Box 100, Brewster, NY 10509. Bulbs and lilies.

George W. Park Seed Co. 1 Parkton Ave., Greenwood, SC 29647-0001. The best selection of flowers. Gorgeous full-color catalog available free.

Peace Seeds. 2385 SE Thompson St., Corvallis OR 97333.

Perennial Vegetable Seed Co. P.O. Box 608, Belchertown, MA 01007.

Phoenix Seeds. P.O. Box 9, Stanley, Tasmania 7331. Organic seed varieties.

Plants of the Southwest. Agua Fria, Rte. 6, Box 11A, Santa Fe, NM 87501. Products for a healthy planet.

Raintree Nursery. 391 Butts Rd., Morton, WA 98356. Berries, plants, fruit and nut trees, books, and supplies.

Ramsey Seed. P.O. Box 351, 205 Stockton St., Manteca, CA 95336. Wide variety of seeds, including those for compost crops.

Redwood City Seed Co. P.O. Box 361, Redwood City, CA 94064. Basic selection of non-hybrid, untreated vegetable and herb seeds. Expert at locating various tree seeds, including redwoods.

Reliable Seeds. 3862 Carlsbad Blvd., Carlsbad, CA 92008. Seeds.

R. H. Shumway Seed Company. P.O. Box 1, Graniteville, SC 29829-0001. Vegetable, flower, herb, grass, grain, fodder, and cover crop seeds; roses, berries, and fruit trees; and supplies.

Richters—Canada's Herb Specialist. 357 Hwy. 47, Goodwood, ON L0C 1A0, Canada. Herb, vegetable, and flower seeds. Plants, supplies, potpourri, natural medicines, and books.

Rocky Mountain Seed Services. Box 215, Golden, BC V0A 1H0, Canada. British Columbia native seeds, including hard-to-find varieties.

Rohrer Seeds. P.O. Box 250, Smoketown, PA 17576. Vegetable and flower seeds plus some cover crops and grains.

Roses of Yesterday and Today. 802 Brown's Valley Rd., Watsonville, CA 95076-0398. Old, rare, unusual, and modern roses.

Russell Graham. 4030 Eagle Crest Rd. NW, Salem, OR 97304. Bulbs, flowers, perennials, ferns, and oriental grasses.

Salt Spring Seeds. P.O. Box 444, Ganges, Salt Spring Island, BC V8K 2W1, Canada. Organic open-pollinated grains, beans, and vegetables.

Sanctuary Seeds. 1913 Yew St., Vancouver, BC V6K 3G3, Canada. Seeds, companion plants, and medicinals.

Sand Hill Preservation Center. 1878 230th St., Calamus, IA 52729. Heirloom seeds and poultry.

Sandy Mush Herb Nursery. 316 Surrett Cove Rd., Leicester, NC 28748-9622. Seeds, plants, herbs, and books.

Sassafras Farms. P.O. Box 1007, Topanga, CA 90290. Two dozen organically grown vegetable varieties and miscellaneous roots.

*Seed Saver's Exchange, 3076 North Winn Rd., Decorah, IA 52101. Exchange listings published yearly for $2. Good source of heirloom varieties. Listing includes seed saving guide. Excellent.

*———. Garden Seed Inventory, 5th edition. Seed Saver's Exchange, 3076 North Winn Rd., Decorah, IA 52101, 2001. 560 pp. Excellent listing of all open-pollinated vegetable seed varieties sold in the United States.

*———. Fruit, Berry and Nut Inventory, 3rd edition. Seed Saver's Exchange, 3076 North Winn Rd., Decorah, IA 52101, 2001. 560 pp.

Seeds of Change. P.O. Box 15700, Santa Fe, NM 87506-5700. Organic seeds.

Self-Reliance Seed Co. P.O. Box 96, Stanley, Tasmania 7331. Vegetable, annual, herb, and tree seeds.

Setropa. A. E. Bussum, P.O. Box 203, 1400, Holland. Seeds for forestry and environmental conservation.

Shepherd's Garden Seeds. 30 Irene St., Torrington, CT 06790-6658. Special vegetable, flower, and herb seeds; supplies and books.

Sonoma Antique Apple Nursery. 4395 Westside Rd., Healdsburg, CA 95448. Fruit trees.

Sourcepoint Organic Seeds. 1349 2900 Rd., Hotchkiss, CO 81419. Organic cereal grains, vegetables, and other seeds from many parts of the world.

Southern Exposure Seed Exchange. P.O. Box 460, Mineral, VA 23117. Apple, vegetable, and flower seeds; supplies and books. Mostly open-pollinated seeds.

Southmeadow Fruit Gardens. Lakeside, MI 49116. Large selection of fruit trees.

Spring Hill Nurseries. 110 W. Elm St., Tipp City, OH 45371. Perennial plants and flowers.

St. Lawrence Nurseries. 325 State Hwy 345, Potsdam, NY 13676. Berries and vines; fruit and nut trees.

Stark Brothers Nurseries and Orchards Co. P.O. Box 510, Louisiana, MO 63353-0510. Fruit tree and landscaping catalog. Hedges, shrubs, vines, berries, ground cover, and roses; fruit, nut, shade, and ornamental trees; supplies and books. Specializes in fruit trees, especially dwarf and semi-dwarf varieties, including many developed by Luther Burbank.

Steele Plant Co. Gleason, TN 38229. Sweet potato starts; onion, cauliflower, cabbage, brussel sprouts, and broccoli seeds.

Stokes Seeds. P.O. Box 548, Buffalo, NY 14240-0548. Carries excellent varieties of many vegetables, especially carrots. Be sure to specify "untreated" seeds.

Suffolk Herbs. Sawyer's Farm, Little Cornard, Sudbury, Suffolk C010 0NY, England. Wide variety of seeds and herbs.

Sunnyboy Gardens. 3314 Earlysville Rd., Earlysville, VA 22936. Herb catalog.

Sunnybrook Farms Nursery. 9448 Mayfield Rd., Chesterland, OH 44026. Scented geranium source.

Suttons Seeds. Hele Rd., Torquay, Devon TQ2 7QJ, England. Catalogue available only in England. Use catalogue for information only. Order seeds through Garden Import, P.O. Box 760, Thornhil, ON L3T 4A5, Canada.

Synergy Seeds. P.O. Box 787, Somes Bar, CA 95556. Open-pollinated, some wildcrafted. Unusual grains.

Taylor Herb Gardens. 1535 Lone Oak Rd., Vista, CA 92084. Herb seeds and plants by mail.

Territorial Seed Co. P.O. Box 157, Cottage Grove, OR 97424-0061. Seeds, tools, and supplies.

Thompson and Morgan. P.O. Box 1308, Jackson, NJ 08527-0308. Wide variety of seeds.

Thunderfoot Earthworks—Sunnyland Seeds. John Munk, P.O. Box 385, Paradox, CO 81429.

Tillinghast Seed Co. P.O. Box 738, LaConner, WA 98257.

Tolowa Nursery. P.O. Box 509, Talent, OR 97540. Berries, grapes, fruit, nut, woodlot, and ornamental trees.

Tomato Growers Supply. P.O. Box 2237, Fort Myers, FL 33902. Tomato and pepper seeds; supplies, books, and cooking equipment.

Tradewinds Bamboo Nursery. 28446 Hunter Creek Loop, Gold Beach, OR 97444. Plants, books, hardgoods, and bamboo products.

True Seed Exchange. R.R. 1, Princeton, MO 64673. Exchange for home-grown seed. To join (i.e., to list your seeds for exchange and to receive listings in return), send $2.

Turtle Tree Seeds. Camphill Village, Copake, NY 12516. Biodynamic, open-pollinated seeds.

Underwood Gardens. Grandma's Garden, 1414 Zimmerman Rd.,

Woodstock, IL 60098. Open-pollinated and heirloom seeds.

Valley Seed Service. P.O. Box 9335, Fresno, CA 93791. Specialty seeds for research.

Van Bourgondien. P.O. Box A, 245 Farmingdale Rd., Babylon, NY 11702. Bulbs, ground cover seeds, and rare perennials.

Vandenberg. Black Meadow Rd., Chester, NY 10918. Bulbs, indoor plants, lilies, perennials, and wildflowers.

Van Engelen. 23 Tulip Dr., Bantam, CT 06750. Bulbs and lilies.

Vermont Bean Seed Co. Computer Operation Center, Vaucluse, SC 29850-0150. All kinds of beans for those who want to start growing more protein crops.

Vesey's Seeds for Short Seasons. P.O. Box 9000, Calais, ME 04619-6102. Vegetable and flower seeds, supplies, tools, books, and natural pest control.

Victory Garden Plants. P.O. Box 867, Mendocino, CA 95460. Landscaping plants.

Vilmorin. 6104 Yorkshire Terr., Bethesda, MD 20814. Vegetable seeds.

Vilmorin Andrieux. 4, quai de la Megisserie, 75001 Paris, France. Old, respected seed house specializing in high-quality gourmet vegetables. Catalog in French. Expensive minimum order.

Volkman/North Coast Seed Co. P.O. Box 5875, Portland, OR 97228. Grass, pasture, and bird seed.

Wayside Gardens. 1 Garden Ln., Hodges, SC 29695-0001. Trees, vines, shrubs, plants, supplies, and books.

Well-Sweep Herb Farm. 317 Mount Bethel Rd., Port Murray, NJ 07865. Herbs, supplies, and books.

White Flower Farm. Litchfield, CT 06759-0050. Plants, flowers, tools, supplies, and books.

Willhite Seed Co. P.O. Box 23, Poolville, TX 76076. Vegetable seeds.

Wilson Brothers Floral Co. Roachdale, IN 46172. Scented geranium source.

Winterthur. Winterthur, DE 19735. Rare plants.

Wolf River Nurseries. Rte. 67, Buskirk, NY 12028. Vines, berries, and trees.

Wood Prairie Farm. 49 Kinney Rd., Bridgewater, ME 04735. Organic seed potatoes.

Yates Vegetable Seed Catalog for Commercial Growers. P.O. Box 616, Toowoomba, Queensland, Australia 4350. Specializes in tropical varieties suitable for the southern hemisphere. Free international seed catalog.

*Yerba Buena Nursery. 19500 Skyline Blvd., Woodside, CA 94062. Native California plants. Excellent.

Seed Saving

Almekinders, Conny, and Niels Louwaars. *Farmers' Seed Production: New Approaches and Practices.* London: Intermediate Technology Publications, 1999. 291 pp.

*Ashworth, Suzanne. *Seed to Seed.* Decorah, IA: Seed Savers Publications (3076 North Winn Rd., Decorah, IA 52101), 1991. 222 pp.

Bubel, Nancy. "Saving Seeds." *Mother Earth News,* September/October 1987, 58–63.

Department of Agronomy, *Seed Saving Project News,* U.C. Davis, Winter/Spring 1991. 13 pp.

Deppe, Carol. *Breed Your Own Vegetable Varieties.* White River Junction, VT: Chelsea Green, 2000. 367 pp.

Dremann, Craig. *Vegetable Seed Production.* Redwood City, CA: Redwood City Seed Co. (P.O. Box 360, Redwood City, CA 94064), 1974. 6 pp.

Gately, Barbara. *Plant Pollination Instructional Manual.* Berkeley, CA: U.C. Instructional Laboratory, Graduate School of Education.

George, Raymond A. T. *Vegetable Seed Production.* New York: Longman, 1985. 318 pp.

————. *Vegetable Seed Production,* 2nd edition. New York: CABI Publishing, 1999. 328 pp.

Jason, Dan. *Save Our Seeds, Save Ourselves.* Salt Spring Island, Canada: Salt Spring Seeds (P.O. Box 444, Ganges, Salt Spring Island, BC V8K 2W1, Canada). 23 pp.

Johnston, Robert, Jr. *Growing Garden Seeds.* Albion, ME: Johnny's Selected Seeds (Albion, ME 04910), 1976. 32 pp. Culture of plants for saving seed.

Justice, Oren L., and Louis N. Bass. *Principles and Practices of Seed Storage: Agriculture Handbook No. 506.* Washington, DC: U.S. Government Printing Office, 1978. 289 pp.

Manual Seed Cleaning Screens Abundant Life Seed Co. (P.O. Box 772, Port Townsend, MA 98368.) Available in the following mesh sizes (in fractions of inches): $\frac{1}{4}$, $\frac{1}{8}$, $\frac{1}{2}$, $\frac{1}{16}$, and $\frac{1}{30}$. Made of stainless steel for long use. Screen mesh and framed screens available at a per-square-foot price.

Miller, Douglas C. *Vegetable and Herb Seed Growing for the Gardener and Small Farmer.* Hersey, MI: Bullkill Creek Publishing, 1977. 46 pp. A good book to start with.

Nabham, Gary Paul. *Enduring Seeds—Native American Agriculture and Wild Plant Conservation.* Berkeley, CA: North Point Press (850 Talbon Ave., Berkeley, CA 94706), 1989. 225 pp.

"New Isn't Necessarily Better." *Harrowsmith Country Life,* January/February 1994.

Roberts, E. H., ed. *Viability of Seeds.* Syracuse, NY: Syracuse University Press, 1972. 448 pp.

*Rogers, Marc. *Saving Seeds: The Gardener's Guide to Growing and Storing Vegetable and Flower Seeds.* Pownal, VT: Storey, 1990. 185 pp.

"Seeds for Life." *ILEIA Newsletter,* March 1994.

U.S. Department of Agriculture. *Seeds—The Yearbook of Agriculture, 1961.* Washington, DC: U.S. Government Printing Office, 1961. 591 pp.

Seeds/Diversity

Benefits of Diversity—An Incentive toward Sustainable Agriculture. New York: United Nations Development Program, 1992. 209 pp.

Cromwell, Elizabeth, and Steve Wiggins. *Sowing beyond the State: NGOs and Seed Supply in Developing Countries.* London: Overseas Development Institute (Regent's College, Inner Circle, Regent's Park, London NWI 4NS, England), 1993. 143 pp.

*"Crop Genetic Erosion in the Field." *The Seed Map* (RAFI, P.O. Box 655, Pittsboro, NC 27312). Large chart.

Fowler, Cary, and Pat Mooney. *Shattering—Food, Politics, and the Loss of Genetic Diversity.* Tucson, AZ: University of Arizona Press, 1990. 278 pp.

"Grain—Genetic Resources Action International." *Grain Publications List,* Summer 1992.

"Plants and Seeds as Intellectual Property." *The Seedhead News,* Winter 1994.

Seeds/GMOs

"A Storm Is Breaking Down on the Farm," *Science and Technology,* December 14, 1992, 98–101.

"Are Gene-Altered Plants an Ecological Threat? Test Is Devised." *New York Times–Science,* June 22, 1993.

Biotechnology—An Activists' Handbook. Montpelier, VT: The Vermont Biotechnology Working Group (Rural Vermont, 15 Barre St., Montpelier, VT 05602), 1991. 47 pp.

"The Conflict Between Farmers' Rights and Breeders' Rights." *RAFI Action,* Spring 1993, 4–5.

"Flaws in the Tailoring." *Christian Science Monitor,* March 21, 1994.

Gendel, Steven M., et al. *Agricultural Bioethics—Implications of Agricultural Biotechnology.* Ames, IA: Iowa State University Press, 1990. 357 pp.

Goldberg, Rebecca, et al. *Biotechnology's Bitter Harvest.* Biotechnology Working Group, 1990. 73 pp.

"High-Tech Farming Sows Misery in the Philippines." *Utne Reader,* October/November 1986, 104–105.

Kneen, Brewster. *Farmageddon— Food and the Culture of Biotechnology.* Gabriola Island, Canada: New Society Publishers, 1999. 231 pp.

Rissler, Jane, and Margaret Mellon. *The Ecological Risks of Engineered Crops.* Cambridge, MA: MIT Press, 1996. 168 pp.

Seeds/Green Revolution

"Green Revolution." *The Elements* (1901 Q St. NW, Washington, DC 20009), June 1975, 1, 14–16.

"Green Revolution Hits Double Trouble." *U.S. News & World Report,* July 28, 1980, 37, 40.

"Green Revolution Is Not Enough, Study Finds." *New York Times– Science,* September 6, 1994.

"Green Revolution #2." *Dollars and Sense Magazine,* December 1985.

"How Green Is the Green Revolution?" *Enfo* (Box 761, Berkeley, CA 94701), September 1973, 1–2.

Lipton, Michael, and Richard Longhurst. *New Seeds and Poor People.* Baltimore, MD: Johns Hopkins University Press, 1989. 464 pp.

Merrill, Richard. *Ecology of the Green Counter-Revolution.* Santa Barbara, CA: Community Environmental Council, 1973.

Mullen, William. "The Green Revolution: Can the World Salvage It?" *San Francisco Examiner and Chronicle,* December 14, 1975, A-13.

Shiva, Vandana. *The Violence of the Green Revolution: Third World Agriculture, Ecology and Politics.* London: Zed Books, 1991. 264 pp.

"Tanzania Corn Taller, Greener but Costlier." *The Oregonian,* February 24, 1993.

"The U.S. Won't Be Shielded in the Event of a Bio-Crisis." *Christian Science Monitor,* November 23, 1994.

Wallace, James N. "Is the Green Revolution Over?" *San Francisco Examiner and Chronicle,* August 17, 1980.

Wilkes, H. Garrison, and Susan Wilkes. "The Green Revolution." *Environment,* October 1972, 32–39.

"The Withering Green Revolution." *Natural History,* March 1973, 20–21.

Seeds/Plant Propagation

Brickell, Christopher, ed. *Plant Propagation.* New York: Simon & Schuster, 1979. 96 pp.

Food and Agricultural Organization of the United Nations. *The Plant—The Flower.* Rome: FAO, 1976. 29 pp. In the United States: UNIPUB, 1180 Ave. of the Americas, New York, NY 10036.

———. *The Plant—The Living Plant and the Root.* 1976. 29 pp.

———. *The Plant—The Stem, the Buds, and the Leaves.* 1976. 30 pp.

Fyfe, Agnes. *Moon and Planet.* Arlesheim, Switzerland: Society for Cancer Research, 1975. 94 pp.

Hartmann, Hudson T., et al. *Plant Propagation—Principles and Practices,* 5th edition. Englewood Cliffs, NJ: Prentice Hall, 1990. 647 pp.

Hawthorn, Leslie, and Leonard H. Pollard. *Seed Production.* New York: Blakiston, 1954. 626 pp. A classic.

Heiser, Charles B., Jr. *Seed to Civilization.* San Francisco: W. H. Freeman, 1973. 243 pp.

Hofstetter, Robert. *Overseeding Research Results, 1982–1984.* Kutztown, PA: Agronomy Department, Rodale Institute Research Center, 1984. 30 pp.

Lawrence, William J. C., and J. Newell. *Seed and Potting Composts.* London: Allen & Unwin, 1941. 136 pp.

Lorenz, Oscar A., and Donald N. Maynard. *Knott's Handbook for Vegetable Growers,* 3rd edition. New York: John Wiley & Sons, 1988. Useful charts for small farmers. Strong chemical orientation.

Powell, Eileen. *From Seed to Bloom.* Pownal, VT: Storey, 1995. 312 pp.

*Reilly, Ann. *Park's Success with Seeds.* Greenwood, SC: George W. Park Seed Co. (Greenwood, SC 29647), 1978. 364 pp.

Robinson, Raoul A. *Return to Resistance—Breeding Crops to Reduce Pesticide Dependence.* Davis, CA: agAccess, 1996. 480 pp.

*Sutton and Sons. *The Culture of Vegetables and Flowers from Seeds and Roots.* London: Simpkin, Marshall. Hamilton, Kent, 1898. 427 pp. Excellent. Out of print.

Soil

Albrecht, William A. *The Albrecht Papers—Vol. III.* Austin TX: Acres U.S.A., 1989. 401 pp.

———. *The Albrecht Papers—Enter Without Knocking.* Austin, TX: Acres U.S.A., 1992. 315 pp.

———. *The Other Side of the Fence.* Austin, TX: Acres U.S.A., 1996. 25-minute video.

American Society of Agronomy, Crop Science Society of America, Soil Science Society of America. "The Role of Phosphorus in Agriculture." Proceedings of a symposium held June 1976. Madison, WI: American Society of Agronomy, Crop Science Society of America, Soil Science Society of America, 1980. 910 pp.

———. "Crop Tolerance to Suboptimal Land Conditions." Proceedings of a symposium, November– December 1976. Madison, WI: American Society of Agronomy, Crop Science Society of America, Soil Science Society of America, 1978. 343 pp.

Balfour, Lady E. B. *The Living Soil and The Haughley Experiment.* London: Faber and Faber, 1975. 383 pp.

Bear, Firman E. *Soils and Fertilizers,* 4th edition. New York: John Wiley & Sons, 1959. 420 pp.

Beatty, Marvin T. *Soil Science at the University of Wisconsin Madison— A History of the Department, 1889–1989.* Madison, WI: University of Wisconsin, 1991. 141 pp.

Berkelaar, Edward, Ph.D. "The Effect of Aluminum in Acidic Soils on Plant Growth." *ECHO Development Notes* (17391 Durrance Rd., North Myers, FL 33917), April 2001, 1–3.

Biofuels, Development and Soil Productivity. Sacramento, CA: Office of Appropriate Technology (1600 9th St., Sacramento, CA 95814), 1982. 109 pp.

*Brady, Nyle. *The Nature and Properties of Soils,* 10th edition. New York: Macmillan, 1990. 621 pp.

Brown, Kirk W., et al. *Sustaining Our Soils and Society.* Alexandria, VA: American Geological Institute, 1999. 64 pp.

Buol, S. W., et al. *Soil Genesis and Classification.* Ames, IA: Iowa State University Press, 1997. 527 pp.

Carter, Martin R., ed. *Soil Sampling and Methods of Analysis.* Boca Raton, FL: Lewis, 1993. 823 pp.

*Carter, Vernon G., and Tom Dale. *Topsoil and Civilization.* Norman, OK: University of Oklahoma Press, 1955. 292 pp. Describes how flourishing civilizations have fallen into decay by not maintaining their agricultural health and soil.

Coleman, David C., and D. A. Crossley, Jr. *Fundamentals of Soil Ecology.* San Diego, CA: Academic Press, 1996. 205 pp.

Crozier, Carl. *Soil Conservation Techniques for Hillside Farms: A Guide for Peace Corps Volunteers.* Springfield, VA: National Technical Information Service (Peace Corps Information Collection & Exchange, Office of Training and Program Support, 806 Connecticut Ave., NW, Washington, DC 20526), 1986. 97 pp.

Dalla Rosa, Karl R. "Building Soils on Pacific Atolls." *Nitrogen Fixing Tree News* (Nitrogen Fixing Tree Assoc., Morrilton, AR), January–March 1993. 2 pp.

Doran, John W., and Alice J. Jones. *Methods for Assessing Soil Quality.* Madison, WI: Soil Science Society of America, 1996. 410 pp.

Farb, Peter. *Living Earth.* New York: Harper Colophon, 1959. 175 pp. Easy-to-read peek at the life under the soil.

Faulkner, Edward H. *Plowman's Folly.* Norman, OK: University of Oklahoma Press, 1943. 155 pp. Classic.

———. *Soil Development.* Norman, OK: University of Oklahoma Press, 1952. 232 pp.

Fenzau, C. J. *An Acres U.S.A. Primer.* Austin, TX: Acres U.S.A., 1979. 435 pp.

Ford, Brian J. *Microbe Power.* New York: Stein and Day, 1976. 181 pp.

Gardner, Gary. *Shrinking Fields: Cropland Loss in a World of Eight Billion.* Worldwatch Paper 131. Washington DC: Worldwatch Institute, 1996. 56 pp.

Glanz, James. *Saving Our Soil: Solutions for Sustaining Earth's Vital Resource.* Boulder, CO: Johnson Books, 1995. 182 pp.

Godderham, P. T. "The Effect on Soil Conditions of Mechanized Cultivation at High Moisture Content and of Loosening by Hand Digging." *Journal of Agricultural Science,* No. 976, 567–571.

Grimshaw, Richard G., and Larisa Helfer, eds. *Vetiver Grass for Soil and Water Conservation, Land Rehabilitation and Embankment Stabilization* (World Bank Technical Paper No. 273). Washington DC: World Bank, 1995. 281 pp.

Hall, Sir A. D. *The Soil—An Introduction to the Scientific Study of the Growth of Crops.* New York: E. P. Dutton, 1920. 252 pp.

Handbook on Soils. Brooklyn, NY: Brooklyn Botanic Garden, 1956. 81 pp. Some photos of root systems in the soil.

Hans Jenny: Soil Scientist, Teacher, and Scholar. Berkeley, CA: Regional Oral History Office (386 Library, University of California, Berkeley, CA 94720), 1989. 372 pp.

Harpstead, Milo I., Thomas J. Sauer, and William F. Bennett. *Soil Science Simplified.* Ames, IA: Iowa State University Press, 1997. 210 pp.

Havlin, John L., et al. *Soil Fertility and Fertilizers,* 6th edition. Upper Saddle River, NJ: Prentice Hall, 1999. 499 pp.

*Hensel, Julius. *Bread from Stones.* Austin, TX: Acres U.S.A., 1991. 102 pp.

Hillel, Daniel. *Out of the Earth: Civilization and the Life of the Soil.* Berkeley and Los Angeles: University of California Press, 1992. 321 pp.

Hopkins, Cyril. *Agricultural Experiment Station, How Not to Treat Illinois Soils.* Urbana, IL: University of Illinois, 1915. 31 pp.

Hopkins, Donald P. *Chemicals, Humus, and the Soils.* London: Faber and Faber Limited, 1945. 278 pp.

*Howard, Sir Albert. *The Soil and Health.* New York: Devin-Adair, 1956. 307 pp. A cornerstone of the organic movement.

*Hyams, Edward. *Soil and Civilization.* New York: Harper & Row, 1976. 312 pp. Reprint from 1952.

Ingham, Elaine. "Life in the Soil—Understanding the Foodweb." *Acres, U.S.A.,* January 1997, 18–23.

Ingham, Elaine R., Andrew R. Moldenke, and Clive A. Edwards. *Soil Biology Primer.* Ankeny, IA: Soil and Water Conservation Society (7515 NE Ankeny Rd., Ankeny, IA 50021), 2000. 48 pp.

Introduction to Soil and Water Conservation Practices. Oklahoma City, OK: World Neighbors (International Headquarters, 5116 N. Portland, Oklahoma City, OK 73112), 1985. 33 pp.

Jenny, Hans. *The Soil Resource: Origin and Behavior.* New York: Springer-Verlag, 1980. 377 pp.

———. *Factors of Soil Formation: A System of Quantitative Pedology.* New York: Dover, 1994. 281 pp.

King, F. H. *The Soil.* New York: Macmillan, 1895. 303 pp.

Kohnke, Helmut. *Soil Science Simplified,* 3rd edition. Prospect Heights, IL: Waveland Press, 1966. 78 pp.

Kruckeberg, Arthur R. *California Serpentines: Flora, Vegetation,*

Geology, Soils, and Management Problems. Berkeley, CA: University of California Press, 1984. 180 pp.

Krupenikov, I. A. *History of Soil Science: From Its Inception to the Present.* New Delhi, India: Oxonian Press Pvt., 1992. 352 pp. Translated from Russian.

Larkcom, Joy. "Deep Cultivation." Subsection of "Soil and Soil Pests." *Journal of the Royal Horticultural Society* 104, Part 6, June 1979, 252–256.

Lewandowski, Ann. *Minnesota Soil Management Series: Soil Management* (21 pp.), *Compaction* (17 pp.), *Manure Management* (17 pp.), *Organic Matter* Management (17 pp.), and *Soil Biology and Soil Management* (17 pp.). St. Paul, MN: Minnesota Institute for Sustainable Agriculture, University of Minnesota Extension Service (405 Coffey Hall, 1420 Eckles Ave., St. Paul, MN 55108-6068), 2000. For large-scale agriculture; very good information also applicable on smaller scales.

Lindert, Peter H. *Shifting Ground— The Changing Agricultural Soils of China and Indonesia.* Cambridge, MA: MIT Press, 2000. 351 pp.

Logsdon, Gene. *The Gardener's Guide to Better Soil.* Emmaus, PA: Rodale Press, 1975. 246 pp.

Lord, Russell. *The Care of the Earth: A History of Husbandry.* New York: The New American Library, 1962. 384 pp.

Lowdermilk, W. C. "Conquest of the Land through Seven Thousand Years." *Agricultural Information Bulletin*, No. 99. (Washington, DC: U.S. Government Printing Office), 1975. 30 pp.

Lyon, T. Lyttleton, et al. *The Nature and Properties of Soils,* 5th edition. New York: Macmillan, 1952. 591 pp.

———. *The Nature and Properties of Soils,* 4th edition. New York: Macmillan, 1943. 499 pp.

———. *Soils: Their Properties and Management.* New York: Macmillan, 1915. 764 pp.

Lyon, T. Lyttleton, et al., and Harry O. Buckman. *The Nature and Properties of Soils.* New York: Macmillan, 1929. 428 pp. 1st edition only for more organic treatment.

Magdoff, Fred, and Harold van Es. *Building Soils for Better Crops.* Burlington, VT: Sustainable Agriculture Network, Sustainable Agriculture Publications (Hills Bldg., Rm. 10), University of Vermont, 2000. 230 pp.

Morgan, Sampson. *Clean Culture— The New Soil Science: An Original and Scientific Treatise on Clean Culture, the Mineralized-Humus Method of Soil Fertilization Without the Use of Animal Manure.* 1908.

Nierenberg, Danielle. "Toxic Fertility." *World Watch,* March/April 2001, 30–38.

No-Digging Report No. 1. Essex, England: Henry Doubleday Research Association, reprint 1972. 40 pp.

Ortloff, Stuart H., and Henry B. Raymore. *A Book about Soils for the Home Gardener.* New York: M. Barrows, 1962. 189 pp.

*Parnes, Robert. *Fertile Soil— A Grower's Guide to Organic and Inorganic Fertilizers.* Davis, CA: agAccess, 1990. 194 pp.

Paul, E. A., et al., eds. *Soil Organic Matter in Temperate Agroecosystems.* Boca Raton, FL: CRC Press, 1997. 414 pp.

Pellant, Chris. *Rocks and Minerals— The Most Accessible Recognition Guides.* New York: Dorling Kindersley Handbooks, 1992. 256 pp.

Pfeiffer, Ehrenfried. "Organic Matter Rebuilt in Pure Sand." *Biodynamics,* Spring 1951, 2–8. **AL**

———. *Soil Fertility: Renewal and Preservation.* East Grinstead, Sussex, England: Lanthorn Press, 1983. 199 pp.

Pimental, David, ed. *World Soil Erosion and Conservation.* Cambridge, Great Britain: Cambridge University Press, 1993. 349 pp.

Ridzon, Leonard, and Charles Walters. *The Carbon Cycle.* Kansas City, MO: Acres U.S.A., 1994. 150 pp.

Robert Parnes Speaks on the Science and Necessity of Organic Residues in the Soil. Gates Mills, OH: Griesinger Films, 1991. 60 mins. Video. **IL**

Russell, E. J. *The Fertility of the Soil.* London: Cambridge University Press, 1913. 128 pp.

Russell, E. John, rewritten by E. Walter Russell. *Soil Conditions and Plant Growth.* New York: Longmans, Green, 1950. 635 pp.

*Sachs, Paul D. *Edaphos: Dynamics of a Natural Soil System,* 2nd edition. Newbury, VT: Edaphic Press, 1999. 201 pp. Excellent for understanding the soil ecosystem.

Shaxson, T. F. *Land Husbandry: A Framework for Soil and Water Conservation.* Ankeny, IA: Soil and Water Conservation Society (7515 NE Ankeny Rd., Ankeny, IA 50021), 1989. 64 pp.

Singer, Michael J., and Donald N. Munns. *Soils, An Introduction.* Upper Saddle River, NJ: Prentice Hall, 1996. 480 pp.

Smith, William C. *How to Grow 100 Bushels of Corn per Acre on Worn Soil.* Delphi, IN: Smith, 1910. 111 pp.

Soil Quality Test Kit Guide. Washington, DC: U.S. Department of Agriculture, Agriculture Research Service, Natural Resources Conservation Service, Soil Quality Institute, 1999. 82 pp. **IL/AL**

Soil Science Society of America, American Society of Agronomy. "Field Soil Water Regime." Proceedings of a symposium held on August 16, 1971. Madison, WI: Soil Science Society of America, American Society of Agronomy, 1973. 212 pp.

———. "Soils for Management of Organic Wastes and Waste Waters." Proceedings of a symposium held March 1975. Madison, WI: Soil Science Society of America, 1977. 650 pp.

———. "Soil Fertility and Organic

Matter as Critical Components of Production Systems." Proceedings of a symposium sponsored by Division S-4, S-2, S-3, and S-8 of the Soil Science Society of America in Chicago, December 3, 1985. Madison, WI: Soil Science Society of America, American Society of Agronomy, 1987. 166 pp.

Soils and the Greenhouse Effect. Sussex, England: John Wiley & Sons, 1990. 575 pp.

Sylvia, David M., et al., eds. *Principles and Applications of Soil Microbiology.* Upper Saddle River, NJ: Prentice Hall, 1999. 550 pp.

*U.S. Department of Agriculture. *Soils and Men—The Yearbook of Agriculture, 1938.* Washington, DC: U.S. Government Printing Office, 1938. 1,232 pp.

The Vanishing Soil. Kimberton, PA: Biodynamic Farming and Gardening Association (P.O. Box 550, Kimberton, PA 19442). Video.

Veldkamp, Tom. *AGRODOK 2, Soil Fertility.* Wagenigen, The Netherlands: Agromisa (P.O. Box 41, 6700 AA Wagenigen, The Netherlands), 1992. 25 pp. Chemical orientation; can be modified for GROW BIOINTENSIVE and organic use.

"The Vetiver System: A Proven Solution." Arlington, VA: The Vetiver Network(3601 N. 14th St., Arlington, VA 22201). Pamphlet.

Waksman, Selam A. *Humus.* Baltimore, MD: Williams and Wilkins, 1938. 526 pp.

———. *Soil Microbiology.* New York: John Wiley & Sons, 1952. 356 pp.

Westerman, R. L., ed. *Soil Testing and Plant Analysis.* Madison, WI: Soil Science Society of America, 1990. 784 pp.

Wildman, William E., et al. *Soil: Physical Environment and How It Affects Plant Growth.* Leaflet No. 2280. Davis, CA: University of California, Division of Agricultural Sciences, June 1975. 10 pp.

Solar Cooking

Como Hacer y Usar Una Caja Solar para Cocinar. Sacramento, CA: Solar Cookers International (1919 21st St., #101, Sacramento, CA 95814), n.d. 27 pp.

Kerr, Barbara Prosser. *The Expanding World of Solar Box Cookers.* Taylor, AZ: Kerr-Cole Solar Box Cookers (P.O. Box 576, Taylor, AZ 85939), 1991. 79 pp.

Kerr Enterprises. (P.O. Box 27417, Tempe, AZ 85281.) A *very* good solar box cooker. Send $4 for plans and other material.

The Solar Box Cooker Manual: How to Make, Use and Teach Others about Them. Sacramento, CA: Solar Cookers International (1919 21st St., #101, Sacramento, CA 95814), May 1990. 66 pp. $10.

*Solar Cookers International. (1919 21st St., #101, Sacramento, CA 95814.) A nonprofit organization with excellent solar oven plans, recipes, and cooking information. Write for publications list.

Still, Dean, and Jim Kness. *Capturing Heat—Five Earth-Friendly Cooking Technologies and How to Build Them.* Cottage Grove, OR: Aprovecho Research Center (80574 Hazelton Rd., Cottage Grove, OR 97424), 1996. 35 pp.

Still, Dean, Mike Hatfield, and Peter Scott. *Capturing Heat Two—Fuel-Efficient Cooking Stoves with Chimneys, A Pizza Oven, and Simple Water Heaters: How to Design and Build Them.* Cottage Grove, OR: Aprovecho Research Center (80574 Hazelton Rd., Cottage Grove, OR 97424), 2000. 48 pp.

Supply Catalogs

Bozeman Bio-Tech. P.O. Box 3146, 1612 Gold Ave., Bozeman, MT 59772. Long-term insect pest control.

Catalog for Cooks, Williams-Sonoma. P.O. Box 7456, San Francisco, CA 94120. Cooking utensils.

Coast Dry Flowers and Baskets. Box 10, San Francisco, CA 94101. Dry flowers, bouquets, baskets, and floral supplies.

Cotton Clouds. Rte. 2, Desert Hills #16, Safford, AZ 85546. Cotton yarn.

Countryside General Store. 103 N. Monroe St., Waterloo, WI 53595.

Cumberland General Store. Rte. 3, P.O. Box 81, Crossville, TN 38555. Old time general merchandise.

De Van Koek Dutch Trader. 3100 Industrial Terr., Austin, TX 78759. Garden tools.

Down to Earth Dist. Garden Products Catalog, P.O. Box 1419, Eugene, OR 97440. Wholesale fertilizers, tools, etc. Minimum order $100.

Dramm. P.O. Box 528, Manitowoc, WI 54220. Professional watering tools.

Duluth Trading Company. 8300 Highland Dr., Wausau, WI 54401, (877) DTC-2345. Sells gel knee pads.

The Earth Store. P.O. Box 2286, Bellaire, TX 77402. Organic products.

Environmental Concerns. 9051-E Mill Station Rd., Sebastopol, CA 95472. Products for a safer, cleaner world, including biodegradable soaps and recycled paper.

Fertile Ground Books. P.O. Box 2008, Davis, CA 95617-2008, books@agribooks.com. Excellent books.

Florist Products Horticultural Supplies. 2242 N. Palmer Dr., Schaumburg, IL 60195. Supplies and tools.

Gardener's Supply, 128 Intervale Rd., Burlington, VT 05401. Garden tools, greenhouses, and supplies.

Gardens for Growing People. P.O. Box 630, Pt. Reyes Sta., CA 94956. Children's gardening supplies.

Good Books Catalog. P.O. Box 419, Intercourse, PA 17534.

Great Lakes IPM Catalog of Insect Monitoring Systems for the Professional Grower. 10220 Church Rd. NE, Vestaburg, MI 48891.

Jacobs Brothers Co. 8928 Sepulveda Blvd., Sepulveda, CA 91343. Fifteen-year shade and pest netting in various percentages of shading capacity.

Magic Garden Supply. P.O. Box 68, Redway, CA 95560. Supplies.

Mountain Rose Herbs—A Catalogue of Herbal Delights. P.O. Box 2000, Redway, CA 95560.

Nasco Farm and Ranch. P.O. Box 901, Fort Atkinson, WI 53538. Farm and ranch supplies.

New England Cheesemaking Supply Company. P.O. Box 85, Ashfield, MA 01330. Supplies and books.

Nitragen, Inc. 3101 W. Custer Ave., Milwaukee, WI 53209. Source of many kinds of inocula for seeds, so you can maximize the fixing of nitrogen in the soil by legumes and obtain higher yields and higher protein contents.

Northeast Carry Trading Company. 110 Water St., Hallowell, ME 04347.

Ohio Earth Food. 13737 Duquette Ave. NE, Hartville, OH 44632. Mail-order organic fertilizers.

*Peaceful Valley Farm Supply. P.O. Box 2209, Grass Valley, CA 95945. Fertilizers, supplies, seeds, and books. Excellent source.

Pratt, Doug, ed. *Real Goods Solar Living Source Book: The Complete Guide to Renewable Energy Technologies and Sustainable Living,* 10th edition. White River Junction, VT: Chelsea Green, 1999. 561 pp. A directory of equipment.

Real Goods. 13771 S. Hwy. 101, Hopland, CA 95449. Renewable energy.

Real Goods Renewables: Utility Inter-tie Systems: How to sell power to your electric utility company (and get yours for free!). 1031 N. State St., Ukiah, CA 95482-3413.

Rocket Chef. P.O. Box 4525, Pacoima, CA 91331, (800) 544-4099. Non-electric food processor.

SelfCare Catalog. 349 Healdsburg Ave., Healdsburg, CA 95448. Products for self-help health care, including key books.

Seventh Generation. Colchester, VT 54460.

Smith and Hawken. Box 6900, Florence, KY 41022-6900. Tools, clothes, bulbs, and books.

Snow Pond Farm Supply. P.O. Box 70, Salem, MA 01970. Soil-building seed, soil amendments, and fertilizers; natural pest controls; and tools.

Timber Press. 9999 SW Wilshire, Portland, OR 97225. Books.

VJ Growers Supply. 500 W. Orange Blossom Trail, Apopka, FL 32703. Six-year clear vinyl 6-ml plastic film for constructing mini-greenhouses. Available in 54-inch-wide, 100-foot-long rolls only.

*Walt Nicke's Garden Talk. P.O. Box 433, Topsfield, MA 01983. Supplies and tools. Good catalog.

Wild Weeds. P.O. Box 88, Redway, CA 95560. Herbal solutions for all purposes, seeds, and books.

Sustainable Agriculture

Appropriate Technology Transfer for Rural Areas (ATTRA). *Sustainable Agriculture Directory of Expertise.* Burlington, VT: Sustainable Agriculture Network, Sustainable Agriculture Publications, University of Vermont, 1996.

Clark, Robert, ed. *Our Sustainable Table.* San Francisco: North Point Press, 1990. 176 pp.

Enriquez, Laura J. *Cuba's New Agricultural Revolution: The Transformation of Food Crop Production in Contemporary Cuba.* Oakland, CA: Food First—Institute for Food and Development Policy (398 60th St., Oakland, CA 94618), 2000. 29 pp.

Gates, Jane Potter. *Tracing the Evolution of Organic/Sustainable Agriculture.* Beltsville, MD: National Agricultural Library, 1988. 20 pp.

Gliessman, Stephen R. *Agroecology: Ecological Processes in Sustainable Agriculture.* Boca Raton, FL: Lewis, 2000. 357 pp.

Jackson, Wes. *New Roots for Agriculture.* San Francisco: Friends of the Earth, 1980. 155 pp. Addresses the importance of developing sustainable agricultural systems including perennial seed-producing plants.

Jason, Dan. *Greening the Garden: A Guide to Sustainable Growing.* Philadelphia, PA: New Society Publishers, 1991. 196 pp.

Kirschenmann, Frederick. *Switching to a Sustainable System.* Windsor, ND: Northern Plants Sustainable Agriculture Society (R.R. 1, Box 73, Windsor, ND 58424), 1988. 18 pp.

Kolisko, E., and L. Kolisko. *Agriculture of Tomorrow.* Bournemouth, England: Kolisko Archive Publications, 1975. 322 pp.

Looking after Our Land. Oxford, UK: Oxfam Publications (274 Banbury Rd., Oxford 0X2 7DZ, U.K.). 20-minute video.

Lowrance, Richard, Benjamin R. Stinner, and Garfield J. House, eds. *Agricultural Ecosystems—Unifying Concepts.* New York: John Wiley & Sons, 1984. 233 pp.

National Research Council. *Alternative Agriculture.* Washington, DC: National Academy Press, 1989. 448 pp.

———. *Sustainable Agriculture and the Environment in the Humid Tropics.* Washington, DC: National Academy Press, 1993. 702 pp.

Peet, Mary. *Sustainable Practices for Vegetable Production in the South.* Newburyport, MA: Focus Publishing (P.O. Box 369, Newburyport, MA 01950), 1996. 174 pp.

Pereira, Winin. *Tending the Earth: Traditional, Sustainable Agriculture in India.* Bombay, India: Earthcare Books (2 Anand, 17 Carmichael Rd., Bombay 400 026 India), 1993. 315 pp.

Petersen, Cass, Laurie E. Drinkwater, and Peggy Wagoner. *The Rodale Institute Farming Systems Trial—The First 15 Years.* Kutztown, PA: The Rodale Institute, 1999. 40 pp.

Pretty, Jules. *The Living Land.* London: Earthscan Publications, 1998. 324 pp.

Sustainable Agriculture for California. Pub. 3349. Oakland, CA: Division of Agriculture and Natural Resources, University of California (6701 San Pablo Ave., Oakland, CA 94608-1239), 1991. 197 pp.

Sustainable Farming. Quebec, Canada: REAP (Box 125, Glenaladale House, Ste.-Anne-de-Bellevue, Quebec H9X 1C0, Canada). Quarterly magazine.

Sustainability of California Agriculture —A Symposium. Davis, CA: U.C. Cooperative Extension, U.C. Davis College of Agricultural and Environmental Sciences, U.C. Santa Cruz Agroecology Program, U.C. Agricultural Experiment Station, American Society of Agronomy California Chapter, n.d. 317 pp.

Towards Sustainable Agriculture. Langenbruck, Switzerland: Agroecol Development (c/o Oekozentrum Langenbruck, CH-4438 Langenbruck, Switzerland). Information of Low-External Input Agriculture (P.O. Box 64, 3830 AB Leusden, The Netherlands), 1988. Two-part series.

The Transition Document—Toward an Environmentally Sound Agriculture. Portland, OR: Oregon Tilth Research and Education Committee, 1989. 77 pp.

What Is Sustainable Agriculture? Davis, CA: University of California, Sustainable Agriculture Research and Education Program, 1991. 5 pp.

United Nations Development Programme (UNDP). *Urban Agriculture—Food, Jobs and Sustainable Cities.* New York: UNDP, 1996. 302 pp.

Terracing

Copijn, A. N. *A-Frames and Other Levelling Instruments.* Leusden, The Netherlands: ETC Foundation, AME Programme (P.O. Box 64, 3830 AB Leusden, The Netherlands), 1986. 13 pp.

———. *Soil Protection.* Leusden, The Netherlands: ETC Foundation, AME Programme, 1987. 16 pp.

How to Farm Hilly Lands. Forestry for People Series. The Philippines: Bureau of Forest Development. 15 pp.

"Kenyans Shore Up Hopes and Topsoil with Terraces." *Christian Science Monitor,* May 9, 1988.

Vetiver Grass—A Thin Green Line Against Erosion. Washington, DC: National Research Council, National Academy Press, 1993. 171 pp. "Living terracing" crop.

Wenner, Carl G. *Trees in Erosion and Soil Conservation.* Nairobi, Kenya: Nairobi Ministry of Agriculture, Farm Management Branch Project and Evaluation Division, 1980. 26 pp.

———. *An Outline of Soil Conservation in Kenya.* Nairobi, Kenya: Kenya Ministry of Agriculture, Soil Conservation Extension Unit. 57 pp.

World Bank. *Vetiver Grass—The Hedge Against Erosion.* Washington, DC: World Bank, 1990. 78 pp.

Testing

National Testing Laboratory. 6555 Wilson Mills Rd., Ste. 102, Cleveland, OH 44143. Water testing.

*Timberleaf Soil Testing Service. 39648 Old Spring Rd., Murrieta, CA 92563-5566, (909) 677-7510. Excellent. Send for information on services and prices. The basic and trace mineral tests are highly recommended.

Wallace, T. M. C. *The Diagnosis of Mineral Deficiencies in Plants.* Long Ashton, Bristol: University of Bristol Agricultural and Horticultural Research Station, 1944. 164 pp.

*Watercheck. 6555 Wilson Mills Rd., Cleveland, OH 44123, (800) 458-3330. Excellent water testing laboratory. Write for information.

Tools

Arts Machine Shop. Harrison at Oregon Trail, American Falls, ID 83211. Good-quality soil corers.

Blackburn, Graham. *Woodworking Handtools.* New York: Simon & Schuster, 1974. 238 pp.

Branch, Diana S. *Tools for Homesteaders, Gardeners, and Small-Scale Farmers.* Emmaus, PA: Rodale Press, 1978. 512 pp.

Carruthers, Ian, and Marc Rodriquez. *Tools for Agriculture: A guide to appropriate equipment for smallholder farmers.* Nottingham, U.K.: Russell Press, 1992. 238 pp.

The C. S. Bell Co. 170 W. Davis St., Tiffin, OH 44883. Grain mills and shellers.

J. A. Cissell Co. Aqunkum-Yellowbrook Rd., Farmingdale, NJ 07727. Five- to ten-year bird netting.

Happy Valley Ranch. P.O. Box 9153, Yakima, WA 98909. Cider, fruit, and wine presses.

Jackson, Albert, and David Day. *Tools and How to Use Them.* New York: Knopf, 1979. 252 pp.

Jones, Bernard E., ed. *The Complete Woodworker.* Berkeley, CA: Ten Speed Press, 1980. 408 pp.

Logan, William Bryant. *The Tool Book: A compendium of over 500 tools for the well-tended garden.* New York: Workman, 1997. 302 pp.

*McCullagh, James C. *Pedal Power—In Work, Leisure and Transportation.* Emmaus, PA: Rodale Press, 1977. 133 pp.

McRobie, George, ed. *Tools for Organic Farming.* London: Intermediate Technology Publications, 1990. 77 pp.

R. Hunt & Co. Ltd. Atlas Works. Earles Colne Colchester, Essex, England CO6 2EP. Manufacturers of mechanical power transmission equipment agricultural machinery, e.g., chaff cutters, winnowers, groundnut decorticators, and grinding mills.

Seymour Hardware Catalog. Seymour Manufacturing Co., 500 N. Broadway, Seymour, IN 47274.

Stratoflex, Inc. 220 Roberts Cut-Off, P.O. Box 10398, Fort Worth, TX 76114. Excellent heavy-duty water hoses. We like the #230-12.

*Tresemer, David. *The Scythe Book— Mowing Hay, Cutting Weeds, and Harvesting Small Grains with Hand Tools.* Brattleboro, VT: Hand and Foot, 1981. 120 pp.

Volunteers in Technical Assistance. Appropriate Technology Materials Information Sheets. Volunteers in Technical Assistance (3206 Rhode Island Ave., Mt. Rainier, MD 20822).

Wells, Malcolm. *Recovering America —A More Gentle Way to Build.* Brewster, MA: Malcolm Wells (673 Satucket Rd., Brewster, Cape Cod, MA), 1999. 143 pp.

Traditional Agriculture

Gliessman, Stephen R., et al. *Un Enfoque Agro-ecologico en el Estudio de la Agricultura Tradicional.* Santa Cruz, CA: Agroecology Program, University of California at Santa Cruz, 1984. 10 pp.

———. "The Ecology and Management of Traditional Farming Systems," from Altieri, M., and S. Hecht, eds., *Agroecology and Small Farm Development*, 1990, 13–17.

Information for Low External Input Agriculture. Understanding Traditional Agriculture. Bibliography. The Netherlands: ILEIA (P.O. Box 64, 3840 AB Leusen, The Netherlands), 1987. 144 pp.

Mountjoy, Daniel C., and Stephen R. Gliessman. "Traditional Management of a Hillside Agroecosystem in Tlaxcala, Mexico: An Ecologically Based Maintenance System." *American Journal of Alternative Agriculture*, Winter 1988, 3–10.

Sattaur, Omar. "The Lost Art of the Waru Waru." *New Scientist*, May 12, 1988, 50–51.

Stevens, William K. "An Eden in Ancient America? Not Really." *New York Times*, March 30, 1993.

Trees

Agroforestry in the United States—Research and Technology Transfer Needs for the Next Millennium. Columbia, MO: Association for Temperate Agroforestry (203 ABNR Bldg., University of Missouri, Columbia, MO), 2000. 23 pp.

Ayensu, Edward S., et al. *Firewood Crops.* Washington, DC: National Academy of Sciences, 1980. 237 pp.

Bailey, L. H. *The Cultivated Conifers in North America.* New York: Macmillan, 1933. 404 pp.

Baker, Richard St. Barbe. *Among the Trees.* London: Man of the Trees, 1935. 96 pp.

———. *The Brotherhood of the Trees.* London: Adelphi, n.d. 64 pp.

———. *Caravan Story and Country Notebook.* Wolverton, Bucks, England: McCorquodale, 1979. 71 pp.

———. *Dance of the Trees.* London: Oldbourne Press (121/128 Fleet St., London EC4, England), 1956. 192 pp.

———. *Famous Trees of New Zealand.* Wellington, New Zealand: A. H. and A. W. Reed, 1965. 150 pp.

———. *Green Glory.* New York: A. A. Wyn, 1949. 253 pp.

———. *I Planted Trees.* London: Lutterworth Press, 1952. 262 pp.

———. *Kabongo—The Story of a Kikuyu Chief.* New York: A. S. Barnes, 1955. 127 pp.

———. *Kamiti.* New York: Duell, Sloan and Pearce, 1958. 117 pp.

———. *Men of the Trees.* New York: Dial Press, 1931. 283 pp.

———. *My Life, My Trees.* Forres, Scotland: Findhorn Publications, 1970. 167 pp.

———. *The Redwoods.* London: Lindsay Drummond (2 Guilford Place, London WC1, England), 1945. 95 pp.

———. *Sahara Challenge.* London: Lutterworth Press, 1954. 152 pp. Important book.

———. *Trees—A Book of the Seasons.* London: Lindsay Drummond, 1940. 113 pp.

———. *Trees in the Environment—Selected Writings of Richard St. Barbe Baker.* Saskatchewan, Canada: University of Saskatchewan Archives. 153 pp. Unpublished manuscript.

Balancing Ecology and Economics: A Start-Up Guide for Forest Owner Cooperation. Madison, WI: Cooperative Development Services (30 W. Mifflin St., Ste. 401, Madison, WI), University of Wisconsin Center for Cooperatives (230 Taylor Hall, 427 Lorch St., Madison, WI), Community Forestry Resource Center, Institute for Agriculture & Trade Policy (2105 First Ave. S., Minneapolis, MN), 2000. 107 pp. plus appendices.

Board on Science and Technology for International Development. *Firewood Crops: Shrubs and Tree Species for Energy Production, Vol. 2.* Washington DC: National Research Council, 1984. 92 pp.

Brinkman, Willemine, ed. *Why Natural Forests Are Linked with Nutrition: Health and Self Reliance of Villagers in Northeast Thailand—A Collection of Papers.* Phu Wiang, Khon Kaen Province: Royal Forest Department, Ministry of Agriculture and Cooperatives (United National Development Programme, Food and Agriculture Organization of the United Nations. Phu Wiang, Khon Kaen Province), 1989. 86 pp.

Broad, Ken. *Caring for Small Woods.* London: Earthscan, 1999. 233 pp.

Brooks, Alan. *Woodlands: A Practical Handbook,* revised edition. Wallingford, U.K.: British Trust for Conservation Volunteers, 1988. 173 pp.

Burkhardt, Hans J. *Maximizing Forest Productivity.* Willits, CA: Burkhardt Books (P.O. Box 117, Willits, CA 95490), 1994. 140 pp.

Camp, Orville. *The Forest Farmer's Handbook: A Guide to Natural Selection Forest Management.* Ashland, OR: Sky River Press, 1990. 72 pp.

Carter, Jane. "Alley Farming: Have Resource-Poor Farmers Benefited?" *Agroforestry Today*, April–June 1996, 5–7.

Cheyney, E. G. *Farm Forestry.* New York: Macmillan.

Cheyney, E. G., and J. P. Wentling. *The Farm Woodlot.* New York: Macmillan, 1919. 343 pp.

Clark, F. B. *Planting Black Walnut for Timber.* Washington, DC: U.S. Department of Agriculture Forest Service, 1976. 10 pp.

Coe, Richard. "Through the Looking Glass: 10 Common Problems in Alley-Cropping Research." *Agroforestry Today,* January–March 1994, 9–11.

Collingwood, G. H., and Warren D. Brush. *Knowing Your Trees.* Washington, DC: American Forestry Association, 1978. 389 pp.

Crawford, Martin. *Chestnuts*. Dartington, Totnes, Devon, U.K.: Agroforestry Research Trust, 1995. 52 pp.

———. *Hazelnuts*. Dartington, Totnes, Devon, U.K.: Agroforestry Research Trust, 1995. 28 pp.

———. *Walnuts*. Dartington, Totnes, Devon, U.K.: Agroforestry Research Trust, 1995. 28 pp.

Evans, D. O., and L. T. Szott. *Nitrogen-Fixing Trees for Acid Soils*. Morrilton, AR: Winrock International Nitrogen Fixing Tree Association, 1995. 328 pp.

Farris, Cecil W. *The Hazel Tree*. East Lansing, MI: Northern Nut Growers Association, Department of Botany and Plant Pathology, Michigan State University, 2000. 74 pp.

Food and Agriculture Organization of the United Nations. "Proceedings of the International Workshop on Community Forestry in Africa." Rome, Italy: FAO (Viale Delle Terme di Caracalla, 00100 Rome, Italy), 2000. 423 pp.

———. *Forest Tree Seed Directory*. New York: United Nations, 1975. 283 pp.

Forest, Farm, and Community Tree Network (FACT Net). *Nitrogen-Fixing Trees for Fodder Production*. Morrilton, AR: Winrock International, 1996. 125 pp.

Forestry and Nutrition—A Reference Manual. Bangkok, Thailand: Regional Forestry Officer (FAO Regional Office for Asia and the Pacific, Maliwan Mansion, Phra Atit Rd., Bangkok, Thailand), 1989. 114 pp.

Forests, Trees and Food. Rome, Italy: Community Forestry Unit (Forestry Department, Forestry Policy and Planning Division, FAO, Via delle Terme di Carcalla 00100 Rome, Italy), 1992. 26 pp.

Foster, Ruth. *Landscaping That Saves Energy Dollars*. New York: David McKay, 1978.

Friends of the Trees. *1988 International Green Front Report*. Chelan, WA: Friends of the Trees, 1988. 97 pp.

Friends of the Trees Society. Star Rte., Box 74, Oroville, WA 98844. Good tree information.

Garrett, H. E., W. J. Rietveld, and R. F. Fisher, eds. *North American Agroforestry: An Integrated Science and Practice*. Madison, WI: American Society of Agronomy, 2000. 402 pp.

*Giono, Jean. *The Man Who Planted Hope and Grew Happiness*. Brooksville, ME: Friends of Nature, 1967. 17 pp. Account of a one-man tree planting program. Inspirational.

The Greenwood Trust—Woodland Courses, Station Rd., Coalbrookdale, Telford, Shropshire TF8 7DR, England. Courses include coppicing. A rare opportunity.

*Gridley, Karen, ed. *Man of the Trees—Selected Writings of Richard St. Barbe Baker*. Willits, CA: Ecology Action, 1989. 144 pp.

Hammond, Herb. *Seeing the Forest Among the Trees: The Case for Wholistic Forest Use*. Vancouver, Canada: Polestar Press, 1991. 309 pp.

Hart, Robert A. de J. *Forest Gardening*. Bideford, England: Green Books (Ford House, Hartland, Bideford, Devon EX39 6EE, England), 1991. 212 pp.

Hartmann, Hudson T., and Karl W. Opitiz. *Olive Production in California*. Berkeley, CA: University of California Agricultural Publications (207 University Hall, Berkeley, CA 94720), 1966. 63 pp.

The Harvard Forest Models. Cambridge, MA: Harvard College, 1941. 48 pp.

Hilliers and Sons. *Hilliers' Manual of Trees and Shrubs,* 4th edition. Newton Abbot, England: David and Charles, 1977. 575 pp. A key publication.

Hilts, Stewart, and Peter Mitchell. *The Woodlot Management Handbook*. Buffalo, NY: Firefly Books, 1999. 282 pp.

How to Grow Your Own Firewood. Cooperative Extension (University of California, Division of Agriculture and Natural Resources), Publication 21484. 6 pp.

Hutchinson, F. *A Guide to the Richard St. Barbe Baker Papers*. Saskatchewan, Canada: University of Saskatchewan Archives, 1988. 26 pp.

Huxley, Anthony, ed. *Deciduous Garden Trees and Shrubs*. New York: Macmillan, 1973. 216 pp.

———. *Evergreen Garden Trees and Shrubs*. New York: Macmillan, 1973. 216 pp.

Institute for Sustainable Forestry. *Landowner Resource Guide*. Redway, CA: Institute for Sustainable Forestry (P.O. Box 1580, Redway, CA 95560), June 2000.

International Institute of Rural Reconstruction (IIRR). *Agroforestry Technology Information Kit*. Silang, Philippines: IIRR, 1998, 650 pp. 6 booklets.

Johnson, Dave. *The Good Woodcutter's Guide: Chain Saws, Portable Mills, and Woodlots*. White River Junction, VT: Chelsea Green, 1998. 215 pp.

Johnson, Hugh. *The International Book of Trees*. New York: Bonanza Books, 1980. 288 pp. Good background.

Josiah, Scott, et al. *Agroforestry in Minnesota: A Guide to Resources and Demonstration Sites*. St. Paul, MN: Center for Integrated Natural Resource and Agricultural Management, University of Minnesota, 1999. 132 pp.

Kang, B. T., A. N. Atta-krah, and L. Reynolds. *Alley Farming*. London: Macmillan, 1999. 110 pp.

Kang, B. T., et al. *Alley Cropping: A Stable Alternative to Shifting Cultivation*. Ibadan, Nigeria: IITA, 1984. 22 pp.

Koppell, Carla R. R., et al. *Guidelines for Integrating Nutrition Concerns into Forestry Projects*. Rome, Italy: Community Forestry Unit (Forestry Department, Food & Agriculture Organization, Via delle Germe di Caracalla, 00100 Rome, Italy), 1991. 41 pp.

*Kyle, H. R., et al. *CCC Forestry*. Washington, DC: U.S. Department of the Interior, Office of Education, 1937. 334 pp.

Lambert, F. *Tools and Devices for Coppice Crafts.* Chatham, U.K.: Mackay, 1957. (Available from the Centre for Alternative Technology, Machynlleth, Powys SY20-9AZ, Wales, U.K.) 48 pp.

Leucaena: Forage Production and Use. Waimanalo, HI: Nitrogen-Fixing Tree Association, 1985. 39 pp.

Leucaena: Promising Forage and Tree Crop for the Tropics. Washington, DC: National Academy of Science, 1977. 102 pp.

Leucaena: Wood Production and Use. Waimanalo, HI: Nitrogen-Fixing Tree Association, 1985. 50 pp.

Leucaena-Based Farming. Oklahoma City, OK: World Neighbors, 1986. 29 pp.

Lindstrom, Jan, and Kingamkono, Rose. *Foods from Forests, Fields and Fallows.* Uppsala, Sweden: Swedish University of Agricultural Sciences (International Rural Development Centre, Box 7005, S-750 07 Uppsala, Sweden), 1991. 133 pp.

Longhurst, Richard. *Dependency on Forestry and Tree Foods for Food Security.* Upsala, Sweden: Swedish University of Agricultural Sciences, 1991.

MacDicken, K., and N. Vergara. *Agroforestry: Classification and Management.* New York: John Wiley & Sons, 1990. 382 pp.

Man of the Trees. Redway, CA: Music for Little People (P.O. Box 1460, Redway, CA 95560). Video. **BL**

The Man Who Planted Trees. (Academy Award, 1987.) Los Angeles: Direct Cinema (P.O. Box 69799, Los Angeles, CA 90069). Excellent animated adaptation of Jean Giono's classic story. In English and French. Video. **BL**

Mann, Rink. *Backyard Sugarin'.* Woodstock, VT: Countryman Press, 1978. 78 pp.

Martz, Jeff. "Multi-Story Cropping System for the Dominican Republic." *The Permaculture Activist,* November 1988, 14–15.

Men of the Trees. *Richard St. Barbe Baker, 1889–1972: A Keepsake Book for All Ages and Generations.* Perth, Australia: Men of the Trees, 1989. 72 pp.

Mitchell, Alan. *The Trees of North America.* New York: Facts on File, 1979. 280 pp.

Nearing, Helen and Scott. *The Maple Sugar Book.* White River Junction, VT: Chelsea Green, 2000. 305 pp.

Neem: A Tree for Solving Global Problems. Washington, DC: National Academy Press, 1992. 141 pp.

Nitrogen-Fixing Tree Association. *Nitrogen-Fixing Tree Research Report,* Vol. 11, 1993. Morrilton, AR: NFTA, 1993. 140 pp.

On the Edge of the Forest. Olney, PA: Bullfrog Films. Excellent video of Dr. E. F. Schumacher, author of *Small Is Beautiful.* A key perception about agroforestry and trees, 1977. **BL**

Pavlik, Bruce, et al. *Oaks of California.* Los Olivos: Cachuma Press (P.O. Box 560, Los Olivos, CA 93441), 1991. 184 pp.

Perry, David A. *Forest Ecosystems.* Baltimore, MD: The Johns Hopkins University Press, 1994. 649 pp.

Pilarski, Michael, ed. *Restoration Forestry: An International Guide to Sustainable Forestry Practices.* Durango, CO: Klvaki Press (585 E. 31st St., Durango, CO 81301), 1994. 525 pp.

Sheat, W. G. *Propagation of Trees, Shrubs, and Conifers.* New York: Macmillan, 1957.

*Sholto Douglas, J., and Roberta A. de J. Hart. *Forest Farming.* London: Intermediate Technology Publications, 1984. 207 pp. Excellent.

Short Rotation Forestry. Oley, PA: Bullfrog Films (P.O. Box 149, Oley, PA 19547), 1982. 29-minute video.

*Smith, J. Russell. *Tree Crops: Key to a Permanent Agriculture.* Old Greenwich, CT: Devin-Adair, 1953. 408 pp. Classic work on an important concept.

Smith, Michael, and Michael Pilarski. *Friends of the Trees: Third World Resource Guide.* Tonasket, WA: Friends of the Trees Society (P.O. Box 1064, Tonasket, WA 98855), May 1993.

Sudworth, George B. *Forest Trees of the Pacific Slope.* New York: Dover, 1967. 455 pp.

Sunset Editors. *Garden Trees.* Menlo Park, CA: Sunset Books, 1975. 96 pp.

Titmuss, F. H. *A Concise Encyclopedia of World Timbers.* New York: Philosophical Library, 1949. 156 pp.

Tree People. *The Simplest Act of Planting a Tree—Healing Your Neighborhood, Your City, and Your World.* Los Angeles: Jeremy P. Tarcher, 1990. 236 pp.

U.S. Department of Agriculture. *Trees—The Yearbook of Agriculture, 1949.* Washington, DC: U.S. Government Printing Office, 1949. 944 pp.

Utah Community Forest Council. *Shigo on Trees: The Video.* Spotlight Visual Communications. Video.

*Weiner, M. A. *Plant a Tree.* New York: Macmillan, 1975. 277 pp. Excellent.

Whitefield, Patrick. *How to Make a Forest Garden.* East Meon, Hampshire, England: Hyden House, The Sustainability Centre, 1998. 168 pp.

Wijewardene, Ray, et al. *Conservation Farming.* Sri Lanka: Marga Publications (61, Isipathana Mawatha, Colombo 5, Sri Lanka).

Yepsen, Roger B., Jr. *Trees for the Yard, Orchard, and Woodlot.* Emmaus, PA: Rodale Press, 1976. 305 pp.

Tropics

*Ackland, J. D. *East African Crops.* London: Longman Group, 1980. 252 pp. Very good.

Appert, Jean. *The Storage of Food Grains and Seeds.* London: Macmillan, 1987. 146 pp.

Asian Vegetable Research and Development Center. P.O. Box 42, Shanhua, Tainan 741, Taiwan ROC. A nonprofit research organization for vegetables.

Atkins, George. "Growing Crops on Mounds in Low Wetlands." The Developing Countries Farm Radio Network (595 Bay St., Toronto, ON M5G 2C3, Canada). 8 pp.

Beets, Willem C. *Raising and Sustaining Productivity of Smallholder Farming Systems in the Tropics.* Alkmaar, Holland: AgBé Publishing (P.O. Box 9125, 1800 GC Alkmaar, Holland), 1990. 738 pp.

Bernhardt, Ed. *Home Gardening in Costa Rica.* San Jose, CA: The Tico Times (P.O. Box 4632, San Jose, Costa Rica), 1985. 88 pp.

Brandjes, Pieter, Peter van Dongen, and Anneke van der Veer. *Green Manuring and Other Forms of Soil Improvement in the Tropics.* Wageningen, The Netherlands: CTA (P.O. Box 380, 6700 AJ Wageningen, The Netherlands), 1989. 49 pp.

CIDICCO. *Technical Report No. 1. The Use of Velvetbean by Village Farmers of Honduras to Produce Corn.* Tegucigalpa, Honduras, August 1993. 4 pp.

————. *Technical Report No. 2. The Use of Lablab Bean by Traditional Farmers in Honduras.* Tegucigalpa, Honduras, August 1993. 4 pp.

————. *Technical Report No. 7. The Use of Velvetbean as Cover Crop in Citrus Plantations.* Tegucigalpa, Honduras, March 1992. 4 pp.

————. *Technical Report No. 8. The Utilization of Velvetbean as a Source of Food.* Tegucigalpa, Honduras, February 1993. 4 pp.

Composting for the Tropics. Bocking, England: Henry Doubleday Research Association, 1963. 288 pp. Useful pamphlet for humid areas.

Dupriez, Hugues, and Philippe De Leneer. *African Gardens and Orchards.* Wageningen, The Netherlands: CTA (P.O. Box 380, 6700 AJ Wageningen, The Netherlands), 1988. 294 pp.

————. *Agriculture in African Rural Communities.* Wageningen, The Netherlands: CTA (P.O. Box 380, 6700 AJ Wageningen, The Netherlands), 1988. 294 pp.

Dynamics of Soil Organic Matter in Tropical Ecosystems. Honolulu, Hawaii: NifTAL Project, University of Hawaii, 1989. 249 pp.

ECHO (Educational Concerns for Hunger Organization), 17391 Durrance Rd., North Fort Myers, FL 33917. A nonprofit organization that provides key seeds to development projects.

Ecology Action Staff. *A Preliminary Guide to Tropical Biointensive Food Raising.* Palo Alto, CA: Ecology Action, 1982. 31 pp. Includes large bibliography.

Enoch, Ivan, and R. E. Holttum. *Gardening in the Tropics.* Singapore: Times Editions, 1991. 384 pp.

Gardening Nutritious Vegetables. Shanhua, Taiwan: The Asian Vegetable Research and Development Center (Shanhua, Taiwan, R.O.C.), 1988. 136 pp.

Gibson, D., and A. Pain. *Crops of the Drier Regions of the Tropics.* Singapore: Longman Singapore, 1985. 157 pp.

Gliessman, Stephen R., et al. "The Ecological Basis for the Application of Traditional Agricultural Technology in the Management of Tropical Agro-Ecosystems." *Agro-Ecosystems* 7, 1981, 173–185.

————. "Local Resource Use Systems in the Tropics: Taking Pressure Off the Forests," in *Tropical Rainforests,* California Academy of Sciences, 1988, 53–70.

————. "Ecological Basis of Traditional Management of Wetlands in Tropical Mexico: Learning from Agroecosystem Models," in *Biodiversity—Culture, Conservation and Ecodevelopment,* Margery Oldfield and Janis B. Alcorn, eds. Boulder, CO: Westview Press, 1991. 211–229.

————. "Understanding the Basis of Sustainability for Agriculture in the Tropics: Experiences in Latin America." *Sustainable Agricultural Systems.* Ankeny, IA: Soil and Water Conservation Society (7515 NE Ankeny Rd., Ankeny, IA 50021), n.d., 378–390.

Goeltenboth, Friedholm, ed. *Subsistence Agriculture Improvement: Manual for the Humid Tropics.* Lanham, MD: Unipub, 1990. 228 pp.

Hill, D. S., and J. M. Waller. *Pests and Diseases of Tropical Crops: Vol. I, Principles and Methods of Control.* Harlow, Essex. England: Longman, 1990. 175 pp.

Hodges, R. D., ed. *Composting in Tropical Agriculture.* Ipswich, England: International Institute of Biological Husbandry, 1979. 32 pp.

Honey Bee—A Voice of Creative Farmers, Artisans, Pastoralists and Other Grassroots Innovators. Ahnedbad, India: Society for Research and Initiatives for Sustainable Technologies and Institutions, Indian Institute of Management. Periodical.

ILEIA Newsletter. (Information for Low External Input Agriculture, P.O. Box 64, 3830 AB Leusden, The Netherlands.) An excellent magazine.

Institute for Tropical Agriculture. University of Florida, Box 13533, Gainesville, FL 32604.

International Institute of Rural Reconstruction. 1775 Broadway, New York, NY 10019. Also: Silang, Cavite, Philippines. Has specialized in Biointensive mini-farming. Information packet *(Agricultural Technologies)*.

International Institute of Tropical Agriculture. 133 Dharmapala Mawatha, Columbo 7, Sri Lanka.

Irvine, F. R. *West African Crops.* Oxford, England: Oxford University Press, 1969. 272 pp.

Janzen, Daniel. "Tropical Agroecosystems." *Science,* Vol. 182, 1973, 1,212–1,219.

*MacKay, Susan E. "Alley Farming in the Humid and Subhumid Tropics. Proceedings of an International Workshop held at Ibadan, Nigeria." Ottwawa, Canada: IDRC (P.O. Box 8500, Ottawa, ON K1G 3H9, Canada), March 1986. 251 pp.

Manor House Agricultural Centre. Private Bag, Kitale, Kenya, East

Africa. A nonprofit organization that specializes in Biointensive mini-farming training.

Martin, Franklin W. *Forages for the Small Farm.* Ft. Myers, FL: ECHO (17430 Durrance Rd., N. Ft. Myers, FL 33917-2200), n.d. 24 pp.

———. *Handbook of Tropical Food Crops.* Boca Raton, FL: CRC Press, 1984. 296 pp.

———. *Primer on Plants and Techniques for Agriculture in Dry Regions of the Tropics.* N. Ft. Myers, FL: ECHO (17391 Durrance Rd., N. Ft. Myers, FL 33917), n.d. 16 pp.

Organic Matter Management and Tillage in Humid and Subhumid Africa. IBSRAM Proceedings, No. 10. Bangkok, Thailand: International Board for Soil Research and Management, 1990. 459 pp.

*Sanchez, Pedro A. *Properties and Management of Soil in the Tropics.* New York: John Wiley & Sons, 1987. 618 pp.

Schwartz, H., and Marcial A. Pastor-Corrales, eds. *Bean Production Problems in the Tropics,* 2nd edition. Cali, Columbia: Centro Internacional de Agricultura Tropical (Apartado Aeréo 6713, Cali, Colombia), 1989. 725 pp.

Soil Management, Compost Production and Use in Tropical and Subtropical Environments. Rome, Italy: FAO of the United Nations (Via delle Terme di Caracalle, 00100 Rome, Italy), 1987. 177 pp.

Sommers, Paul. *Low-Cost Farming in the Humid Tropics: An Illustrated Handbook.* Metro Manila, Phillipines: Island Publishing House (STA Mesa P.O. Box 406, Metro Manila, Philippines), 1984. 38 pp.

Srivastava, Jitendre, et al. *Conserving Soil Moisture and Fertility in the Warm Seasonally Dry Tropics.* Washington, DC: The International Bank for Reconstruction and Development (1818 H St., NW, Washington, DC 20433), 1993. 75 pp.

Steiner, Kurt G. *Intercropping in Tropical Smallholders Agriculture with Special Reference to West Africa.* Eschborn, Germany: Deutsche Gesellschaft für Technische Zusammenarbeith (Postfach 5180, D-6236 Eschborn/ Ts. 1, Germany), 1984. 304 pp.

Stoll, Gabriele. *Natural Crop Protection in the Tropics.* Weikersheim, Germany: Margraf Verlag (P.O. Box 1205, 97985 Weikersheim, Germany), 2000. 376 pp.

Thurston, H. David. *Slash/Mulch Systems: Sustainable Methods for Tropical Agriculture.* Boulder, CO: Westview Press, 1997. 196 pp.

UNICEF. *The UNICEF Home Gardens Handbook.* New York: UNICEF, 1982.

USDA, ARS Tropical Agriculture Research Station. 2200 Pedro Albizu Campos Ave., Ste. 201 Mayaguez, Peurto Rico 006800-5470 (formerly, Mayaquez Institute of Tropical Agriculture, SEA, Box 70, Mayaquez, Puerto Rico 00681).

Wicherley, W. *The Whole Art of Rubber Growing.* Philadelphia: J. B. Lippincott, 1911. 151 pp.

Vegetables

Aaron, Chester. *The Great Garlic Book: A Guide with Recipes.* Berkeley, CA: Ten Speed Press, 1997. 146 pp.

Allan, Ken. *Sweet Potatoes for the Home Garden.* Kingston, Canada: Green Spade Books, 1998. 204 pp.

Allen, C. L. *Cabbage, Cauliflower and Allied Vegetables.* New York: Orange Judd, 1918. 125 pp.

Bailey, L. H. *Principles of Vegetable Gardening.* New York: Macmillan, 1901. 450 pp.

Barnes, James, and William Robinson. *Asparagus Culture: The Best Methods Employed.* New York: George Routledge & Sons, n.d. 84 pp.

Basse, H., et al. *Variétés de Laitues.* Wageningen, Holland: Instituut Voor De Veredeling Van Tuinbourwgewassen, 1960. 228 pp.

Blasdale, Walter C. "Some Chinese Vegetable Food Materials and Their Nutritive and Economic Value." *Bulletin No. 68.* Washington, DC: USDA Office of Experiment Stations, July 15, 1899, 48 pp.

Brewster, J. L. *Onions and Other Vegetable Alliums.* Wallingford, Oxon, U.K.: CAB International, 1994. 236 pp.

Brickell, Christopher, ed. *Vegetables.* New York: Simon & Schuster, 1980. 96 pp.

Burrage, Albert C. *Burrage on Vegetables.* Boston: Houghton Mifflin, 1975. 224 pp. Good notes on scheduling for continuous harvest.

Burton, W. G. *The Potato,* 3rd edition. New York: Halsted Press, 1989. 724 pp.

Decoteau, Dennis R. *Vegetable Crops.* Upper Saddle River, NJ: Prentice Hall, 2000. 464 pp.

DeWitt, Dave and Paul W. Bosland. *How to Grow Peppers—The Pepper Garden.* Berkeley, CA: Ten Speed Press, 1993. 240 pp.

———. *Peppers of the World: An Identification Guide.* Berkeley, CA: Ten Speed Press, 1996. 219 pp.

Engeland, Ron L. *Growing Great Garlic.* Okanogan, WA: Filaree Productions (Rte. 2, P.O. Box 162, Okanogan, WA 98840), 1991. 213 pp.

Garnham, Peter. "Cut-And-Come-Again Lettuce Sampler." *Kitchen Gardener,* February/March 1999, 10–14.

Gregory, James J. H. *Cabbages: How to Grow Them.* Salem, MA: Observer Steam Printing Rooms, 1870. 73 pp.

———. *Onion Raising: What Kinds to Raise and the Way to Raise Them.* Marblehead, MA: Messenger Steam Printing House, 1878. 42 pp.

Greiner, T. *Celery for Profit.* Philadelphia, PA: W. Atlee Burpee, 1893. 85 pp.

Hand, F. E., and K. L. Cockerham. *The Sweet Potato.* New York: Macmillan, 1921. 261 pp.

Harrison, S. G., et al. *The Oxford Book of Food Plants.* New York: Oxford University Press, 1969. 207 pp.

Herklots, G. A. C. *Vegetable Cultivation in Hong Kong.* Hong Kong: The South China Morning Pos, 1947. 208 pp.

Ivins, J. D., and F. L. Milthorpe, eds. *The Growth of the Potato—Proceedings of the Tenth Easter School in Agricultural Science, University of Nottingham, 1963.* London: Butterworths, 1963. 328 pp.

Jeavons, John. *How to Grow More Vegetables*, 2nd edition. Los Altos, CA: Sixth District PTA Braille Group (P.O. Box 326, Los Altos, CA 94023-0326).

Kains, Maurice G. *Chicory Growing as an Addition to the Resources of the American Farmer.* Washington, DC: Government Printing Office, 1898. 52 pp.

Langsner, Louise. "The Many Faces of Asian Greens." *Kitchen Garden,* June/July 1998, 20–25.

Larkcom, Joy. *Creative Vegetable Gardening.* New York: Abbeville Press, 1997. 208 pp.

Macself, A. J. *The Vegetable Grower's Treasury.* London: W. H. & L. Collingridge, n.d. 320 pp.

Maynard, Donald N., and George J. Hochmuth. *Knott's Handbook for Vegetable Growers,* 4th edition. New York: John Wiley & Sons, 1997. 582 pp.

Ohio Agricultural Experiment Station. *The Relation of Weather to the Date of Planting Potatoes in Northern Ohio.* Wooster, Ohio: Ohio Agricultural Experiment Station, 1926. 43 pp.

Omohundro, John T. "One Potato, Two Potato." *Natural History Magazine,* June 1985, 22–27.

Robinson, R. W., and D. S. Decker-Walters. *Cucurbits.* New York: CAB International, 1996. 226 pp.

Rodale Institute. *Legumes for Lasting Benefits. Information Sheet #2.* Kurtztown, PA: International Ag-Sieve (Rodale Institute, 611 Siegfriedale Rd., Kutztown PA 19530), n.d. 4 pp.

*Rubatzky, Vincent, and Mas Yamaguchi. *World Vegetables*, 2nd edition. New York: Chapman & Hall, 1997. 842 pp. Very good.

Sanders, T. W. *Vegetables and Their Cultivation.* London: Q. H. & L. Collingridge, 1928. 508 pp.

Sherf, Arden F., and Alan A. MacNab. *Vegetable Diseases and Their Control.* New York: John Wiley & Sons, 1986. 728 pp.

Solomon, Steve. *Water-Wise Vegetables.* Seattle: Sasquatch Books, 1993. 93 pp.

Staub, Jack. "Faux Spinaches Can Stand the Heat." *Kitchen Gardener,* August/September 1999, 12–15.

Stiles, Shelly. "Hot Potatoes." *National Gardening,* July/August 1994, 29–34.

*Vilmorin-Andrieux, M. M. *The Vegetable Garden.* London: John Murray, 1905. 782 pp. Softcover edition: Berkeley, CA: Ten Speed Press, 1981. 620 pp. Hardcover edition: Willits, CA: The Jeavons-Leler Press (5798 Ridgewood Rd., Willits, CA 95490). 620 pp. Reprint of the excellent 1885 English edition by John Murray. This classic is still one of the most useful works on cultural directions in existence today.

Weaver, William Woys. *Heirloom Vegetable Gardening.* New York: Henry Holt, 1997. 439 pp.

Wickson, Edward J. *The California Vegetables in Garden and Field.* San Francisco: Pacific Rural Press, 1917. 319 pp.

Zuckerman, Larry. *The Potato: How the Humble Spud Rescued the Western World.* New York: North Point Press, 1998. 320 pp.

Water

Cocannouer, Joseph A. *Water and the Cycle of Life.* Old Greenwich, CT: Devin-Adair, 1962. 142 pp. All his books are fascinating and easy to read.

Cummings, Ronald, et al. *Waterworks: Improving Irrigation Management in Mexican Agriculture.* Washington, DC: World Resources Institute (1709 New York Ave., NW, Washington, DC 20006), 1989. 51 pp.

Davies, Rodney. *Dowsing.* London: The Aquarian Press (77-85 Fulham Palace Rd., Hammersmith, London W6 8JB, England), 1991. 112 pp.

DripWorks, 190 Sanhedrin Circle, Willits CA 95490, (800) 616-8322. Complete line of drip irrigation.

Ingram, Colin. *The Drinking Water Book.* Berkeley, CA: Ten Speed Press, 1995. 198 pp.

James, I. C., et al. "How Much Water in a 12-Ounce Can?" Washington, DC: U.S. Geological Survey, 1976. 18 pp.

———. *Principles of Irrigation Practice.* New York: Macmillan, 1920. 496 pp.

King, F. H. *Irrigation and Drainage: Principles and Practice of Their Cultural Phases.* New York: Macmillan, 1906. 502 pp.

Kourick, Robert. *Graywater Use in the Landscape: How to Make Your Landscape Prosperous with Recycled Water.* Santa Rosa, CA: Metamorphic Press, 1988. 28 pp.

Ludwig, Art. *Greywater Information: How to Manage Greywater and Rainwater in the Landscape.* Santa Barbara, CA: Developer of Oasis Biocompatible Laundry Detergent, 1991. 17 pp.

Matson, Tim. *Earth Ponds Sourcebook: The Pond Owner's Manual and Resource Guide.* Woodstock, VT: The Countryman Press, 1997. 171 pp.

Mellin, Bob. *Waterhole: A Guide to Digging Your Own Well.* San Anselmo, CA: Balboa Publishing (11 Library Place, San Anselmo, CA 94960), 1991. 71 pp.

Pimental, David, et al., "Water Resources: Agriculture, the Environment, and Society." *BioScience,* Vol. 47, No. 2, February 1997, 97–106.

Postel, Sandra. *Pillar of Sand: Can the Irrigation Miracle Last?* New York: W. W. Norton, 1999. 313 pp.

Richardson, Gail, and Peter Mueller-Beilschmidt. *Winning with Water: Soil-Moisture Monitoring for Efficient Irrigation.* New York: Inform, 1988. 173 pp.

Riotte, Louise. *Catfish, Ponds and Lilypads.* Pownal, VT: Storey, 1997. 186 pp.

Romanelli, Vince. "How to Drive a Well." *Countryside and Small Stock Journal*, July/August 1994, 34–35.

Stadelmann, Peter. *Water Gardens.* Haupauge, NY: Barron's Educational Series (250 Wireless Blvd., Haupauge, NY 11788), 1994. 143 pp.

Swindells, Philip. *Container Water Gardens.* Pownal, VT: Storey, 1998. 128 pp.

The Urban Farmer Store. 2833 Vicente St., San Francisco, CA 94116. Drip irrigation products.

Van den Heuvel, Kick. *Wood and Bamboo for Rural Water Supply.* Delft, The Netherlands: Delft University Press, 1983. 76 pp.

Vogt, Evon, and Ray Hyman. *Water Witching USA.* Chicago: The University of Chicago Press, 1918. 248 pp.

Walters, Gregg L., ed. *Hach Water Analysis Handbook.* Loveland, CO: Hach, 1989. 691 pp.

Yeomans, Ken B. *Water for Every Farm.* Australia: Griffin Press, 1993. 261 pp.

Weeds

Cocannouer, Joseph A. *Weeds: Guardians of the Soil.* New York: Devin-Adair, 1948. 179 pp. How weeds help your garden. **BL**

Cramer, Craig and Staff of The New Farm, eds. *Controlling Weeds with Fewer Chemicals.* Emmaus, PA: Rodale Institute, 1991. 138 pp.

Hatfield, Audry W. *How to Enjoy Your Weeds.* New York: Sterling , 1971. 192 pp. Delightful. Includes an herbal lawn, flower salads, and other charming ideas.

Kummer, Anna P. *Weed Seedlings.* Chicago: The University of Chicago Press, 1951. 435 pp.

Martin, Alexander C. *Weeds.* New York: Golden Press, 1972. 160 pp. Inexpensive identification guide.

Muenscher, Walter C., and Peter A. Hyypio. *Weeds.* Ithaca, NY: Cornell University Press, 1980. 586 pp.

Pleasant, Barbara. *The Gardener's Weed Book: Earth-Safe Controls.* Pownal, VT: Storey, 1996. 201 pp.

Robbins, W. W., et al. *Weeds of California.* Sacramento, CA: Department of Agriculture, 1951. 547 pp.

Walters, Charles, Jr. *Weeds—Control Without Poison.* Austin, TX: Acres U.S.A. (P.O. Box 91299, Austin, TX 78709), 1991. 320 pp.

Whitson, Tom D., et al. *Weeds of the West.* Jackson, WY: Pioneer of Jackson Hole, 1991. 630 pp.

Who Is Ecology Action?

Ecology Action is a nonprofit, tax-exempt, environmental research and education organization located at 5798 Ridgewood Road, Willits, California 95490-9730, U.S.A. Formed in the early 1970s, the organization acted as a catalyst in recycling glass and metal wastes in the city of Palo Alto. This project, for which Ecology Action won 3 awards, was taken over by the city to be run as an ongoing service.

Currently, Ecology Action consists of 4 self-supporting projects: (1) *An organic garden supply store and educational center,* Common Ground (see caption below for address), offering inexpensive seeds, tools, books, fertilizers, and gardening advice. Store sales pay for 2 full-time staff persons and support periodic classes on the GROW BIOINTENSIVE method and other gardening topics. (2) *A repository of urban and rural homesteading information and supplies.* Adjoining the store is a library on topics such as cheesemaking, blacksmithing, raising chickens and bees, tending goats, and other farming skills. (3) *A mini-farming demonstration and research garden area.* Currently the mini-farming staff includes 5 paid staff positions and 4 interns. Salaries and stipends are paid out of sales of this book and other publications, supporting memberships, and contributions from foundations, corporations, and individuals. (4) *A mail-order service,* Bountiful Gardens (18001 Shafer Ranch Road, Willits, California 95490-9626), which offers GROW BIOINTENSIVE and key food-raising publications, open-pollinated seeds, and supplies to gardeners around the world.

Ecology Action maintains files of experienced people, publishes a newsletter of GROW BIOINTENSIVE information (about 4 issues a year), and offers periodic workshops and classes. Membership fees ($30 per year, tax-deductible) support its ongoing work, library, newsletter, and mini-farming work.

One Ecology Action project is a nonprofit store and educational center, where seeds are sold by the piece, like penny candy. Start a bulk seed-buying group in your community. The savings are tremendous when you package your own. Our store, Common Ground, is located at 559 College Avenue, Palo Alto, California 94306. It is open 10 A.M. to 5:30 P.M. on Tuesday through Saturday, and 10 A.M. to 5:00 P.M. on Sunday. We can be reached at (650) 493-6072.

Ecology Action Offerings

Ecology Action offers:

1. Periodic class series on the GROW BIOINTENSIVE method and urban homesteading topics, on Saturday mornings in Palo Alto, California.

2. Periodic tours of the research site in Willits, California.

3. Short mini-farming workshops, plus a few long-term apprenticeships to people who are sincere, committed, and responsible. The 2 key questions asked of interested workers are: "Can you make a 3- to 5-year commitment?" and "How do you expect to use the skills and knowledge when you leave?"

4. We will answer short questions by mail if a stamped self-addressed envelope is enclosed. We continue to develop information sheets covering the most commonly asked questions.

   Our main work is the continued testing of GROW BIOINTENSIVE method yields, spacings, timing, varieties, resource consumption, economic viability, and sustainability.

Perhaps it is unfair to compare the yields we obtained in our hard clay subsoil in Palo Alto with commercial agricultural yields. The stunted broccoli plant on the *left* was grown using *normal backyard techniques*, loosening the soil and adding chemical fertilizer. The broccoli shown in the *middle* was obtained by loosening the soil *12 inches deep* and incorporating a 3-inch layer of aged manure with some compost. The broccoli on the *right* demonstrates the superiority of the GROW BIOINTENSIVE method, with soil loosened 24 inches deep and compost incorporated.

GROW BIOINTENSIVE Applications

The GROW BIOINTENSIVE method, with its high yields, low water and fertilizer consumption, and soil-building techniques, is eminently practical for serious small-scale food production. Some possible applications are:

• One mini-farmer may be able to net $5,000 to $20,000 a year on a ⅛-acre mini-farm. He or she might work a 40-hour week and take a 4-month vacation each year. (For more details, see Ecology Action's *Backyard Homestead, Mini-Farm and Garden Log Book* and *Cucumber Bonanza*, a Self-Teaching Mini-Series Booklet.)

• A backyard gardener in the United States could grow a year's supply of vegetables and soft fruits (322 pounds) on

200 square feet in a 6-month growing season, assuming GROW BIOINTENSIVE intermediate yields. This food would be worth more than $200 and could eventually be grown in about 30 minutes (for 2 beds) a day, making the gardener's time worth $6.50 to $13.00+ per hour.

- An entire balanced diet could be grown on as little as 1,000 square feet per person in an 8-month growing season with another 1,000 square feet needed to make it sustainable. (See David Duhon and Cindy Gebhard's *One Circle*, published by Ecology Action.) Using commercial agricultural techniques, it takes approximately 22,000 square feet per person in India, 7,000 square feet in the United States, and 3,400 square feet in Japan to grow similar diets.

- Eventually we hope to produce as much food per hour by hand as commercial agriculture produces with machines.

Key points such as the low start-up cost, low water usage, and diversity of crops make the GROW BIOINTENSIVE approach especially viable for small farmers in the developing world. This decentralized, self-sufficient approach is consistent with the current emphasis on enabling countries and communities to provide their own food.

Sustainability

The most important element in assessing agricultural systems is whether or not the yields are sustainable in an environmentally balanced way. For thousands of years the Chinese practiced a manual, organic form of intensive farming using only fertilizers grown or produced on the farmstead. They were able to feed 1.5 to 2 times more people per acre than the United States presently does with mechanized chemical or mechanized organic techniques (assuming similar non-meat diets). In addition, chemical techniques deplete the soil's capacity to produce. Wilson Clark, in the January 1975 issue of *Smithsonian*, noted: "Even though more corn was produced per acre in 1968 than in the 1940s, the efficiency with which crops used available [nitrogen] fertilizer actually declined fivefold."

Chemical agriculture requires ever-increasing amounts of fertilizer at an increasing cost as petroleum supplies dwindle. The use of chemical fertilizers depletes beneficial microbial life, breaks down soil structure, and adds to soil salinity. Impoverished soil makes crops more vulnerable to disease and insect attack and requires increasing amounts of pesticides to sustain production. "A modern agriculture, racing one step ahead of the

POTENTIAL OF SMALL-SCALE GROW BIOINTENSIVE FOOD-RAISING AS INDICATED BY ECOLOGY ACTION'S RESEARCH TO DATE

Production as compared to U.S. commercial averages, per unit area

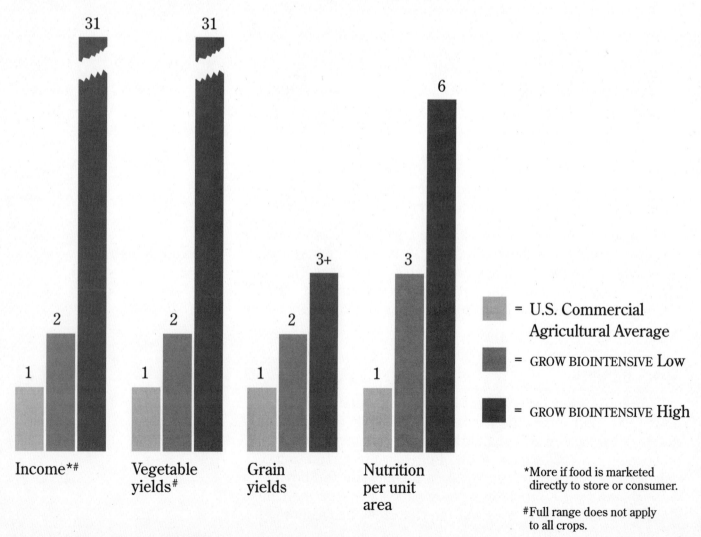

Income*#   Vegetable yields#   Grain yields   Nutrition per unit area

= U.S. Commercial Agricultural Average

= GROW BIOINTENSIVE Low

= GROW BIOINTENSIVE High

*More if food is marketed directly to store or consumer.

#Full range does not apply to all crops.

Pounds of food produced per hour

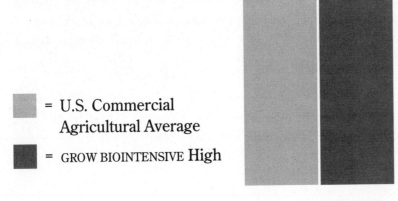

■ = U.S. Commercial Agricultural Average

■ = GROW BIOINTENSIVE High

Potentially can reach the same as with machines as soil and practitioner's skills improve and yields increase, and through the use of new, simple, labor-saving hand devices—when *all* labor inputs for both approaches are evaluated.

Resource use as compared with U.S. commercial average, per pound of food produced

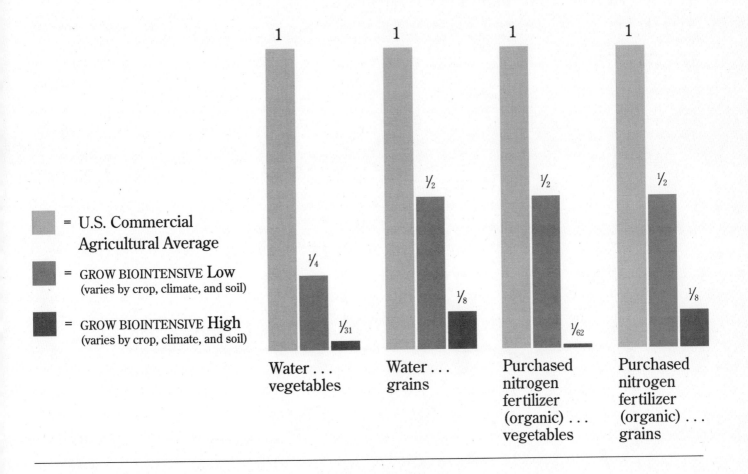

■ = U.S. Commercial Agricultural Average

■ = GROW BIOINTENSIVE Low (varies by crop, climate, and soil)

■ = GROW BIOINTENSIVE High (varies by crop, climate, and soil)

apocalypse, is not ecologically sane, no matter how productive, efficient, or economically sound it may seem" (John Todd, in *The New Alchemy Institute Bulletin*, No. 2). Biological agriculture can sustain yields because it puts back into the soil those elements needed to sustain fertility. A small-scale personal agriculture recycles the nutrients and humus so important to the microbial life-forms that fix atmospheric nitrogen and produce disease-preventing antibiotics.

Preliminary studies by soil scientists at the University of California, Berkeley, indicate that in as little as a 6-month period (and in as many as 8 years), the soil involved in our tests (which was only a "C-horizon" subsoil material at the beginning) was built up to a humified carbon level equal to hundreds of years of natural soil development! If maintained, this improvement may make possible not only the maintenance of sustainable soil fertility, but also the reclamation of deteriorated and marginal lands. (See the following graph.) The GROW BIOINTENSIVE method also nurtures the soil life and structure, utilizes renewable resources, can be productive economically on a small manual scale, and provides higher yields.

SOIL BUILD-UP RATE WITH GROW BIOINTENSIVE PRACTICES AT PALO ALTO SITE COMPARED WITH NORMAL BUILD-UP RATE

A. ■ ■ ■ ■ ■ ■ ■ ■

Observed increase (build-up) in carbon soil (which was subsoil to begin with) at Ecology Action Research Site (tentative figures). The program began in June 1972.

Question: What would the fate of the carbon curve (or nitrogen curve) be if the bed were now left fallow after the normal "intense" organic mater input?

1. ☐ ☐ ☐ ☐ ☐ ☐ ☐ ☐ ☐

Remains at "natural" steady state level?

—Unlikely.

2. ● ● ● ● ● ● ● ● ●

Substantial drop, but leveling off, then rising again under "natural development"?

—Most likely. Accelerated gain of hundreds of years of soil development (in as little as 6 months' or as much as 8 years' time with Ecology Action–type cultivation).

3. ○ ○ ○ ○ ○ ○ ○ ○ ○

Drastic drop back down to zero?

—Unlikely.

B. ▬▬▬▬▬

Normal build-up of soil by natural processes.

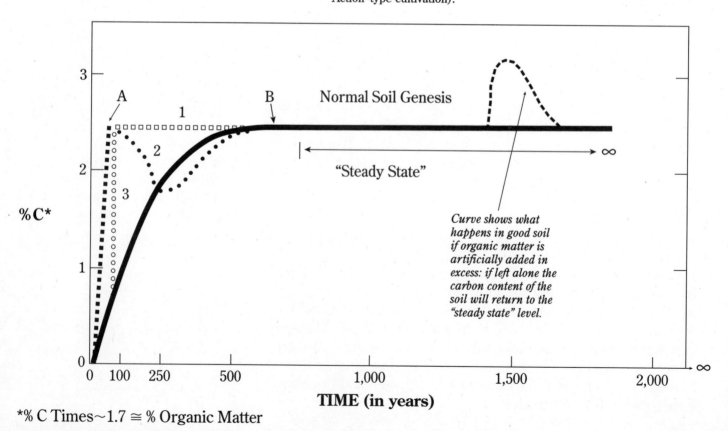

%C*

Curve shows what happens in good soil if organic matter is artificially added in excess: if left alone the carbon content of the soil will return to the "steady state" level.

*% C Times~1.7 ≅ % Organic Matter

Ecology Action Publications

Beeby, John. *Future Fertility: Transforming Human Waste into Human Wealth*. Willits, CA: Ecology Action of the Midpeninsula, 1995. 168 pp.

Duhon, David, and Cindy Gebhard. *One Circle: How to Grow a Complete Diet in Less Than 1,000 Square Feet*. Willits, CA: Ecology Action of the Midpeninsula, 1984. 200 pp. This book helps you to explore your nutritional needs and to design and produce a smallest-scale complete diet.

Gridley, Karen, ed. *Man of the Trees: Selected Writings of Richard St. Barbe Baker.* Willits, CA: Ecology Action of the Midpeninsula, 1989. 120 pp. This collection of excerpts from Richard St. Barbe Baker's most important writings provides a fascinating glimpse of one of this century's most farsighted individuals. Beyond mere human interest, however, the book carries an urgent message about the vital role of trees in planetary survival. (Also in Spanish.)

Jeavons, John. *How to Grow More Vegetables Than You Ever Thought Possible on Less Land Than You Can Imagine.* Revised 6th Edition. Berkeley, CA: Ten Speed Press, 2002. 272 pp. Ecology Action's popular primer gives the most complete instructions and information for the GROW BIOINTENSIVE method.

————. *Cultivo Biointensivo de Alimentos.* Willits, CA: Ecology Action of the Midpeninsula, 1991. Spanish translation of the *fourth* edition of *How to Grow More Vegetables*.

————. *Comment faire pousser.* Berkeley, CA: Ten Speed Press, 1982. 192 pp. French translation of the *second* edition of *How to Grow More Vegetables* with updated data in metric units.

————. *Mehr Gemuse Im Eigenen Garten.* Willits, CA: Ecology Action of the Midpeninsula, 1981. 82 pp. German translation of the *first* edition of *How to Grow More Vegetables*.

————. *Kak Vyraschivat' Bol'she Ovoschei.* Moscow: BVL Publishers, 1997. 220 pp. Russian translation of the *fifth* edition of *How to Grow More Vegetables*.

————. Arabic translation of the *fifth* edition of *How to Grow More Vegetables*. Willits, CA: Ecology Action of the Midpeninsula, 1997. 300 pp.

Mini-greenhouses fit right over the growing beds. Plans for this one are available in Ecology Action's *Backyard Homestead, Mini-Farm and Garden Log Book*. Send for a current publications list.

————. Braille version of the *third* edition of *How to Grow More Vegetables*. Willits, CA: Ecology Action of the Midpeninsula, 1981. For details on how to obtain a copy, write: Monterey County Braille Transcribers, P.O. Box DF, Pacific Grove, CA 93950.

————. Hindi translation of the *first* edition of *How to Grow More Vegetables*. Willits, CA: Ecology Action of the Midpeninsula, 1987. 70 pp.

————. *1972 Preliminary Research Report*. Palo Alto, CA: Ecology Action of the Midpeninsula, 1973. 22 pp. Ecology Action's first data report on the Biointensive method and implications for small farmers.

————. *1972–1975 Research Report Summary*. Palo Alto, CA: Ecology Action of the Midpeninsula, 1976. 19 pp. Summary of data and projections of Ecology Action's first 4 years of research with Biointensive techniques.

————. "Quantitative Research on the Biodynamic/French Intensive Method." In *Small Scale Intensive Food Production—Improving the Nutrition of the Most Economically Disadvantaged Families*, pp. 32–38. Workshop proceedings prepared on behalf of the Office of Nutrition, Bureau for Technical Assistance, U.S. Agency of International Development. Published by the League for International Food Education, Washington, D.C., 1977.

Jeavons, John, and Carol Cox. *The Sustainable Vegetable Garden*. Berkeley, CA: Ten Speed Press, 1999. 118 pp. The basic GROW BIOINTENSIVE book for those just starting. Also gives specific recommendations on the best crops to grow and how much to grow for an entire family.

Jeavons, John, J. Mogador Griffin, and Robin Leler. *Backyard Homestead, Mini-Farm, and Garden Log Book*. Berkeley, CA: Ten Speed Press, 1983. 224 pp. A handbook for everyday use in developing greater self-sufficiency in a backyard homestead or in actually earning an income from a small farm. There is material covering tools and crop testing, as well as calendars, graphs, charts, and plenty of space for record keeping. It also includes updated information on creating your own self-fertilizing herbal lawns.

Roberts, Hugh, ed. *Intensive Food Production on a Human Scale—Proceedings of the Third International Conference on Small Scale and Intensive Food Production*. Willits, CA: Ecology Action of the Midpeninsula, 1982. 224 pp. The result of a gathering of 100 people representing projects in 16 countries.

————. *Proceedings of the Soil, Food, and People Conference*. Willits, CA: Ecology Action of the Midpeninsula, 2001, 180 pp. The result of a gathering of 276 people from 26 countries focusing on the role of Biointensive food raising in the new century.

Shepard, Michael, and John Jeavons. *Appropriate Agriculture.*
Menlo Park, CA: Intermediate Technology, 1977. 14 pp.
Paper given by Peter N. Gillingham at a "Small Is Beautiful"
conference featuring Dr. E. F. Schumacher at the University
of California at Davis.

Self-Teaching Mini-Series Booklets

An Ecology Action Reading Guide. 36 pp. Design your own
curriculum.
Annual Report. 1993. 30 pp.
Another Way to Wealth. 16 pp.
A Perspective. Speech given by John Jeavons at the Second
International Conference on Small-Scale Intensive Food
Production, October 1981.
Backyard Garden Research. 32 pp. Improving your garden's
performance through observation. (Also in Spanish.)
Biointensive Apprentice Possibilities. 21 pp.
Biointensive Composting. 12 pp. (Also in Spanish.)
Biointensive Mini-Farming: A Rational Use of Natural Resources.
15 pp. Explains what Ecology Action is doing and why. (Also
in Spanish, French, German, Russian, Portuguese, and
Chinese.)
Biointensive Mini-Farming: A Seventeen-Year Perspective.
20 pp. (Also in Spanish.)
*The Complete 21-Bed Biointensive Mini-Farm: Fertility, Nutrition
and Income.* 39 pp. Explores sustainably growing all your
own food, making a small income, and composting crops, in
as little as 2,100 square feet. (Also in Spanish and Russian.)
Cucumber Bonanza. 24 pp. Takes cucumbers as an example
of a crop history and goes through 7 years of work, bringing
the 1973 yield of 140 pounds of marketable cucumbers per
100 square feet to over 400 pounds in 1979. An excellent
introduction to mini-farming and the variables that can be
examined in obtaining improved yields. (Also in Spanish.)
"Cultivating Our Garden." A detailed article on GROW
BIOINTENSIVE methods. 4 pp. (Also in Spanish, Russian,
Arabic and Japanese.)
Dried, Cut, and Edible Flowers for Pleasure, Food and Income.
61 pp. (Also in Spanish.)
Ecology Action's Comprehensive Definition of Sustainability. 4 pp.
(Also in Spanish.)
*Examining the Tropics: A Small-Scale Approach to Sustainable
Agriculture.* 31 pp. (Also in Spanish.)
Foliar Feeding. 9 pp. (Also in Spanish.)
GROW BIOINTENSIVE *Sustainable Mini-Farming Teacher
Training and Certification Program—Revised.* 33 pp.
Grow Your Compost Materials at Home. 17 pp. An approach to
sustainable organic matter production and soil fertility on a
"closed system" basis. (Also in Spanish.)

Using a U-bar digging tool cuts digging
time and helps make GROW
BIOINTENSIVE mini-farming competitive
with mechanized techniques.

Grow Your Manure for Free. 32 pp. Summary of compost crops to grow for improving your soil's fertility. (Also in Spanish.)

Growing and Gathering Your Own Fertilizers. 125 pp. (Also in Russian.)

Growing Medicinal Herbs in as Little as Fifty Square Feet—Uses and Recipes. 40 pp.

Growing to Seed. Revised. 45 pp. How to grow your own seed in the smallest possible area while preserving genetic diversity. (Also in Spanish.)

Learning to Grow All Your Own Food: One-Bed Model for Compost, Diet and Income Crops. 25 pp.

Micro-Farming as a Key to the Revitalization of the World's Agriculture and Environment. 13 pp.

One Basic Kenyan Diet: With Diet, Income and Compost Designs in a Three-Growing-Bed Learning Model. 28 pp.

One Basic Mexican Diet. 32 pp. Explores complete nutritional self-sufficiency in a small area with one Mexican diet as a focal point. (Also in Spanish.)

One Crop Test Booklet: Soybeans. 24 pp., plus Data Sheet & Log Form. Contains step-by-step instructions for conducting comparative tests for spacing and yield (with optional water monitoring) for soybeans—an important protein crop throughout the world. This booklet lets you participate in Ecology Action's research or simply grow better soybeans for yourself.

The Smallest Possible Area to Grow Food and Feed. 45 pp.

Test Your Soil with Plants. 86 pp.

Information Packets

Topical treatments on the latest information from our garden research, and our work around the world. Topics range from "Data for Common Compost Crops" (in the Sustainable Soil Fertility packet) to "Double-Digging vs. the U-Bar" (in the Gardening Techniques packet) to "About Amaranth and Quinoa" (in the Crops packet). The information is presented as short complete articles on a given subject area, and the information tends to be interrelated.

Children's Gardening Resources. 3 pp.

Cooking with Sunshine. 2 pp.

Crops. 9 topics, 15 pp. Information on specific crops and things to look for in certain useful crops.

Data Report for One Crop. 2 pp., free. The form to use to send data from your garden to Ecology Action.

Gardening Techniques. 12 topics, 31 pp. Some greening-edge techniques and observations on the art of gardening.

GROW BIOINTENSIVE Projects. 5 topics, 14 pp. Profiles of some of the major Biointensive projects around the world.

Insect and Animal Life. 5 topics, 10 pp. Useful hints and tips for dealing with our wilder neighbors.

Inspiration. 6 topics, 13 pp. The bigger picture. Articles that are Ecology Action's key position papers and put our work in perspective.
Limited Water Growing. 4 topics, 6 pp. Articles on water-saving techniques.
Small Cabin/Land Trust Information. 2 pp.
Sustainable Soil Fertility. 16 topics, 41 pp. The heart of our work—finding out how to have a really sustainable garden or mini-farm.

A Slide Show: 65 slides and the written script describing Ecology Action's many years of research with GROW BIO-INTENSIVE food-raising techniques. Briefly covers: basics of the methods; impact upon backyard food production; potential for truck farming; water, fertilizer and resource use; new tools such as mini-greenhouses and the U-bar; the herbal lawn; and more.

Reprints:

Composting for the Tropics. 28 pp.
Living Quarters for Plant Roots. 6 pp.
Plant Species Index for the Pacific Northwest and General Reference. 20 pp.

Related Publications by Other Organizations

A Preliminary Assessment of the Applicability of French Intensive/Biodynamic Gardening Techniques in Tropical Settings. Santa Barbara, CA: Direct International Development/Direct Relief Foundation, 1978. 47 pp. Report from on-site visits to 4 intensive demonstration gardens in Central America.
Intensive Small Farms and the Urban Fringe. Sausalito, CA: Landal Institute for Small Farm Research, 1976. 93 pp. Based in part on Ecology Action's research.
Martinez, Juan Manuel. *Huertos Familiares.* ECOPOL, c.o. Edif. H10-1-2. Col. Lomas de Plateros, Mexico, D.F. CP 01480, Mexico. 1992. Booklet used by the nationwide program in Mexico to teach Biointensive mini-farming at the introductory level.
———. *Rotofolio Huertos Familiares.* ECOPOL, c.o. Edif. H10-1-2. Col. Lomas de Plateros, Mexico, D.F. CP 01480, Mexico. 1992. Flipchart used for teaching Biointensive mini-farming in villages in Mexico.
Seshadri, C. V., et al. *Bio-Dynamic Gardening.* Vol. 4. Shri A. M., M. Murugappa Chettiar Research Centre, Tharamani, Madras, 600 113, India, 1980. 38 pp.
———. *Bio-Dynamic Horticulture—Improvements & Extension.* Vol. 15. Shri A. M., M. Murugappa Chettiar Research Centre, Tharamani, Madras, 600 113, India, 1983. 43 pp.

Yang, Y. K. "Home Gardens as a Nutrition Intervention." *Small Scale Intensive Food Production—Improving the Nutrition of the Most Economically Disadvantaged Families*, pp. 60–80, Washington, D.C.: League for International Food Education, 1977.

Accredited Classes in Biointensive Mini-Farming

Dr. Ed Glenn and Dr. Mary Olsen of the *Environmental Research Laboratory* (the University of Arizona) give a Biointensive course for arid areas each semester based on their 10 years' experience. Contact them at 2601 E. Airport Drive, Tucson International Airport, Tucson, AZ 85706-6985 or fax (602) 573-0852.

Videotapes of Our Work
(Available from Bountiful Gardens)

Two award-winning PBS specials documenting our work have been televised nationally.

Gardensong (1983) is a beautiful film about Alan Chadwick's work, our own work, and that of others.

Circle of Plenty (1987) is about our Willits garden and the *Menos y Mejores* project in northern Mexico. *Circle of Plenty* addresses some serious problems in world agriculture and shows that the Biointensive method is a viable solution even under Third World conditions with poor soil.

A Journey in Kenya—Biointensive Farmers (1993). Sandra Mardigian and Doug Burck revisit graduates from Manor House Agricultural Centre whom they sponsored, and document the amazing, positive changes that have resulted from Biointensive gardens—both for individuals and for whole villages! Wonderful, hope-filled scenes of African gardens and gardeners. About 20 minutes.

El Huerto Ecologico (1992). This video is used to introduce Biointensive practices in Mexico.

The Living Land (1999). This PBS-TV special is available from the Foundation for Global Community, 222 High Street, Palo Alto, CA, 94301, phone (800) 707-7932. The program focuses on the bases of our lives: the soil, farming, and food. Beautifully done. Interviews with John Jeavons of Ecology Action, Wes Jackson of the Land Institute, Alice Waters of Chez Panisse, and Mas Masumoto, author of *Epitaph for a Peach* and *Harvest Son* are woven into a beautiful fabric.

Help in Kenya

You can help support a Kenyan villager's training at a
5-day Basic Biointensive Skills Workshop at Manor House
Agricultural Centre. To make this happen, send an $85 tax-
deductible donation to the Kilili Self-Help Project, 490 Yale
Road, Menlo Park, California 94025. Help the world grow!

Help in Russia

To assist Biointensive work in Russia, contact: Biointensive
for Russia, 831 Marshall Drive, Palo Alto, California 94303-3614,
fax (650) 424-8767, e-mail cvesecky@igc.org, or visit
www.igc.org/biointensiveforrussia.

Bountiful Gardens

International gardening and mini-farming mail order
catalog. An Ecology Action project. For a free catalog of
gardening publications, fertilizers, tools, and seeds, write
to Bountiful Gardens, 18001 Shafer Ranch Road, Willits,
California 95490-9626, or call (707) 459-6410, or fax
(707) 459-1925. Visit us at www.bountifulgardens.org.
Also, visit www.growbiointensive.org.

Please Join Us.

Membership donations provide a reliable financial base that secures continued education and research programs for sustainable GROW BIOINTENSIVE food-raising worldwide. Our thanks to all of our friends who are investing in the future by making this work possible.

I would like to be part of Ecology Action's work. Enclosed is my membership donation for one year, which includes Ecology Action's newsletter.

- ❏ $15 Newsletter   ❏ $30 Supporting   ❏ $60 Family
- ❏ $100 Sustaining—choose one ★ gift from below
- ❏ $250 Corporate Membership—choose two ★ gifts from below
- ❏ $400 Research Supporter—sponsor a 100-square-foot research growing bed at Willits Research Center for one year—choose two ★ gifts from below.
- ❏ $1,000 Lifetime Membership—choose three ★ gifts from below.
- ❏ Gift membership at $_____   ❏ Other _____

Please send the following gift(s), valid for the term of my membership:

- ★ ❏ *10%-off coupon* for one-time order for seeds (except peas, beans, and corn) from Bountiful Gardens catalog.
- ★ ❏ *Two free admissions* to our Saturday/Sunday classes at our Common Ground Educational Center in Palo Alto.
- ★ ❏ *10%-off certificate* for one-time order from Common Ground store.
- ★ ❏ *Complimentary admission for two* to a scheduled Research Garden Tour in Willits, California (see Bountiful Gardens Catalog for dates).
- ★ ❏ *25%-off certificate* for one-time order from our Rare Seed Catalog.
- ❏ Free Bountiful Gardens Catalog of seeds, books, and supplies.

Please also send:

- ❏ *How to Grow More Vegetables*, 2002 edition, by John Jeavons, $17.95 (U.S. funds). California residents add $1.30 tax. For shipping and handling please add $4 for U.S., $6.00 for Canada, $9 for Mexico, and $14 for all other countries.
- ❏ *The Sustainable Vegetable Garden*, 1999 edition, by John Jeavons and Carol Cox, $11.95 (U.S. funds). California residents add $0.87 tax. For shipping and handling please add $3 in U.S. and $8.50 for all other countries.
- ❏ *Proceedings of the Soil, Food, and People Conference: A Biointensive Model for the New Century*, $30 (U.S. funds). California residents add $2.18 tax. For shipping and handling please add $4 for U.S., $6.00 for Canada, $9 for Mexico, and $14 for all other countries.
- ❏ Sample Newsletter, $1.50 postpaid.
- ❏ Rare Seeds Catalog, $2.50 postpaid.
- ❏ Membership brochures, free.

Name _____

Address _____

_____

Send to: ECOLOGY ACTION, 5798 Ridgewood Road, Willits, CA 95490-9730

MEMBERSHIP

Index

More Gardening Books from Ten Speed Press

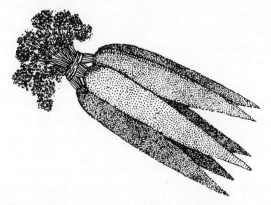

THE SUSTAINABLE VEGETABLE GARDEN
*A Backyard Guide to Healthy Soil
and Higher Yields*

by John Jeavons and Carol Cox

This quick-and-dirty introduction to Ecology
Action's gardening methods shows how easy
it is to grow healthy, organic fruits and vegetables
in almost any plot of land.
128 pages, $11.95, ISBN 1-58008-016-2

THE GARDENER'S TABLE
*A Guide to Natural Vegetable
Growing and Cooking*

by Richard Merrill and Joe Ortiz

Noted horticulturist Richard Merrill and award-
winning cookbook author Joe Ortiz team up to
deliver the ultimate no-nonsense guide to cultivating and cooking from a kitchen garden,
including 50 creative, healthful recipes.
464 pages, $24.95, ISBN 0-89815-876-1

ALLERGY-FREE GARDENING
*The Revolutionary Guide to
Healthy Landscaping*

by Thomas L. Ogren

After researching the role that urban landscaping
plays in the allergy health crisis, horticulturist
Tom Ogren compiled this extensive reference
that will help gardeners and landscapers make
landscaping choices to drastically reduce exposure to harmful allergens.
288 pages, $19.95, ISBN 1-58008-166-5

And, after you grow those vegetables . . .

ECO-CUISINE
*An Ecological Approach to Vegan
and Vegetarian Cooking*

by Ron Pickarski

Using his flair for fresh ingredients, lovingly
prepared and beautifully presented, Ron Pickarski,
author of *Friendly Foods,* advocates healthful,
nutritious food based on the simplest components and flavored with the juices of fruits and
vegetables.
288 pages, $19.95, ISBN 0-89815-635-1

RECIPES FROM A KITCHEN GARDEN
by Renee Shepherd and Fran Raboff

Unique recipes to help you make the most of
your garden's bounty.
176 pages, $11.95, ISBN 1-89815-540-1

MORE RECIPES
FROM A KITCHEN GARDEN
176 pages, $11.95, ISBN 1-89815-730-7

TEN SPEED PRESS / CELESTIAL ARTS / TRICYCLE PRESS
P.O. Box 7123, Berkeley, CA 94707
Phone (800) 841-2665 / Fax (510) 559-1629
order@tenspeed.com / www.tenspeed.com

[continued from inside front cover]

1984

The Peace Corps uses the French translation of *How to Grow More Vegetables* for training in Togo, West Africa. *Growing and Gathering Your Own Fertilizers,* a booklet, is published in response to an appeal from Eastern Europe for more detailed gardening advice. A 3-year apprentice program begins at the Willits site. The Manor House Agricultural Centre Biointensive Program begins in Kenya, East Africa, with Ecology Action's assistance. The East Coast site sponsors a Biointensive conference for agronomists and university professors. A successful Biointensive training project is reported in Tanzania. Mexico's Social Security Program reports 2,000 Biointensive growing beds established in 67 communities in northeastern Mexico as part of its Menos y Mejores ("Fewer Is Better") program. Ecology Action emphasizes complete diet mini-farming.

1985

Ecology Action publishes *One Circle: How to Grow a Complete Diet in Under 1,000 Square Feet,* by David Duhon and Cindy Gebhard. *How to Grow More Vegetables* is translated into German. Segments of *Circle of Plenty,* a PBS-TV special of Ecology Action's work, is taped in Willits. Staff and apprentices at the Willits site begin terracing mountainside growing beds and soil upgrading. Ecology Action acts as advisor to a garden project in Zambia and to a California restaurant garden. Visitors to the California site include people from Tibet, Trinidad, Kenya, Brazil, the Philippines, the Dominican Republic, Canada, England, Mexico, Australia, Zambia, Nepal, and Ethiopia. Timberleaf Farm becomes Ecology Action's official East Coast site, emphasizing economic mini-farming and soil research. Gary Stoner completes a 1-year apprenticeship at Willits and begins the Living Soil Garden Project with the Menos y Mejores program in Tula, Mexico.

1986

Growing to Seed is published, and PBS-TV segments are taped in Tula, Mexico. The International Institute of Rural Reconstruction Biointensive Gardening Project establishes 300 Biointensive beds on the island of Negros in the Philippines as part of a UNICEF project for malnourished children.

1987

Circle of Plenty, the PBS documentary on Ecology Action's work in Willits and Gary Stoner's work in Tula, Mexico, is broadcast nationwide. A feature article appears in *The Christian Science Monitor* on World Food Day. Ecology Action staff visit and advise the Menos y Mejores project in Mexico. *The Complete 21-Bed Biointensive Mini-Farm* booklet is published. Steve Rioch begins a Biointensive mini-farm demonstration, research, and education project at Ohio University in Athens, Ohio. Work at the Timberleaf Farm site is postponed until the Ohio University project is completed. John Jeavons is named a member of the Giraffe Project, honoring people who stick their necks out for the common good, and he receives a Santa Fe Global Village Living Treasure award. Ecology Action emphasizes sustainable soil fertility.

1988

The *One Basic Mexican Diet, Foliar Feeding,* and *Backyard Garden Research* booklets are published. The first 3-week workshop is offered in the Common Ground mini-farm in Willits, California. The workshop is based on hands-on demonstration and a preliminary curriculum/workbook, which is the distillation of 16 years of Ecology Action's learning and experience. The Manor House Agricultural Centre in Kenya, East Africa, initiates an active 2-year apprentice program. The Philippines Department of Education mandates teaching of Biointensive gardening in all primary and secondary schools. The director of the Menos y Mejores program in Mexico visits the Common Ground mini-farm for advanced training, which results in upgraded training for 250 key teachers in Mexico. An article on sustainable soil fertility, economic mini-farming, and Biointensive approaches is published in *California Farmer.* John Jeavons is presented with the 19th Boise Peace Quilt Award.

1989

A 4-year bachelor of science degree program is approved (subject to funding) at Ohio University, under the auspices of the Botany Department. The first accredited class in Biointensive mini-farming is taught during the summer session. Feature articles appear in *Mother Earth News, Vegetarian Times,* and a United States Information Agency publication. There is a second national broadcast of *Circle of Plenty.* Thirty-five agronomists from Guatemala, El Salvador, Honduras, and Costa Rica tour the Willits site. The first 5-day workshop is held at the Willits site with participants from the United States and Mexico. Lectures are held at Stanford University, Clemson University, and Ohio University at Athens. *Micro-Farming: A Seventeen Year Perspective, A Reading Guide, Micro-Farming as a Key to the Revitalization of the World's Agriculture and Environment,* and *Green Manure Crops,* new booklets, are published. *Man of the Trees: Selected Writings of Richard St. Barbe Baker,* edited by Karen Gridley, is published. St. Barbe Baker inspired the planting of trillions of trees worldwide during his lifetime. Lectures are given in Mexico to farmers, students, agronomists, and professors. Talks are sponsored by Mexico's Menos y Mejores program. Over 63,000 Biointensive gardens are reported in Mexico.

1990

Biointensive Composting, A Comprehensive Definition of Sustainability, and *Dried, Cut and Edible Flowers for Pleasure, Food and Income,* three booklets, are published. The first 6-week workshop is given at the Willits site with advanced participants from Mexico, Kenya, the Soviet Union, and the United States. A 5-day workshop is given at Stanford University for participants from Mexico and the United States. A 5-day workshop is given at Stanford University for 9 participants from the Soviet Union and another another is given at the Willits site for particpants from Mexico and the United States. United States Agricultural Extension agents are given a class on sustainable soil fertility. Two classes are given at Ohio University during the summer session. A Latin

American Biointensive mini-farming demonstration, research, and educational site is established at Tizapan, Hildago, Mexico. Translation of the Mini-Series booklets into Spanish is begun. Forty-four agronomists from El Salvador, Nicaragua, Guatemala, Costa Rica, and Honduras attend a tour at the Willits site. Representatives from Mexico's University of Chapingo visit Willits and Ohio University to prepare for a Biointensive program they will initiate in Mexico. A project in Ethiopia reports success in combining Biointensive practices with aquaculture ponds. After 13 years of testing, the Shri A.M. M. Murugappa Chettiar Research Centre in India reports it is ready to teach Biointensive mini-farming throughout India.

1991

The Kenyan Minister of Agriculture expresses support for Biointensive training. Fifty-two apprentices are reported to be enrolled in the Manor House Agricultural Centre 2-year Biointensive Training Program. The Center for Biointensive Mini-Farming is established in Moscow, Russia. The Mexican president's Solidarity Program funds additional training for Biointensive promoters. The *Huertos Familiares* video on Biointensive practices in Mexico is produced. The University of Chapingo creates a Department of Biointensive Mini-Farming. A 5-day workshop is given at Mexico's University of Chapingo, a class series is held at Mendocino College in California, an accredited course is offered at Stanford University, a workshop is held at Mexico's University of Oxochimilco, including Bolivian and Haitian participants, and courses continue at Ohio University. A 7-day workshop is offered at Willits, with participants from Mexico, Togo, Ireland, and the United States. Presentations are made in Portland, Oregon; Seattle, Washington; and Vancouver, British Columbia. Classes and presentations are given throughout the year. Three new Ecology Action booklets are written. *How to Grow More Vegetables* is expanded and revised, and the 4th edition is published in English and Spanish.

1992

IIRR in the Philippines publishes illustrated Biointensive gardening booklets in the Tagalog and Cebuano languages. The Mexican Institute of Social Security/Solidarity Program reports 70,000 new Biointensive family gardens are initiated in 1991. The Mexican National Institute for Adult Education distributes 1,100 copies of the Biointensive video *Heurtos Ecologicos* (The Ecological Garden) throughout Mexico. The Colombian Ministry of Agriculture uses some Biointensive techniques for their vegetable garden programs. The Janus Project in North Carolina begins training single mothers in Biointensive economic mini-farming. The Ford Foundation makes a $221,000 3-year grant to the Manor House Agricultural Centre's Biointensive Training Program in Kenya so the program can be more effectively expanded nationwide. Presentations on Biointensive mini-farming are given at the Congress of National Academy of Sciences in Cuba. The United Nations Food and Agriculture Organization representative in Ethiopia commends Ecology Action on its work. Biointensive sustainable mini-farming classes and workshops are given: a 6-week workshop at Willits; courses at Ohio University; a 7-day workshop in Willits; a 3-day workshop in Seattle, Washington; and a 5-day workshop in Saltillo, Coahuilla, Mexico, cosponsored by ECOPOL, Ecology Action, and Ohio University.

1993

Three-day workshops are given at Stanford University and in San Diego, with 55 participants from 7 states, Canada, Mexico, Iran, Argentina, and Nepal. Linda Sickles of Pennsylvania attends the March 3-day workshop; begins using her farm for Biointensive demonstration, research, and teaching; and gives workshops at the Philadelphia Community Gardens and at Graterford State Prison. Helene Huber turns her enthusiasm for Ecology Action's work into a gardening network, Gardeners in Community, and encourages Habitat for Humanity to establish Gardens for Humanity—gardens to accompany the houses that it helps to build. Gardening

classes are given almost weekly at Ecology Action's Common Ground Education Center in Palo Alto. John Jeavons gives public presentations for the Sierra Club Agriculture Committee and delivers a keynote speech at The American Horticultural Society's National Symposium, Washington, D.C. Four half-day garden tours are held at Willits Research Garden, several series of classes are given for Mendocino College for Beginning and Intermediate/Advanced gardeners, and 2 Ohio University 5-day courses are taught. A 7-day workshop is held in Willits, with participants from the United States and Mexico. A Russian translation of *How to Grow More Vegetables* is completed, and *Lazy-Bed Gardening* is published by Ten Speed Press. Training Centers have now been established on each of 5 continents— the fulfillment of a 1983 goal. The new goal is to catalyze the establishment of training centers in each country in the world. Biosphere II, using techniques based on Ecology Action's work, raises 80% of its food needs for the last 2 years within a "closed system." This experience demonstrates that a *complete* year's diet for one person could be raised on 3,403 square feet ($1/6$–$1/13$ of what commercial agriculture is using to feed one person). In India, village women gardening with Biointensive methods on their own small plots raise enough food to feed their families *and* bring in a whole year's income. In Mexico thousands of new people each year are taught Biointensive methods for nutrition intervention for themselves and their families. Publications and videos in Spanish spread Biointensive techniques in Latin America. The Manor House Agricultural Centre in Kenya is directly and indirectly responsible for training over 30,000 mini-farmers during the past 7 years. The Centre opens its training programs to international students.

1994

Biointensive research focuses on producing complete nutrition, sustainable soil fertility, income, resource conservation, and the preservation of genetic diversity. Classes, tours, and lectures are given throughout the year, including presentations at the Social Ventures Network,

Bioneers, the University of California at Davis, and the New Haven Ecology Project. Two 3-day workshops are given at Willits, California, with 72 participants from 14 states, Mexico, and Siberia. A workshop is given to staff at the Seeds of Change in New Mexico. A 6-week workshop is taught in Willits, California, with key Biointensive practitioners from Kenya and Mexico. Biointensive courses are given at Ohio University. Two Kenyans intern for 6 months at Ecology Action's mini-farm in Willits. A 7-day workshop is taught in Willits for participants from Kenya, Mexico, Argentina, and the United States. Willits Research Garden Tour participants include a representative of Global 20/20, who is working with projects in South Africa and Mali. The PBS-TV program *Market to Market* nationally airs a 10-minute segment about Ecology Action's sustainable Biointensive mini-farming work. Twenty thousand copies of the Russian translation of *How to Grow More Vegetables* are reported sold. Ana Maria Vasquez helps establish Biointensive gardens at 17 drug rehabilitation centers in Colombia. Technical assistance is continually given worldwide, including projects in: drought-stricken India, the Caribbean island of Montserrat, the Stockholm Environmental Institute of Boston, Massachusetts, Guatemala, Kenya, Mexico, and Russia.

In Kenya, 35 farmer groups (536 people) are trained in 5-day workshops at the Manor House Agricultural Centre. This training improves many aspects of villagers' lives. Earnings from vegetable sales by women's farmer groups in the Local Outreach Program (LOP) are used to construct water tanks, start poultry projects, and build family shelters. Nineteen 2-year apprentices graduate from Manor House. In one province, 125 displaced people are reported to be practicing the Biointensive method. Thirty groups in Kenya's Cheptobot area request to be incorporated into LOP's extension visits. Most LOP target group participants and their follower farmers have significantly improved their diet and level of income over the past 9–17 months. Kenya's Minister for Agriculture, Simeon Nyacae, states that organic farming

methods need to be adopted and developed in Kenya, since food items have become expensive and hazardous due to the use of chemicals.

In Mexico, sustainable Biointensive workshops are given regularly throughout the country, including classes taught at Antonio Narro Agricultural University and the University of Chapingo. The new tropical demonstration/training center in Chiapas is further developed. Six more Ecology Action booklets are translated into Spanish. A 3rd edition of *Huertos Familiares* and 9 videos (in Spanish) on different environmental topics are completed. UNESCO and the Public Education Department express interest in including the Biointensive method in a study program of 197 high schools and as a subject in 5 research centers. Antonia Dodero Salinas teaches Biointensive techniques to 40 forest guards and other villagers and students in the Lacandon jungle area of Chiapas.

1995

Future Fertility: Transforming Human Waste into Human Wealth, by John Beeby, *Growing Medicinal Herbs,* by Louisa Lenz, and the 5th edition of *How to Grow More Vegetables,* by John Jeavons, are published. Bountiful Gardens initiates a Small Seed Company Conference at the Asilomar Eco-Farm Conference. Biointensive presentations are made to: a Smith and Hawkens class, at Cornell University, Syracuse University; the Northeast Organic Farming Association of New York, in Berkeley, California; the Coyote Point Environmental Center in San Mateo, California; the National Geographic Research and Exploration Committee in Santa Fe; and the Bioneers Conference in San Francisco, California. Ecology Action gives two 3-day workshops in Willits, California, for a total of 50 people from 15 states and 5 countries. John Jeavons presents 2 workshops in Hawaii to over 200 people, and teaches an accredited Biointensive class on Hawaiian television. John Jeavons also presents a 3-day workshop at Sol y Sombra in Santa Fe, New Mexico. People from Mexico, Kenya, Haiti, and the United States take part in a 6-month internship at the Willits mini-farm. Three educational

mini-farm tours are held. The first 7-day teachers workshop is given at the mini-farm, with 20 participants from 6 states and 5 countries. A mini-farm tour is given for the Director and staff of Fetzer Vineyard Garden. Materials are provided to a group of Cuban farmers who tour the mini-farm under the auspices of Food First. A 1-day workshop is given at the mini-farm. In Kenya, the Local Outreach Program (LOP), a project of Manor House Agricultural Centre, holds 4 separate meetings with the Kenya Ministries of Health and Agriculture, working out ways to collaborate to avoid duplication of effort. Through using Biointensive methods, maize yields for the Kaisagat Women's Group increased from an average of 4 bags per hectare to 10. After seeing demonstration gardens, farmers realize it is better to work a small, well-fertilized piece of land than a larger unfertilized piece. LOP receives requests from 30 farmer groups who want to be incorporated into LOP training programs. A Peace Corps member videotapes LOP activities with Kenyan farmer groups to show key business practices to others. The Kenyan Ministry of Agriculture joins LOP for farm research trials that emphasize Biointensive practices. In Mexico, Padre Julio Cesar de la Garza of *La Milpa* group gives week-long workshops monthly to an average of 30 people per session. These workshops are given at Linares and Mier y Noriega, an arid region where the group maintains demonstration centers. Coordinators from 16 coastal communities in Chiapas state in Mexico report the establishment of 2 mini-demonstration centers. Under DIF (an organization in each state comparable to the US WIC program) in Mexico, 15 1-week theoretical and practical courses are held in 10 states for 375 participants. Ing. Moises Cuevas in Texcoco, Mexico, prepares "A Technical Package for the Production of Organic Vegetables" for use among unions of producers and other interested people. Dr. Jose Francisco Rodriguez of the University of Antonio Narro initiates the process to create a 6-semester course in "Technician in the Biointensive Method." Ing. Gaspar Mayagoitia gives 8 1-week courses to *promotores* and residents of mestiza and indigenous communities in Chihuahua state. The Ecological Groups of Uruapan, Mexico, start to include Biointensive methods in their work with indigenous communities. An intermediate work-shop is held in 7 states in Mexico, under the auspices of SEMARNAP. The Instituto Nacional Indigenista teaches Biointensive methods to all its interns and charges in 120 shelters. ECOPOL, Ecology Action's counterpart for Latin America, gives work-shops in San Luis Potosi, Oaxaca, and Tizapan to a total of 89 *promotores* from 20 states. ECOPOL also gives a 5-day work-shop in Aguascalientes state to 36 agronomists, *promotores,* biologists and civil engineers from 8 states, sponsored by the United Nations Development Program.

1996

Technical advice is given to Ecological Soil Management in West Bank, Israel. Information on Ecology Action and the Biointensive philosophy appears on PBS's *New Garden* program, in *Garden Design* magazine, and in Rodale's *Vitamin A+ Sieve* newsletter. John Jeavons participates in a panel at the Eco-Farm Conference at Asilomar. The Rodale Book Club offers the 5th edition of *How to Grow More Vegetables* as a main selection. Ecology Action gives a 3-day workshop in Willits, California, with 45 participants and 3 translators from 10 states, Russia, Mexico, and Uganda. One of the Russians is the director of the Russian Ministry of Agriculture's Teaching and Methodological Center near Moscow, which serves 292 agriculture technology schools and colleges. John Jeavons presents a 3-day workshop at Green Gulch Center Farm near San Francisco, with 64 people attending from 6 states and 2 countries. Ecology Action staff teach another 3-day workshop in Seattle with 29 participants from 10 states and Kenya. Fairhaven College in Washington approves a 5-year plan for a Biointensive program of 25 beds a year. The U.S. Peace Corps orders *One Circle* for use in Turkmenistan. Fernando Pia, director of CIESA in Argentina, reports that, given their excellent results with Biointensive methods,

they now have farming plans that allow an individual working only 35 hours a week to provide between 60% and 80% of a vegetarian diet for a family of four, plus a reasonable income, on as little as 8,600 square feet. CIESA is visited by 25 agronomic engineers from the National Institute of Agricultural Technology, who are surprised and impressed by the Center and its yields. The Republic of Georgia establishes its first Biointensive beds in the Samtredia region and Tbilisi. ECODOM and Biointensive for Russia host a 3-day workshop in Siberia, cosponsored by the Novisibirsk State Agrouniversity and its farmers' extension service; 68 people participate. It is reported that the yields of Biointensive experiments in Siberia average 287% of U.S. average yields. A rural service center in Zimbabwe is awarded a grant for the 2nd year of its 5-year Biointensive Development Program. A resource center in India receives a grant to help local women in 10 villages start Biointensive gardens for home consumption and income. In Chiapas state, Mexico, Enrique Reyna conducts four Biointensive workshops for pioneers in new population centers. He also gives a workshop for 60 rural people in Tabasco state. Gaspar Mayagoitia gives 7 workshops in Chihuahua state for 110 participants from agricultural high schools and members of Rural Development who work in the Tarahumara mountains. John Jeavons gives Biointensive presentations and meets with farmers, teachers, and officials in Chihuahua and Nuevo Leon states. The *Biointensivistas* (Mexican Biointensive teachers who have trained at the Willits mini-farm) initiate their first annual meeting in Nuevo Leon state.

1997

Ecology Action gives a 3-day workshop in Willits with 42 participants from 5 states, Mexico, and Russia. Nine of the 12 participants from Mexico stay on for 3 days of advanced training at the mini-farm. A second 3-day workshop in Willits has 40 participants from 8 states and Puerto Rico, Togo, Kenya, and Japan. Some of the participants have strong connections with the Phillipines, Russia, Ladakh,

Ghana, the Virgin Islands, Colombia, Mexico, the Dominican Republic, Nigeria, and the Ivory Coast. John Jeavons presents a 3-day workshop in Hawaii for 29 participants, including many indigenous people. The second 7-day teachers workshop is given at the Willits mini-farm. An advanced-level 10-week course is given at the mini-farm, with participants from Mexico, Kenya, and Togo. Ecology Action gives technical assistance to Katalysis/ Honduras, Watts Growing, The Mass Education Library Service in Mumias, Kenya, and the Instituto Rural Valle Grande in Peru. A 3-day workshop participant, comparing soil samples, is amazed at the difference that double-digging makes. Another 3-day workshop participant works with the University of California at Santa Cruz to test the nutritional value of foods he is growing in Biointensive field tests. Carol Cox coteaches at a joint ECODOM/Ecology Action workshop in Siberia. Carol Vesecky, director of Biointensive for Russia, reports that since Biointensive was introduced to Russia in 1990, 18 Eurasians have trained at 3-day workshops in Willits, 1,568 people have been taught, 30 articles have been written, and 25 radio/TV programs have been broadcast. Forty-nine thousand copies of the Russian translation of *How to Grow More Vegetables* are distributed throughout Russia. In Kenya, Manor House gives two 3-month courses for agricultural agents from Tanzania and Uganda. The Environmental Action Team teaches Biointensive methods to 17 farmer groups in western Kenya. Four farmer groups attend 1-week workshops at Manor House with assistance from the Kilili Self-Help Project. People from Uganda ask Manor House trainers about the possiblity of starting a Biointensive training center in their country. Manor House reports that as a result of its 13 years of training, 40 other NGO's in Kenya are initiating Biointensive projects and over 70,000 people have been trained directly and indirectly. An independently commissioned study asserts that between 1992 and 1996, as a result of Biointensive training in Kenya, among the farmers studied, self-sufficiency in maize production was boosted from 22% to 48%, hunger was reduced from 57% to 24%, and the proportion of farmers needing to buy vegetables was reduced from 85% to 11%. In Mexico, the Ministry of the Environment, Natural Resources and Fisheries gives a Biointensive workshop for 25 people, funded by the U.N. The Tizapan Demonstration/Training Center in Hidalgo state gives a course for 16 IMSS *promotores* who work with 80 communities, another to 40 community leaders, and a third to 30 IMSS *promotores*. Gaspar Mayagoitia reports that he and Maristas priests are establishing Biointensive modules in 16 boarding schools in the Chihuahua mountains for Tarahumara children. Moises Cuevas of the University of Chapingo gives a 5-day course to people from 7 Mexican states and Peru.

1998

Ecology Action gives a 3-day workshop in Willits for 42 people from 5 states and Mexico. Two of the Mexican participants work for the Mexican Ministry of Natural Resources, the Environment and Fisheries (SEMARNAP), and 4 other participants later give workshops in Uzbekistan. John Jeavons presents 3-day workshops in Austin, Texas; Chambersburg, Pennsylvania; Santa Fe, New Mexico; and Vancouver, British Columbia. Ecology Action gives a 3-day workshop in Santa Barbara, California, for 41 people from California and Italy. Earth Day presentations are made at Humboldt State University and Mendocino College, both in California. Technical assistance is given to the Kentucky Department of Health, a California PBS food and farming show, the director of a hospital in Tijuana, and Proyecto Esperanza in Mexico, which trains people to stay on their land, return to their land, or learn new skills. The first 5-day basic-level teachers workshop is held at the Willits mini-farm for 16 participants, Ecology Action's first step toward implementing its Certification Program. Two interns from Kenya and 2 Huichol trainees from Mexico receive 6 months of training at the Willits mini-farm. Steve Moore of Wilson College in Pennsylvania is invited to the UN's Commission on Sustainable Development and acts as Biointensive

representative there. CIESA in Argentina gives 3 Biointensive workshops for a total of 72 people, some of whom are very poor farmers from arid Patagonia. In Kenya, Manor House staff help produce a Sustainable Agriculture Extension Manual. Oxfam reports that over 80% of its projects in Kenya employ Manor House graduates or students on field attachment. Manor House gives 2 advanced follow-up workshops, collaborating with the Peace Corps and the Environmental Action Team. Manor House gives a 1-week workshop to 8 participants from Rwanda, Holland, Uganda, and Kenya, and presents many other 1-week workshops for farmer groups. A representative from the Tanzanian Ministry of Agriculture visits Manor House to learn about Biointensive. Two people from the Zimbabwe Orphans Trust take 6 weeks of specialized training at Manor House. Manor House reports that within one year of receiving training, one farmer's income surpassed that of her husband's teaching salary. In Mexico, Patricia Munoz and Salvador Morelos give a 3-month course at Aguascalientes University plus another course for the children of university teachers and employees. A course is given at the Tizapan, Mexico, demonstration/training site for 35 IMSS doctors and *promotores*. The La Milpa group in Nuevo Leon, Mexico, reports that it has trained 570 people in basic courses in 3½ years. Juan Manuel Martinez, director of ECOPOL, gives bimonthly courses for politicians and government employees who can influence agricultural policy at high levels and trains a group of 25 indigenous women, all community leaders, in the mountains of Puebla state. Chihuahua state establishes an Academy of Biointensive and Sustainable Agriculture to oversee schools where Biointensive is a required subject. The 2 employees of SEMARNAP who attended the Willits workshop initiate a Biointensive awareness program for high-level government employees. Empresas en Solidaridad, a government social organization in Tabasco, Mexico, adopts the Biointensive method in 4 communities after Enrique Reyna gives trainings in the area. A 5-day basic-level national Biointensive workshop is given at the University of Chapingo in Mexico.

1999

The terms GROW BIOINTENSIVE® and CULTIVE BIOINTENSIVAMENTE^MR are registered with the United States and Mexican trademark offices respectively to denote the type of Biointensive food-raising practices developed by Ecology Action and to assure the quality of GROW BIOINTENSIVE and CULTIVE BIOINTENSIVAMENTE workshops, publications, and produce.

Three apprentices are in residence at the Willits mini-farm. Ecology Action gives 2 GROW BIOINTENSIVE^SM 3-day workshops in Willits for a total of 75 people from 10 states, Russia, and Sri Lanka. John Jeavons presents GROW BIOINTENSIVE^SM 3-day workshops in Chambersburg, Pennsylvania; Fairfield, Iowa; Boulder, Colorado; and Austin, Texas. A summer course is held for Ecology Action apprentices and interns. Ecology Action gives its second GROW BIOINTENSIVE^SM basic-level teachers workshop at the mini-farm. Booklet #13, *Growing to Seed,* is revised and updated. Four new worksheets are created to help make data and teaching reports easier. A survey form is developed to gather information for the International GROW BIOINTENSIVE™ Directory. A PBS special, *The Living Land,* features John Jeavons, Wes Jackson, Alice Waters, and Mas Masumoto. The upper knoll section of Ecology Action's mini-farm/research garden is converted to a closed-system basis in order to monitor soil sustainability. Former 3-day workshop participants start a GROW BIOINTENSIVE workgroup in Austin. A basic-level teachers workshop participant gives three 1-day seminars at his ranch for farmers, academics, and gardeners. A farmer in Honduras reports that after 52 hours of rain, when other farmers had crops washed away, his Biointensive beds stayed in place. A 3-person team holds a 1-week follow-up workshop review in Uzbekistan, then gives a 3-day workshop for 50 people in Russia. In Argentina, CIESA gives two 3-day workshops for a total of 45 people. CIESA Director Fernando Pia reports that he travels monthly to arid Patagonia, where many indigenous people live, to advise Biointensive projects developed by former apprentices; the area has extremely difficult growing conditions.